LEARNING THEORIES
A TO Z

David C. Leonard

An Oryx Book

Greenwood Press
Westport, Connecticut • London

Library of Congress Cataloging-in-Publication Data

Leonard, David C.
    Learning theories, A to Z / David C. Leonard.
        p.   cm.
    Includes bibliographical references and index.
    ISBN 1–57356–413–3 (alk. paper)
    1. Education—Dictionaries.   I. Title.
LB15.L4695   2002
370′.3—dc21   2001058792

British Library Cataloguing in Publication Data is available.

Library of Congress Catalog Card Number: 2001058792
ISBN: 1–57356–413–3

First published in 2002

Greenwood Press, 88 Post Road West, Westport, CT 06881
An imprint of Greenwood Publishing Group, Inc.
www.greenwood.com

Printed in the United States of America

The paper used in this book complies with the
Permanent Paper Standard issued by the National
Information Standards Organization (Z39.48–1984).

10 9 8 7 6 5 4 3 2 1

Contents

This book is dedicated to God and my family and to all those who have prayed for me while I fight Hodgkin's Disease. At the submission of this book to the publisher, I am still undergoing chemotherapy.

Preface

The purpose of this book is to provide reference information on learning theories about K–12 education, higher education, and industry education and training environments. The book defines over 500 terms related to learning theories and environments. My intent is that it will be helpful for anyone studying learning theories or applying learning theories to their current educational environment.

Each term is placed in the following categories: *cognitivism*, *constructivism*, *behaviorism*, and *humanism*. Of course, a single term may embody characteristics of more than one category. Nevertheless, it is placed within the context of the most predominant category to which it belongs. Within definitions, words in *italics* are those defined elsewhere in the work. The assumption is that you will follow the various cross-references and paths to obtain a better knowledge of the context for each term.

Also noted are learning theories and environments that are currently specific to industry education and training. These are categorized as *organizational learning*—even though they contain elements of theories from the four main categories noted above.

Though not strictly learning theories, also defined are terms related to *educational technology* environments. Examples are *electronic campus*, *virtual communities*, and *videoconferencing*. Without getting into the "bits" and "bytes" of educational technology, these terms are defined within the context of our main categories because they are changing the landscape of how educators educate.

One of the most important aspects of learning theorists' work currently is "catching up" with the swift changes in educational technology that are transforming the landscape of our society and of how we transfer knowledge in a digital world. It is one thing to have new educational software, technologies, and networks available to educators and trainers. It is another thing entirely—something that has not as yet been fully accomplished—to provide learning theories and methods that take complete advantage of the swift advances in educational technology. It is my intent that this reference work will help educators and trainers better understand past and current learning theories, so that they can apply them to new theories that will likely arise in response to the new digital age we are entering.

> New knowledge is built upon past and current thinking.

In addition to the definitions, this book also provides (1) at the front of the book, a list of all terms defined; (2) at the end of the book, an appendix, "Paths through the A-to-Z Content," which groups the terms under each of the six main categories with which the term is predominantly identified; and (3) a selected annotated bibliography of books and articles (print and electronic) relevant to the focus of study. Almost all of the individuals cited in the term definitions will be found in this bibliography, along with annotated listings for their pertinent articles, books, and other writings. The bibliography's purpose is to provide a further depth of knowledge about the terms and their sources within the learning theorist community. Indeed, the terms in this book owe something to all of these sources.

Introduction

Through age and wisdom one discovers that all work builds upon that done by others. This is no less true of this work, even though I have spent countless hours in the analysis, research, and writing of the reference work under circumstances that were certainly more than trying. Nevertheless, my goal throughout has remained to be instructive and useful to you, the readers.

In addition to my own research and study, the genesis of this book is a result of graduate course research work of my technical communication students (over a period of five years) at Mercer University. These adult learners are industry professionals whose job is to transfer knowledge to their customers. They are distance learners and industry practitioners, and my goal was to have them look at the learning theories "out there" and to try to make sense of them. Their mission was to learn about selected theories and then apply them to their *knowledge management* work in industry.

A second group of practitioners also looked at learning theories in use. These were pre-service and in-service K–12 educators, who were in the process of obtaining their certification, their master's degrees, or their specialist's degrees at Mercer University. Their mission, through a course that I taught over several summers, was to look at the learning theories and to apply them to learning units that they would create for their classrooms. I am indebted to both groups for their

intelligence and insight. They forced me to think differently about the terms than I would have otherwise done without having had their participation in the research process.

What the students did find in their research work was a somewhat confusing array of learning theories, a language unique to learning theorists, and a good deal of overlap of information between one category (constructivism, cognitivism, behaviorism, humanism) and the next.

In the course of my attempt to arrive at categorizations, I sought to define the terms within the context of learning paradigms. In general, learning paradigms are classifications of learning theories into schools based upon their most dominant traits. Though there is not universal agreement about what constitutes the learning schools, learning theories defined in this book are categorized under the following learning paradigms: behaviorism, cognitivism, constructivism, humanism, and organizational learning. By classifying the theories into these learning paradigms, the book seeks to provide a context and framework for the theories. The goal is to give the reader a point of reference for comparison and contrast.

Though some learning theories, such as Jean Piaget's *genetic epistemology* and Jerome Bruner's *discovery learning*, could easily fall under two schools, such as cognitivism and constructivism, those theories are categorized herein as primarily constructivist. The approach taken is to categorize a particular theory within what is regarded by the author as the most dominant school or learning paradigm for that theory. Argument could be made for several theories that they may fall under a different category or multiple categories than the ones noted in this book. Cognitivists (as well as behaviorists, humanists, and constructivists) often classify a theory and place it within their own learning paradigm because they see traits that apply to their own view and perspective. Some adherents of learning theory schools or learning paradigms even deny the existence of other learning paradigms. Nevertheless, an attempt has been made here to provide a classification to the theories based upon what the author regards as their most dominant traits in order to provide the reader with a contextual definition of the term.

This attempt at providing a framework, a point of reference is also complicated by the fact that the theories themselves are often confusing and not easily differentiated from one another. For example, *cooperative learning* and *collaborative learning* are often confused, yet they both fall clearly under the learning paradigm of constructivism, based upon their most dominant traits. The hope is that the reader will be able to see patterns and trends to the theories that match with the general characteristics of the learning paradigms under which they are classified.

Having been in education and training in both higher education and industry for 27 years, I have learned that there is a lot that I don't know. Though I have done the best I could by providing a fairly complete sample of terms and bibliographic items related to learning theories and environments, I am certain that there are entries that need to be added. I thus invite you to provide terms and entries that should be included or notations of current terms that should be enhanced. I hope that in a future edition of this work these additions and enhancements can be addressed.

All work of this nature is iterative and incomplete. Nevertheless, I hope I have provided you with a reference book that you can use and refer to as you seek to provide the best content and the best curriculum for your audiences in the new digital learning age in which we live and work.

A good learning theory, like a good book, is one that you can use. May this book be useful to you, the reader. If it is, then I have served my purpose, as I have sought to teach others and to learn in the process.

Alphabetical List of Terms Defined

academic rationalism
accommodation
accretion
ACT theory
action learning
action research
active learning
active processing
activity theory
adaptive coping
adaptive response
adult education
advance organizers
Adventures of Jasper Woodbury
affordance
agents
algo-heuristic theories of emotion
altered states of consciousness
analogical learning
anchored instruction
andragogy
appraisal theories of emotion
apprenticeship learning
aptitude-treatment interaction
artificial intelligence
artificial life
ASK systems
assimilation
assistive technology
asynchronous learning
Atkinson-Shriffrin memory model
audio-conferencing
autoclitic behavior
automatic subgoaling (new)

barriers to learning
behavior control
behavior modeling

behavior modification
behavioral repertoire
behaviorism
bodily kinesthetic intelligence
bounded rationality
brain-based learning
building shared vision
business transformation

Cabri-geometry
case–based reasoning
categorization
cell assembly (Hebb)
Chain of Response model
change adept organization
chaos theory
chat
chunking
class Web site
classical conditioning
CMN-GOMS
co-emergence
cognition
cognitive apprenticeship
cognitive architecture
cognitive array model
cognitive artifacts
cognitive behaviorism
cognitive coaching
cognitive complexity theory
cognitive consistency
cognitive dissonance
cognitive flexibility
cognitive load
cognitive load theory
cognitive map
cognitive overhead
cognitive processes

Alphabetical List of Terms Defined

cognitive psychology
cognitive robotics
cognitive structure
cognitively guided instruction
cognitivism
cohort groups
collaboration
collaborative learning
common sense reasoning
communication rules
community of practice
complete rationality
complex systems
component display theory
computational linguistics
computer-assisted instruction
computer-based training
computer-lexicography
computer-mediated communication
concept acquisition
concept mapping
conceptual dependency theory
conceptual landscape
conceptual map
conceptualization
conditions of learning
connectionism
consciousness
constructionism
constructivism
constructivist learning environment
contextual awareness
contextual dependency theory
contiguity theory
contingency schedule
continuity-noncontinuity controversy
contribution
control of variables strategy
conversation theory
cooperative learning
CoRT thinking
CPM-GOMS
creativity
crisscross landscape
criterion-referenced instruction
critical consumerism
critical theory
critical thinking
crystallized intelligence
cultural reproduction
culture of mathematics
curriculum design
curriculum as experience
curriculum as prescription
cybernetics

data chunking
data mining
decentering
decision making
decision support systems
declarative knowledge
declarative memory
deductive learning
deschooling
developmental learning
dialectic method
differentiation
digital age educational paradigm
digital library
digital objects
digitize
direct attention thinking tools
direct instruction
directed behavior
disconfirmation
discourse theory
discovery learning
disequilibrium hypothesis
disorientation
distance learning
distributed network system
double loop learning
drive reduction theory
drive stimulus reduction theory
dual coding theory
dynamic assessment
dynamic memory

Ebbinghaus experiments
echoic behavior
echoic memory
educational technology
elaboration theory
elaborative rehearsal
electronic campus
electronic learning environment
electronic performance support system
elicited behavior
e-mail
embedded training
emitted behavior
emotion control
emotion theory
empiricism
enactivism
enactment effect
enculturation
engaged learning
enterprise-wide learning
episodic memory

law of effect
law of exercise
law of frequency
law of Pragnanz
law of readiness
laws of association
layers of necessity
learner-centric
learner control
learning and performance
learning by being told
learning environment
learning objectives
learning objects
learning organization
learning outcomes
learning paradigms
learning styles (Kolb)
learning web
legitimate peripheral participation
level of competence
level of processing
lifelong learning
life space
logic theorist
logical deductive
logical-mathematical intelligence
long-term memory

machine learning
machine tractable dictionary
magical number seven
mail list
maintenance rehearsal
management thinking
mands
mastery learning
mathematical metacognition
mathematical problem solving
maximum rationality hypothesis
means-ends analysis
Memex
memory
mental constructs
mental models
metacognition
metadata
metamathematics
mind mapping
mindtools
minimalism
minimalist model
Model Human Processor
modes of learning
molar behavior

molecular behavior
motivation
multimedia
multimedia applications
multiple intelligences
musical intelligence

natural GOMS language
natural language
natural language processing
naturalist intelligence
navigation
negotiated belief structures
negotiation
network model
neural networks
neuron
nonlinearity
Nurnberg funnel

objects with attributes and values
observational learning
olfactory system
one-trial learning
on-the-job training
operant chamber
operant conditioning
operative rules
originality theory
organizational cognition
organizational learning
organizational memory
orchestrated immersion
overt responding

pansophism
parallel processing
parallel thinking
passive learning
PDP memory model
pedagogy
perceptual field
perceptual learning
perceptual organization
performance objectives
performance tracking
personal curriculum design
personal mastery
phase sequence
phenomenonology
physical artifacts
PIGS
place learning
power law of practice
practice field
Premack principle

primary reinforcer
principle of closure
probability differential hypothesis
problem-based learning
problem solving
problem spaces
procedural knowledge
procedural memory
production rules (new)
productions
productive thinking
programmed learning
progressive education
project zero
psychological tools
purposive behaviorism
puzzle box

radical behaviorism
rational analysis
reaction potential
reactive system
recency principle
reception learning
reciprocal determinism
reductive bias
reflective mode of cognition
reinforcement theory
reinforcer
relaxed alertness
repair theory
response learning

scaffolded knowledge integration framework
scaffolded learning
scenario planning
schema
schemata
script theory
search controls
secondary reinforcer
self-directed learning
self-efficacy theory
self-pacing/self-paced instruction
self-reflection
self-regulated learning
self-regulation
semantic encoding
sensory memory
sequencing of instruction
serial processing
shaping
shared cognition theory
shared cognitive maps
short-term memory
signatures

single loop learning
situated cognition theory
situated learning
Six Thinking Hats
skills management
Skinner box
small steps
Soar
social and cultural artifacts
social cognitive theory
social development theory
social learning theory
socio-cognitive conflict
socio-constructivist theory
sociocultural theory
solo taxonomy theory
spatial intelligence
spatial reasoning
speed up learning (new)
spiraled organization
spoken language systems
spreading activation
staged self-directed learning model
Stanford-Binet Intelligence Scale
stimulus array
stimulus intensity dynamism
stimulus-response association
stimulus sampling theory
structuralism
structural learning theory
structure of intellect model
structuring
subsumption theory
survival anxiety
symbol systems theory
symbolic concept acquisition
symbolic interaction
synchronous learning
systems thinking

tabula rasa
tacit knowledge
tact
taskability
taxonomy
taxonomy of educational objectives
teachback
team learning
technical curriculum design
technology integration
telecommuting
theory of action
theory of teaching in context
Theory X/Y
Theory Z

Alphabetical List of Terms Defined

think aloud protocol
thinking mathematically
thought control
tractable
transactive memory
transformational learning
trial-and-error learning
triarchic theory
tuning

unified theories of cognition
universal campus network

verbal behavior
verbal-linguistic intelligence
vestibule training

videoconferencing
virtual learning community
virtual learning environment
visual texture perception
voice recognition
voluntarism

Waterlogic
Web-based education
Web-based knowledge transfer
Web-based training
Wechsler Adult Intelligence Scale
working memory

Xanadu

zone of proximal development

A

They know enough who know how to learn.
—Henry Adams, nineteenth-century
American writer

academic rationalism (humanism)

One of the early *curriculum design* orientations elaborated upon in the mid–1970s by Elliot W. Eisner and Elizabeth Vallance, academic rationalism is the belief that there are certain disciplines (within the liberal arts and sciences) with specific intellectual, cultural, and aesthetic content that must be passed on from one generation to the next. Academic rationalism is aligned to the "back to the basics" movement, in which becoming educated involves an initiation into ways of thinking in the culture represented by the content of the liberal arts and science disciplines. It is related to William H. Schubert's curriculum design orientation of *cultural reproduction*, in which the culture of a society is passed down from person to person within the society through *enculturation*. Enculturation is the process of learning about a culture through interactions and communications at home, at school, and elsewhere in society.

accommodation (constructivism)

One of two *developmental learning* processes espoused by Jean Piaget, accommodation involves the process of changing the child's *cognitive structure,* to make sense of the new events occurring in the environment. The other developmental process, *assimilation*, involves the child interpreting environmental events within the context of already existing *cognitive structures*. Accommodation and assimilation work together as the child develops and interacts with the environment. Strongly influenced by laws of biological development, Jean Piaget, the father of *genetic epistemology*, observed that as the child grows older and becomes an adult, the combined process of accommodation and assimilation increases cognitive growth and maturation intellectually, socially, morally, and emotionally. Thus, the key to the cognitive growth and maturation of the person within the intellectual, social, moral, and emotional spheres is through his or her accommodation and assimilation of experiences that occur throughout a lifetime in the environment. It should be noted that learning theorists who view Piaget as a cognitivist emphasize more Piaget's process of accommodation over assimilation. Those who regard him as a constructivist focus on Piaget's process of assimilation over accommodation. It could easily be argued that Piaget falls under both categories.

accretion (cognitivism)

This is one of three *modes of learning* (a general human learning model) delineated by D.E. Rumelhart and Donald A. Norman in the late 1970s and early 1980s. The main point of modes of learning is that *instructional design* and *curriculum design* should match with these three learning modes: accretion, *structuring*, and *tuning*. Accretion, the most common mode, is a process of *knowledge acquisition*, whereby new knowledge enters into human *memory*. Structuring (and re-structuring), the most difficult mode, involves the creation of new *schema* or *knowledge structures*, which involves reflection that leads to a state of *metacognition*. Tuning, the most time-consuming mode, is the process of taking the new knowledge and using it to perform tasks to facilitate expert human performance.

ACT theory (cognitivism)

John Robert Anderson in 1976 espoused a complete theory of human *cognition* called ACT (Adaptive Control of Thought) theory, a *cognitive architecture*, in which human cognition is an interplay of declarative, procedural, and working *memory*. According to Anderson, currently a professor of psychology and computer science at Carnegie Mellon University, *declarative memory* is a type of *long-term memory* that stores facts and ideas in a semantic network structure (i.e., a *network model*). *Procedural memory*, another type of *long-term memory*, takes sequences of *declarative knowledge* in the form of *productions* and makes further logical inferences about them. Each production contains a set of conditions and actions found within declarative memory. *Working memory*, or short-term conscious thought, retrieves declarative information of facts and ideas, carries out task sequences found in procedural memory, and adds new information gathered from the environment, forming new sequences that are then stored in procedural memory.

Dr. Anderson's continued research focuses on two primary activities: (1) the enhancement of the ACT theory, which is essentially a *production* system architecture for learning, memory, and human *problem solving*, and (2) the application of the ACT theory to the creation of *artificial intelligence* learning systems for mathematics and computer systems programming. Anderson calls

the enhancements to ACT theory that relate to item 1, ACT* (pronounced ACT-star). Enhancements to ACT Theory that relate to item 2 are under the umbrella of ACT-R (in which R stands for rules of cognition).

action learning (organizational learning)

Created originally by Dr. Reg Revans of the International Management Centres in the UK, action learning is an executive training and development strategy in which a management team, guided by a facilitator, works collaboratively on the following actions:

1. Analyze a management problem
2. Develop a plan to address the problem
3. Apply the solution
4. Study the effects of the decision to determine what aspects were effective and ineffective
5. Determine how to handle similar problems in the future.

The purpose of action learning is to help managers and executives learn how to handle more effectively new management situations that continually occur in the workplace. Action learning is a *collaborative learning* activity in which managers compare notes on how they handle new situations and learn from each other to find better methods for *problem solving*. Though an organizational learning theory, it fits as well within *constructivism* in which knowledge is discovered through social interaction.

action research (organizational learning)

Based upon Chris Argyris's *theory of action*, action research, also referred to as action science, is a strategy to help managers move from *single loop* learning (learning that corrects errors by changing routine behavior) to *double loop* learning (learning that corrects errors by examining the underlying culture of the organization) in order to enhance *decision making* within a fluid work environment. The strategy goes back to World War II and was used to make command and control decisions in the military during wartime. The goal of action research is to integrate action and reflection for the management practitioner in the midst of great organizational change. Its method is useful in helping managers make more reflective, informed decisions and to develop a culture of inquiry in decision-making activities. Action research emphasizes *collaboration*, cooperation, and sharing of information and experiences among management peers. Action research, also sometimes referred to as action science, focuses on managers examining practical work problems within certain *theories of action*. These theories of action are composed of values, theories, beliefs, rules, policies, and procedures that people in organizations follow to plan and carry out all work actions. By developing high levels of action research skills, managers within organizations can more easily innovate and deal with organizational change, promote *organizational learning*, and respond more productively to problem situations that require their attention and action.

active learning (constructivism)

Also known as *discovery learning*, active learning emphasizes the intrinsic motivation and self-sponsored curiosity of the learner who fashions content and is actively involved in its formation. Active learning shifts the focus of content structuring from the teacher (i.e., an *instructor-centric* orientation) to the learner (i.e., a *learner-centric* orientation). By being actively involved in the shaping of the content, the learners gain a far better understanding of the information than they would otherwise have. The opposite of active learning (i.e. *passive learning*) occurs when the teacher shapes the content for the students completely and provides that information to the student, usually in a lecture format. The student takes notes, memorizes the content, and feeds it back to the teacher for the test. In the fifth century B.C., the Chinese philosopher, Lao-tse, simply defined the essence of active learning when he said: "If you tell me, I will listen. If you show me, I will see. But if you let me experience, I will learn."

active processing (cognitivism)

One of the three types of instructional methods for *brain-based learning*, active processing takes place when the learner analyzes and becomes aware of the form, meaning, and motivation behind *knowledge acquisition*. The other two types of brain-based learning methods are *orchestrated immersion* (immersing students in a rich learning environment) and *relaxed alertness* (minimizing learner fear, while retaining a rich educational experience). In Renate Caine and Geoffrey Caine's book, *Making Connections*, the close relationship between the way the brain works and the way people like to learn is explicated within a brain-based learning approach. Active processing is closely allied to *metacognition*, which is being conscious of and aware of what one has learned. In short, the brain is an immensely powerful processor. Active processing seeks to get the brain working the way it should work. As long as the brain is not constrained from doing its normal work, learning will take place. Traditional rote learning (from *the industrial age educational paradigm*), however, inhibits learning by punishing the brain's natural processing activity. For active processing to take place, teachers must create a realistic context for learning, they must let students work in teams and work through mistakes themselves, and they must allow for students' continual self-assessments of how they learn and why they learn.

activity theory (constructivism)

Arising out of Lev Semyonovich Vygotsky's *social development theory*, activity theory is a learning framework in which individuals act on objects (through *social and cultural artifacts* that include language, norms, and modes of behavior) to achieve specific *learning outcomes*. He and his Russian colleagues, Alexander Luria and Alexei Leont'ev, formulated in the 1920s and 1930s the concept of an activity as a unit of analysis within a social and cultural framework. The three elements of activity theory are the actor, the object, and the community. The actor's activities are different from each other as a result of the object focused upon. The actor transforms the object into an outcome. The actor's relationship with the object is mediated through the social and cultural artifacts. *Consciousness* exists in the individual as a result of the actor working with the object and moving toward an outcome within the culture. Personality formation and learning cultural meanings and modes become intrinsically intertwined. The term "object" is thus an object of a learning exercise and is related to the motivation of the actor in achieving a particular outcome. The core of activity theory is that thinking, reasoning, and learning is a culturally and socially mediated phenomenon.

adaptive coping (organizational learning)

As a response to an organization's resistance to change, adaptive coping is a management learning strategy in which the individual does not challenge past, pre-set assumptions within a company or institution regarding its policies, procedures, and culture. Instead, one works within the old framework and seeks to provide small, incremental enhancements to the organization. With adaptive coping, the manager tries to improve and perfect the company or institutional practices that are built on the past policies and culture of the organization without challenging these old assumptions in order to seek systemic organizational change. Adaptive coping is thus an opposite strategy of *transformational learning*, in which old assumptions, policies, and practices are challenged to adapt to the changes and fluidity occurring in the business environment. Adaptive coping is an effective strategy if the company is working in a fairly stable and non-fluid environment, where change occurs slowly, with technologies that evolve relatively slowly. In the current business and technological environment, adaptive coping is not a very good organizational learning strategy in contrast to transformational learning.

adaptive response (educational technology)

A common feature built into current technology-based *learning environments*, adaptive response is a method in which the application is customized in response to the learner's continued interactions with it. A learner is in an adaptive response learning environment if, from the user's perspective, the application literally changes to reflect the increase in knowledge or skills gained by the learner. Once new concepts and skills are mastered, the program "adapts" and provides more sophisticated "responses" at a greater level of difficulty, given the increase in knowledge and skill base of the learner. As one learns more, the program provides a richer environment to move the learner to a higher knowledge and skill level. Adaptive response technology also monitors learner progress through the program, keeps track of the knowledge and skill level of that learner, and adapts the program to the learner's strengths and weaknesses, in order to customize lessons to fit that learner's set of needs. The adaptive response method has been utilized and adapted in many common computer games, in which the user masters one level of the game and then moves on to the next level to master a new set of challenges.

adult education (humanism)

In the mid–1920s, well before Malcolm Knowles's *andragogy* theory, Eduard Christian Lindeman, a contemporary and colleague of John Dewey, published a book entitled *The Meaning of Adult Education*. This work is Lindeman's espousal of his forward-thinking views of education for adults. To Lindeman, education is not preparation for life. "Education is life." By that Lindeman means that the essence of education for adults is situations and experiences, not the subjects they study. It is these situations and experiences that need to be brought into the adult educational experience. From Lindeman's perspective, "the situation-approach to education means that the learning process is at the outset given a setting of reality." Given this belief, Lindeman feels that college graduates are in most need of adult education, for they have been most negatively affected by a school system that is authoritarian and *instructor-centric* versus *learner-centric*.

For Lindeman, the purpose of education is "to put meaning into the whole of life." "Authoritative teaching, examinations which preclude original thinking, rigid pedagogical formula—all of these have no place in adult education." To Lindeman, life is also education. "Small groups of aspiring adults who desire to keep their minds fresh and vigorous; who begin to learn by confronting pertinent situations; who dig down into the reservoirs of their experience before resorting to texts and secondary facts; who are led in the discussion by teachers who are also searchers after wisdom and not oracles: this constitutes the setting for adult education, the modern quest for life's meaning." Believing very much in the social aspects of adult education, Lindeman declares that adult education is essentially friends educating each other, led by an instructor who is also seeking answers along with his or her colleagues in the quest for truth. Finally, Lindeman notes that genuine education involves adults "doing and thinking together." As such, Lindeman's philosophy of adult education is similar to Dewey's *instrumentalism* and his belief in *lifelong learning* as well as Jean Lave's later theory of *situated learning*.

advance organizers (cognitivism)

A term from David Ausubel's *subsumption theory* of learning, advance organizers are abstracts, outlines, and introductions of a large body of content that help structure and organize the content to be taught. Advance organizers are used to help students learn a large body of new content more readily by relating it up front to previously learned information within the learner's existing *schema*. Advance organizers not only structure the information, but also provide initial contextual information already familiar to the learner (the existing *schema*). This helps the learner take existing knowledge and relate it to new content to be learned.

Adventures of Jasper Woodbury (educational technology)

A research and development project of the Cognition and Technology Group, Learning Technology Center at the Peabody College of Vanderbilt University, the goal of the Adventures is the creation of shared *learning environments* in which students and teachers interact and solve problems. The theory behind the Adventures is *anchored instruction*, whereby *cooperative learning* and realistic *problem solving* are anchored to four episodic videodisc adventures in which a series of narrative events set up real-life scenarios and difficulties to be resolved by the students in a cooperative fashion. Anchored instruction is based to a large extent on Lev Vygotsky's *social development theory*. The role of the teacher is as participant and guide to help the students resolve the problems set up in the narrative. The *cooperative learning* method has been successfully transferred to the business environment as well for industry training courses.

affordance (humanism)

Within James J. Gibson's *information pickup theory*, affordances refer to the physical environment that we perceive and that make up the *stimulus array*. These environmental affordances include the physical landscape, the land, sky, and water. Also within the stimulus array are *invariants*, such as shadow, texture, color, and layout that help determine what we perceive. As espoused in Gibson's information pickup theory, the act of perception is a dynamic between the organism and the physical environment.

Developed by Gibson from the 1950s through the1970s, information pickup theory is a *Gestalt theory* and approach to perception and learning. Gestalt, the German word for shape or configuration, is a way of describing how humans perceive the world, as a meaningful whole rather than as isolated stimuli. Human beings see complete shapes, such as buildings, houses, mountains, trees, and lakes. Humans do not see merely lines, incomplete shapes, and patches of color. To adherents of Gestalt theory, dissection and analysis of individual parts is a distortion of reality. To Gestaltists, the whole is greater than the sum of the parts. Thus, given this philosophical background, Gestaltists study *molar behavior* (i.e., the whole) versus *molecular behavior* (i.e., the parts). In terms of learning, Gibson postulates that the learner must have a rich, complex learning environment within which to interact. Learning should be based upon visual cues that the learner obtains from interacting in the environment. To increase learning, the instructor must provide environmental affordances within which the learners can learn and perform a series of activities.

agents (educational technology)

A relatively new type of software technology, agents guide software users and provide *electronic performance support* as they seek to complete software tasks online. According to the *Agent Sourcebook* by Colin Harrison and Alper Caglayan, three basic types of agents occur in computer systems: (1) desktop, (2) *Internet*, and (3) intranet. The first type, desktop agents, are categorized into operating system, application, and suite agents. Operating system agents guide users of desktop operating systems, application agents guide users of applications, and suite agents guide users for a suite of software applications. The second of the three basic types, *Internet* agents, are Web search agents that filter information and provide automatic information retrieval on particular preselected topics that are then "pushed" to users without their having to actively search for additional information. The third type, intranet agents, are categorized into four types. Collaborative customization agents help automate workflow among several business units. Process automation agents automate workflow within a business unit. Database agents search out data within enterprise-wide databases. Resource-brokering agents define resource

allocation configurations among servers within a business organization. Agents are a practical application of electronic performance support, where learners gain access to information at the precise moment of need, while they are on the job.

algo-heuristic theory (cognitivism)

Lev Nakhmanovich Landa's algo-heuristic theory, first postulated in the mid–1970s, focuses on identifying *cognitive processes* that learners undergo while performing learning tasks and *problem-solving* activities to obtain knowledge to perform new operations. To Landa, there are three types of knowledge: images, concepts, and propositions. Images are visualizations of a *knowledge object*, such as a mental image of a baseball. Concepts focus on the form of an object with its defining set of features and characteristics, such as the size, hardness, and the red stitching around the baseball. Propositions are the relationships between an object and another, such as a baseball in relation to a baseball bat or glove. Propositions would include rules and laws, such as the laws of physics that operate when a baseball is hit using a baseball bat.

Knowledge can be viewed in relation not only to objects but also to operations. To perform a task or solve a problem, the learner must follow either algorithmic or heuristic processes or sets of operations. Algorithmic processes are regular operations performed under a defined, simple set of conditions. An example of an algorithmic process is throwing a baseball to another person with a baseball glove. If the process is one that the learner does not know how to do beforehand or is one that is not performed in a regular, simple manner and that involves *decision making* and skill, then this is known as a heuristic process. An example of a heuristic process is a pitcher throwing a curve ball to the inside part of the home plate to the catcher in order to strike out the batter with a count of one ball and two strikes.

A key aspect of the theory is that algo-heuristic principles can be taught through prescriptions (sets of specific instructions for problem solving) and demonstration of operations that follow the prescriptions. As a final note, instructing students to discover how to perform the processes through their own initiative and practice is far better than having them learn by observing only.

altered states of consciousness (behaviorism)

While philosophical debate has ensued for centuries on the nature of mind and brain and on what constitutes a state of *consciousness*, behaviorists have more recently focused their attention on altered states of consciousness, which are different from a normal, wakeful, and alert state. Examples of altered states are dreams, daydreams, prayer, meditation, or even trances induced by hypnosis and/or mind altering drugs. Altered states of consciousness are particularly important to behavior therapists, who seek to apply *behavior modification* to control and redirect a patient's undesirable behavior. Subliminal suggestion is often used to redirect the *stimulus response association* from bad behavior to good behavior.

analogical learning (cognitivism)

Used by good teachers since the time of Socrates (and before), analogical learning involves comparing a familiar situation with a new, unfamiliar situation so that the new situation can be better understood within a more familiar context. Analogical learning occurs when the instructor delineates a particular scenario, abstracts details from that scenario, and defines a solution to the particular problem presented in that scenario. Then the instructor applies the solution from this known problem to a new, but similar, scenario and problem. The students' job is to apply the problem/solution set from the original scenario to the new scenario and come up with a solution for the new scenario. Analogical learning thus involves the creation of a set of feature mappings of the two scenarios. (X situation is similar to Y situation, with these similarities and differences in de-

tails, problems, and outcomes.) Analogical learning is closely allied to *case-based reasoning*, which is the process of applying previous experience to *problem solving* in which an old case is compared to a new case that has similar features and elements.

anchored instruction (cognitivism)

Based upon the technology-based learning theory of John Bransford and others at Vanderbilt University, anchored instruction is a method of linking (or anchoring) new concepts to the learner's knowledge and experience to help make these new concepts easier to learn and remember. In the case of the *Adventures of Jasper Woodbury*, the anchors are the videodisc narrative episodes, which provide a simulated realistic scenario for the learner to grapple with (along with the teacher as guide) and provide solutions to problems that arise. The anchor itself is a contextual representation, a simulated real-life trigger that reminds the learner of previous experiences and concepts learned. As a result of this anchor, the new information about to be learned has a framework and is more meaningful to the student as well as easier to be recalled again at a later date. Thus, the key thing about anchored instruction is context, in which the teacher provides, often through a technology-based application (such as the Adventures of Jasper Woodbury), an anchor, which bonds the content to a true-to-life frame of reference to enhance the learning and retention of the new content.

andragogy (constructivism)

Previously dominated by the *instructor-centric* theories of *pedagogy* that pretty much ignored for years how adults learn best, adult learning became a major focus when Malcolm Knowles in 1968 pioneered the learning theory of andragogy, a *learner-centric* approach to learning, based on the following six assumptions:

1. "Need to Know." Adults require that the instructor provide a rationale for why they need to learn the new infor-

7

mation prior to learning it. Otherwise, they lack a motivation for learning, which is a key to the adult learning experience.

2. "Self-Concept." Adults have a defined identity that involves being responsible for their own lives, decision, and actions. They dislike being told what to do, as is often the case in a pedagogic learning environment.

3. "Life Experience." Adults have gained life experiences from both a qualitative and quantitative perspective and have taken on roles not as yet taken on by children, such as that of spouse, parent, worker, manager, etc. They bring this knowledge and experience to the learning experience.

4. "Readiness to Learn." Adults are ready to learn when they make a decision that the content to be provided in the learning experience will be helpful for their real-life activities.

5. "Orientation to Learning." Adults approach learning from a very practical perspective. They seek it to improve their lives and to be more productive. Thus, they expect learning to be task-oriented and related to their jobs versus passively obtaining subject-oriented information unrelated to their work. Thus, they will learn the content only as it applies to activities that they need to learn about to perform useful tasks. For adults, providing contextual information is key to the effectiveness of the learning experience.

6. "Motivation to Learn." Adults are, for the most part, self-motivated to learn. Internal forces are at work that make them self-motivated, such as better lifestyle, better work environment, better job, increased self-esteem, etc. Adults are highly motivated to learn in a positive adult learning environment. They become fearful when placed in a pedagogic learning environment where the teacher seeks to be an authority figure, rather than a facilitator of knowledge.

Many of Knowles's postulates for adult learning are currently being applied to traditional pedagogic learning environments with positive results. It could be argued that one of the main problems with public education at the K–12 level is the perpetuation of the pedagogic model, with its emphasis on passive, rote, nonsocial, non-contextual learning from an authoritarian type of instructor, whose primary means of student motivation is the grade. It could also be argued that at all levels, the use of andragogic elements, including anchors, case studies, role playing, simulations, self-evaluations, and peer evaluations are most helpful to the pedagogic learning process. Instructor adoption of the andragogic role of coach and facilitator can be viewed as an improvement to the learning experience for all learners at no matter what level over that of the traditional role of the teacher as authoritarian dispenser of information as lecturer, grader, and primary source of knowledge.

Children today seem far more mature, far more knowledgeable and worldly, than their parents were as children. Students seem to thrive when placed in an andragogic learning environment. Many of the reforms being attempted in K–12 schools involve the movement from pedagogy to andragogy for all learning levels. From Knowles's perspective, andragogy was a way to improve education for adults. Thirty years later, andragogic learning methods are being applied on a fairly broad basis to pedagogical learning environments. The success of this approach for all levels of learners is still a subject of debate and discussion. Without Knowles's initial distinction of andragogy and pedagogy, there never would have been a debate. With Knowles, a paradigm shift has occurred from *instructor-centric* to *learner-centric learning*.

appraisal theories of emotion (constructivism)

Part of Albert Bandura's *social learning theory*, appraisal theories of emotion attempt to predict what kinds of situations and emotional states elicit specific types of emotional responses from learners that can either enhance or inhibit the quality and effectiveness of the learning experience. Social learning theory defines learning behavior as a continuous reciprocal interaction of cognitive, behavioral, and environmental factors. Emotions play an important factor in the receptivity of the learner to the learning experience. For example, a learner in an emotional state of anger and tension will have far more difficulty absorbing information and sharing ideas with fellow learners than a learner whose emotional state is one of relative calmness and serenity. In short, appraisal theories consider the impact of emotional states and responses on learning.

apprenticeship learning (humanism)

Used on a widespread basis for centuries going back to the medieval guilds, apprenticeship learning is a structured system of one-on-one training between a mentor and an apprentice that leads to certification in a particular discipline or trade. It is sometimes supplemented by classroom instruction on the concepts of the discipline that are required to be learned in relation to the trade. From a modern educational perspective, apprenticeship learning occurs when the teacher works alongside the student and assists in the performance of a set of very hands-on tasks. With this approach, teachers give students practice situations before having them do more challenging work tasks on their own. Apprenticeship learning is allied to *cognitive coaching,* a nonjudgmental mentoring process between an instructor and a student, in which the ultimate goal is that the learner can accomplish tasks independently of the instructor. In business, apprenticeship learning is used often, in which the mentor is a practitioner who works in the field and shows the apprentice "the ropes" of how to do the job. In any apprenticeship learning environment, mastery of a set of tasks results in mastery of that trade or discipline. Other current terms for apprenticeship learning are *on-the-job training* and *direct instruction.* Though in widespread use during the Middle Ages, apprenticeship learning was in fact practiced

among Egyptian scribes in 2000 B.C. and rules for how apprenticeships should be handled were included in the Code of Hammurabi in Babylon around the same time period.

aptitude-treatment interaction (constructivism)

Sometimes referred to simply as ATI, aptitude-treatment interaction postulates that learning content and interaction should be adapted to the varying aptitudes and emotional states of the students. Optimal learning occurs when the instructional content matches the learner's aptitude. Like Howard Gardner's theory of *multiple intelligences,* aptitude-treatment interaction emphasizes the individual differences and *learning styles* of students and how learning content should be tailored to take into consideration these differences. ATI was first presented in the mid–1970s by Lee Cronbach and Richard Snow who identify three basic principles of ATI, which are the following: (1) Student aptitudes and instructional content interact and are highly influenced by both task variables and situational variables. (2) The lower the students' ability, the more highly structured the learning content needs to be. The higher the students' ability, the more loosely structured the learning content can be, since this is more effective for the learners. (3) Students who are anxious and seek to conform also learn better in highly structured environments, whereas less anxious and more independent-minded students do better in low-structured learning environments.

artificial intelligence (cognitivism)

In its simplest definition, artificial intelligence (also referred to as "AI") is the study of how to make computers think like humans. The difficulty is that, despite the millions of words written and projects done on *intelligence,* researchers are still not all that clear on how humans think. The value of artificial intelligence within the context of studying cognition is this: The study of AI allows us to better understand how humans think. Thus, by attempting to provide computers with the ability to do things such as provide expert advice, understand natural language, speak, and recognize handwriting, it is hoped that we will learn better how humans reason, learn and speak language, and have complex thoughts. AI has sometimes been criticised as being impractical and unable to yield specific results. However, the three most useful areas for AI are the following: (1) Building *expert systems* (to have computers solve real-life problems by following "if/then" rules of logic). (2) Building *natural language processing* systems (to allow computers to understand spoken and typed language). (3) Building *neural networks* (to create a digitized model of the human brain by utilizing the binary memory of the computer).

From a learning theory perspective, there are several ongoing projects involving AI including, but not limited to, the *General Problem Solver* (GPS) program built on the *logic theorist*, an architecture for human problem solving; *Soar*, an architecture for human cognitive processing; and *GOMS*, an architecture for human-computer task completion. As one can see, there are many and varied approaches taken on AI, each of which attempts to model a part of what we think we know about human intelligence, how we think, communicate, and learn. We have a long way to go, but we do seem to be getting a bit closer regarding understanding the process. The problem goes back to our definition of intelligence. Is it reasoning ability? Is it the ability to perceive and process data from the real world? Is it the ability to learn itself? Thus, ultimately AI has a twofold purpose: to make computers more useful and to understand better how humans think.

artificial life (cognitivism)

Coined and first studied by Christopher G. Langton, Director of the Artificial Life Program at Sante Fe Institute, artificial life, sometimes called Alife, is the study of man-made systems that perform behaviors characteristic of living beings. More specifically, artificial life is the attempt to explain the behavior of existing carbon-based life forms by creating man-made, computerized "life" forms, within a computer simulated model, that are able to adapt to that environment and perform actions independent of an external human agent. Alife and *artificial intelligence* are generally regarded as two separate fields of research, though a portion of AI research has joined with Alife research in terms of creating relatively simple human made systems that "evolve," learn, adapt, and become more complex as they increase in "intelligence." Where *artificial intelligence* researchers tend to come from backgrounds in psychology, computer science, and computer engineering, artificial life researchers tend to come from backgrounds in biology, chemistry, physics, and mathematics. As there is a convergence currently occurring in the fields of engineering and biology, so too is there a convergence of artificial life and artificial intelligence research.

ASK systems (educational technology)

Developed by Roger Schank and his students at the Institute for Learning Sciences at Northwestern University, ASK systems are a set of *hypermedia applications* that contain a *knowledge base* of video clips by teacher experts on various topics of interest. A hypermedia application is an exploratory system that allows the user to select from a menu of topics that the students wish to know more about. As an example, the *Internet* itself is one huge hypermedia *learning environment*. In the ASK learning environment, which is in effect an *expert system*, the students query the hypermedia knowledge base and have a dialogue with the experts. The net result is that students have questions on topics and, in response, teachers provide stories (through the video clips) of their own experiences that illustrate and expand upon the topics. It is akin to the elder of the tribe telling stories and providing wisdom while the tribe's children sit around the campfire and ask questions. In such a manner, knowledge is transferred and experiences are shared between experts and novices by means of the expert system.

assimilation (constructivism)

One of two *developmental learning* processes espoused by Jean Piaget, assimilation involves the child interpreting environmental events within the context of already existing *cognitive structures*. The other developmental process, *accommodation*, involves the process of changing the child's cognitive structures to make sense of the new events occurring in the environment. Accommodation and assimilation work together as the child develops and interacts with the environment. As the child grows older and becomes an adult, the combined processes of assimilation and accommodation increase cognitive growth and maturation intellectually, socially, morally, and emotionally. Learning theorists who view Piaget as a cognitivist emphasize Piaget's process of accommodation over assimilation. Those who regard him as a constructivist focus on Piaget's process of assimilation over accommodation. It is probably true that Piaget falls under both categories.

assistive technology (educational technology)

Primarily for individuals with disabilities, assistive technology refers to any type of computer or other technology products, such as *voice recognition* hardware and software, that help people with mental or physical difficulties overcome them in order to accomplish learning activities and tasks. Assistive technology also refers to the services that help the disabled select and use the appropriate technology to meet their learning goals.

asynchronous learning (educational technology)

A type of *distance learning*, asynchronous learning is *computer-mediated communication* in which the learners and the instructor are NOT communicating over the *Internet* at the same time as part of their course activities. Instead, interactions and communications are occurring nonsimultaneously through the use of *e-mail, mail lists, class Web sites* (where lectures, lecture notes, *chat* text, syllabus, case studies, video and audio files, and research deliverables are posted) for consumption at any time. Asynchronous learning derives its meaning from the data processing world, in which the term asynchronous refers to computer interactions or processes that occur at various points in time, rather than at the same time. Asynchronous learning is opposed to *synchronous learning*. Synchronous learning is computer-mediated communication in which the learners and the instructor are communicating over the *Internet* at the same time as part of their course activities. With synchronous learning, interactions and communications are occurring simultaneously through the use of *videoconferencing*, voice or text chat, *or audio-conferencing*. Typically, most Internet-based distance learning courses employ both asynchronous learning and synchronous learning methods and techniques. Both are of value for the creation of *virtual learning communities*, the *electronic campus*, and the *universal campus network*.

Atkinson-Shiffrin memory model (cognitivism)

This is the first significant *levels of processing* memory model delineated in the middle-to-late 1960s, in which it is postulated that humans process sensory data and information from the environment through three distinct levels: *sensory memory, short-term memory*, and *long-term memory*. Previous theories of how people remember and learn focused on a simple model in which information either goes directly into short-term memory or long-term memory. The Atkinson and Shiffrin model, though the core idea of it remains current, has been superseded by Craik and Lockhart's *level of processing* theory that postulates that the human mind processes information and learns at a number of different levels simultaneously. The more levels experienced, the deeper the processing that occurs. Rote memorization (as experienced in the *industrial age educational paradigm*) is unsuccessful because deep processing does not occur and the information remains (only temporarily) in short-term memory. When information is given a context, then the information can be processed and fixed in long-term memory.

audio-conferencing (educational technology)

An example of a *multimedia application* used for *distance learning*, audio-conferencing involves using in effect a digital audio phone to allow instructors and learners in multiple locations to hear one another in conference in real time (i.e., live) and interact. With the advent of the *Internet*, audio-conferencing has moved to the PC desktop, wherein each learning participant has mounted on his or her own personal computer a microphone and speakers. As each participant speaks, the others in the audio-conference can hear one another as the voice and sound data is carried over the network and delivered to each participant's computer and speakers.

autoclitic behavior (behaviorism)

This term refers to the fourth of four categories of human *verbal behavior* delineated by B.F. Skinner. According to Skinner, verbal behavior (i.e., language) of humans can be entirely defined and explained within the context of *reinforcement theory*. For Skinner, both human talking and listening are actions that are directly influenced, just like any other behavior, by reinforcement from the environment. Skinner classified verbal behaviors that are responses to reinforcement into four categorizations: (1) *Mands*. These are commands and utterances that require an immediate response. An example of a mand is, "Watch out for that car." (2) *Tact*. These are words that represent specific objects recognized by the human in the environment, expressed out loud, and reinforced not only by the sound of the word but also by an observer's recognition that the word corresponds to the object and to the sound of the word itself. (3) *Echoic Behavior*. When the human repeats exactly same the set of words stated verbatim by another, this action is known as echoic behavior. It is a beginning stage toward learning more complex verbal behavior beyond repetition of another's

words. (4) *Autoclitic Behavior*. This is behavior that is entirely dependent upon other verbal behavior to qualify responses, to express relationships, and to provide a grammatical frame to the verbal behavior. Overall, Skinner's view of human verbal behavior is that it is based entirely upon the environment and environmental responses. He rejects the cognitive processes that are delineated by cognitivists as they seek to define natural language processing of humans.

automatic subgoaling (cognitivism)

An element (along with *problem spaces, search control, data chunking, objects with attributes and values,* and *production rules*) in Allen Newell's *Soar,* a *cognitive architecture* and *artificial intelligence* programming language, automatic subgoaling is a single mechanism for generating goals. Within the program, a goal is a result that an operator seeks to achieve from completing a set of tasks (i.e, the operator moving from an initial state to a final state or result). Arguing for a *unified theory of cognition,* Newell developed a set of principles for *cognitive processing* and human *problem solving* with Soar. Soar stands for State, Operator, And Result. The other elements in Soar, besides automatic subgoaling, are defined as follows. Problem spaces are a single framework within which all tasks and subtasks associated with achieving a goal are to be resolved. As such, problem solving in Soar is a search through the problem space in which the program applies an Operator (set of operations) to a State to get a Result. Search control is the process of selecting appropriate problem spaces, states, and operators by comparing alternative paths to take. Data chunking is the process by which the program recalls information in *working memory* outside of the context that the information first appeared. Objects with attributes and values provide a single representation of temporary knowledge in *working memory*. Production rules provide a single representation of permanent knowledge in *long-term memory*. As an attempt to construct a *unified theory of cognition,* Soar focuses on analyzing a task and all related subtasks and developing an effective and efficient means for completing the task and subtasks. Current Soar research is being conducted at Carnegie Mellon University, Ohio State University, University of Michigan, University of Southern California, University of Hertfordshire, and University of Nottingham.

B

barriers to learning (constructivism)

A reference to a set of constraints that can prevent the learning from becoming actively involved in the adult learning process, barriers to learning are discussed at length in Patricia Cross's *Chain of Response* model. In that model, adult learners can be greatly inhibited by a set of dispositional, situational, and institutional barriers to learning that can negate the individual's positive attitude, motivation, and desire to participate in the learning experience. Examples of dispositional barriers to learning include lack of self-esteem, perceived negative learning experiences from a traditional school environment during childhood, and lack of family emotional support. Examples of situational barriers to learning include lack of money, transportation, and family care. Institutional barriers to learning come from schools that do not have an adult-learner-friendly policy toward education. Schools can provide institutional barriers to learning by making it difficult for adult students to apply, register, and participate in the classes. Thus, in Cross's Chain of Response model, participation in the learning experience is a direct result of a complex chain of responses originating within and outside of the adult learner. Barriers to learning can break off the links in the chain of responses and ultimately stop the adult learner from achieving his or her learning goals.

behavior control (behaviorism)

This is the control of an individual's entire physical existence through rewards and punishments. With behavior control, the coercive agent seeks to control all aspects of the person's life: where one lives; what one eats, wears, sleeps; duties performed, etc. It typically involves a set of coercive techniques used to alter both the behavior and the attitude of the subject. Critics of *behaviorism* claim that those who seek to manipulate individuals through behavior-control techniques are using *behavior-modification* and *operant-conditioning* methods to accomplish their mission. Leon Festinger in the 1950s argued that to avoid *cognitive dissonance*, humans will sometimes subject themselves to behavior control, *thought control* (i.e., control of an individual's thought processes), and *emotion control* (i.e., the control of an individual's emotional life).

behavior modeling (behaviorism)

The goal of B.F. Skinner's *operant conditioning* is to achieve behavior modeling (sometimes called behavior shaping), so that the animal is rewarded for following a particular path or set of actions that is desired by the behavioral scientist. Albert Bandura, a student of B.F. Skinner, studied behavior modeling in humans by noting how we learn by observing. More specifically, Bandura studied how violence portrayed in mass media can negatively affect the behavior of some children who watch violent television shows. What he noted was that certain types of children will observe and then imitate behavior of characters seen on the television screen. Subsequent research has shown that most children will from time to time imitate behavior seen on television, though not necessarily violent behavior. Those children most at risk to imitate violent behavior from television shows (and movies) have the following characteristics: (1) a strong identification with the character portrayed in the show; (2) persistent fantasy thoughts about the program, with the child envisioning himself or herself in the role of the character; and (3) the capacity to commit a violent physical act. From Bandura's original observations of children and media effects on them, he developed his *social learning* theory. He determined that certain types of children learn to perform violent and aggressive actions by observing and then modeling their behavior after what they have seen. He referred to this as direct learning through instantaneous matching of the observed behavior to the modeled behavior.

behavior modification (behaviorism)

Also referred to as behavior therapy, behavior modification is a discipline that focuses on methods of changing human behavior, in particular, dysfunctional behavior. Behavior modification is based upon a series of assumptions regarding human behavior. These include the following: We can predict human behavior because it follows certain laws and patterns and we can change human behavior through *operant conditioning* and other behavioral science techniques. Other assumptions of behavior modification are that the mechanisms of human behavior are the same for both functional and dysfunctional human action and that the internal state or thoughts of the individual are not the concern of the behavioral scientist seeking to alter the dysfunctional behavior. Behavior modification of an individual undergoing therapy is achieved when a change of behavior is induced in that individual by the behavioral scientist manipulating the environment within which the patient's actions are performed. As such, behavioral scientists pay a great deal of attention in their therapy to targeting the dysfunctional behavior, describing the behavior within the environmental context, and documenting the effectiveness of the attempted interventions to modify the behavior within that environment. From these detailed observations of human behavior within a particular environmental context, emerge patterns of how humans behave in given situations.

behavioral repertoire (behaviorism)

Animals are limited by their specific range of actions they can perform (their behavioral repertoire), which is predominantly based upon the structure and function of their bodies. For example, no matter how much coaxing or conditioning, elephants cannot be taught to fly nor can birds be taught to swim given their body structures. In *operant conditioning*, animals are limited by their behavioral repertoire to be taught and to perform particular sets of actions. A behavioral scientist sets up a *stimulus-response association* within the constraints of the behavioral repertoire of the species. However, no amount of coaxing, cajoling, conditioning, or training will yield the result of the animal performing actions it is incapable of doing given its physiological makeup. The more closely a desired response can be connected to the natural behavior and motion of the animal (its behavioral repertoire), the more likely the behavioral scientist will achieve a positive result.

behaviorism

One of the four major learning theory schools, behaviorism is the belief that instruction is achieved by observable, measurable, and controllable objectives set by the instructor and met by the learners who elicit a specific set of responses based upon a controlled set of stimuli. Based upon B.F. Skinner's initial research work with mice in the 1930s, behaviorism made the assumption that by controlling the lab environment of mice, they could be trained to behave consistently. Humans also, if provided with a correct stimulus, would be able to be trained to respond in a particular manner exhibited by a set of behavioral outcomes.

In the world of behaviorism, instructors drive specific behavioral outcomes from learners through a defined set of *learning objectives*. Learning tasks are structured from simple to complex activities. Assessing the success of the educational experience is based completely upon the achievement of a set of behavioral outcomes predicted by the learning objectives. By systematically adjusting the stimuli throughout a course of study, the instructor can alter and fine-tune the behavior of the learners and modify the outcomes.

Behaviorism does not concern itself with the learner's internal mental states, constructs, and symbols that *cognitivism* considers in its focus on learning *schemas*. With cognitivism, the focus of research is on how the brain receives, internalizes, and recalls information. Behaviorism is not interested in internal mental states, but only in external outputs, learning products, and behavioral change.

Behaviorism is not concerned with the willfulness, *creativity*, and autonomy of the learners that *constructivism* considers in its focus on the learning process. With constructivism, the focus of research is on how to help learners construct, rather than be controlled by the learning experience. Behaviorism is not interested in any behavior from the students that is not predicted beforehand by the learning objectives and demonstrated by the behavioral outcomes. Unlike *humanism*, behaviorism is not interested in the self-direction or self-actualization of the learner. It is not concerned about whether individual or social human needs are met through the educational process, as is humanism. Behaviorism is concerned with learning outputs, with a set of single events controlled by the stimulus-response mechanism versus the *learning* and thinking that is the focus of humanism.

Nevertheless, despite its detractors and opposing schools of learning (cognitivism, constructivism, and humanism), behaviorism is still a powerful force in how children and adults are taught nearly seventy years after Skinner began his research with animals.

bodily kinesthetic intelligence (constructivism)

One of Howard Gardner's eight *multiple intelligences*, bodily kinesthetic intelligence is the ability to hold objects and to control one's own body movements, as well as to have coordination. One who posseses bodily-kinesthetic intelligence can integrate body movements with thoughts, feelings, and ideas. Examples of bodily-kinesthetic activities are all sports (e.g., baseball, basketball, football, soccer, etc.), dance, mime, drama, and martial arts. Individuals who possess this type of intelligence and who are provided with the right cultural and educational background in this area are apt to pursue careers as baseball, basketball, football, or soccer players, as well as dancers or actors. Gardner suggests that bodily-kinesthetic intelligence needs to be developed in the individual and must not be given less focus in favor of *verbal-linguistic intelligence* and *logical-mathematical intelligence*, which most schools tend to emphasize in their *curriculum design*.

bounded rationality (cognitivism)

A term from the *artificial intelligence* community, bounded rationality refers to the limited cognitive abilities, based upon its *cognitive architecture*, that a computer *agent* has within an artificial intelligence system to approximate the human ability to synthesize knowledge and solve problems. Examples of limitations include *memory* and time. In *Soar,* and in other artificial intelligence systems, the limits of the architecture become apparent as one increases the complexity and amount of the body of knowledge that is required to complete the set of tasks and as the tasks themselves are made more complex and diverse. The better the architecture of the artificial intelligence system, the more closely it approximates human *cognitive processes* to achieve what is considered *complete rationality*. This assumes, of course, that humans themselves are completely rational (though Herbert Simon, in his *Models of Man* assumes they are not) as they go about solving complex, task-based problems in the environment. In short, bounded rationality refers to a computer agent's ability, as well as a human's ability, to achieve *complete rationality*.

brain-based learning (cognitivism)

Based upon the research of Renate and Geoffrey Caine, brain-based learning is a theory that focuses on the close relationship between the way the brain works and the way children and adults learn. According to the Caines, the first twelve years of a child's life determine how intelligent the adult will be later. By analogy, the brain is a complex and vast human computer hardware mechanism that has millions of built-in patterns and inputs. As the human learns and works in the environment, millions of software programs are created and enhanced over time. The three instructional methods for achieving brain-based learning are: *orchestrated immersion* (immersing students in a rich, hands-on learning environment), *active processing* (helping the students become aware of the form, meaning, and motivation behind *knowledge acquisition* through various hands-on learning tasks), and *relaxed alertness* (minimizing learner fear, while retaining a rich, hands-on educational experience). In short, brain-based learning de-emphasizes memorization, listening to lectures, and textbook reading and emphasizes instead hands-on learning tasks that actively engage the learner

in the learning process through active *problem solving*.

building shared vision (organizational learning)

One of the disciplines for the *learning organization* in Peter Senge's *The Fifth Discipline*, building shared vision is a process of sharing multiple visions that different people within the organization have of themselves and the business world. It is a future-oriented activity, in which individuals within the organization build a consensus of how they want things to be in the near and not-so-near future. Its goal is to foster among the participants compliance and commitment to the vision of the future that the group strives for within the organization.

business transformation (organizational learning)

An important aspect of *knowledge management, organizational learning*, and *transformational learning*, business transformation involves using technology, especially communications and *collaboration* technology, to enhance every aspect of how the business enterprise operates. Business transformation is primarily concerned with spearheading enterprise-wide *organizational learning*, innovation, and the application of breakthrough digital age technologies to create new products and services. In the recent past, data processing primarily handled structured information to run the financial and accounting aspects of the business. With the rise of the Web and the *digitization* of the *knowledge base* (e.g., image, audio, video, and animation files) within various types of digital *knowledge objects* (e.g., white papers, design documents, policies and procedures, and technical specifications), enterprises can shift their product focus from physical to *knowledge assets*.

In both high-tech and low-tech industries, knowledge managers working with computer hardware and software engineers provide the digital glue that helps link the bits—the rich data types within the *knowledge objects* — to the physical products (automobile, airplane, software programs) being created. Knowledge managers are on the front lines of companies' business transformation and *organizational learning* initiatives. They ulti-mately help move enterprises from an *industrial age educational paradigm* to a *digital age educational paradigm* by their involvement in the creation of a vast library of electronic information that support the products and services offered by these enterprises.

C

I am a part of all that I have met.
—Alfred, Lord Tennyson, nineteenth-century English poet laureate

Cabri-geometry (educational technology)

As noted in their Web site (http://www-cabri.imag.fr/a-propos/index-e.html), Cabri-geometry is an extremely popular educational software application used by secondary school geometry students, as well as by university mathematics and science students and researchers worldwide. It is a visualization tool allowing students and researchers to actively explore the properties of geometric objects and to modify their shapes and interrelationships. Cabri-geometry is a product of a collaborative research project at the University Joseph Fourier of Grenoble and the Centre National de la Recherche Scientifique in the Laboratoire de Structures Discrètes et de Didactique, along with EIAH (Environnements Informatiques d'Apprentis-sage Humain) in the laboratory LEIBNIZ. The application runs under DOS, Windows, Mac, and Texas Instrument calculator operating systems (TI-92 and TI-89). It has received numerous awards worldwide and is an important tool for *active learning, discovery learning,* and *collaborative learning* activities. Examples of simple visualizations and animations are provided at the following Cabri-geometry Web site page (http://www-cabri.imag.fr/a-propos/fonctions-e.html). In addition to sponsoring an international conference devoted to the promotion and development of *active-learning*-based geometry exercises, the consortium sponsors Cabri online activities, including forums, *chat* groups, Cabri-Java applets (for *Web-based training*), and bulletin boards. Cabri-geometry is one of the most popular, widespread educational technology products used by learners worldwide. Its value to the learning theory school of *constructivism* is that the learner has direct control over the behavior of the geometric objects he or she has constructed in a highly visual, fast feedback oriented way.

case-based reasoning (constructivism)

Part of both organizational learning and the learning theory school of *constructivism*, case-based reasoning is a method for human *problem solving* and learning as well as a method for building *knowledge management* and *expert systems*. In its simplest form, case-based reasoning is the process of taking the remembered experiences and solutions of previous problems we encounter in the environment and applying and adapting them to solve new problems that occur. A case-based reasoning system stores previous experiences that are categorized in memory, retrieves them as it applies to a new situation, reuses the experience in the new situation and then categorizes and records the new result in memory.

In Roger Schank's *Script theory* of learning, human beings follow a similar case-based reasoning approach. We learn to perform new activities by creating scripts that contain sequential procedures for given situations. We store these in memory and "pull out" specific scripts for situations that are similar to previous scenarios we have encountered and adapt them to the new situation. In Schank's world, scripts govern our memories, learning, and actions. Through *active learning*, we build scripts and develop a memory system that allows us to act again in similar situations. By creating scripts, we integrate what we have learned with new situations that demand solutions to problems. From a case-based reasoning perspective, we store and categorize a series of cases from previous situations and we recall and reuse them for new problem situations that require a solution in the environment. The genesis of case based reasoning is the case method of Christopher Langdell, dean of Harvard Law School, who in the 1880s practiced the approach of teaching students about the law, not by reading legal texts, but by studying previous court verdicts and opinions and applying those to current cases.

categorization (cognitivism)

Within John Anderson's postulate for *rational analysis* (human cognition optimizes the behavior adaptation of the organism to accomplish tasks in the environment), categorization is one of three basic *signature* data for studying human *memory*, thinking and behavior which is part of his *ACT theory*. The other two signatures are the *power law of practice* and the *fan effect*. The power law of practice, simply stated, is that the more often one performs a particular task, the less time it takes to accomplish it. The fan effect is that the larger and tighter the fan of conceptual links there are in the brain to the task to be achieved, the more likely the central concept to accomplish that task will be activated in memory. Categorization, in this *schema*, is

the Web (fan) of information that is organized in the brain, based upon the feedback obtained from the act of completing the task. The forming of categories of information in the brain is strictly tied to the predictive usefulness of categorization to the mission of accomplishing the task.

Critics of Anderson's theory, like Herbert Simon, state that *rational analysis* is flawed because humans are not optimal and operate more under *bounded rationality* than anything else, and because human behavior across task domains are not constant, not easily predictable, and not always rational. Signature data alone do not define how humans think and solve problems in the environment. Rather, a whole series of data, some of which may appear to be irrelevant to researchers, can play a part in how we form concepts and seek to accomplish tasks in the environment. In a more general sense, categorization is very important to human learning and behavior. It helps us reduce the complexity of all of the input provided by the environment. It helps us identify objects in relation to one another by their features and in some sort of hierarchy. It reduces the need for relearning. And it helps us decide on an optimal or nearly optimal set of actions to apply in a given situation that takes place in the environment.

cell assembly (cognitivism)

According to Donald O. Hebb, all infants are born with a *neural network* that is loosely organized with random *neuron* interconnections. As the child develops, the neural network becomes more organized and is better able to interact with the environment, from which the child obtains a multitude of inputs. Each environmental object the child encounters through the senses fires a package of neurons known as a cell assembly. Cell assemblies are organized sets of neurons linked together and activated by an environmental object or event. Just as reactions to environmental objects form cell assemblies, so too do cell assemblies interconnect to form *phase sequences*. Cell assemblies that consistently follow one another sequentially in time form a phase sequence. A phase sequence is a sequence of cell assemblies, a sequence of thought that follows a logical order. Once cell assemblies and phase sequences become more fully developed in the human, a framework for learning is built and the human is able to learn with relative ease and quickness. Once these learning building blocks are fully formed, the adult is able to think and learn with creativity and insight.

Chain of Response model (constructivism)

In Patricia Cross's Chain of Response model, sometimes simply referred to as COR, participation in the adult learning experience is a direct result of a set of variables that are determining factors for the successfulness of the adult learning activity. The variables that make up the Chain of Response model are: (1) the learner's self esteem; (2) the learner's attitude toward the educational experience; (3) the learner's pre-conceived goals and expectations coming into the learning experience; (4) life changes that may be occurring at the time of the learning experience; (5) *barriers to learning* that can negate the desire and ability to participate in the learning experience; (6) the learner's awareness of adult learning opportunities that meet learner goals; (7) previous participation in positive adult learning activities. All of these variables form links in the process that can predict how successfully adult learners will perform in their upcoming *adult education* experience.

change adept organization (organizational learning)

According to Rosabeth Moss Kanter, author of fifteen books and numerous scholarly articles and currently professor of management at Harvard University, the change adept organization is defined as one that anticipates, responds to, and adapts to ongoing changes that continuously occur within the business enterprise. According to Kanter, the ways to foster a change adept organization are by using the three Cs, which are concepts, competence, and connections. Concepts encourage imagination that lead to new innovations. Competence encourages skill development through *knowledge sharing* and exchange. Connections encourage *collaboration* as well as joint ventures that are both internal and external to the organization. Kanter emphasizes that managers of a change adept organization must continuously encourage, in particular, collaboration and knowledge sharing. Without these connections, innovations and skills development quickly wither and die. As such, Kanter's change adept organization principles are closely allied to *action science*, *action research*, and *collaborative learning*, and fall under the learning paradigm of *constructivism*.

chaos theory (constructivism)

One of the important principles behind *artificial life*, chaos theory asserts that behind apparently random events within the natural world (such as the weather) as well as human-made systems (such as the stock market) lies an inherent, but complex order, based upon simple mathematical computations. Small changes that occur at the beginning of a *complex system* can later produce dramatic results to that system. In a chaotic system, an organism placed immediately in an unfamiliar, complex environment will not be able to survive. There will not be time for Piaget's *developmental learning* processes of *accommodation* and *assimilation* to occur to allow for the successful growth of that individual's mental or physical capacity to cope with the situation. If that same entity is placed in an environment that gradually becomes more complex, the organism will adapt, evolve, and survive and will also become a more complex entity as a result of its interactions with the increasingly complex environment.

Chaos theory is the study of whole, dynamic sets of systems that develop over time and follow distinct patterns, though on the surface, the events occurring within the system appear to be quite random, nonlinear, and far from orderly. The *nonlinearity* and apparent randomness of chaos-based systems place chaos theory within the learning paradigm of *constructivism*, especially given the interrelationships between chaos theory, complex systems, and *co-emergence*. Co-emergence is an important aspect of *complex systems* in which enhancements to the entire system occur as a result of repeated *knowledge sharing* interactions that develop between as few as two entities (e.g., human beings or *agents*) over time. These interactions and *collaborations*, though apparently insignificant when viewed individually, are in fact significant catalysts to change for the entire complex system (and for the entities within the system) over a given time.

chat (educational technology)

An important *synchronous learning* aspect of many *Internet*-based *distance learning* courses, chat is real-time (i.e., at the same time) *computer-mediated communication* in which participants can communicate with each other via the computer by means of typing text and/or voice. Text chat involves each participant typing on his or her own PC, while others across the Internet network respond by typing on their own PC, with all communications between the parties appearing on each person's computer screen. The result is that everyone in the chat can read the text of all of the participants' comments and responses in real time (i.e., live) and respond accordingly. Voice chat, sometimes referred to as *audio-conferencing*, or digital audio-conferencing, involves each party "chatting" (i.e., talking) into a microphone attached to the PC and listening to the communications of the other parties through the PC speakers or headphones. With advances in *voice recognition* technologies, individuals in voice chats will note the appearance on their PC screens of a text version of the chat session as they speak. Chats can become asynchronous learning activities, if the text of the entire chat session is posted to a *class Web site* after the interaction takes place. This allows participants in vastly different time zones (i.e., the United States and Japan) who could not attend the live chat to view the content of that chat asynchronously (i.e., at their own time and leisure).

chunking (cognitivism)

In a general sense, chunking is the process of breaking up information into smaller units so that it is easier for the human brain to remember and process. An example of chunking is assigning the telephone area code "770" to phone numbers in metropolitan Atlanta, Georgia. People repeatedly dialing phone numbers with a "770" prefix will know that the person to be dialed lives in metropolitan Atlanta. Within Allen Newell's *Soar* theory, chunking is a learning process that involves analyzing and committing to *memory* a particular resolution to a previously encountered situation or problem. When the individual encounters a similar impasse, he or she recalls the "chunk" and reuses it to solve this new problem.

class Web site (educational technology)

Becoming ubiquitous to the online academic landscape, the class Web site is the central location where the instructor and the learners, participating in a Web-based *distance learning* course, access, share, and post information related to the class they are taking online. The class Web site is a clear-cut example of *asynchronous learning, computer-mediated communication* in which the learners and the instructor are NOT communicating over the *Internet* at the same time as part of their course activities. Instead, interactions and communications are occurring nonsimultaneously via the class Web site (where lectures, lecture notes, *chat* text, syllabus, case studies, video and audio files, and research deliverables are posted) for consumption at any time. Asynchronous learning derives its meaning from the data processing world, in which the term asynchronous refers to computer interactions or processes that occur at various points in time, rather than at the same time. Asynchronous learning is opposed to *synchronous learning*. Synchronous learning is computer-mediated communication in which the learners and the instructor are communicating over the *Internet* at the same time as part of their course activities. With synchronous learning, interactions and communications are occurring simultaneously through the use of *videoconferencing*, voice or text *chat, or audio-conferencing*. Typically, most *Internet*-based distance learning courses employ both asynchronous learning and synchronous learning methods and techniques. However, all Web-based distance learning courses employ the class Web site, for without it, there is no central point online from which learners can obtain the asynchronous and synchronous components of the course. The class Web site, a key component for *Web-based knowledge transfer,* is crucial to the creation of *virtual learning communities*, the *electronic campus*, and the *universal campus network*.

classical conditioning (behaviorism)

The most basic and simple type of behavioral conditioning is classical conditioning. Classical conditioning occurs when two unrelated stimuli are provided simultaneously to a subject, whereby the subject begins to associate the two stimuli together and the subject provides an involuntary, reflexive response (*elicited behavior*) without being mentally aware of why the response is occurring. The classic example of this type of conditioning is the feeding of Pavlov's dog, in which the dog is provided with two unrelated stimuli (food at the sound of the bell). After a time, the dog, upon hearing the bell, begins to salivate, even though food is withheld from the subject. The dog "learns" that the bell sound means food, without the dog undergoing any *cognitive processing* or thinking about the activity.

CMN-GOMS (cognitivism)

This is one of a family of GOMS techniques that includes *keystroke level model, natural GOMS language,* and *CPM-GOMS*. CMN stands for Card, Moran, and Newell, the original developers of GOMS in the mid–

1980s. GOMS stands for Goals, Operators, Methods, and Selection rules. CMN-GOMS is an enhancement to the keystroke level model technique of GOMS. CMN-GOMS provides a hierarchical structure to the keystroke level model, which is the simplest of GOMS techniques that focuses on the measurement of discrete observable events and task times. A later enhancement to the *logic theorist* and GPS, *General Problem Solve*r, GOMS is a *cognitive architecture* (i.e., a model of cognitive processing for human *problem solving*, human learning, and task completion). The GOMS family is a prominent model for *human-computer interaction* and human learning used currently to measure the usefulness of computer user interface designs and human task performance. Goals refer to the desired result that the learner seeks to achieve. Operators are sets of operations that the learner constructs to meet the goal. Methods are operator sequences grouped together to achieve goal completion. Selection rules are decision points for particular methods to be used for particular situations that arise during the goal-seeking activity. Through the observation of human task performance with computers, GOMS seeks to model human *cognitive processing* and *memory* that occur in defined stages (i.e., *sensory memory, working memory,* and *long-term memory*).

co-emergence (constructivism)

A central principle of *enactivism*, co-emergence is the product of the interactions and communications that occur within a *collaborative learning* and *discovery learning* environment of learners, in which the stronger and weaker partners grow and help each other throughout the learning process. As in Vygotsky's *social development theory*, co-emergence is an important aspect to the development of human *consciousness* and *cognition* through the shared activity of learning occurring within the social relationships of the individuals participating in the process. Co-emergence is also an aspect of *complex systems* in which enhancements to the entire system occur as a result of repeated information-sharing interactions over time between as few as two entities. These interactions, though apparently insignificant, are in fact significant catalysts to change of the entire system as in *chaos theory*.

cognition (cognitivism)

In the seventeenth century, French philosopher and scientist René Descartes declared: "I think, therefore I am." Philosophical debate has ensued for centuries on the nature of mind and brain, what constitutes a state of consciousness, and what constitutes knowledge (e.g., *epistemology*) and thinking. Modern cognitivists seek to explore cognition. They seek to discover how humans and machines "think." As it is closely related to consciousness, cognition is a state of being through which passes individual thoughts and feelings making up one's personality and character. Self-awareness, awareness of beliefs and influences, and awareness of the external environment are important aspects of cognition, which involve a foundation and a mental framework for one's ability to think and learn.

cognitive apprenticeship (constructivism)

Closely allied to *apprenticeship learning* and *cognitive coaching*, this term refers to a model for hands-on instruction that seeks to redress the incorrect assumptions often made by schools about how people learn. These incorrect assumptions are as follows: (1) Learners automatically transfer school knowledge to everyday practice. (2) Learners are passive receivers of knowledge. (3) Learning is a direct result of providing the right stimulus to obtain the right response. (4) The minds of learners are blank slates with no context for learning. (5) Knowledge can be acquired independent of its context. According to Allan Collins, John S. Brown, and S.E. Newman, the cognitive apprenticeship model is based upon the following four elements: content,

methods, sequence, and sociology. Content refers to not merely the absorption of facts, but more importantly to *problem-solving* strategies, planning and revision management strategies, and learning strategies to reconfigure content. Method refers to a *scaffolded learning* approach, where the instructor initially supports the learners only to help them gain independence to carry out learning and *problem-solving* tasks later. Sequence refers to providing information first that is simple, straightforward, and familiar. Then more complex tasks with divergent problem solving scenarios that the learner must grapple with and resolve are provided. Sociology refers to utilizing *collaborative learning* techniques allowing students to learn and work in teams, as they will do when they leave the classroom.

cognitive architecture (cognitivism)

Closely related to a *unified theory of cognition*, cognitive architecture refers to a model of mental processing for human *problem solving*, learning, and task completion. An example of a cognitive architecture is Newell's *Soar,* which is a framework for understanding how humans and *artificial intelligence* computer systems "think" and learn. This is a widely recognized cognitive architecture that uses concepts such as *chunking* and *problem space* to describe how the human brain works to solve problems and complete tasks. Another example of a cognitive architecture is Anderson's *ACT theory*, in which computer system simulations of how the human brain works are utilized to assess the accuracy of the model.

cognitive array model (behaviorism)

Sometimes simply called the array model, William Kaye Estes's cognitive array model is his approach to *cognition, learning and performance*, and *memory*. Though a proponent of *behaviorism*, Estes in a fairly recent book entitled *Classification and Cognition* (1994) espoused the theory that *categorizations* and classifications of stimuli features encountered in the environment are stored by humans in sets or arrays. Estes's array model focuses not on past stimuli events, but on present events that will be encountered again and reused in the future. To Estes, the essence of human thinking and memory is classification and categorization. The purpose of his array model is to predict how humans fit particular stimuli into specific categories for later use. Unlike his earlier *stimulus sampling theory*, which was a behaviorist approach to learning in which mental events are not considered, Estes's cognitive array model clearly falls into the *learning paradigm* of *cognitive behaviorism*. Like Edward Chace Tolman's *purposive behaviorism*, Estes's cognitive array model declares that humans learn what is observed in the environment. These observations (which are classified and categorized) are translated into specific behaviors that are the result of the goals of the learner. Like *information processing theory*, Estes in his later years believes that inputs from the environment (i.e., stimuli) interact with multiple cognitive processes prior to a particular behavior or set of behaviors occurring.

cognitive artifacts (humanism)

These belong to one of two types of artifacts that aid human *cognition*. The other type of artifact is the *physical artifact*. In his mid–1990s book, *Things that Make Us Smart*, Donald A. Norman describes cognitive artifacts, such as reading, math, and language that are important for the *reflective mode of cognition*, as well as physical artifacts that we interact with, such as pencils, calculators, and computers that are important for the *experiential mode of cognition*. The experiential mode of cognition is more of a subconscious mode of thinking that occurs as we experience events and objects in our contemporary work and *learning environment*. The reflective mode of cognition refers to a higher-order thinking, similar to *metacognition*, in which the learner takes in ideas encountered from the world, thinks through them, reflects

upon them, and reuses them to construct new ideas and knowledge. According to Norman, contemporary education focuses on the use of computers, technology, and *multimedia* (the physical artifacts) that help us in regard to the experiential mode of cognition. Yet, he feels that these same physical artifacts can often inhibit learners with regard to thinking creatively and constructively by means of the reflective mode of cognition through reading, math, and language (the cognitive artifacts). Norman's concern about technology and its use in education is that it overemphasizes the experiential mode of cognition and seeks to immerse and entertain students instead of getting them to be thoughtful and reflective, thus strengthening their reflective mode of cognition.

cognitive behaviorism (behaviorism)

This is a hybrid of both *cognitivism* and *behaviorism* in which the focus is not only on the external behavior of the subject, but also on that subject's internal mental state and *cognitive processes*. In their research and observations, cognitive behaviorists seek to differentiate between actions that are the result of reflex and those that are the result of thinking and the development of internal *schemas*. Typically, behaviorists are not concerned with the internal thought processes of their subjects. This is not the case with cognitive behaviorists, who make the assumption that there exists behavior that involves the processing of internal *schemas* as well as behavior that is the result of *classical conditioning*, which was most famously described in the study of Pavlov's dog. In that study, the dog came to associate involuntarily the sound of a bell with obtaining food. After a short time in which the dog was given food at the sound of the bell, the dog began to salivate at the sound even when the food was not provided. In short, cognitive behaviorism, breaks one of the most important assumptions of behaviorism, which is that internal mental processes should not be the focus of study and experiment because they cannot be observed.

cognitive coaching (constructivism)

Similar to *cognitive apprenticeship, apprenticeship learning,* and *collaborative learning,* cognitive coaching is a type of multiple mentoring in which the learners become more and more aware of their own mental processing (*metacognition*) activities, through the process of guiding each other and sharing insights, information, and problem solving approaches. If the coach (instructor) is not an equal, but has greater knowledge than that of the learners, then the goal of this "expert" is to foster even greater independence in the learners by providing personal insights on the expert's own thinking processes that relate to the problem solving activity. This coach seeks to foster the further sharing of information between the learners as they go about the process of exchanging ideas and problem solving methods.

cognitive complexity theory (cognitivism)

CCT (i.e., cognitive complexity theory) is an important part of the *GOMS* (*G*oals, *O*perators, *M*ethods, *S*election) model by Card, Moran, and Newell, in which human learning task times are predicted for completing online computer-related activities. GOMS itself seeks to predict the impact of errors and error recovery on computer task completion. CCT seeks to decompose user goals for completing computer tasks with a greater degree of granularity than GOMS in order to obtain more accurate predictions of how long it will take users to learn to complete tasks online with fewer errors. CCT is also related to John Carroll's *minimalism,* in which it is postulated that learning occurs more readily when a learner can build on past experience and knowledge and apply it to the computer task at hand.

cognitive consistency (humanism)

The opposite of cognitive dissonance, cognitive consistency is a state that individuals seek to achieve and maintain a balance between their ideas and beliefs and their life experiences. When there arises a conflict between these beliefs and experiences, *cognitive dissonance* occurs. Cognitive consistency is the individual's attempt to make sense out of the experiences that occur in the world around him or her. It is central to achieving psychological well-being and is related to Piaget's two *developmental learning* processes, that is, *accommodation* and *assimilation.*

cognitive dissonance (humanism)

The opposite of cognitive consistency, cognitive dissonance, first coined by Leon Festinger in 1957, is that state that individuals do not wish to remain in for long given the imbalance that exists between their ideas and beliefs and their life experiences. Cognitive dissonance causes psychological instability in the individual and makes it difficult for learning to occur. An example of cognitive dissonance is the millennialist who believes that the world will end at a certain time and when it does not end at the appointed hour, cognitive dissonance occurs. Various rationalizations, which may appear to outsiders or nonbelievers as illogical, are used to reattain cognitive consistency. To avoid cognitive dissonance, people ultimately find a way to adjust their beliefs to fit the new experience, no matter how weak the logic or rationalization may appear to others. In attempting to avoid cognitive dissonance, some individuals may become easily subjected to *behavior control* (i.e., the control of an individual's entire physical existence), *thought control* (i.e., the control of an individual's thought processes), and *emotion control* (i.e., the control of an individual's emotional life).

cognitive flexibility (constructivism)

First espoused by R.J. Spiro, R.L. Coulson, P.J. Feltovich, and D. Anderson in the late 1980s and early 1990s, cognitive flexibility theory focuses on the construction of knowledge by learners who build structure and context within the *learning environment* they are studying. Typically, within the *conceptual landscape,* learners navigate through a nonstructured hypermedia environment (also known as the *crisscross landscape*) via the Web or via an application, and then create their own representations and maps *(conceptual maps)* of that *knowledge base* they are traveling through. The instructor's role is to provide case studies and multiple perspectives of the *knowledge base*, with the learners applying that information to their own learning contexts as they build the conceptual map of the unstructured information. It should also be pointed out that oversimplification and memorization are de-emphasized within cognitive flexibility learning theory. The instructor should not try to reduce the information to a formula, oversimplify it, or try to structure it for the learners. Doing so defeats the entire purpose of the learners constructing the content and learning through the process and also leads to a state of learner oversimplification known as *reductive bias*.

cognitive load (cognitivism)

This has to do with the human capacity to remember and process information simultaneously. Most humans can only process five to nine information items at a time (i.e., G.A. Miller's *magical number seven*). This constraint puts a severe limit on how we can think and learn, especially with regard to processing multiple items that exceed our cognitive load. *Schema* acquisition and *chunking* are two methods that allow us to process multiple information items more efficiently and effectively. Bombarding learners with too much information all at once will cause information overload and it is certainly one of the main obstacles to learning—especially in an age when we already suffer from a glut of information (i.e., *infoglut*) that is readily available to us. If our cognitive load is at capacity and we are attempting to do "multitasking," it is unlikely we will be able to perform additional mental processes and complete tasks without making serious errors and omissions.

cognitive load theory (cognitivism)

Espoused by John Sweller in the late 1980s, cognitive load theory's emphasis is on the limitations of human *working memory*. Its principles are the following: (1) Working memory is limited, and once exceeded, no learning can take place. (2) *Long-term memory* is unlimited. (3) Learning involves actively engaging the working memory so that information is transferred, processed, and stored in *long-term memory*. In relation to *instructional design*, information should be presented to the student through working examples that have all of the data, diagrams, and steps included to provide the learner with a clear, simple view of the essential information needed in order to keep cognitive load at a minimum. Extensive searching and sifting through information as well as complex *problem-solving* scenarios carry a high cognitive load and should not be utilized. Novice learners, without a well-developed *schema* or context for learning, require a simplified set of instructional materials that keep cognitive load down. This allows the working memory to focus on the business of transferring the information to long-term memory.

cognitive map (behaviorism)

This is the body of knowledge that an organism or *agent* has about the surrounding environment. It is a mental picture that allows the organism to navigate through various paths within that environment. For proponents of *cognitive behaviorism*, a cognitive map is important for studying *learning and performance*. In their studies, behaviorists found that animals do not respond randomly to stimuli. Through trial and error, they follow various paths, creating a cognitive map along the way, and work toward obtaining the desired reward. Without the cognitive map, the animal would be unable to adapt behavior to obtain the reward. An example of an adherent of the creation of cognitive maps in organisms is Edward Chace Tolman and his belief in *purposive behaviorism*, also known as *cognitive behaviorism*.

cognitive overhead (educational technology)

In a *hypermedia application*, cognitive overhead is the mental effort that the learner must engage in to follow the structure of the application. Typically, *hypermedia* has a high degree of *nonlinearity* that easily causes user *disorientation*. To reduce cognitive overhead, authors typically include in the application a textual or graphical table of contents, a *cognitive map*, that provides an overview of the landscape of the nonlinear environment so that the learners do not get lost between all of the various links in cyberspace.

cognitive processes (cognitivism)

Generally speaking, cognitive processes are the mental processes that individuals undergo as they think, learn, and perform *problem-solving* and *decision-making* activities. As they relate to Robert Gagne's *conditions of learning*, cognitive processes are mental processes tied to the nine *instructional events* elaborated upon in the theory. The nine instructional events and their respective cognitive processes (in parentheses) are:

1. Gain attention (reception) in order to focus upon the task at hand.
2. Inform learners of the objective (expectancy) in order to provide up front what are the projected *learning outcomes* for the course or module.
3. Stimulate recall of prior learning (retrieval) in order to stimulate prior knowledge previously remembered and gained.
4. Present the stimulus (selective perception) in order to initiate new information.
5. Provide learning guidance (*semantic encoding*) in order to structure the new information in a form that can be stored and remembered.
6. Elicit performance (responding) in order to stimulate learner recall through learners' active responses.
7. Provide feedback (reinforcement) in order to ensure that learning has occurred.
8. Assess performance (retrieval) in order to determine if the learners' performance is appropriate, correct, and in line with the projected learning outcomes.

9. Enhance retention and transfer (generalization) in order to place the new knowledge gained into *long-term memory*.

Cognitive processes are a primary area of focus within *cognitive psychology*.

cognitive psychology (cognitivism)

Thoroughly within the realm of the *learning paradigm* of *cognitivism*, cognitive psychology is the scientific discipline that deals with the study of *cognitive processes*. Cognitive psychologists focus their studies on the internal mental states of human beings and *agents* versus the behaviorists who are concerned with exhibited behaviors only of various organisms and who are wholly unconcerned with studying the *cognitive processes* of the brain. Unlike behaviorism, cognitive psychology is a discipline that seeks to detail what specifically occurs in the mind when a stimulus is presented and a response is made. Behaviorists, on the other hand, have no interest whatsoever in delineating what occurs between the introduction of the stimulus and the response of the organism. Key areas of study within cognitive psychology are perception, learning, and *memory*. Another important focus of study within cognitive psychology is how human and computer information processing systems are similar and different from each other.

cognitive robotics (cognitivism)

Within the realm of *cognitive psychology*, and more specifically, *artificial intelligence*, research in cognitive robotics focuses on the theory and creation of robots that can think, learn, and act within changeable and unpredictable environments. The ultimate goal of cognitive robotics is the creation of robots that are like us with regard to human intelligence, learning, and behavior. The only difference between us, theoretically speaking, would be that the robot would be a nonbiological entity. Whether or not the robots would have emotions, social relationships, and an ability to cooperate is a subject thus far of considerable theoretical debate.

cognitive structure (constructivism)

Jean Piaget's conception of cognitive structure is inextricably linked to an understanding of an organism's set of *schemata* that it utilizes to interact with the environment. To Piaget, all organisms have cognitive elements that manifest themselves into overt (e.g., grasping) and covert (e.g., thinking) behavior. These sets of behaviors determine how an organism interacts with the environment as it develops. The more schemata utilized by the organism, the more it can respond to the environment. In Jean Piaget's *genetic epistemology*, the cognitive structure of the organism is modified through the dual processes of *assimilation* and *accommodation*. As the organisms interact with the environment, as they develop, the schemata themselves are modified in order to allow the individuals to deal with the changes occurring as a result of interactions with the environment through the process of development.

cognitively guided instruction (cognitivism)

Also referred to as CGI, cognitively guided instruction, which is closely related to a number of other theories for learning mathematics, is based on initial research done by Carpenter and Moser in the 1970s examining how children learn basic mathematics between first and third grade as they move from an understanding of simple, concrete objects to abstract mathematical concepts. CGI is closely related to *scaffolded learning*, in which the student is initially provided a great deal of support and basic knowledge of the subject by the instructor. Then gradually, as information is learned and built up over time, the student is encouraged to combine the previous knowledge and solve more complex problems independently. It is also related to *thinking mathematically*, in which the entire approach to mathematical problem solving is carried over into other problem solving

scenarios that occur in life. The basic learning process is similar for CGI, scaffolded learning, and thinking mathematically. The learner moves from simple, concrete *mathematical problem-solving* situations, where the learner is guided by the instructor, to more complex ones, in which the learner is "on one's own." As a result, he or she now has and is able to draw upon a body of knowledge from previous learning experiences.

cognitivism

One of the four major learning theory schools, cognitivism is the belief that human thinking and learning are similar to that of computer information processing. As such, the focus of cognitivism is on learning inputs and outputs that are processed by the human mind, much as the computer processes information.

In the world of cognitivism, the external world is composed of a series of objects that have specific properties and are interrelated. Learning takes place when the individual gathers information from the external world and builds within the mind a mental construct of that world, a representation of how that world appears to the individual. These mental constructs are, it is hoped, accurate representations of real-world objects that include their properties and their interrelationships. Within this context, individual human knowledge is a large collected database of information, organized into some sort of logical model in the mind, which can be accessed and then described through human language. Human thinking is a process of collecting data (inputs) from the external world, manipulating the objects and transforming them into symbolic representations in the mind that depict logically what is perceived in the external world, and describing them through speech, writing, and drawing (outputs).

In education, cognitivism focuses on the accurate transmission of knowledge of the objective reality of the world from a teacher (expert) to students. Success is achieved when, at the end of the lesson, the students have the same mental construct of the objects being studied as that of the teacher. The key question that causes difficulty for cognitivism as a learning theory is this: "How can we be sure that the mental construct mutually envisioned at lesson's end by the teacher and students is an accurate depiction of reality?"

Unlike *behaviorism*, which involves no interest in studying internal mental states, but rather in external outputs, learning products, and behavioral change, cognitivism is completely concerned with an internal, symbolic mental processing system that focuses on learning *schemas* and that focuses on how the brain receives, internalizes, and recalls information. Cognitivism is not concerned with the willfulness, *creativity*, and autonomy of the learners that *constructivism* considers in its focus on the learning process. Where constructivism focuses on how to help learners construct content that is highly iterative, subjective, and not fixed according to a single symbol system or mental construct, cognitivism focuses on finding better depictions of the human information-processing model and better methods of transmitting *schemas* from teachers to students. In constructivism, learners build their own meaning from new knowledge that they help construct. In cognitivism, learners have their knowledge built by someone else, an expert, whose job it is to convey as best as possible the mental construct that describes the objects being studied. Unlike *humanism*, cognitivism is not interested in the self-direction or self-actualization of the learner. It is not concerned about whether individual or social human needs are met through educational processes, as is humanism. Cognitivism is concerned with learning inputs, outputs, and the accurate depiction of the internal processing of the human mind versus *holistic learning* and thinking and the attainment of psychological balance that is the focus of humanism. Despite its detractors and opposing schools of learning (behaviorism, constructivism, and humanism), cognitivism is still a powerful force in delineating how humans think, learn, transmit information, and solve problems.

cohort groups (constructivism)

From the perspective of *collaboration* in education, cohort groups represent particular sets of individuals who go through a particular program of study and graduate at the same time. More often than not, the cohort group is participating in a *constructivist learning environment* and is performing *collaborative learning* activities. The group itself may represent either a diverse group of individuals or, as is more often the case, individuals that are similar either in terms of age, work experience, or status. An example of a cohort group would be executives going through an Executive MBA program. With a program that is pretty much "lock step," the cohort group members attend the same sets of classes and work together in teams. The shared experience creates a sense of bonding among the members of the cohort group. Mentoring, *cognitive coaching*, and *apprenticeship learning* activities are often enhanced as a result of the collaboration of the members of the cohort group as they go through the program of study together.

collaboration (constructivism)

This is the *collaborative learning* activity that occurs in a *constructivist learning environment* in which team members, who may represent a *cohort group*, work together on a shared learning project or set of projects. Each person in the group provides his or her contribution to the joint learning effort. All members are directed in a cooperative effort toward the overall goal of a successful learning project completion. It is the *collaboration* itself of the group that moves the group toward the goal, rather than simply the individual efforts of the team members. All have a shared vision and all strive toward the completion of the final work product, with iterative learning milestones and checkpoints occurring along the project path. With the advent of *distance learning*, much of this collaboration occurs in a *virtual learning community* where interaction occurs in cyberspace within a *virtual learning environment*.

collaborative learning (constructivism)

This is a strategy for learning that has as its basis Lev Vygotsky's *social development theory*, in which it is postulated that social development and interaction play a fundamental role in the development of the individual learner's cognitive abilities, including thinking, learning, and communicating. Through the act of *collaboration*, learners share knowledge, pool resources, and interact within the learning group to produce deliverables that are theoretically more complete and robust than that which would be created by an individual learner working alone. Closely related to the theory of *enactivism*, and *co-emergence*, collaborative learning also takes as a given the fact that positive changes and better learning results occur through the simple but continuous interactions among the learners over a period of time. Stronger and weaker members are paired to encourage *cognitive coaching* and *apprenticeship learning* within a *constructivist learning environment*. As *distance learning* becomes more widespread, in which *virtual learning communities* will interact in a *virtual learning environment*, much of the collaborative learning activity will occur in cyberspace.

common sense reasoning (cognitivism)

Within the *artificial intelligence* community, common sense reasoning is an important attribute that is sought within *machine learning*. Humans observe the world of objects and their interrelationships and make inferences about that world using what is often referred to as *inductive learning* and logic. Typically, artificial intelligence programs use more formal *deductive learning* and reasoning, which has as its basis mathematical logic. Human inferential logic is very fluid and flexible. It is based greatly on observations of the physical world and the immediate environment and of sharing that information with other humans. In the process of learning and interacting with the world and with other people, humans sort out what inferences are correct and incorrect. This is an important aspect of how people learn. Until computers or robots can expand their input capabilities (take in information from the real world) and be able to make inferences based upon these inputs, communicate them to us, and truly share information, common sense reasoning will be beyond their reach. From a learning theory perspective, human communication and interaction play a key role in the achievement of common sense reasoning. Our human ability to learn, to communicate, and to use common sense knowledge that we obtain from the world of experience is a result of our ability to use common sense reasoning and inferential logic to shape our perception of that world.

communication rules (organizational learning)

In a study of cultural, learning, and communication aspects of organizations, Linda Smircich in 1983 defined organizational cognition as a system of shared knowledge and beliefs of individuals within the organization that are based upon common *knowledge structures* and *communication rules*. According to Maryan Schall, also writing in 1983, communication rules are tacit understandings among work groups within an organization that are based primarily on soft and transitory choices rather than on strict and everlasting laws. According to Schall, there are two types of communication rules: *operative rules* and *formal rules*. Operative rules are those rules that members of a group agree upon as being relevant and "happening here" within their aspect of the organization. As such, operative rules are similar to the concept of *tacit knowledge* as it is defined within *knowledge management* circles. Formal rules are more explicit rules found in corporate documents and *knowledge bases* and *Web-based knowledge transfer systems*. As such, formal rules are similar to the knowledge management concept of *explicit knowledge*.

community of practice (constructivism)

In Jean Lave's *situated learning* theory, learners' participate in a community of practice, which is a social, interactive group of seasoned practitioners who provide *cognitive coaching* and *apprentice learning* to novices who are in the process of learning a particular skilled craft or trade. Based upon her anthropological studies of cross-cultural *knowledge sharing* among skilled tradespeople, including midwives, meat cutters, tailors, and others, Lave's observations became the basis of her *situated learning* theory. In her observations, she noted that as the novice gains knowledge and moves closer to the community's center, he or she begins to take on the role of mentoring new, uninitiated individuals into the community of practice. The social interaction process that occurs between newcomers and old-timers within the community of practice Lave refers to as *legitimate peripheral participation*. Through this participation process and within the community of practice, knowledge and skills are transferred among the members of the society. Lave's conclusion is that knowledge transfer is closely tied to the social situation in which the knowledge is learned. Out of the social context, the knowledge itself is meaningless. Lave's further conclusion is that classroom learning, by its very nature, is out of context and irrelevant. Knowledge gained within the work setting, within the community of practice, is in context and relevant.

complete rationality (cognitivism)

A term from the *artificial intelligence* community, complete rationality refers to the cognitive abilities, based on its *cognitive architecture*, that a computer *agent* has within an artificial intelligence system to get as close as possible to the human ability to synthesize knowledge and solve problems. However, most systems, including the human system, are unable to attain this idealized state of complete rationality. Examples of system limitations include *memory* and time. Examples of human limitations include feelings and emotions. In *Soar,* and in other artificial intelligence systems, the limits (i.e., *bounded rationality*) of the system architecture become apparent as one increases the complexity and amount of the body of knowledge required to complete the set of tasks and as the tasks themselves are made more complex and diverse. The better the architecture of the artificial intelligence system, the more closely it approximates an idealized state of human *cognitive processes* to achieve what is considered complete rationality. This assumes, of course, that humans themselves are completely rational (Herbert Simon in his *Models of Man* assumes they are not) as they go about solving complex task-based problems in the real versus the system environment.

complex systems (constructivism)

In *chaos theory*, random events occur within two basic types of complex systems: the natural world (such as the weather), and human-made systems (such as the stock market). Though apparently chaotic on the surface, these complex systems are guided by an inherent order, which has as its basis simple mathematical computations. Small, incremental changes that occur at the beginning of a complex system can later produce dramatic results to that system. In a chaotic system, an organism placed immediately in an unfamiliar, complex environment will not be able to survive. There is not time for Piaget's *developmental learning* processes of *accommodation* and *assimilation* to occur to allow for the successful growth of that individual's capacity to cope with the environment—and to survive through *trial-and-error learning*. If, on the other hand, that same individual is placed in an environment that gradually becomes more complex, the "organism" will adapt, evolve, and survive.

The *nonlinearity* and apparent randomness of chaos-based, complex systems place chaos theory within the learning paradigm of *constructivism*, especially since there are interrelationships among chaos theory, complex systems, and *co-emergence*. Co-emergence, an important aspect of *complex systems,* is when enhancements to the entire system occur as a result of repeated *knowledge-shar-*

ing interactions that develop between as few as two entities (e.g., human beings or *agents*) over time. Although they seem insignificant when viewed individually, these interactions and *collaborations* are in fact significant catalysts to change of the entire complex system (and of the entities within the system) over a given time.

component display theory (cognitivism)

Developed by David Merrill in the early 1980s, component display theory, also known by the acronym CDT, emphasizes that the learner should have control over the *sequencing of instruction*, based upon the instructional components (e.g., presentation forms) provided by the lesson. Merrill's CDT has two learning dimensions: content and performance. Along the performance continuum, Merrill has "find," "use," and "remember." Along the content continuum, Merrill has "fact," "concept," "procedure," and "principle." CDT also specifies four primary presentation forms: "expository presentation of generality," "expository presentation of instances," "inquisitory generality," and "inquisitory instance," as well as four secondary presentation forms: "prerequisites," "objectives," "helps," "mnemonics," and "feedback." The most effective lesson according to Merrill would include within it all primary and secondary presentation forms. The cognitive basis of Merrill's CDT are associative memory (a hierarchical network structure) and algorithmic memory (using *schema*). Both of these are essential to the individual's capacity to recall and use information. A lesson constructed according to CDT principles offers a great degree of learner individualization, since the learner has control over the *sequencing of the instruction*, which matches with his or her individual *learning styles*. Thus, the *sequencing of instruction* is *learner-centric*, though the presentation of the materials is highly structured and strictly defined in terms of the presence of the presentation components, though the order of consuming the materials is left up to the user's preference.

computational linguistics (cognitivism)

In short, computational linguistics is the use of the computer to create statistical and computational models that simulate various types of linguistic and *natural language* phenomena that occur in *natural language processing*. An important *artificial intelligence* research focus, natural language processing is an attempt to make computer programs able to understand spoken or written natural languages (e.g., English). This would mean that computers would be able to understand meaning. Research is currently being conducted into compiling dictionaries of words and their meanings that are *tractable*. Tractable refers to a body of textual material that a computer can "read" and "understand." Tractability occurs through statistical sampling of word patterns and recurrences. Thus, an objective of computational linguistics and *computer lexicography* is the development of *machine tractable dictionaries* to facilitate computer-based natural language processing. Closely associated with *voice recognition*, which is sometimes referred to as natural language recognition, computational linguistics along with natural language processing has as its "holy grail" the goal of making the computer able to understand meanings of human words and to allow computers and humans to communicate. The path to that "holy grail" in the minds of more than a few AI researchers is through the creation of the machine tractable dictionary. The method that allows for the computer to read and understand natural language is through statistical sampling via computational linguistics of the dictionary and its definitions.

computer-assisted instruction (educational technology)

Also known by the acronym CAI, computer-assisted instruction, along with *computer-based training* and now *Web-based training*, all refer to educational and training software programs that utilize the computer as an instructional tool versus as an automation machine. CAI is one of the earliest terms used to describe these types of programs. The CAI programs that ran on early PCs were primarily limited to simple text and graphics. This term was later replaced by the term computer-based training (CBT).

computer-based training (educational technology)

Also known by the acronym CBT, computer-based training has as its most common educational application guided walkthroughs and exercises for users learning computer software applications, such as word processing, database management, spreadsheet, and accounting. Generally speaking, computer-based training is reserved for describing second-generation interactive educational technology, with *computer-assisted instruction* the term describing first-generation applications. With the advent of the *Internet* as an educational technology delivery method, computer-based training is being superseded by the third-generation term and technology, *Web-based training*.

computer lexicography (cognitivism)

Computer lexicography is the creation of dictionaries that are written in *natural language* (i.e., English) and yet are *tractable* by computers. A *machine tractable dictionary* is one that a computer can use to communicate with humans in their natural language. An important *artificial intelligence* research focus, *natural language processing* is an attempt to have computer programs understand spoken or written natural languages. This would mean that computers would be able to understand meaning. Research is currently being conducted into compiling dictionaries of words and their meanings that are *tractable* (that a computer can "read" and "understand"). Thus, an objective of *computer lexicography* is the development of *machine tractable dictionaries* to facilitate computer-based natural language processing. This area of AI research is also closely associated with *computational linguistics,* which involves the use of statistics and statistical programs to identify word patterns and recurrences.

Closely associated with *voice recognition*, which is sometimes referred to as natural language recognition, natural language processing is the ultimate goal of AI research, so that the computer is able to understand meanings of human words and communicate with humans. According to many AI researchers, that goal will be reached through the creation of the machine tractable dictionary, the focus of computer lexicography.

computer-mediated communication (educational technology)

Also known by the acronym CMC, computer-mediated communication is a term popularized by John December, who since 1992 has provided a comprehensive collection of *Internet* resources on this area of study. CMC is human communication via the computer. Primarily *Internet*-based, CMC focuses on the group dynamics, team-based learning activities, and associated *collaboration* and communication technologies that closely dovetail with the constructivist learning theories embodied in *collaborative learning, cooperative learning*, and *situated learning*, among other theories within the educational *learning paradigm* of *constructivism*. CMC is a process and a technology whereby humans can create, exchange, and access information over the *Internet* to enhance communication and *collaboration*. *Virtual learning communities, virtual learning environments, Web-based education, Web-based training, Web-based knowledge transfer, videoconferencing*, and *telecommuting*, are several of many topics covered under the umbrella of CMC.

concept acquisition (cognitivism)

In *Soar* (State, Operator And Result), which is a *unified theory of cognition* developed by Newell and colleagues at Carnegie Mellon University in the 1990s, concept acquisition is a process of labeling objects perceived in the environment, within a *problem space*. The activity of concept acquisition involves associating an object (e.g., a round, spherical, smooth three-dimensional circle) with a label (e.g., a ball). Associating the spherical object with a ball is a type of abstraction activity and is related to the process of *chunking* in which the brain breaks up information into smaller units so that it is easier to remember and process. Concept acquisition is closely related to *inductive learning*, in which inferences are made and then tested to see whether or not they are correct.

concept mapping (constructivism)

This is a learning process originally developed by Joseph D. Novak and enhanced as a software program by William Trochim at Cornell University, in which learners, often in a *cooperative learning* situation, work together to produce a graphical or pictorial view of the concepts being studied and how they are interrelated. The steps for performing concept mapping are: (1) select participants and focus, (2) generate statements, (3) structure the statements, (4) pictorially represent the statements on a graphical map, (5) interpret the map, and (6) use the map. At the end of the learning activity, the maps themselves become a visual framework and a record of the thought processes of the group that includes their final results. An important by-product of the activity is that learners assess the status of the map and determine what future enhancements need to be made to it and to the learning process itself. Concept mapping is related to Tony Buzan's *mind mapping,* which is another learning process that uses visualizations to depict concept networks. Both have roots in David Ausubel's *subsumption theory*, in which a great deal of emphasis is placed on prior knowledge providing an important foundation for the development of new concepts. Though the term could be classified under the *learning paradigm* of cognitivism, concept mapping, with its emphasis on learner *collaboration* and construction of knowledge, is primarily within the learning paradigm of *constructivism*.

conceptual dependency theory (cognitivism)

In the mid–1970s, Roger Schank delineated his conceptual dependency theory, which states that all *conceptualizations* can be defined in terms of a set of acts performed on objects in the environment by actors (i.e., by humans). This theory was Schank's initial attempt to define how knowledge is structured and how humans think and remember. A correlative theory first elaborated upon by Schank in the mid–1970s, *contextual dependency theory*, looked at how humans represent meaning in sentences within the context of language understanding. Both led to Schank's fully elaborated *script theory*, a delineation of how language processing and higher thinking work. Script theory postulates that human *memory* (which Schank regards as *episodic memory)* is based upon personally remembered episodes and experiences, i.e., *scripts* (a sequence of events and actions) that we call upon and apply to a *schema*. Scripts allow human beings to make inferences. *Schema* refers to a *knowledge structure* that gets created as we experience new things in the environment from which we create more scripts. This knowledge structure (schema) is dynamic and continually enhanced over time. As additional experiences occur, new scripts get written, and the schema becomes enhanced as a result of an ever-growing set of personal life episodes and experiences. With both conceptual dependency theory and script theory as their theoretical basis, a number of *natural language processing* computer programs are being tested and developed.

conceptual landscape (constructivism)

In *cognitive flexibility theory,* the conceptual landscape is the *learning environment* of the *hypermedia application* that the learners navigate through to obtain information and to construct a *schema*, or *conceptual map* of the content to be learned. As the learners traverse through the landscape multiple times, they soon acquire multiple and layered perspectives of the concepts being studied. By crisscrossing through the conceptual landscape (which is sometimes referred to as the *crisscross landscape*) the learners deal with the content from many directions and perspectives, so that the knowledge gained provides a flexible *schema* to be used and reused in many learning and life situations.

conceptual map (constructivism)

In *cognitive flexibility theory,* the conceptual map is the learner's mental representation or *schema* of the *conceptual landscape* that is traversed while crisscrossing through the *learning environment* of the *hypermedia application* and begin to make sense of the content being studied. Typically, there is a good deal of complexity to the *knowledge base*. The conceptual map is thus the learner's attempt to make sense of the nonlinear and multidimensional traversal of the complex content.

conceptualization (cognitivism)

In Roger Schank's *script theory,* a conceptualization is an action performed by a human on an object within the environment. These actions are recorded as scripts in the mind. From these scripts, a *schema*, or *knowledge structure,* is created. As new conceptualizations are recorded as scripts, the *schema* is enhanced and further developed over time. From scripts, humans can make logical inferences and understand oral and written communication.

conditions of learning (cognitivism)

Robert Gagne's *conditions of learning* theory describes a hierarchy of different types of learning, which require different instructional strategies and *instructional designs* based upon specific *learning outcomes*. As delineated in the conditions of learning theory, there exists a hierarchical set of *cognitive processes* that occur in relation to instructional events. The nine instructional events and their respective cognitive processes (in parentheses) are as follows: (1) Gain attention (reception) in order to focus upon the task at hand. (2) Inform learners of the objective (expectancy) in order to provide up front what are the projected *learning outcomes* for the course or module. (3) Stimulate recall of prior learning (retrieval) in order to stimu-

late prior knowledge previously remembered and gained. (4) Present the stimulus (selective perception) in order to initiate new information. (5) Provide learning guidance (*semantic encoding*) in order to structure the new information in a form that can be stored and remembered. (6) Elicit performance (responding) in order to stimulate learner recall through learners' active responses. (7) Provide feedback (reinforcement) in order to ensure that learning has occurred. (8) Assess performance (retrieval) in order to determine if the learners' performance is appropriate, correct, and in line with the projected learning outcomes. (9) Enhance retention and transfer (generalization) in order to place the new knowledge gained into *long-term memory*. For Gagne, these hierarchies provide a rationale for *sequencing of instruction*.

connectionism (behaviorism)

Edward Thorndike's behaviorist learning theory proposes that learning occurs through the close associations that occur between stimuli and responses without any consideration of the internal mental states (that the cognitivists are so concerned about) which, by their very nature, are unobservable and therefore irrelevant. Thus the "connection" in connectionism is the S-R *stimulus-response association* that guides all behavior, including learning. Connectionism, according to Thorndike, follows three basic laws: the *law of effect*, the *law of readiness*, and the *law of exercise*. The law of effect states that responses to stimuli become habits when the effect of the response is rewarding to the "organism." The law of readiness states that there exists a chain of responses from the "organism" as it pursues an externally rewarded goal. If this chain is blocked at any point, it causes the organism a great deal of frustration and annoyance. The *law of exercise* states that the more connections become stimulated over time, the stronger (and more habitual) they become and vice versa. Based upon these three basic laws, Thorndike concludes that intelligence can be measured by how many connections have been learned by the "organism."

consciousness (cognitivism)

In the seventeenth century, French philosopher and scientist René Descartes declared: "I think, therefore I am." Philosophical debate has ensued for centuries on the nature of mind and brain, what constitutes a state of consciousness, and what constitutes knowledge (e.g., *epistemology*). Behaviorists have been interested in *altered states of consciousness*. Cognitivists, in their attempts to delineate internal mental states and to simulate them with *artificial intelligence* systems, have sought to define consciousness as well. Constructivists have considered consciousness, especially in relation to *creativity*. Consciousness is a state of being in which pass individual thoughts and feelings that make up one's personality and character. Self-awareness, awareness of beliefs and influences, and awareness of the environment are important aspects of being conscious that form a foundation and a mental framework for one's ability to learn.

constructionism (constructivism)

Constructionism is a term coined by Seymour Papert, developer of the Logo programming language for children-oriented, computer-aided instruction (CAI) applications, and currently a professor at MIT. Constructionism is a minimalist approach to teaching with the goal of producing in the learners the most learning for the least teaching. It is in the same vein as Bruner's *discovery learning* approach with its emphasis on a *learner-centric* orientation, in which the learner is actively engaged in constructing knowledge. Its focus is on a *curriculum design* that is expansive, that allows the learner to reach out beyond the limits of the traditional classroom environment to construct his or her own *learning environment* and to build a little school of discovery within a school. To Papert, the content of the average school curriculum represents a small fraction of human knowledge that is now available to children via the *Internet* and

through computers to children. However, merely putting a computer in front of a child is not a solution to the problems facing schools still caught up in the *industrial age educational paradigm*. To move to the *digital age educational paradigm*, schools must embrace *constructivism*, the larger *learning paradigm* within which constructionism fits.

The goal of Papert's constructionism is to allow students to build things. By analogy, constructionism is a process that encourages the students to fish by giving them the rod and the reel, and taking them to the lake where the fish are, rather than merely telling them how to fish or reading them a fishing story in the classroom. Opposed to constructionism is what Papert coins *instructionism*, which takes us back to the traditional methodology of too much instruction and too little learning. To Papert, there is too much emphasis on the teacher constructing content, too little on the student constructing his or her own world using tools and technology made available via computers and the Internet.

constructivism

One of the four major learning theory schools, constructivism is the belief that learners, having some prior knowledge and experience as a basis from which to test out their hypotheses, build their own set of content to solve a particular set of problems posed by the instructor. Constructivism is a *learner-centric* educational paradigm, in which content is constructed by the learners in a team-based *collaborative learning, constructivist learning environment* rather than by the instructor. Learner-centric theories embodied in constructivism focus on the importance of the learners over the instructor to the instructional activity. In the *active learning* educational paradigm of constructivism, the instructor is no longer a primary intermediary and single conduit of knowledge between the learners and the learning experience. All knowledge need not pass first through him or her. The instructor instead becomes a catalyst, a coach, and a program manager directing projects that center upon solving a particular problem, not an intermediary or a barrier between the content and the students. With constructivism, learner inquiry and discovery, learner autonomy, and self-motivation of the learner are critical elements to the success of the learning process.

There are many learning theories that fall under the educational paradigm of constructivism, such as Len Vygotsky's *social development* theory, Jean Lave's *situated learning*, and a host of others. Two that are most often cited as preeminent examples of constructivism are Piaget's *developmental learning* theory and Bruner's *discovery learning* theory.

In Piaget's *development learning* theory, the key to the growth and maturation of the person is through a twofold learning process. Through the process of *accommodation*, existing *cognitive structures* change to make sense of the new events occurring in the environment. Through *assimilation*, the individual interprets environmental events based upon existing cognitive structures. Both are integral to the success of the individual's development.

The key concept of Bruner's *discovery learning* theory is that learners are more likely to remember concepts if they discover them on their own, apply them to their own *knowledge base* and context, and structure them to fit into their own backgrounds and life experiences. In the process of discovery, the learners make errors, but these are intregral to the learning process. The key assumption of discovery learning is that learners are mature enough, self-motivated enough, and experienced enough to actively take part in the formation and structuring of the learning content. The opposite of discovery learning occurs when the instructor does so much shaping and structuring of the content (as occurs in many learning theories under *cognitivism*) that little room is left for the learners' own self-discoveries, errors, adjustments, and enhancements.

Ironically, both Piaget and Bruner are sometimes claimed as well by cognitivists. Cognitivists embrace those aspects of the theories in which the learners work from a *schema*, an existing mental framework, that they can refer to and then build additional content from as they make their inferences, interconnections, hypotheses, and learning decisions. Constructivists embrace the learning theories of Piaget and Bruner because of the *learner-centric* versus *instructor-centric* framework in which the learners are actively engaged in the creation of the knowledge framework.

The key difference between the cognitivists and constructivists is that the constructivists see knowledge as extremely relativistic, where nothing can be taken for granted or regarded as objective truth. The cognitivists, on the other hand, focus on what they regard as the accurate transmission of objective knowledge (i.e., of the objective reality of the world) from the teacher (who is the expert) to students (who are not). The key question that differentiates the constructivists from the cognitivists is: "How can we be sure that the cognitivist's mental construct mutually envisioned at lesson's end by the teacher and students is an accurate depiction of reality?" The constructivist assumption is that one has a better chance of grasping "the truth" or at least multiple perspectives of "the truth" by the group of learners working together.

This is the key emphasis for "social" constructivists, like Vygotsky, Lave, and others, who emphasize the social aspects, the *collaborative learning* aspects of the construction of the content within a *community of practice*. Where cognitivism focuses on finding better depictions of the human information-processing model and better methods of transmitting *schemas* from teachers to students, constructivism focuses on how to help learners construct content that is highly iterative, subjective, and not fixed according to a single symbol system or mental construct.

Unlike *behaviorism*, where learners are placed in a very controlled environment in order to be directed toward a specific set of behavioral changes based upon a set of predetermined, instructor-based objectives, constructivism seeks to place the learners in an open-ended learning environment in which they build their own meaning from new knowledge, new content that they construct. Constructivism and *humanism* are similar in that they both focus on the self-direction, autonomy, and growth of the individual through the learning process. Humanism simply focuses more on the learners' self-actualization, on the *holistic learning* and thinking and the attainment of psychological balance that is central to the humanist educational paradigm.

Despite its detractors and opposing schools of learning (primarily behaviorism and, to a certain extent, cognitivism), constructivism is a very prominent theory espoused and utilized today in traditional as well as in nontraditional educational settings.

constructivist learning environment (constructivism)

Based primarily upon the constructivist learning theories of Piaget and Bruner, a constructivist learning environment is one in which learners, either in a more traditional classroom setting or in a *virtual learning environment*, build information in a team-based manner that emphasizes learner *knowledge sharing* and *collaboration*. They acquire knowledge, share knowledge, and structure the knowledge among their teammates, with the instructor acting as a guide, co-collaborator, and coach. Other theories that provide a basis for a constructivist learning environment include *collaborative learning, cooperative learning*, and *situated learning*. With the advent of the *Internet*, the constructivist learning environment may be part of a larger *virtual campus network* that includes *Web-based education, videoconferencing*, and *Web-based knowledge transfer*. Whether a virtual or a real classroom environment, the goal of the constructivist learning environment is to simulate a real-world setting in which the learners, using their previous training and experiences, perform discovery learning activities and come up with a solution to a problem initially posed by the instructor.

contextual awareness (humanism)

In Carl Rogers's *experiential learning*, contextual awareness is the instructor's ability to factor into the *instructional design* process the learner's environment, personal experiences, beliefs, values, and overall predisposition to the learning activities. As the instructional designer creates the course content, he or she must be cognizant of these factors that have an important influence on the learner's capacity to learn effectively. In certain instances, the designer must alter the learner's negative pre-dispositions and influences (i.e., *barriers to learning*) often resulting from being previously engaged in the *instructor-centric learning* activity that is prevalent in the *industrial age educational paradigm*, before the learning event itself can begin satisfactorily.

contextual dependency theory (cognitivism)

A corollary of Roger Schank's *conceptual dependency theory* and an important precursor of his *script theory,* contextual dependency theory looks at how humans represent meaning in sentences within the context of language understanding in order to determine how knowledge is structured. Both conceptual dependency theory and contextual dependency theory led to Schank's fully elaborated script theory, a delineation of how language processing and higher thinking work in humans.

contiguity theory (behaviorism)

This is Edwin Ray Guthrie's theory, which postulates that learning is a result of the organism's association between a specific stimulus and a specific response. The classic study that Guthrie performed was on cats trying to escape the maze of a *puzzle box*. Trial and error is important to escape. By photographing the cat's movements, Guthrie observed that the cats learned to repeat their movement sequences based upon their last escape from the puzzle box. The cats improved their escape ability by unlearning movements that were not successful to their mission.

The key thing about the theory is that learning occurs immediately at the time of the response to the stimulus. Rewards and punishments are insignificant to learning. Forgetting what is learned is not a result of passage of time, but rather a result of interference. For the learner, as the stimulus becomes associated with other incorrect responses, the interference occurs. Within a human (versus cat) learning situation, contiguity theory stresses having the learners perform very specific tasks and making sure that their last response in the learning situation is correct, for that is what will be remembered and learned. The downside of the theory is that just as specific actions are quickly learned, so too are they quickly unlearned.

contingency schedule (behaviorism)

Important within the context of *reinforcer* and *reinforcement theory*, a contingency schedule is a method used to increase *behavior modification* in an organism by denying access to a specific action. In early reinforcement theories, a reinforcer is anything that reinforces behavior. For Hull, a reinforcer is anything that causes *drive reduction* in an organism. Generally speaking, a reinforcer is a stimuli, of which there are two types. A *primary reinforcer* is one that has as its basis the survival of the organism. A *secondary reinforcer* is a stimulus that is paired with a primary reinforcer. According to William Timberlake, the *disequilibrum hypothesis* postulates that each and all activities of an organism can be a reinforcer if the experimenter provides a *contingency schedule* whose sole purpose is to constrain the organism from accessing a particular activity. The contingency schedule creates in the organism a disequilibrium in which the restriction to activity access is itself a reinforcer. By providing a contingency schedule, the least probable activity that could be reinforced is reinforced in the organism.

continuity-noncontinuity controversy (behaviorism)

Not necessarily associated with any one *learning paradigm*, but most often debated among behaviorists, the continuity-noncontinuity controversy is a debate about whether learning occurs in small steps on a gradual, incremental basis or occurs all at once in an all-or-none fashion. In Edwin Ray Guthrie's *contiguity theory* and his *one-trial learning*, he accepts all of Aristotle's *laws of association*, except the postulate regarding frequency. Aristotle's postulate regarding frequency is that the more often two objects are experienced by an organism simultaneously, the more likely they will be remembered and learned. Guthrie rejected this notion.

With Guthrie, one trial, one successful pairing of a stimulus with a response is sufficient for learning to occur by the organism. Given both his contiguity theory and his postulate regarding one-trial learning, Guthrie had to come up with his *recency principle*, which states that whatever the organism did last in the presence of a fixed set of stimuli will be repeated again when those same stimuli recur.

Opposing Guthrie and his one-trial learning and recency principle, Thorndike in his theory of *connectionism* postulates that learning occurs gradually in small increments. According to Thorndike's *law of exercise* within his theory of connectionism, the more often an organism repeats a response to a particular set of stimuli, the more likely the organism will become "intelligent" and able to repeat the task again successfully, more quickly, and with fewer errors. Thus, learning does not really "stick" or become strengthened through one trial, but through several repeated trials over time.

In an attempt to quantify Guthrie's contiguity theory and his postulate regarding one-trial learning, William Kaye Estes's *stimulus sampling theory* used statistics and probabilities to predict the behavior of the organisms, though he included both one-trial learning and an incremental approach to learning in his formulation. To Guthrie, learning occurs all at once. To Thorndike, it occurs in small increments. To Estes, it occurs (for small sets of stimuli) all at once, but for larger sets, it occurs gradually in increments. This debate as to whether learning occurs all at once or in increments is known as the *continuity-noncontinuity controversy*.

contribution (organizational learning)

An important aspect of thinking and sharing techniques within Edward de Bono's various learning theories, including *lateral thinking, Six Thinking Hats*, DATT (*Direct Attention Thinking Tools*), and *CoRT thinking*, a contribution is the enhancement of an idea originally conceived of, primarily by a group. A positive contribution to the idea provides additional support and points out its benefits. A negative contribution to the idea provides cautions to full implementation of the idea, without changes to make the idea work. All of de Bono's paradigms, whether for *organizational learning* in an industry setting or for traditional teaching in a school environment, emphasize the teaching of thinking as a basic skill. The role of the contribution is to provide improvement to the original idea. As such, the whole method of idea contribution is closely allied to *collaborative learning, cooperation*, and *social development theory,* all of which fall under the *learning paradigm* of *constructivism*.

control of variables strategy (cognitivism)

As a recent four-year pilot project led by Carnegie Mellon University psychology professor David Klahr and postdoctoral fellow Zhe Chen, control of variables strategy (CVS) seeks to teach at the primary school level the scientific method of experimentation. With CVS, all possible variables in an experiment are identified and controlled with one variable being tested to determine various results. By keeping all variables but one constant in the experiment, the children are able to draw conclusions that would be impossible to de-

termine in a more open-ended experiment when all variables are left open to chance.

CVS directly opposes Bruner's *discovery learning* process and insists that the cognitive process skills of the scientific method must be overtly taught. The goal of CVS is that children at a relatively early age become scientific thinkers who are able to use logic and reason to run simple scientific experiments and make educated conclusions. The instructor, as with most cognitivist-oriented *learning paradigms*, is most important to the process of teaching this method and must be actively involved in training the children to be scientific thinkers.

conversation theory (constructivism)

In the mid–1970s, Gordon Pask espoused his *conversation theory* that for both living organisms and *artificial intelligence* machines, learning results from the continuing conversations on a focused subject matter that these entities engage in over time on several language levels. Similar to *social development* theory, *cognitive coaching*, and *apprenticeship learning*, conversation theory emphasizes *teachback*, which is the process in which one entity teaches another entity what has been learned. Pask's theory also emphasizes the entities' joint learning activities that focus on the relationships between concepts. Learners come to understand these concept relationships in one of two ways. They either obtain information sequentially, or they look at the complete set of information and seek a higher-order relationship that is not necessarily sequential. Conversation theory is an outgrowth of *cybernetics*, in which it is postulated that learning is completely determined by the subjective social interaction of the learners and enhanced as the conversation continues.

cooperative learning (constructivism)

A type of collaborative learning, cooperative learning as elaborated by two brothers, Roger T. Johnson and David W. Johnson (both of the Cooperative Learning Center at the University of Minnesota), is characterized by the acronym *PIGS*, which stands for *P*ositive interdependence, *I*ndividual accountability, *G*roup interaction, and *S*ocial skills. Positive interdependence occurs when the learners become aware that they need each other to complete the learning task successfully. Individual accountability refers to the individual effort and instructor assessment required for the individual learner to complete successfully his or her role within the overall group mission.

Group interaction is the *cognitive coaching* and sharing of information that the learners engage in during the learning activity. Social skills refer to techniques, methods, and traits that promote group interactions, including, but not limited to, leadership, decision making, trust-building, communication, and conflict management. The fruits of collaborative learning include learners being better able to think for themselves, think with others, investigate topics and share information, and make judgments and assessments about the information learned.

CoRT Thinking (organizational learning)

Though a quarter century old, Edward de Bono's CoRT thinking, still in wide global use in industry and in the classroom, provides sixty thinking lessons to help motivate and direct learners to develop creative solutions to problems, write more creatively, and become more active, self-confident, and effective thinkers. According to de Bono, Western culture thinking is often adversarial and negative instead of constructive and cooperative. The goal of CoRT thinking is to accomplish something positive, to create something useful for the group and for society. As such, CoRT thinking could easily fall into the *learning paradigms* of both *constructivism* and *humanism*.

The 60 thinking lessons are broken up into the following categories: CoRT 1 Breadth (10 lessons); CoRT 2 Organization (10 Lessons); CoRT 3 Interaction (10 Lessons); CoRT 4 *Creativity* (10 Lessons); CoRT 5 Information and Feeling (10 Lessons); and CoRT 6 Action (10 Lessons). CoRT thinking is not

based upon IQ, for according to de Bono, one can have a high IQ, but be a very poor thinker with poor thinking skills. And, on the contrary, an individual with a lower IQ can be quite effective in practical, real-life and work situations, if he or she has developed the CoRT thinking skills necessary to be an effective thinker.

CPM-GOMS (cognitivism)

This is one of a family of GOMS techniques that includes *keystroke level model, natural GOMS language,* and *CMN-GOMS.* CPM stands for Cognitive Perceptual Motor. CPM-GOMS is based upon CMN-GOMS. The distinguishing feature of CPM-GOMS is the following. Where other GOMS techniques make the assumption that humans perform one task at a time, CPM-GOMS assumes that humans will multitask. CPM-GOMS thus includes models and charts of multiple-task execution times that following a critical path leading toward the overall learning goal.

creativity (organizational learning)

The subject of much thought, speculation, and print, creativity from an *organizational learning* perspective involves helping individuals at work to become innovative thinkers, to break loose from the bounds of thinking "inside the box" that has been taught in the traditional school system. One of the most prolific learning theorists who has explored extensively the creative thinking process, Edward de Bono, in his *lateral thinking* approach, focuses on the process for generating new creative ideas to solve business problems. In lateral thinking, there are four steps to creativity: (1) Focus on dominant ideas that come to mind in order to polarize perception of a problem. (2) Look at multiple perspectives of the problem. (3) Relax the logical thinking process taught in schools as part of the scientific method. (4) Allow "outside of the box" ideas to come to mind and be considered even though they do not fit into the logical, scientific thinking pattern.

In the recent past, organizations tended to try to teach their employees how to define a problem and then immediately focus on a specific solution. Lateral thinking, and other similar theories that try to teach creative thinking, seek methods to break through the problem-solution rigidity that characterizes the logical thinking processes taught in schools and later applied at work. Howard Gardner's *multiple intelligences* is another perspective seeking to free learners from the process of the *logical-mathematical intelligence* paradigm that tended to dominate the schools and the testing process. Recognizing that there are many different types of intelligence, Gardner seeks to reform the educational system to allow students who do not fit into the logical-mathematical paradigm to succeed.

In de Bono's *Six Thinking Hats*, the purple hat tends to be most dominant in organizations. This is the doubting and *critical thinking* hat that essentially is characterized by the statement: "That won't work. We have never done that before. It is crazy and stupid." The green hat, on the other hand, is the creative hat that is donned when the group or an individual in the group seeks to follow the lateral thinking process and brainstorm new ideas, where nothing is quickly dismissed or diminished as a possible solution to the problem. Sometimes an individual who is thoroughly ingrained in the purple-hat approach to thinking is asked to don the green hat and to take on the role of creative thinking and brainstorming as outlined in lateral thinking. The Six Thinking Hats approach essentially is to get employees to think differently from the way they normally think and to get individuals who are most purple in orientation to think green. Others have looked at creativity and intelligence, how to measure creativity, and how to increase creativity for the benefit of organizations. Still others seek to determine the nature of creativity itself, while all search for ways to enhance it and to create a positive environment for it in order to solve problems that continually occur in the twenty-first-century workplace.

crisscross landscape (cognitivism)

In *cognitive flexibility theory,* the crisscross landscape (also known as the *conceptual landscape*) is the *learning environment* of the *hypermedia application* that the learners traverse back and forth to obtain information and to construct a *schema* or *conceptual map* of the content to be learned. As the learners traverse through the landscape multiple times, they soon acquire a multiple and layered perspective of the concepts that they are studying. As the learners crisscross through the *conceptual landscape* and deal with the content from many directions and perspectives, the knowledge gained provides a flexible *schema* that can be used in many learning and life situations.

criterion-referenced instruction (organizational learning)

Robert Mager's criterion-referenced instruction, known by the acronym CRI, developed in the mid–1970s. It is a method used primarily in industry training development of instructional content, which lays down specific *learning objectives* and *learning outcomes* in the *curriculum design* of the *computer-based training* or standard training course materials being developed. The CRI process includes the following activities: (1) Perform a task analysis of content to be learned. (2) Determine learner performance objectives and outcomes. (3) Set up tests and evaluations of the learner outcomes based upon the objectives. (4) Develop the content.

As an *organizational learning* approach, CRI focuses on the job activities of the learners and seeks to determine the specific competencies (knowledge and skills) needed to perform the job successfully. As in Gagne's *conditions of learning, sequencing of instruction* is to a great extent left up to the learners and is based upon their mastery of the objectives and of their self-progress. CRI is also compatible with Knowles's *andragogy* and other constructivists who emphasize the self-initiative and self-management of the learners as they go through the learning content. Most learning modules developed according to CRI are self-paced and often involve mixed media, including workbooks, videotapes, *computer-based training* modules, and group discussions, among others.

critical consumerism (organizational learning)

In the 1920s, W.E. Warner developed a curriculum for schools within the industrial arts and technologies area that emphasized teaching children how to be more effective consumers and users of products they will buy as adults. With the advent of the *Internet*, critical consumerism in the early twenty-first century has become an important focus of many Web sites that evaluate consumer products and services with regard to price, performance, safety, and quality. Whether for health information, autos, electronics, or travel (among many other examples), a plethora of Web sites has sprung up whose primary purpose is to supply important instructional information to consumers that will ostensibly make them better purchasers of goods and services. Many organizations, aware of the popularity of and need for critical consumerism, devote significant portions of their Web sites to providing detailed instructional information on their products and services—as objectively as possible. In the past, this type of information would be parceled out sparingly, by the organizations that create the products and services, via TV commercials and print media. It would be left to third parties to provide more detailed and objective product and service explications and evaluations thereof.

critical theory (constructivism)

In the world of literary criticism, critical theory involves defining, classifying, analyzing, interpreting, and evaluating works of literature. In educational and learning theory circles, critical theory is an aspect of Albert Bandura's *social learning* theory, in which the learner assesses and appraises the model being observed by internalizing it and trying to imitate it. Social learning theory postulates that we humans learn by observing others in the environment and modeling ourselves after them. In the words of Yogi Berra, infamous and oft-quoted New York Yankee catcher, coach, manager, and baseball World Series great, "You can observe a lot by watching." Translated, this means that young baseball players can learn a great deal by observing other players play the game and by modeling their behavior after those observed. Though he may not have been aware of it at the time, Yogi Berra, a student of the game, was a firm advocate and practitioner of critical theory.

critical thinking (organizational learning)

Closely related to the concept of *metacognition*, critical thinking is the process of collecting information, processing it, and using the information for wise *decision making* and informed *problem solving*. It involves the conscious awareness of one's thinking and thought processes. It is the ability to exercise control over one's *cognitive processes* as well as the ability to communicate effectively what one has learned. Critical thinking is the blue hat in Edward de Bono's *Six Thinking Hats* paradigm. In exercising critical thinking, one reviews the situation, asks pertinent questions, weighs the facts, interprets the data, and makes clear judgments. Similar to reading and writing, critical thinking is a skill that can be developed with time and practice. From an *organizational learning* perspective, critical thinking is allied to *management thinking* and *systems thinking*. In his book *How We Think*, John Dewey 90 years ago defined critical thinking as "reflective thought," whereby one withholds judgment, remains skeptical, and questions assumptions, yet keeps an open mind to solutions that will surface through a close intellectual and emotional examination of the problem and its social context.

crystalized intelligence (cognitivism)

Most intelligence tests seek to measure crystallized intelligence, which is the accumulation of knowledge and reasoning skills obtained from the culture and applied to *prob-

lem-solving situations. It is based upon an individual's capacity to use the knowledge previously acquired and to follow problem solving approaches previously learned and apply them all to a current problem under consideration. Another type of intelligence, *fluid intelligence* is a measure of how quickly one's mind can adapt to new problems and situations not previously encountered. Fluid intelligence is not dependent upon the previous store of knowledge and experience one has in reserve to bear upon the current problem. Debate has ensued as to whether crystallized intelligence or fluid intelligence advances or declines with age. Janet Belsky argued in 1990 that crystallized intelligence declines with age as a result of a cumulative effect of losses in health, job, and relationships. Jack Horn argued in the 1970s that crystallized intelligence increases if the individual is relatively healthy and engages in new ideas, relationships, and experiences despite the obvious effects of aging on the physical aspects of existence.

cultural reproduction (humanism)

In the mid–1980s, William H. Schubert regarded cultural reproduction as one of the important orientations for curriculum design that is similar to academic rationalism. The goal of cultural reproduction is enculturation, which is the process of learning about a culture through our interactions and communications at home, at school, and in society at large. In education, cultural reproduction is the means by which important elements of the culture must be passed down from one generation to the next.

culture of mathematics (humanism)

Closely related to *cultural reproduction*, the culture of mathematics is a social orientation toward *thinking mathematically*, which is being able to look at the world from a mathematical point of view. It involves achieving over time a level of competence with the mathematical theorems, postulates, and their applications while using them to better understand our world and our society. Within a *constructivist learning environment*, novice learners are introduced into the culture of mathematics through *social development, apprenticeship learning*, and *cognitive coaching*. They participate in the process of acquiring mathematical knowledge within a cultural, interactive context. Through a series of *mathematical problem-solving* activities within the group and guided by the instructor, the novice learners slowly become part of the culture of mathematics. Similar to the process of *enculturation* and similar to the learning process described in Jean Lave's *situated learning*, the learners over time come to participate in a *community of practice*. As novices gain mathematical knowledge and move closer to the community's center, they become more actively engaged in the culture of mathematics and eventually take on the role of mentor, helping new, uninitiated individuals into the community of practice.

curriculum as experience (constructivism)

This phrase refers to a *problem-based learning* method that opposes the *curriculum-as-prescription* approach. Curriculum as prescription focuses on the instructor as a transmitter of information with the learners as receivers of information that is provided linearly within a very structured environment. Curriculum as experience, on the other hand, focuses on the learners as constructors of knowledge. In this context, the teacher acts as a facilitator of activities that focus on the whole rather than on the parts. The learning environment is flexible, informal. Problem-based learning, which is a fundamental aspect of curriculum as experience, is a curriculum design approach in which learners are expected to synthesize and construct knowledge to resolve problems based upon objectives and conditions that they themselves establish at the beginning of the class or module.

Problem-based learning is developed and maintained by the Center for Problem-Based Learning, which was created by the Illinois

Mathematics and Science Academy to provide *curriculum design* support for K–16 instructors who seek to do research, *knowledge sharing*, and training in problem-based learning methods and skills. The method of problem-based learning is in opposition to the traditional *industrial age educational paradigm*, with its emphasis on lecture-based, *instructor-centric* curriculum. As such, problem-based learning, with its corresponding curriculum-as-experience approach, is much in the same family of constructivist methods as that of Jerome Bruner's *discovery learning*, in which the emphasis is on the learner setting the objectives and creating and structuring the knowledge set to be learned.

curriculum as prescription (cognitivism)

This phrase refers to an anti–*problem-based learning* method that opposes the *curriculum-as-experience* approach. Curriculum as prescription focuses on the instructor as a transmitter of information and organizer of the content, with the learners as passive receivers of information that is provided linearly within a very structured *learning environment*. Curriculum as experience, on the other hand, focuses on the learners as constructors of knowledge. In this context, the teacher acts as a facilitator of activities that focus on the whole rather than on the parts. The learning environment is flexible, informal. Curriculum as prescription is essentially the traditional *industrial-age-educational-paradigm* approach to learning, with the emphasis on the teacher as the sage on the stage lecturing on content, while the students passively receive the information and feed it back to the instructor on the test.

curriculum design (cognitivism)

Though not strictly limited to *cognitivism*, this term refers to the planning activity that occurs in the *instructional design* process, in which the developer of the content typically performs the following: (1) Assess user needs. (2) Define learning objectives. (3) Determine the tasks to be learned. (4) Define the pro-

cess and *sequencing of instruction*. (5) Determine the nature of the content and the media to be used. (6) Delineate the method of evaluating the curriculum delivery. Learning theorists and instructional designers have come up with a plethora of curriculum design approaches to fit with their own particular *learning paradigm*. Nevertheless, all of the approaches are similar to the process defined in Mager's *criterion-referenced instruction*, whereby up-front planning ensures that the goals, objectives, and mission of the curriculum are accomplished to satisfy the needs of the users and match the tasks that the users must learn to perform. In the late 1980s, Ornstein and Hunkins grouped a myriad of curriculum designs into three broad categories: (1) subject-oriented curriculum designs, (2) learner-centric curriculum designs, and (3) problem-centered curriculum designs. In essence, curriculum design spans all of the *learning paradigms* of *cognitivism, constructivism, behaviorism,* and *humanism*.

cybernetics (constructivism)

Coined in 1948 by Norbert Wiener in his book with the same name, cybernetics is the study of control and communication in animals, machines, humans, and society. Cybernetics, which means "steersman" in Greek, has its roots in Claude Shannon's *information theory,* which was an attempt in the late 1940s to solve the problem of communicating information efficiently over noisy data and communication lines by using statistics and probability as well as various types of feedback and control mechanisms.

Cybernetics is closely related to *chaos theory*, which postulates that no matter how complex and disordered our world appears to be, there lies an inherent self-organizing order that is self-adapting, self-regulating, and based upon mathematical principles and statistical calculations. As it relates to chaos theory, cybernetics has influenced studies and research in *artificial intelligence* and *artificial life*. Though the roots of cybernetics are in mathematics and engineering, adherents of cybernetics seek to include a variety of disciplines, including but not limited to biology, neurophysiology, anthropology, psychology, and education.

Very much in sync with the *learning paradigm* of *constructivism*, cybernetics also considers how observers construct and interact with knowledge taken in from the real world, which is by its very nature subjective and based upon the individual and the collective perceptions and experiences of the participants. This subjective and human social interactive aspect of cybernetics is exemplified in Gordon Pask's *conversation theory*, in which learning is completely determined by the subjective social interaction of the learners and is modified as the conversation and interaction continue. Opposite to an analytical and objectivist perspective and approach to the real world as seen by the cognitivists, cybernetics can be best characterized by a quote from the American naturalist John Muir. "When we try to pick up anything by itself, we find it is attached to everything in the universe." With its emphasis on synthesis and its seeking to look at the whole picture of things, cybernetics also shares common beliefs with *Gestalt theory* and *humanism*.

D

data chunking (cognitivism)

In Allen Newell's *Soar*, data chunking is the process by which learners recall information about objects in *working memory* outside of the context that the information was first perceived. For example, if a child picks up a small red, plastic pickup truck from a sandbox, the data chunks (i.e., attributes of the object) that are placed in working memory are: "small," "red," "plastic," and "pickup truck shape." When that same child sees a large, black pickup truck on the street in front of the house, the data chunks between the two perceived objects are compared and contrasted. Thus, each attribute of the pickup truck is noted. In the case of the pickup truck, it would be size, color, wheels, etc. The new object perceived is thus placed in the context of the old object where comparisons and contrasts are made. Data chunking, as opposed to chunking, involves objects rather than situations. *Chunking* is a learning process that involves analyzing and committing to memory a particular resolution to a previously encountered problem. When the learner encounters a similar situation, he or she recalls the "chunk" and reuses it for the new problem.

data mining (cognitivism)

Closely related to *agents* that guide software users and provide *electronic performance support* to them, data mining is a function of sophisticated database and *knowledge base* applications that automatically search out hidden spatial and textual patterns within a large set of data. Data mining typically uses statistical methods to determine similarities and patterns within the set. It is closely related to *machine learning*, in which knowledge is extracted from databases in order to simulate and model how knowledge is acquired by humans and by *agents*. Data mining does not change the information in the database. It simply combs through the information and discovers previously unknown relationships among the set. Data mining is an important function of many *artificial intelligence* applications and the building of *neural networks* that simulate how the mind works with regard to retrieving, sifting through, and processing information.

decentering (educational technology)

In a *hypermedia application*, decentering refers to its characteristic of not typically having a permanent center or central point of organization. By its very nature, *hypermedia* has a high degree of *nonlinearity* that can easily cause user *disorientation*. Decentering is the process whereby the learner shifts the center of the application as the area of focus shifts. In other words, whatever is the learner's particular interest at a given point in the program becomes the center of the application. To reduce the effects of decentering and to reduce the learner's *cognitive overhead*, authors typically include in the application a textual or graphical table of contents, a *cognitive map*, which provides an overview of the landscape of the nonlinear environment. This helps the learners so that they will not get lost between all of the various links in cyberspace.

decision-making (organizational learning)

Related to Chris Argyris's *action research,* decision making is an important aspect of *management thinking* involving several stages of action that should occur before informed choices that will affect the organization are made. Oftentimes, issues that affect the decision-making process go unrecognized. Lack of conscious awareness of these issues often causes poor decision making. With a clear knowledge of the issues involved, the manager should record his or her thought processes regarding the issues and the impacts on those affected by the decision. An important aspect of decision making is that the results of it should involve a business transformation and a new way of looking at the situation and business culture. This is a central aspect of *organizational learning* and *action learning.* Decision makers must pay careful consideration to how to introduce the changes that will occur as a result of the decision. Decision making is often a team-based activity and is a crucial element of a *collaborative learning* process that involves *critical thinking, problem solving,* and *cognitive coaching* activities. Decision making is not simply a manager making correct choices. It is a process that should occur within a social and *organizational learning* context.

decision support systems (organizational learning)

An important tool for *collaboration* and *collaborative learning* activities in a business organization, decision support systems allow managers and employees to be more effective regarding *decision-making, problem-solving,* and *cognitive coaching* activities. Part of a corporate-networked computer system, the decision support system usually has a facilitator who monitors and controls the group interactions and communications as issues are raised (often anonymously) and suggested solutions are provided electronically. Typically all issues and responses are displayed for all participants to see and reflect upon. Also an important tool for *action research, action learning,* and *organizational learning,* decision support systems are critical to the social interaction aspects of *management thinking* and Chris Argyris's *double loop learning.*

declarative knowledge (cognitivism)

An important component of John Anderson's *ACT theory,* which is a *cognitive architecture* describing how humans think and perform tasks, declarative knowledge is essentially knowledge of concepts. Declarative knowledge is stored in a specific format, which can be further subdivided in *memory* and reused as needed. Another type of knowledge in Anderson's theory, *procedural knowledge* is that which is needed by individuals to perform tasks. It is skills knowledge. Declarative knowledge is stored in *declarative memory*; whereas procedural knowledge is stored in *procedural memory*. Both declarative and procedural memory are types of *long-term memory* as opposed to *working memory.* Though declarative knowledge is stored in declarative memory, sequences of declarative knowledge (i.e., *productions*) are stored in procedural memory where further inferences related to task completion are made.

declarative memory (cognitivism)

In John Robert Anderson's *ACT theory,* declarative memory stores *declarative knowledge*, which is in a particular format and can be further analyzed and broken down, as opposed to *procedural memory,* which stores *procedural knowledge* used by an individual to perform tasks that over time become routine. John Anderson's ACT theory is a *cognitive architecture,* which states that human *cognition* is an interplay of procedural, declarative, and working memory. *Declarative memory* is a type of *long-term memory* that stores facts and ideas in a semantic network structure (i.e., a *network model*). *Procedural memory,* another type of long-term memory, takes sequences of declarative knowledge in the form of *productions* and makes further logical inferences about them. Each production contains a set of conditions and actions found within declarative memory. *Working memory,* or short-term conscious thought, retrieves declarative information of facts and ideas, carries out task sequences found in procedural memory, and adds new information gathered from the environment, forming new sequences that are then stored in procedural memory.

deductive learning (cognitivism)

A form of *machine learning* in *artificial intelligence* systems, deductive learning involves rote learning based upon direct external inputs that do not result in the gain of any new knowledge or concepts. Deductive learning is opposed to inductive learning, which is the acquisition of new concepts and methods without direct external input from an outside source. Generally speaking, inductive learning is more difficult for *machine learning* because it involves the addition of new information and concepts based upon educated inferences, which may in fact be incorrect. In most *artificial intelligence* systems, such as *Soar,* the *cognitive architecture* employs both inductive and deductive learning attributes as a model for mental processing.

deschooling (constructivism)

A concept from Ivan Illich, deschooling is a process that refocuses education on the learner and his or her *personal curriculum design,* wherein the choice of curriculum is, at least to a certain extent, a result of the learner's choice. Deschooling's primary emphasis is on the individual's pursuit of knowledge. In the 1970s, Illich argued that education's top-down management style, which was typical of modern technological organizations, was robbing students of their *creativity* and personal *decision-making* abilities. Learners, in effect, needed to be deschooled, that is, deprogrammed from the *industrial age educational paradigm* whose principles and policies get in the way of the natural curiosity and self-motivation of the learner. Deschooling is thus a definite precursor to Bruner's *discovery learning* and other constructivist paradigms, wherein the focus is on the learner and the learner's construction of content and meaning in the educational curriculum.

developmental learning (constructivism)

From a generic perspective, this is the umbrella term, also referred to by learning experts as *genetic epistemology,* for the developmental learning theories of Jean Piaget, including *assimilation, accommodation,* and *equilibration.* Epistemology is the study of knowledge. Piaget's studies were concerned with how children attain knowledge into adulthood. He was concerned with how *cognitive structures, schemata,* are developed through individuals' environmental interactions. Typically, the term "genetic" refers to inheritance. However, in this instance, the term "genetic" refers to the developmental learning processes of individuals. In total, genetic epistemology is the study of how individuals attain knowledge through intellectual development and experience. In Jean Piaget's genetic epistemology, the cognitive structure of the organism is modified through the dual developmental learning processes of assimilation and accommodation. As the organisms interact with the environment, as they develop, the schemata themselves are modified in order to allow the individuals to deal with the changes occurring as a result of interactions with the environment through the process of development.

dialectic method (constructivism)

Also known as the Socratic method, and utilized by Socrates and later Plato around 400 B.C., the dialectic method is a teaching approach that is a dialogue between an expert and a searcher or a set of searchers on a particular topic or range of topics. Though insisting that he knows nothing or nearly nothing, the expert asks a series of questions of the searchers so that they may gain a better understanding of the topic by exposing gaps in reasoning, fallacies, and other misconceptions. As a result, the group arrives at a closer approximation of true knowledge of the topic through this collective activity of intellectual debate and discussion. In fact, the dialectic method is an early, yet most prominent example of what we now refer to as *constructivism*.

In modern times, constructivism is a *learner-centric* educational paradigm, in which the content is constructed by the learners rather than by the instructor. In the *active learning* educational paradigm of constructivism, the instructor is not the primary intermediary and single conduit of knowledge between the learners and the learning experience. Rather, the instructor acts as a coach, guiding the learners toward their own answers, their own solutions to a problem or issue posed by the instructor. As an active learning approach, the dialectic method, a method to help students learn through self-generated understanding, is thus an important precursor of constructivism.

differentiation (constructivism)

In gifted education, differentiation is a method of *curriculum design* customization and enhancement to satisfy the needs of learners who have special abilities and talents over and above that of other students. Differentiation occurs along three areas: (1) content (what is learned). (2) process (how it is learned). (3) product (net outcome and deliverable based upon the learner's special abilities). In the mid-to-late 1990s, Carol Ann Tomlinson of the University of Virginia argued that in differentiating the curriculum for gifted students, teachers must no longer be dispensers of knowledge, but must instead be organizers of learning opportunities. As such, differentiation is closely related to the principles and practices of Bruner's *discovery learning*. In a sense, all students to Tomlinson are gifted in certain areas. All have unique abilities and talents. Thus, in differentiated classrooms, teachers must make sure that each student competes against himself or herself as learning and development progresses, rather than competing against other students who have varying abilities, learning styles, and aptitudes.

digital age educational paradigm (organizational learning)

An important aspect of *knowledge management* and *organizational learning*, the digital age educational paradigm represents a critical shift in thinking about how learners learn and how schools should teach. With the *industrial age educational paradigm*, the focus is *instructor-centric*. The instructor supplies the content to the learners. With the digital age educational paradigm, the focus is *learner-centric*. The learners construct the content, with the instructor acting as a facilitator rather than an information disseminator. Given this context, in the digital age educational paradigm, schools shift the focus of their expenditures from building school (i.e., brick-and-mortar edifices) that house traditional classrooms. Schools focus on the learners using technology as integral to the process of acquiring and sharing information inside and outside of the classroom with or without the instructor's guidance. Schools shifting to this new paradigm are: (1) reviewing their present faculty, their educational philosophy, and orientation to determine if they can teach effectively in the digital age; (2) re-training existing instructors or hiring new ones that are knowledgeable about technology and *technology integration*; (3) re-evaluating what constitutes good methods of *knowledge transfer* in this digital age; (4) focusing on providing their schools with the necessary computer resources and support to build and maintain an *electronic campus*; (5) investing in an electronic learning environment for the students.

Of late there is much ado about "integrating technology into the curriculum" (i.e., *technology integration*). What this often means, however, is "technologizing" traditional teaching methods that worked well in the *industrial age educational paradigm*, do not work now in the digital age. In the current work environment, most knowledge workers are not producing widgets nor are they creating atoms. Instead, they are working with bits. Their work is a result of a collaborative effort of a team of knowledge workers who use technology to produce processes and programs that transform the business itself and provide knowledge to customers who, more often than not, are business partners.

Before Gutenberg, knowledge was shared primarily by monks in medieval monasteries. Retrieval of this information was difficult, copying was laboriously slow, and cataloguing of information was virtually nonexistent. After Gutenberg, information was published and disseminated more readily, but the cataloguing and indexing of information was still slow and laborious, making information retrieval difficult at best. In more recent predigital times—the era of print publishing, analog media, and manual cataloging—information is still not easily cataloged, indexed, and shared.

In this early digital age in which we are working and learning, a vast array of unstructured digital information (i.e., *knowledge objects*) is available via the computer. The problem is that most business organizations that seek to be learning organizations are choking on *infoglut*—too much information that is not easily indexed, cataloged, retrieved, or shared by the knowledge workers. Unfortunately, in education, many institutions are still in the pre-Gutenberg stage where information is not yet in digital form. Nevertheless, in the more mature phase of the digital age (a state that no one in industry or education has quite reached yet), infoglut will be alleviated as knowledge objects are cata-

logued, indexed, and made more accessible to the knowledge worker (and student) via the *machine tractable dictionary* and the *digital library*.

digital library (educational technology)

In its simplest definition, a digital library is a library of information provided in various electronic forms (text, audio, video, graphics), and available to a geographically dispersed group of users by means of a *distributed network system*. Various types of digital forms of information within the digital library are referred to as *digital objects*. Digital objects contain *digitized* information along with a unique identifier that provides a means for cataloging the object. These unique identifiers are referred to as *handles*.

The primary goal of the digital library is to provide users with universal access to a network of libraries and information servers that include a wide array of *knowledge objects* and *metadata* that define what the objects are. Metadata is information about the information. Metadata includes information like title, subject, file formats, author(s), date, summary or abstract, etc. A handle is the mechanism that provides the digital objects with metadata. Basic naming and storage conventions for digital objects are used to identify the digital object, register intellectual property, and link digital objects together within the digital library. Multiple digital library projects are currently in process. A good example of a prominent project is that of the Library of Congress. This project, known as the National Digital Library, has the mission of digitizing public domain literary and historic works and early photographs pertaining to the United States to be provided to the public via computer.

The digital library is a key element of the *electronic campus* that many universities are seeking to build for their students. The digital library is a key element of the *electronic learning environment* that corporations are seeking to build for their employees. It is key to the successful deployment of *distance learning* and the transformation from the *industrial age educational paradigm* to the *digital age educational paradigm*. It is central to the mission of *Web-based education*, *Web-based training*, and *Web-based knowledge transfer*. Without the digital library, self-directed learners seeking to use *hypermedia* and *multimedia* content to build information within a *constructivist learning environment* will find themselves unable to do so.

digital objects (educational technology)

These are various types of digital forms of information (text, audio, video, graphics) stored within the *digital library* and made available to a geographically dispersed group of users by means of a *distributed network system* of computers. Digital objects contain *digitized* information along with a unique identifier (i.e., a *handle*) that provides a means for cataloging the object. Digital objects are also sometimes referred to as *knowledge objects* or *learning objects*.

digitize (educational technology)

Important for building the *digital library*, digitize refers to the process in which analog media (pictures, slides, VHS videotape, audiotape, hard copy text) are converted into a digital format that can be stored electronically, processed, and distributed across a network of computers.

direct attention thinking tools (organizational learning)

Edward de Bono's ten simple strategies for thinking smarter, direct attention thinking tools also referred to as DATT, are exercises to guide learners toward sharper perceptual abilities and more focused thinking. Tool 1 is plan ahead. Tool 2 is consider all sides of the issue. Tool 3 is divide up the problem into smaller units. Tool 4 is consider every consequence of considered actions. Tool 5 is determine goals and objectives of considered actions. Tool 6 is consider all possible alternatives. Tool 7 is consider other parties' perspectives. Tool 8 is make sure that your considered actions match your values. Tool 9 is prioritize actions to be taken. Tool 10 is focus your attention on the outcomes of the actions. Edward de Bono is the prominent learning theorist who is also the developer of other thinking methods, including *lateral thinking, CoRT thinking,* and *Six Thinking Hats.*

direct instruction (organizational learning)

Another term for *on-the-job training*, which is sometimes simply referred to as OJT, direct instruction is the more modern, industry-oriented reference to *apprenticeship learning*. Direct instruction is one-on-one instruction at the job site, in which an expert who already knows how to perform a set of job tasks is directly training a novice on how to complete the job. This method of corporate instruction is still in wide use and is quite popular, for the likelihood of successful skills transfer is quite high. Its downside is that direct instruction is human resource intensive and expensive, especially if many trainees need to learn the same set of job tasks at a time. Another downside of direct instruction is that both the trainer and the trainee are, during the instruction, off the production line or away from the normal course of business activities to be accomplished on the job.

directed behavior (cognitivism)

In a number of learning theories, directed behavior is a term used for learner (or computer *agent*) actions that are goal-oriented and led by specific *learning objectives* and progress milestones. As a result, learner (or agent) progress can be better determined in a more quantitative manner by both the developer of the content and the learner. In *Soar*, for example, the purpose of the agent or learner is to perform a set of actions that lead to a final result. Since directed behavior is more readily quantifiable, the Soar program can analyze a task and all related subtasks and develop an effective and efficient means for completing the task and subtasks to reach a directed goal. With the Soar *artificial intelligence* application, the computer programmer must set up beforehand the goal that the learner or agent is to achieve.

disconfirmation (organizational learning)

In Peter Senge's *organizational learning* paradigm, disconfirmation is the process that helps motivate employees as learners who need to begin sharing information within the enterprise so that it can be more successful. Disconfirmation is a state of dissatisfaction with the current state of the organization's learning capabilities. It involves initially a sense of frustration from the employee who is not reaching a level of self- and group expectation, of not meeting a set of goals for the organizational learning activity. As an employee develops patterns for sharing information among colleagues and customers within and outside of the enterprise, he or she is better able to satisfy the needs of the *community of practice* where *collaboration* is to occur.

discourse theory (cognitivism)

This is the study of how coherent, connected, and extended discourse occurs. In *artificial intelligence* studies on *natural language processing* and *hypermedia*, researchers use discourse theory to create models of the structures and the enhancements to the structures that underlie extended discourse. Another goal of discourse theory is to find ways of improving navigation of *hypermedia applications* that match the way learners think and process information. By looking at the number and structure of hypermedia links accessed in the application, discourse theorists attempt to determine a discourse history generated by the learner transversing through the *nonlinear* cyberspace. Each move through a set of hyperlinks is interpreted as a digression from the main topic of discussion. Undetermined as yet is whether hypermedia is a dialogue, a monologue, or another form of discourse.

discovery learning (constructivism)

Also known as *active learning*, discovery learning, a term attributed to Jerome Bruner, is perhaps the preeminent theory for *constructivism*. The key concept of discovery learning is that learners are more likely to remember concepts if they discover them on their own, apply them to their own *knowledge base* and context, and structure them to fit into their own background and life experiences. The assumption of discovery learning is that the learner is mature enough, self-motivated enough, and experienced enough to actively take part in the formation and structuring of the learning content. The instructor's role is as a facilitator, a coach, and a guide, who points the way and assists the learners through their active learning activities.

Though primarily a proponent of constructivism, Bruner is so popular among learning theorists that he is claimed by both constructivists and cognitivists alike. Cognitivists embrace that part of Bruner's theory of instruction which maintains that the learners need a *schema* they can refer to and then build additional content as they make their inferences, interconnections, hypotheses, and learning decisions. Constructivists embrace his theory that, by being actively involved in the shaping of the content, the learners gain a far better understanding than they would otherwise of the knowledge that they are in the process of transforming. The opposite of discovery learning occurs when the instructor does so much shaping and structuring of the content that little room is left for the learners' own self-discoveries and enhancements. Discovery learning matches well with the basic character and design of the *Internet* and *hypermedia*, in that both rely upon the associative thinking patterns of the naturally curious inquiring learner.

disequilibrium hypothesis (behaviorism)

This *reinforcement theory* of William Timberlake states that restricting access to a particular response from an organism makes that response even more reinforcing. Conversely, providing excessive access to a response makes that response even more punishing to the organism. Timberlake's disequilibrium hypothesis is a response to David Premack's *probability differential hypothesis*, otherwise known as the *Premack principle*. Both William Timberlake and David Premack seek to respond to and elaborate upon B.F. Skinner's behaviorist notions about *reinforcers*, *operant conditioning*, and *reinforcement theories* within the *learning paradigm* of *behaviorism*. The question that Premack and Timberlake try to answer is "what is a reinforcer?" In early reinforcement theories, a reinforcer is anything that reinforces behavior. For Hull, a reinforcer is anything that causes *drive reduction* in an organism.

Generally speaking, a reinforcer is a stimulus, of which there are two types. A *primary reinforcer* is one that has as its basis the survival of the organism. A *secondary reinforcer* is a stimulus that is paired with a primary reinforcer. David Premack (and his *Premack principle*) regards all of the organism's responses as potential reinforcers for behavior. According to the Premack principle, an oft-repeated activity of an organism can be utilized to reinforce an activity occurring less frequently.

However, with regard to reinforcers and their frequency of occurrence, the Premack principle has been questioned by Timberlake's disequilibrium hypothesis. This theory postulates that each and all activities of an organism can be a reinforcer if the experimenter provides a *contingency schedule* whose purpose is to constrain the organism from accessing a particular activity. The contingency schedule creates in the organism a disequilibrium in which the restriction to activity access is itself a reinforcer. Thus, according to Timberlake, the more restricted the organism is to responding to the reinforcement, the greater the disequilibrium, which correspondingly creates an even greater reinforcement to perform and to complete the action in order to reattain a sense of balance.

disorientation (educational technology)

In a *hypermedia learning application*, disorientation refers to the act of getting lost within cyberspace. By its very nature, *hypermedia* has a high degree of *nonlinearity* that can easily cause user disorientation. To reduce the effects of disorientation, authors typically include in the application a textual or graphical table of contents, a *cognitive map*, which provides an overview of the landscape of the nonlinear environment. This helps the learners so that they will not get lost between all of the various links in cyberspace. Otherwise, user disorientation will result. This can have a detrimental effect on the learning experience. The learners spend so much time selecting and attempting to navigate through the application that they have little energy left for absorbing the information. However, disorientation can also be regarded as a positive effect, in which the act of trying to recover from being lost is a catalyst for the users to learn and structure the content.

distance learning (educational technology)

A ubiquitous term currently bandied about a great deal in educational and business circles, the term distance learning refers to a set of distribution options that permit a wider geographic span of instruction than is typically available on a traditional brick-and-mortar campus. The term formerly referred to the use of analog broadcast media, but now it more commonly refers to the use of digital media, such as *multimedia* and *hypermedia* for *Web-based education*, and *Web-based training* provided on an *electronic campus* in education or in an *electronic learning environment* in business. With distance learning, class interactions occur between instructors and students across multiple locations over a wide geographic area. Traditional teaching methods (i.e., standard lecture) do not usually work well for distance learning. Constructivist learning approaches, such as *discovery learning*, are favored for distance learning, whereby learners access information through the *Internet*, communicate with each other via *chat* sessions, *e-mail*, and *mail lists*, and where the instructor acts as a facilitator and coach rather than as a fount of knowledge and lecturer. For Internet-based distance learning classes, both *asynchronous learning* (i.e., *e-mail, mail lists, class Web sites*, etc.) and *synchronous learning* (*audioconference, videoconference,* and *chat*) techniques and technologies are employed.

distributed network system (educational technology)

This is a computer network or series of networks in which *knowledge objects* are distributed across many computers that work together to provide information to geographically dispersed users and learners within a corporate *knowledge base*. The *Internet* itself is a vast array of distributed network systems that essentially represent a huge distributed computing environment spread globally. The distributed network system that schools and businesses build for *distance learning* is a crucial infrastructure that is necessary for the creation and maintenance of the *digital library*, the *electronic campus*, and the *universal campus network*.

double loop learning (organizational learning)

Chris Argyris's double loop learning is the second and most important of two types of learning that must take place in organizations in order for them to undergo successful transformation. Double loop learning is part of Argyris's *action research*. Action research, part of Argyris's *theory of action*, is a strategy to help managers move from *single loop* learning (learning that corrects errors by changing routine behavior) to *double loop* learning (learning that corrects errors by examining the underlying culture of the organization) in order to enhance corporate *decision making*.

Argyris's theories of action are underlying rules by which the organization operates. Often these rules are unstated and even un-

known. As such, double loop learning attempts to bring to the surface, examine, and point out certain actions (and most importantly their underlying theories) that occur within the organization that are just and competent and distinguish them from actions that are unjust and incompetent. Once these actions are deemed unjust and incompetent, double loop learners next attempt to make systemic changes to the organization by correcting these underlying rules and their embodiments in individual behaviors that are harmful to the business and its culture. Examples of individual actions in use that are harmful to the organization, to organizational change, and to *organizational learning* are: (1) Maintaining control. (2) Winning. (3) Suppressing negative feelings. (4) Remaining rational. These four underlying rules that govern behavior have a great deal to do with corporate ossification. Becoming aware of them and their outward manifestations in individual behavior is central to Argyris's action research and to double loop learning.

drive reduction theory (behaviorism)

This theory states that organisms, especially humans, learn to perform behaviors that have the effect of reducing their biological drives. Hull's drive reduction theory is based upon his mathematical formulation known as *Hull's law*. The equation reads as follows:

$E = H \times D$, where

D = **Drive:** the strength of a biologically-based homeostatic need.

H = **Habit:** the strength of a particular stimulus-response association.

E = **Energy or Response Potential:** the energy for performing the behavior, which is directly related to the probability of the behavior being completed.

This formula helps to explain *behaviorism* in humans better than earlier theories of Skinner and Thorndike, which were able to look fairly accurately at the *stimulus-response association* of animals. By means of this equation, Hull was able to consider the drive and motivation of humans more explicitly by taking in such factors as environment, emotion, and prior training (*habit strength*) that would affect the *stimulus-response association*.

drive stimulus reduction theory (behaviorism)

Hull in later years decided to rename his *drive reduction theory* and instead call it drive stimulus reduction theory. He did so to emphasize the reduction or complete removal of stimuli elements from the drive that occurs upon the organism completing a correct response sought after on the part of the experimenter. For example, a thirsty organism that obtains water in response to a particular desired action in an experiment will have a reduced thirst drive eventually. However, before that drive is completely satisfied, certain physiological effects of obtaining water will occur, such as reduced dry mouth, lips, and throat. In other words, the effect of drinking water must reach the brain before the thirst drive is reduced. In the meantime, the animal keeps drinking water, even though his physical symptoms of thirst (dry mouth, lips, throat) are alleviated.

dual coding theory (cognitivism)

Allan Paivio's dual coding theory is a theory of human *cognition* that states that human recognition and recall is enhanced by the *parallel processing* of verbal (i.e., spoken and textual) information along with non-verbal (i.e., image) information. Information recognition and recall is by contrast weakened if only one channel is used. If both verbal and image stimulation is provided to the learner, recognition and recall is enhanced. Proponents of *multimedia* have subsequently argued that Paivio's dual coding theory is further justification of why *multimedia applications* that employ text, image, audio, and video elements are far more effective than traditional teaching methods that are primarily verbal in orientation. The verbal processing level focuses on language, while the non-verbal processing level focuses on representations of non-verbal events. Each level is important to human learning, and when

combined, provide stimuli for enhanced human cognition and understanding.

dynamic assessment (constructivism)

A *constructivist* learning activity that is used most often in a *situated learning* environment, dynamic assessment is a process whereby students self-assess and peer assess their own work, rather than have the instructor perform the assessment activity and provide a grade. In situated learning, the learners participate in a *community of practice*. As the novice gains knowledge and moves closer to the community's center, he or she becomes more actively engaged in the culture and eventually takes on the role of mentor, helping new, uninitiated individuals into the community of practice. The instructor's role changes from that of an evaluator to that of a coach and a facilitator that perhaps provides at most some guidelines for the dynamic assessment activity.

Situated learning was further developed by Brown, Collins and Newman in their theory of *cognitive apprenticeship,* in which learners acquire skills and knowledge within a particular environment through a process of mentoring. An important aspect of *cognitive apprenticeship* as well, dynamic assessment refocuses the learning activity away from the instructor as primary evaluator and grade-giver and puts it into the hands of the individual learner and the situated learning community of practice. The learner deliverable that is commonly reviewed and "dynamically" assessed over the duration of the course as well as in the final assessment is a student portfolio that contains work samples representing the tangible achievements of the individuals participating in the learning activity.

dynamic memory (cognitivism)

In Roger Schank's *script theory,* dynamic memory is an important concept for describing how our *long-term memories* are not static but ever changing and fluid as a result of the constant input and processing of new life and learning experiences. Opposed to the notion that memory is a warehouse that is basically static, dynamic memory within Schank's script theory emphasizes how we make decisions and have particular sets of expectations based upon prior experiences that we have incorporated into a set of scripts. In short, script theory postulates that life events are understood and processed in terms of scripts, plans, and other *knowledge structures* that reside within dynamic memory. In Schank's paradigm, dynamic memory is by its very nature self-adjusting in order to accommodate the new knowledge and experiences being processed. As dynamic memory is involved in the process of incorporating new information and experiences, learning takes place. It is not simply the process of adding information to a static, long-term memory warehouse.

E

Ebbinghaus experiments (behaviorism)

In the mid-to-late nineteenth century, Hermann Ebbinghaus sought to separate the study of human learning and memory from philosophy by performing a series of behavioral experiments that followed Aristotle's *laws of association*, in particular by studying the effects of the *law of frequency*. Aristotle's postulate regarding frequency is that the more often two events occur together, the stronger will be the association between them. Or, from a learning theory perspective, the more often two objects are experienced by an organism simultaneously, the more likely they will be remembered and learned.

For Ebbinghaus, the greater the number of trials one experienced, (e.g., the greater the number of successive exposures to a list or a group of syllables), the better was the association, as well as the rate of learning and remembering. Later, Edwin Guthrie rejected this notion. With Guthrie, one trial, one successful pairing of a stimulus with a response is sufficient for learning to occur by the organism. This is known as *one-trial learning*. Nevertheless, Ebbinghaus's experiments dra-matically changed the study of the associative process and led the way toward later empirical studies by the behaviorists. Rather than make theoretical assumptions about the law of frequency, Ebbinghaus used experiments to chart how the law of frequency functioned, especially in relation to what Skinner would later refer to as *verbal behavior*.

echoic behavior (behaviorism)

This term refers to the third of four categories of human *verbal behavior* delineated by B.F. Skinner. According to Skinner, verbal behavior (i.e., language) of humans can be entirely defined and explained within the context of *reinforcement theory*. For Skinner, both human talking and listening are actions that are directly influenced, just like any other behavior, by reinforcement from the environment. Skinner classified verbal behaviors that are responses to reinforcement into four categorizations: (1) *Mands*. These are commands and utterances that require an immediate response. An example of a mand is, "Watch out for the baseball." (2) *Tact*. These are words that represent specific objects recognized by the human in the environment, expressed out loud, and reinforced not only by the sound of the word but also by an observer's recognition that the word corresponds to the object and to the sound of the word itself. (3) Echoic Behavior. When the human repeats exactly the same set of words stated verbatim by another, this action is known as echoic behavior. It is a first step toward learning more complex verbal behavior beyond repeating what another has said. (4) *Autoclitic Behavior*. This is behavior that is entirely dependent upon other verbal behavior to qualify responses, to express relationships, and to provide a grammatical frame to the verbal behavior. Overall, Skinner's view of human verbal behavior is that it is based entirely upon the environment and environmental responses. He rejects the cognitive processes that are delineated by cognitivists as they seek to define natural language processing of humans.

echoic memory (cognitivism)

Coined in 1967 by Ulric Neisser, currently professor of *cognitive psychology* at Cornell University, echoic memory, one of three *sensory memories* along with *haptic memory* and *iconic memory*, is the aspect of human cognitive processing that deals with auditory stimuli from the outside world. Once the sound is perceived and enters the sensory memory (also known as the sensory store or the sensory registry), echoic memory information then moves from *short-term memory* to *long-term memory*. According to Nelson Cowan of the University of Missouri, there are two different auditory sensory stores where aural information first enters after it is picked up by our ears: a short one of 200 milliseconds and a long one of up to 10 seconds. *Memory* itself is an important aspect of learning theory, for it is generally regarded that learning takes place through memory as sensations and other information pass from the sensory store to short-term memory to long-term memory. The important thing to note about echoic memory is that it is not generally under conscious control and that the sensation remembered is very brief in duration.

educational technology

Within the world of education and business and in support of all of the *learning paradigms* discussed in this book, especially as it relates to the *digital age educational paradigm*, educational technology, also called *instructional technology*, is an umbrella term that refers currently to any form of computer products or *computer-mediated communication* tools that support or are intrinsic to the learning process. Using a plethora of currently available computer hardware and software solutions that make up a school's instructional technology mix (including *multimedia* and *hypermedia*), learners can create, exchange, enhance, and access information through the computer, and increasingly in this digital age through the *Internet,* to enhance their learning activities. A current goal of many instructional technology products and solutions is the creation of the *virtual learning community*, the *electronic campus*, and the *universal campus network.*

elaboration theory (cognitivism)

Charles Reigeluth's elaboration theory developed in the 1980s is an *instructional design* method utilized for organizing and sequencing instruction. Reigeluth's key point is that instructional information should be provided to the learners in increasing order of complexity, which he refers to as an elaborative sequence. This component is the most critical to Reigeluth. Other components of instructional information should be as follows: learning prerequisite sequences, summary, synthesis, analogies, cognitive strategies, and learner control. The theory utilized what Reigeluth calls content structure in three forms (concepts, procedures, and principles) to organize and sequence the instructional information. Thus, the learner masters the information by moving from simple to complex tasks. In each task sequence, the learner is referred back to the previous task in order to keep information in context. Another important point of the theory, then, is that the learner should be provided with a meaningful context and foundation for learning the information at each step of the way toward increasing levels of complexity.

elaborative rehearsal (cognitivism)

An important aspect of Craik and Lockhart's *level of processing* theory, elaborative rehearsal is a means of committing knowledge to *long-term memory* and achieving deep processing by putting the information in context through *chunking, cognitive coaching*, and *analogical learning* activities. In contrast to *maintenance rehearsal*, which is basically rote repetition of information that places it temporarily in *short-term memory*, elaborative rehearsal involves deep processing of knowledge to create items in *memory* that are long lasting. As such, Craik and Lockhart's levels of processing model matches with cognitivist approaches, such as Bransford's *anchored instruction* and the Caines's *brain-based learning* as well as constructivist approaches, such as Vygotsky's *social development theory* and the Johnsons' *cooperative learning*. Examples of ways to process information more deeply through elaborative rehearsal are creating summaries of information, linking the content to one's life while providing personal examples that are discussed out loud with fellow students, and generating questions for discussion with colleagues who are also studying the information. The key point regarding deep processing (i.e., learning) through the method of elaborative rehearsal is putting knowledge gained into conceptual, personal, and social context. By doing so, knowledge gained will be remembered and committed to long-term memory.

electronic campus (educational technology)

An electronic campus is not a physical place but a virtual space, where learners access, share, and post information to take classes online and ultimately to complete a course of study and obtain a degree. Typically utilizing the *Internet*, electronic campus learners interact within an *electronic learning environment*, which allows working adults who seek either training in business organizations or education (most typically, advanced degrees) in academic ones to attend classes online via *distance learning* without having to set foot on a physical campus. Ideal for working adults, the electronic campus, an important aspect of the *digital age educational paradigm*, is transforming our notion of training and education at the beginning of the twenty-first century. It encourages *learner-centric* education and is a most effective environment for self-motivated, busy adults.

electronic learning environment (educational technology)

A critical component of a business or academic organization's *distance learning* initative, an electronic learning environment is a *distributed network system*, a corporate *electronic campus*, where knowledge workers and learners gain and share information from and among each other. It typically and most currently employs digital media, such as *multimedia* and *hypermedia* for *Web-based knowledge transfer* and *Web-based training* to provide an enterprise-wide *knowledge management* system for all of the employees within the organization, whether they are located in Tennessee or Tibet. Within a corporate electronic learning environment, interactions occur between experts and novices across multiple locations over a wide geographic area. Typically, learners within the electronic learning environment access information and communicate with each other via *chat, e-mail*, and *mail lists*. Often an important component of the electronic learning environment is a *digital library*, where the *knowledge objects* of the organization are stored.

electronic performance support system (organizational learning)

Coined by Gloria Gery and referred to by the acronym EPSS, an electronic performance support system is a *computer-based training* system, most typically within a corporate enterprise, designed to provide employees with on-the-job access to training information as needed while job tasks are being performed online. The primary goal of most EPSSs is to provide knowledge workers with learning information just when they need it. Of late, many EPSSs are *Web-based training* and *Web-based knowledge transfer* applications, incorporating both *multimedia* and *hypermedia* components, which are part of a larger *knowledge management* system that the organization employs to allow its employees to communicate and share information more effectively. In the current *digital age educational paradigm*, in which an important goal is the creation of a corporate *electronic learning environment*, the EPSS represents a critical technology for knowledge management in three key areas: (1) *business transformation*, (2) *organizational learning*, and (3) *Web-based knowledge transfer*.

elicited behavior (behaviorism)

In the experiments of B.F. Skinner, elicited behavior is the particular reflexive action that the animal involuntarily makes, such as salivating at the sight of a lever in an *operant chamber* in anticipation of receiving food through the voluntary action of pressing a lever. Elicited response is an important aspect of operant conditioning. Operant conditioning is a behavioral learning theory in which a stimulus (e.g., food for the pigeon or rat) and a *reinforcer* (e.g., a light) is used by the experimenter to generate an animal behavior and response (e.g., pressing a lever). By pressing the lever, the animal receives food. The goal of B.F. Skinner's *operant conditioning* is to achieve behavior shaping, or *behavior modeling*, so that the animal is rewarded for following a particular path or set of actions that is desired by the behavioral scientist.

e-mail (educational technology)

An *asynchronous learning* technology, e-mail, or electronic mail, is an important method of *computer-mediated communication* for *distance learning* in which the learners and the instructor are able to communicate with each other over the *Internet* as part of their course activities. With e-mail, users send each other messages over computer networks and are able to attach *multimedia* files that can be

perused by the recipients of the message. These files can contain audio, video, and graphics files that the recipient can open up and read at will. With e-mail, communications are occurring nonsimultaneously for perusal of the contents by the learners and instructor at any time.

Besides e-mail, other examples of asynchronous learning are *class Web sites* and *mail lists*. A form of e-mail, mail lists are a very effective way for an instructor and the learners to communicate with each other in the group, even though they are geographically dispersed, since an individual can broadcast a message or document to everyone in the class (including the instructor) at once. Asynchronous learning derives its meaning from the data processing world, in which the term asynchronous refers to computer interactions or processes that occur at various points in time, rather than at the same time.

Asynchronous learning is opposed to *synchronous learning*. Synchronous learning is computer-mediated communication in which the learners and the instructor are communicating over the *Internet* at the same time as part of their course activities. With synchronous learning, interactions and communications are occurring simultaneously through the use of *videoconferencing*, voice or text *chats, or audio-conferencing*. Typically, most Internet-based distance learning courses employ both asynchronous learning and synchronous learning methods and techniques. Both are of value for the creation of *virtual learning communities*, the *electronic campus*, and the *universal campus network*.

embedded training (educational technology)

An important aspect of current thinking in *instructional design*, embedded training is learning information provided in either *computer-based training* or *Web-based training* modules in a *just-in-time* fashion to working adults in a business organization. Embedded training is an important aspect of *electronic performance support systems*. It is regarded as a far better training method than classroom-type training, which is provided all at once in a more traditional lecture manner. It employs a *learner-centric* versus *instructor-centric* approach to learning. Embedded training is a key element of the *digital age educational paradigm*.

emitted behavior (behaviorism)

Unlike Pavlov's *classical conditioning*, Skinner's *operant conditioning* involves providing an animal with a stimulus that does not necessarily elicit an involuntary or reflexive response (i.e., *elicited behavior*). Within a Skinnerian *behavior modification* experiment, an emitted behavior is a response from an animal that is voluntary, but nevertheless possible to control by the experimenter through the arrangement of various stimuli and *reinforcers* to achieve behavior *modeling*. The voluntary response of a rat pressing a lever to obtain food in an *operant chamber* is an example of an emitted behavior.

emotion control (behaviorism)

This is the control of an individual's emotional life typically within a group or cult through coercive techniques that often involve *behavior modification* and *operant conditioning* methods. It often occurs in cult situations in which the coercive agents attempt to control the subjects' emotions through fear, guilt, or abuse. Fear is instilled in the subject by creating an outside enemy who is declared to be a persecutor of the group. Fear is also instilled in the subject by the coercive agent who will often claim that the subject is not ideologically perfect, not willing to go along with the group mission and goals. Perhaps the most powerful emotion control technique is instilling a phobia in the subject if the subject leaves the group. The *elicited behavior* response sought in the subject is a panic attack at the thought of leaving the group.

Critics of *behaviorism* sometimes claim that coercive agents seeking to control an individual's behavior, thoughts, and feelings use *behavior modification* and *operant conditioning* methods. In fact, emotion control is sometimes confused with behavior control, though they are in fact different. *Behavior control* is a set of coercive techniques used to alter the behavior, attitude, and thoughts of the subject whether they are deemed functional or dysfunctional. The control is occurring against the will of the subject. With emotion control, the subject is willingly subjected to the coercive agent's methods because of a desire to change and often to become part of the group or cult. With behavior control, the coercive agent seeks to control all aspects of life: where one lives; what one eats, wears, sleeps; duties performed, etc. In behavior control, the victim knows who is the "enemy" attempting to exert control. In emotion control, the victim does not really know if the controlling agent is a friend or a foe.

In emotion control, the victim willingly goes along with the process of control because he or she is seeking a change of behavior, and more important, wanting desperately to conform to the group or cult mission. To avoid *cognitive dissonance*, people ultimately find a way to adjust their beliefs to fit the group experience and situation no matter how poor the logic or rationalization may be to others for remaining in the group. According to Leon Festinger, in attempting to avoid cognitive dissonance, some individuals are easily subjected to *behavior control* (i.e., the control of an individual's entire physical existence), *thought control* (i.e., the control of an individual's thought processes), and emotion control (i.e., the control of an individual's emotional life).

emotion theory (constructivism)

Part of Albert Bandura's *social learning theory*, emotion theory (also referred to as *appraisal theories of emotion*) predict what kind of situations and emotional states elicit specific types of emotional responses from learners to enhance or inhibit the quality and effectiveness of the learning experience. Social learning theory defines learning behavior as a continuous reciprocal interaction of cognitive, behavioral, and environmental factors. Emotions play an important factor in the receptivity of the learner to the learning experience. For example, a learner in an emotional state of anger and tension will have far more difficulty absorbing information and sharing ideas with fellow learners than a learner whose emotional state is one of relative calmness and serenity. In short, emotion theory considers the impact of emotional states and responses on learning.

empiricism (behaviorism)

Not really part of any one *learning paradigm*, but an influence on all, empiricism is the philosophical belief that the basis for the understanding and attainment of human knowledge (i.e., *epistemology*) is through sensory experience. Through the senses, humans gather information and process it. The human mind is thus a direct result of life and learning experiences. From sensory experience, humans derive simple ideas. From a combination of simple ideas, complex ideas are formed.

Empiricism's most obvious and ardent expositor in relatively modern times was the seventeenth-century English philosopher John Locke. He believed that the human mind at birth was a blank slate (*tabula rasa*) upon which experience writes. In the eighteenth century, David Hume, often regarded as a radical empiricist, argued that we can be sure of nothing, for all of our knowledge is based upon subjective and personal sensory experience. From a philosophical perspective, empiricism, especially in its most radical form, was a tremendous influence on *behaviorism*, in which the study of mental events was regarded as irrelevant and off-limits. Instead, human behavior, not human thought, should be the focus of learning research. To the behaviorists, behavior can be scientifically observed and analyzed. This is not the case with human thought.

Opposed to this radical form of empiricism is *cognitivism*, whose philosophical roots go back to Immanuel Kant. Immanuel Kant, directly opposing Hume, stated that there are *innate categories of thought* or faculties that are not derived from sensory experience. These faculties influence and provide meaning to our sensory experiences. For Kant, the mind itself is the source of knowledge. For empiricists, the source of knowledge is the sensory world.

enactivism (constructivism)

This is a thoroughly *constructivist* theory of *cognition* which attempts to explain how people obtain knowledge and interact with the environment and with others. Enactivism is primarily a social phenomenon and is related to *collaborative learning*. A central principle of enactivism is *co-emergence*, which is the product of the interactions and communications that occur within a collaborative learning and *discovery learning* environment of learners, in which the stronger and weaker partners grow and help each other as they learn. As in Vygotsky's *social development theory*, both enactivism and co-emergence are important to the development of human *consciousness* and cognition through the shared activity of learning occurring within the social relationships of the individuals participating in the process. Enactivism is also an aspect of *complex systems* in which enhancements to the entire system occur as a result of repeated information sharing interactions between as few as two entities over time. These interactions, though apparently insignificant, are in fact significant catalysts to change of the entire system, as in *chaos theory*.

enactment effect (organizational learning)

In order for learners to recall information more readily, it is far better to have them perform instructional tasks than it is to provide them with instructions without having them put the instructions into action. This concept is what is known as the enactment effect. Important for *instructional design, computer-based training,* and *Web-based training,* the enactment effect is central to the development of *electronic performance support systems* and other learning systems in which the learner is obtaining new information that is procedural in nature.

enculturation (humanism)

The process of learning about a culture through social interactions at home, school, and work, enculturation is an important related concept to *academic rationalism, curriculum design,* and *cultural reproduction*. One of the early *curriculum design* orientations elaborated upon in the mid–1970s by E.W. Eisner and E. Vallance, academic rationalism is the belief that there are certain disciplines (within the liberal arts and sciences) with specific intellectual, cultural, and aesthetic content that must be passed on from one generation to the next. Academic rationalism is aligned to the "back-to-the basics" movement, in which becoming educated involves an initiation through enculturation into ways of thinking represented by the content of the liberal arts and science disciplines.

Enculturation is also related to William H. Schubert's curriculum design orientation of *cultural reproduction*, in which the culture of a society is passed down from person to person by means of the enculturation process. Enculturation is also a central aspect of Len Vygotsky's *social development theory*, which is an attempt to define human *cognition* in relation to the social interaction of the individual within his or her culture. To Vygotsky, human *consciousness* is completely a result of socialization and enculturation.

engaged learning (constructivism)

Developed by a set of researchers at the North Central Regional Education Laboratory in the mid–1990s, engaged learning is a learning method that focuses on engaging students in learning projects based upon real-world situations. Engaged learning is made up of eight elements: (1) Involve the learners in setting goals for the learning project. (2) Make the learning project tasks realistic, meaningful to the learners, and multidisciplinary; and design the tasks to allow for *collaboration* among the learners, their parents, and the instructors as mentors. (3) Design assessment activities based upon the performance of the learners for their work on the project. (4) Emphasize the co-construction of knowledge by learners, instructors, and other experts brought in to help with the task. (5) Provide a learning environment that enhances collaboration. (6) When grouping learners together for teams, make sure the teams are heterogeneous (i.e., sex, age, culture, socioeconomic background). (7) Shift the role of the instructor from lecturer to a co-collaborator, mentor, coach, and facilitator(8) Shift the role of the learner from passive recipient of content to an active learner who engages in *discovery learning* activities as well as *cognitive apprenticeship* activities through mentoring and reviewing with peers the fruits of the work as it is developed and enhanced in an ongoing, iterative fashion. Learners, not instructors, become knowledge creators. In short, engaged learning seeks to apply and combine many learning theories that fall under the *learning paradigm* of *constructivism*, including, but not limited to, *situated learning, collaborative learning, active learning,* and *cognitive apprenticeship*.

enterprise-wide learning (organizational learning)

Within current *knowledge management* circles, enterprise-wide learning is a much-touted, much-repeated reference to building a *Web-based knowledge transfer* system, to building an *electronic learning environment* that promotes *business transformation, organizational learning,* and the achievement of a state of corporate *metacognition*. Through *agents, electronic performance support systems,* and other *just-in-time training* approaches, organizations can move from the *industrial age educational paradigm* to the *digital age educational paradigm*. With the advent of the *Internet*, organizations can now build and maintain a *distributed network system* for enterprise-wide learning, which includes a *digital library* that contains *multimedia* and *hypermedia* components to support the *learning organization*. As such, organizations create an infrastructure for a *virtual learning environment* that is used by internal employees, customers, and even the public, while being entirely separate from the brick-and-mortar organization.

episodic memory (cognitivism)

In Roger Schank's *conceptual dependency theory* and *script theory*, episodic memory is regarded as the sum total of experiences that an individual experiences in life and recalls as scripts. Script theory postulates that human memory (which Schank regards as primarily *episodic memory*) is based upon personally remembered episodes and experiences, i.e., *scripts* (a sequence of events and actions) that we call upon and apply to a *schema*. Scripts allow human beings to make inferences. *Schema* refers to a *knowledge structure* that gets created as we experience new things in the environment, from which we create more scripts. This knowledge structure (schema) is dynamic and continually enhanced over time. As new experiences occur, new scripts get written, and the schema become enhanced as a result of an ever-growing set of personal life episodes and experiences recorded in episodic memory. With both conceptual dependency theory and script theory as their theoretical basis, a number of *natural language processing* computer programs are being tested and developed.

epistemology (humanism)

Not really belonging to any one *learning paradigm*, but perhaps closest to *humanism*, epistemology is a branch of philosophy that focuses on the nature of human knowledge. A sampling of questions asked in epistemology include: What is the source and nature of Knowledge? What does it mean to know? What are the limits of knowledge? What is the relationship between the knower and that which is known?

Going back to the ancient Greeks, Plato believed that for every object of the physical world, there is a corresponding abstract idea of that object. Humans cannot experience the abstract idea through sensory experience. All humans have a soul. Each soul before becoming part of a physical body has pure and complete knowledge. Once placed in a physical body, the soul becomes contaminated and loses focus over the abstract ideas it once possessed. By turning from the physical world of sensory experience and looking inward into one's mind, one recollects when it was a pure spirit able to conceive of pure knowledge and all of the abstract ideas not available to the senses. For Plato's student, Aristotle, knowledge is obtained through sensory experience and reasoning according to the *laws of association*. These laws of association were to have a tremendous influence on current learning theorists, especially the behaviorists.

In more modern times, René Descartes in the seventeenth century, influenced by Platonism and the separation of mind and body, believed that innate ideas were integral to the mind and not derived from the sensory world. Examples of innate ideas are God, the self, and concepts of space, time, and motion. To Descartes, the body is a machine that can be dissected and analyzed to determine its functions. Also in the seventeenth century, John Locke believed that all things in the mind are a direct result of sensory experience. The mind is a blank slate upon which the life experiences are written. This philosophy is known as *empiricism*.

In the eighteenth century, David Hume argued that we can be sure of nothing, for all of our knowledge is based upon subjective and personal sensory experience. To Hume, all knowledge of the physical world is based upon personal impressions, feelings, and ideas aroused and organized according to *laws of association*. Also in the eighteenth century, Immanuel Kant, opposing Hume, stated that there are *innate categories of thought* or faculties that are not derived from sensory experience. These faculties influence and provide meaning to our sensory experiences. For Kant, the mind itself is the source of knowledge. In a sense, John Locke with his empirical view of knowledge is the father of *constructivism*. Immanuel Kant, with his philosophy of innate knowledge, is the father of *cognitivism*. David Hume, with his skeptical view of what we can know, is the father of *behaviorism*.

As noted by the twentieth-century founder of behaviorism, John B. Watson, since *consciousness* cannot be reliably studied, then we should not bother studying it at all. Behavior is observable and therefore behavior is what should be studied only. Watson felt that the study of epistemology, the study of *consciousness,* should be left to the philosophers. To Watson, the thousands of years of study of what is knowledge (i.e., epistemology) is a waste of time and scientific effort. From Watson's perspective, only the *laws of association,* specifically contiguity and frequency, are useful to the study of learning and behavior. Nevertheless, debate about what constitutes knowledge from both a philosophical and a psychological perspective continues today.

equilibration (constructivism)

An important concept to Jean Piaget, equilibration is a stabilizing process that the individual seeks to achieve through the dual developmental processes of *accommodation* and *assimilation.* Accommodation involves the process of changing *cognitive structures* to make sense of the new events occurring in the environment. Assimilation involves interpreting environmental events within the context of already existing cognitive structures. Accommodation and assimilation work together as the child develops and interacts with the environment in order to achieve a state of equilibrium. Strongly influenced by laws of biological development, Jean Piaget, the father of *genetic epistemology,* observed that as the child grows older and becomes an adult, these combined processes increase cognitive growth and maturation intellectually, socially, morally, and emotionally.

error factor theory (behaviorism)

Harry Harlow's error factor theory states that learning is more a result of eliminating errors than it is of strengthening correct responses. Harlow, a psychologist at the University of Wisconsin until his death in 1981, performed a series of experiments with monkeys in which he discovered the following result. The more times that monkeys were able to solve problems posed by the experiment (e.g., picking correct objects from among incorrect ones), the more likely they were to select the correct object in subsequent trials.

At the beginning of the experiment, the monkeys made a tremendous amount of errors among the 344 discrimination problems they were to solve. It is important to note that each of the 344 problems included a different set of objects. The monkeys slowly improved until they reached a point toward the end of the experiment at which they were providing accurate responses 95 percent of the time. From these experiments, Harlow believed that the monkeys were, in effect, learning to learn. They were in the process of forming what Harlow called learning sets. If a monkey, after forming a learning set, selected the correct object on one round, it was highly likely that the monkey would select the correct object on the next round, as well as on succeeding rounds.

Harlow concluded from his data that over time the monkeys were gaining insight and speed in problem resolution in a very rapid fashion. In the *continuity-noncontinuity controversy,* Harlow responded that organisms at first learn slowly, incrementally. Later, once they have developed learning sets that allow them to discriminate between objects, learning is very rapid as the correct responses are provided very quickly. To explain his results, Harlow used the term error factors (hence, error factor theory). In other words, strategies that the monkeys tried that produced errors would first need to be eliminated before the discrimination problems could be solved with accuracy and speed later on, once the monkey had developed learning sets. Then once the learning sets had been formed, the monkeys were able to resolve the next problem posed correctly on the very first trial (i.e., *one-trial learning*). To Harlow, the monkeys had learned to learn.

experience-based learning (constructivism)

Related to John M. Carroll's *minimalism,* experience-based learning, like Albert Bandura's *observational learning,* focuses upon the learner's previous experience that is applied to new knowledge and concepts to be learned. Rather than taking an *instructor-centric* approach in which the teacher provides content to the learner, experience-based learning is *learner-centric* in orientation. The instructor is a facilitator who describes a problem situation that prompts the learners to undergo a series of *problem-solving* and *decision-making* activities. Using this method, instructors prod learners to use their own past experiences to plan, define goals, make educated inferences, and take a particular path leading to a solution to a problem or a series of problems. The process is as follows. Knowledge is acquired. It is applied to past knowledge and experiences. It is then translated to the current situation and assessed once the solution has been applied. Through thoughtful reflection, the learner is able to reapply what has been learned to life situations not as yet experienced.

experiential learning of Carl Rogers (humanism)

From the humanistic psychotherapist, Carl Rogers, experiential learning has as its focus the personal involvement and personal experience of the learner as a primary shaping influence over the individual's learning activity. A pioneering psychotherapist, Rogers began in the 1940s the practice (still current) of transcribing verbatim the therapy sessions of his patients. His focus was on client-centered therapy, which is one of the most widely used methods practiced today. The catch phrase "How do you feel about X?" is a result of this type of humanistic therapy approach. In one of his most famous books, *On Becoming a Person,* Rogers states:

> Experience is, for me, the highest authority. The touchstone of validity is my own experience. No other person's ideas, and none of my own ideas, are as authoritative as my experience. It is to experience that I must return again and again, to discover a closer approximation to truth as it is in the process of becoming in me. Neither the Bible, nor the prophets—neither Freud nor research — neither the revelations of God nor man— can take precedence over my own direct experience.

As one might expect, Rogers's experiential learning theory has as its basis his humanistic approach to psychotherapy. Four basic principles of Rogers' experiential learning are: (1) the personal involvement of the learner who has complete control over the direction and focus of the learning experience, (2) the learner-initiated activity of the active learner who is more often than not a self-motivated adult, (3) the self-assessment and self-evaluation processes of the learner (versus instructor assessment) regarding his or her work, and (4) the pervasive effects on the learner of the learning event that is based upon real-life experiences and concerns. In terms of methodology, experiential learning focuses on *case-based reasoning*; the learners' self-initiation of the learning activity; their self-appraisal of the value of the learning activities accomplished and the work performed; and the emphasis on a non–threatening, nonjudgmental learning environment to limit the possibility of threats to the selfhood, which are by nature, harmful to the learning experience. To Rogers, there are two types of learning: (1) cognitive learning, which is unimportant to the self because it is based on academic knowledge that does not address the needs and wants of the learners and (2) experiential learning, which is significant because it is related to learning that has relevance to the individual's life or work experiences.

Experiential Learning of David Kolb (cognitivism, organizational learning)

Providing a historical perspective on experiential learning, David A. Kolb, in his book *Experiential Learning: Experience as the Source of Learning and Development,* outlined in the mid–1980s how experiential learning has its roots in Kurt Lewin's *Gestalt theory* and his concept of *life space,* John Dewey's *instrumentalism,* and Jean Piaget's *genetic epistemology.* Kurt Lewin's view of Gestalt theory states that whatever occurs to a human individual shapes that individual and influences all aspects of that individual (i.e., influences his or her *life space*). Dewey's instrumentalism states that learning is developing and that developing is learning. In Jean Piaget's genetic epistemology, the cognitive structure of the human is modified through the dual processes of *assimilation* and *accommodation*. As humans interact with the environment, as they develop a heightened sense of *cognition* through sets of life and learning experiences, they further develop intellectually, emotionally, and morally to deal with the changes occurring internally and externally as a result of these interactions with the environment.

David Kolb in his book goes on to create a model for experiential learning by matching types of *cognitive processes* with specific types of *instructional design* strategies that are based upon his four *learning styles*. These four learning styles are tied to four types of learners: reflectors, theorists, pragmatists, and activists. (1) Reflectors observe, watch, and take in information from the environment and reflect upon these experiences often in a visual manner. They are characterized as imaginative types. (2) Theorists also observe and watch, and take in information from the environment, but they process the information abstractly and play with the idea of it in an analytical fashion. They are thus characterized as analytical types. (3) Pragmatists take in the experiences from the external environment and process them by testing them out in an active fashion. They are characterized as practical, common sense types. (4) Activists are intimately tied to their senses and sensory experiences. They process what they see, hear, touch, and feel. They are characterized as dynamic, intuitive types.

From an *instructional design* perspective, the following learning strategies should be employed for each learning style type. (1) Reflectors need instruction that is discussion- or simulation-oriented. They need to see patterns, probe, question, and reflect. They seek to answer the question, "Why." The instructor's role for reflectors is to motivate and witness. (2) Theorists need instruction that is structured, factual, and challenging. They need to analyze, organize, classify, and use logic to see the interrelationships between concepts. They seek to answer the question, "What." The instructor's role is to give them the facts. (3) Pragmatists need instruction that is practical, involving *problem-solving* activities, with the instructor acting as a facilitator and a coach. They seek to answer the question, "How." And they desire to discover on their own the links between content and opportunities to solve real-life problems. (4) Activists need instruction that focuses on self-discovery with the instructor being an assessor of process and product. Activists prefer to focus on evaluations, summaries, and syntheses. They enjoy role-playing and competitive tasks. They seek to answer the question, "What if."

In more recent books, Kolb has applied his perspectives on experiential learning and learning styles to organizational behavior and *organization learning*. Kolb's *Organizational Behavior: An Experiential Approach,* published in 2000, provides group learning exercises and *problem-solving* situations and simulations to promote experiential learning for the various types of learning styles of employee audiences he addresses. Its twin goals are to have employees learn specific, new work-related content and through the experience to learn more about oneself, one's learning style, as well as one's learning strengths and weaknesses.

experiential mode of cognition (humanism)

One of two modes of *cognition* including the *reflective mode of cognition*, the experiential mode of cognition is more of a subconscious mode of thinking that occurs as we experience events and objects in our contemporary work and *learning environment*. The reflective mode refers to a higher-order thinking, similar to *metacognition*, in which the learner takes in ideas encountered from the world, thinks through them, reflects upon them, and reuses them to construct new ideas and knowledge.

According to Donald A. Norman's book from the mid–1990s, *Things that Make Us Smart: Defending Human Attributes in the*

Age of the Machine, contemporary education focuses on the use of computers, technology, and *multimedia* that help in regard to the experiential mode of cognition, yet often inhibit learners with regard to thinking creatively and constructively by means of the reflective mode of cognition. Norman goes on to describe *physical artifacts* that we interact with, such as pencils, calculators, and computers that are important for the experiential mode of cognition as well as *cognitive artifacts,* such as reading, math, and language that are important for the reflective mode of cognition. Thus, Norman's concern about technology and its use in education is that it overemphasizes the experiential mode of cognition and seeks to immerse and entertain students instead of getting them to be thoughtful and reflective, thus strengthening the reflective mode of cognition.

expert system (cognitivism)

An expert system is an *artificial intelligence* application that uses a *knowledge base* in which the computer helps humans perform *problem-solving* activities by following "if/then" rules of logic. Roger Schank and his colleagues' *Ask systems* serve as a good example of an expert system or set of expert systems. Developed by Roger Schank and his students at the Institute for Learning Sciences at Northwestern University, ASK systems are a set of *hypermedia applications* that contain a *knowledge base* of video clips by teacher experts on various topics of interest. A hypermedia application is an exploratory system that allows the user to select from a menu of topics that the students wish to know more about. As an example, the *Internet* itself is one huge hypermedia learning environment.

In the ASK *learning environment,* the students query the hypermedia knowledge base and, in effect, have a dialogue with the experts. The net result is that students have questions on topics and, in response, teachers provide stories (through the video clips) of their own experiences that illustrate and expand upon the topics. It is akin to the elders of the tribe telling stories and providing

wisdom while the tribe's children sit around the campfire and ask questions. In such a manner, knowledge is transferred and experiences are shared between experts and novices.

explanation-based generalization (cognitivism)

Sometime referred to as EBG, the explanation-based generalization is a rule of thumb used for *problem solving* within *Soar.* An example of an explanation-based generalization is *chunking.* Within Allen Newell's *Soar,* chunking is a learning process that involves analyzing and committing to memory a particular resolution to a previously encountered situation or problem. When the individual encounters a similar impasse, he or she recalls the "chunk" and reuses it to solve this new problem.

explicit knowledge (organizational learning)

From a *knowledge management* perspective, explicit knowledge is knowledge that is extant in the form of corporate memos, reports, policies, and procedures within the business enterprise. Thus, explicit knowledge resides in formal documents of the organization. Even though these documents may be *digitized* and provided to employees within a *digital library,* they are often less important than *tacit knowledge.* Tacit knowledge is knowledge that is stored in people's heads and shared among immediate colleagues. It is often harder to capture, yet it contains more valuable information that needs to be disseminated throughout the organization.

explicit memory (cognitivism)

In the mid–1980s, Peter Graf and Daniel L. Schacter defined explicit memory as the mind's conscious recall of a past event. Data stored in explicit memory relates to a specific event that occurred at a particular place and time. This is opposed to *implicit memory,* which Graf and Schacter regard as the effects of a previous event on a particular task not requiring conscious recall. Implicit memories cannot be recalled and used for actions and reasoning. Examples of tasks in which implicit memory is involved are driving an automobile or hitting a baseball. Learning the rules and techniques of driving a car or hitting a baseball involves explicit memory. Explicit and implicit memory can be dissociated. For example, patients suffering from amnesia typically have greatly impaired explicit memory, while their implicit memory remains relatively intact.

exploration/exploitation (organizational learning)

According to James G. March, a professor at Stanford University, exploration/exploitation is a dual process that defines how organizations learn and perform *problem-solving* and *decision-making* activities in order to implement new ideas and innovations within the company. To March, organizations that learn, decide, and act too quickly tend to "exploit" rather than "explore" the innovation. By exploiting, the organization locks itself into quick decisions and routines that are less than optimal. By implementing in a more incremental fashion (i.e., exploration), organizations can act on their innovations in a more reasoned manner without being bounded by quick decisions that immediately limit the choices and adjustments that need to be made.

expository teaching (cognitivism)

This is a term referred to in David Ausubel's subsumption theory, which he first delineated in the 1960s and further elaborated upon in the 1970s. Subsumption theory states that new material learned in a school setting should be related to previously presented ideas and concepts that become processed and extant in the *cognitive structure* of the brain. Opposing somewhat Bruner's *discovery learning* process, in which the student discovers and shapes content on his or her own, Ausubel believes that instructors must provide to the students contextual information, as well as *advance organizers,* which act as a bridge between new material and previous material studied.

Thus, Ausubel's learning paradigm is more *instructor-centric* versus *learner-centric*. In fact, he refers to the instructional aspects of the subsumption process as expository teaching. Ausubel further defines, from the learner's perspective, the subsumption process (new ideas placed by the instructor within the context of old ideas within some sort of conceptual structure) as *reception learning,* which opposes *discovery learning,* in which the students construct and organize the content. Besides reception learning, Ausubel also refers to subsumption theory as meaningful verbal learning, which is learning (of primarily textual information) determined by the organization of the learner's prior knowledge that allows for the facile incorporation and reception of the new knowledge. As noted, much of Ausubel's focus is on the reception of verbal and textual information.

Followers and adherents of David Ausubel and his theory, in an attempt to provide graphical depictions of words and idea linkages, developed visual word and idea maps of concept families and linkages to provide a pictorial, contextual structure to the information being studied. These are exemplified in *concept mapping, mind mapping,* and *knowledge mapping* techniques. All are based upon subsumption theory, a process in which new concepts and ideas enter the learner's *consciousness* and fit within a broader context and categorization.

extinction (behaviorism)

An important concept in Pavlov's *classical conditioning,* extinction is the disappearance of a response from the organism due to a lack of *reinforcement*. Classical conditioning is the most basic and simple type of behavioral conditioning, in which two unrelated stimuli are provided simultaneously to an organism, whereby the organism begins to associate the two and provides an involuntary, reflexive response (*elicited behavior*) without being mentally aware of why the response is occurring. The classic example of this type of conditioning is the feeding of Pavlov's dog, in which the dog is provided with two unrelated stimuli (food at the sound of the bell). After a time, the dog, upon hearing the bell, begins to salivate, even though food is withheld from the subject. The dog "learns" that the bell sound means food, without the dog undergoing any mental processing or thinking about the activity. However, if the food is continually withheld from the dog several times, the dog will eventually stop salivating, will stop unconsciously associating the bell with food. This disappearance of the dog's response (salivating) to the sound of the bell is known as extinction.

F

Education is not filling a pail but the lighting of a fire.
—William Butler Yeats, twentieth-century Irish writer

facial action coding system (constructivism)

Developed by P. Ekman and W.V. Friesen, and delineated in their "Manual for the Facial Action Coding System" in 1978, the facial action coding system is an attempt to measure precisely by means of facial muscular action the emotional response of the subject. Facial expressions are measured with this system in terms of location, duration, and intensity. A time-consuming activity, the coding of one minute of facial activity with this system can take as long as one hundred minutes, depending upon the complexity of the facial expression. An *artificial intelligence* system, videotape, and slow motion are used to attempt to record and code the activity with painstaking precision.

This system is useful to the study of the effects of emotions on learners and the learning experience. As an example, Albert Bandura's *appraisal theories of emotion,* a part of his *social learning theory,* seeks to predict what kinds of situations and emotional states elicit specific types of emotional responses from learners to enhance or inhibit the quality and effectiveness of the learning experience. Social learning theory defines learning behavior as a continuous, reciprocal interaction of cognitive, behavioral, and environmental factors. Emotions play an important factor in the receptivity of the learner to the learning experience. For example, a learner in an emotional state of anger and tension will have far more difficulty absorbing information and sharing ideas with fellow learners than a learner whose emotional state is one of relative calmness and serenity. Bandura's emotion theory considers the impact of emotional states and responses on learning.

The facial action coding system is an attempt to measure in a scientific, precise manner the exact emotional state that the subject is in as well as the subject's emotional responses to various stimuli by measuring small, muscular movements in the human facial expression.

fan effect (cognitivism)

Within John Anderson's postulate for *rational analysis* (human *cognition* optimizes the behavior adaptation of the organism to accomplish tasks in the environment), the fan effect is one of three basic *signature* data for studying human memory, thinking, and behavior which is part of his *ACT theory*. The other two signatures are the *power law of practice* and *categorization*. The fan effect states that the larger and tighter the fan of conceptual links there are in the brain to the needed task to be achieved, the more likely the central concept to accomplish that task will be activated in memory. The power law of practice, simply stated, is that the more often one performs a particular task, the less time it takes the system or organism to accomplish it. *Categorization*, in this *schema*, is the Web (the fan itself) of information organized in the brain, based upon the feedback obtained from the act of completing the task.

field dependent thinking (cognitivism)

According to T. Witkin and colleagues, who studied in the 1970s, how students learn, field dependent thinking is characterized by learners who are sensitive to the social environment, who view problems from a global perspective, and who are more inclined to take in information as it is presented by the instructor. Field dependent thinkers are influenced by an external reward system (i.e., grades) and tend to work well within an *instructor-centric* learning environment. They tend to have greater difficulty in problem solving than *field independent thinkers*.

field independent thinking (cognitivism)

The converse of *field dependent thinking*, field independent thinking, as elaborated by T. Witkin and colleagues, is characterized by learners who are analytical, individual problem solvers, not greatly influenced by social context or a reward system, more independent-minded, and able to think outside of the box. Field independent thinkers prefer to supply their own structure and organization to the learning activity and tend to work well within a *learner-centric* learning environment.

Fifth Discipline (organizational learning)

In the 1990s, Peter Senge's book entitled *The Fifth Discipline* elaborated upon a new way for companies to perceive themselves, grow, and develop a sense of self-awareness, a state of *metacognition*. Metacognition is a state in which the organization becomes conscious of its own processes and decisions and more acutely aware of the skills of its knowledge workers. In Peter Senge's paradigm for the *learning organization*, a way to achieve a state of metacognition is through the development of *systems thinking*, the *Fifth Discipline*. This is a mode of thinking, a process in which one not only analyzes the entire organization and breaks it down into its constituent parts, but also considers carefully the relationships between all of the parts. With systems thinking, one must focus on all or almost all of the interactions and interrelationships that occur within the organization being studied.

Systems thinking is an important and necessary milestone to be achieved for the enterprise to become a learning organization. It allows one to look more carefully at the overall corporate situation and make informed decisions that are based upon an understanding of how the entire organization operates within a social context. In short, with systems thinking, one looks at all of the aspects and interrelations occurring within the system (i.e., the enterprise) before making judgments about the direction that the organization should take to be effective as a whole and within the society at large.

fluid intelligence (cognitivism)

As opposed to *crystallized intelligence*, fluid intelligence is a measure of how quickly one's mind can adapt to new problems and new situations not previously encountered or experienced. Fluid intelligence is not at all dependent upon the previous store of knowledge and experience one has in reserve (as in crystallized intelligence) to bear upon the current problem encountered. It is directly related to one's ability to perform on-the-spot reasoning quickly and efficiently. Fluid intelligence is thus different from *crystallized intelligence*, which is the accumulation of knowledge and reasoning skills obtained from the culture and applied to *problem-solving* situations that have been previously experienced.

Debate has ensued as to whether fluid intelligence or crystallized intelligence advances or declines with age. Janet Belsky in 1990 argued that fluid intelligence is at its highest level when the central nervous system is performing at its peak in early adulthood. As the central nervous system declines in function due to aging, so too does fluid intelligence decline. Others, like Jack Horn in the 1970s, have argued that central nervous system structures continue to develop (despite some losses) and do not overall appreciably decline with age.

formal discipline theory of transfer (humanism)

Opposing Edward Thorndike's *identical elements theory of transfer* (i.e., as an increasing number of common elements applied in one learning situation is applied to another learning situation, the likelihood of transfer increases), the formal discipline theory of transfer regarded the human mind as composed of specific faculties that must be exercised and developed. As an example, according to the formal discipline theory, the act of learning mathematics automatically should improve one's reasoning faculty. Thorndike felt that this general transfer is not applicable, that learning must take place in terms of very specific skills. According to Thorndike, a good mathematician is not necessarily a highly rational person. A good musician may be less than intelligent.

This formal discipline theory is sometimes referred to as the "mental muscle" approach to learning, whereby the individual learner exercises specific mental faculties (i.e., memory, reasoning, judgment, etc.) the same way that an athlete might perform specific exercises to increase the size of the biceps or triceps. Reasoning and other faculties could thus be increased through practice, repetition, and exercise of specific mental muscles. The theory goes back to that of Thomas Reid, who postulated in the eighteenth century that there were 27 faculties of mind that he considered innate and that we use to perceive the outside world. In fact, Reid believed that reality is based entirely upon our perception of it through the 27 faculties of mind. Later psychologists believed that these faculties get stronger with increased practice and use. To this day, the formal discipline theory is still regarded as an effective means of education.

formal rules (organizational learning)

This term refers to a set of communication rules within an organization that are quite similar to the *knowledge management* concept of *explicit knowledge*. In a study of cultural, learning, and communication aspects of organizations, Linda Smircich in 1983 defines organizational cognition as a system of shared knowledge and beliefs of individuals within the organization that are based upon common *knowledge structures* and *communication rules*. According to Maryan Schall in 1983, communication rules are tacit understandings among work groups within an organization, which are based primarily on soft and transitory choices rather than on permanent laws. Schall says that there are two types of communication rules: *operative rules* and *formal rules*. Operative rules are those rules that members of a group agree upon as being relevant and "happening here" within the organization. Operative rules are then similar to the concept of *tacit knowledge* as it is defined within *knowledge management* circles. Formal rules are more explicit rules found in corporate documents and *knowledge bases*. Formal rules are often shared through *Web-based knowledge transfer* systems. Formal rules are more easily identified and available across the organization than are operative rules, which tend to reside within the work group or set of allied work groups working on a project.

functional context training (cognitivism)

Thomas Sticht's functional context training is an approach developed originally for the U.S. military and later enhanced for the U.S. Department of Labor and Department of

Education for adult technical training, reading, and literacy training in the late 1970s and 1980s. The method focuses first on providing a familiar context for a set of new information. The learner then builds from simple and well-known concepts and procedures to more complex concepts and tasks. Functional context training bears a resemblance to Charles Reigeluth's *elaboration theory,* which was developed in the 1970s. It is an *instructional design* method used for organizing and sequencing instruction. Reigeluth's key point is that instructional information should be provided to the learners in increasing order of complexity, which he refers to as an elaborative sequence.

Thus, in both functional context training and elaboration theory, the learner masters the information by moving from simple to complex concepts and tasks. Functional context training also bears some resemblance to *situated learning,* with its focus on knowledge presented in the context of work settings and applications. For both functional context training and situated learning, the learning activity must be relevant to the learner's prior knowledge and work experience so that new knowledge can be more quickly and easily understood and applied.

functionalism (humanism)

Not really a part of any modern *learning paradigm,* though closest to that of humanism, functionalism, a late-nineteenth-century learning theory espoused by William James, opposed its contemporary theories of *voluntarism* and *structuralism* that sought to discover the basic elements of *consciousness.* William James's functionalism stated that consciousness cannot be reduced to elements, but rather functions as a unity that allows the individual to adjust to his or her environment. To James, consciouness had a specific purpose, which was primarily to improve the human condition. Functionalism had a tremendous influence on John Dewey, the founder of *instrumentalism.* Under the influence of Darwinian evolutionary thought, functionalism focused on how human thoughts and behaviors related to the survival of the individual and of the species.

fuzzy logic (cognitivism)

Initiated in the mid–1960s and still elaborated upon and applied to a variety of engineering, *cognitive psychology,* and *organizational learning* situations, fuzzy logic is the brainchild of Lotfi A. Zadeh. Zadeh is a professor at the University of California at Berkeley within the graduate school of computer science in the department of electrical engineering and computer sciences. His theory at its core deals with sets. Normally, in mathematics, an object either does or does not belong to a set (e.g., 0 or 1). However, in the world of fuzzy logic, an object can belong and not belong to a set. In effect, an object can have a degree of belonging to a set. Take, for instance, the example of a pile of rocks. Is the pile of rocks still the same set if one rock is removed? What if two, three, four, or five rocks are removed? Is it still a pile of rocks? At what point does the pile become a "non-pile" of rocks? In a classical set theory framework, the rock either belongs or does not belong to a set (i.e., to the pile of rocks).

From a fuzzy set framework, there exists a degree of membership of the rock to a set. It may both belong and not belong to a set. It thus partially belongs to a set. At its core, fuzzy logic is an attempt to deal with the impreciseness, uncertainty, vagueness, and complexity of knowledge in the real world. Fuzzy logic has been applied to control systems in engineering; to *cognitive robotics, artificial intelligence, artificial life, machine learning, natural language processing, neural networks,* and *expert systems in cognitive psychology;* and to *problem solving, decision making, knowledge bases,* and *knowledge management* in *organizational learning.* Fuzzy logic, in short, provides an adaptive method to model complex systems. It is closely allied to *chaos theory* and assumes that we live in an imprecise, complex, multivariable-oriented, dynamic world at a variety of levels (physically, mentally, and socially).

Systems that seek to mirror this complex world must be adaptive. A system or a model that follows fuzzy logic typically uses *adaptive response* technology. A common feature built into current technology-based *learning environments*, adaptive response is a method in which the application is customized in response to the learner's continued interactions with it. A learner is in an adaptive response learning environment if, from the user's perspective, the application literally changes to reflect the increase in knowledge or skills gained by the learner. Once new concepts and skills are mastered, the program "adapts" and provides more sophisticated "responses" at a greater level of difficulty, given the increase in knowledge and skill base of the learner. As one learns more, the program provides a richer environment to move the learner to a higher knowledge and skill level.

Fuzzy logic systems applied to *learning and performance* are closely allied to the discipline of *intelligence augmentation*.

G

For every problem, there is one solution which is simple, neat and wrong.
    —H.L. Mencken, twentieth-century
                American writer

game theory (cognitivism)

As it relates to individuals working in organizations, game theory is a mathematical model based upon probability and statistics, in which *decision making* is studied to determine how individuals work together either in a cooperative or uncooperative fashion to complete *problem-solving* activities effectively. Also an important aspect of *artificial intelligence* and game-oriented *multimedia applications,* game theory is researched to determine probabilities that an *agent* will be able to follow a set of rules to complete an action or set of actions. In its simplest, least complicated definition, a game is a set of rules that are followed by humans or agents to complete a task or set of tasks successfully. Game theory researchers have noted that humans (and agents) work in patterns that emerge out of what is apparently a nonlinear, sometimes illogical set of circumstances and decisions. From this perspective, game theory follows rules and patterns that are noted in *chaos theory*.

One of the flaws inherent in game theory research relates to the concept of *complete rationality* and *bounded rationality*. The better the *cognitive architecture* of the artificial intelligence system, the more closely it approximates human cognitive processes to achieve what is considered *complete rationality*. This assumes, of course, that humans themselves are completely rational (Herbert Simon, in his *Models of Man,* assumes they are not) as they go about solving task-based problems set up in the game. Bounded rationality refers to a computer agent's ability as well as a human's ability to achieve *complete rationality*. The problem, however, is that humans often do not behave rationally, especially when interacting with others in which opposing tendencies toward cooperation and absence of cooperation during problem solving are inextricably intertwined.

General Problem Solver (cognitivism)

Sometimes referred to by the acronym GPS, the General Problem Solver is an enhancement to Allen Newell and Herb Simon's the *logic theorist*, which some consider to be the first *artificial intelligence* program. Both programs are from the middle 1950s. The goal of GPS was twofold: (1) to solve problems that require intelligence and (2) to understand better how humans perform *problem-solving* activities. GPS made a clear-cut differentiation between problem solving (people solve problems in relation to knowledge) and domain knowledge (the collection of knowledge people need to solve generic tasks). GPS also introduced *means-ends analysis,* which is a method for problem solving that involves comparing the current state to a goal state, with subgoals noted in between the two, that are needed to meet the overall goal. GPS is an important foundation for *GOMS,* which was developed in the mid–1980s by Newell, Card, and Moran. GOMS is an acronym for Goals, Operators, Methods, and Selection and is a prominent model for *human-computer interaction* used today to measure the usefulness of computer user interface designs.

generative learning (constructivism)

First developed by Marvin Whittrock in the mid–1970s and still being discussed and updated, generative learning is an approach toward learning and instruction that emphasizes the learner's engagement in active mental processing in which the learner creates new structures and new understandings of the content. Closely related to *constructivism, active learning,* and *cooperative learning,* generative learning emphasizes higher-order skills development, including *problem solving,* reasoning skills, and team work skills. It is a *learner-centric* orientation to instruction in which learners generate their own learning, their own knowledge, while the instructor acts as a facilitator, rather than as a knowledge disseminator. New mental connections occur as the learner integrates existing knowledge with new information from the environment and from the group of peer learners. When students generate new understandings, new content structures, new approaches to a given topic or set of topics, generative learning occurs.

genetic epistemology (constructivism)

This is an umbrella term for the developmental theories of Jean Piaget, including *assimilation, accommodation,* and *equilibration.* Epistemology is the study of knowledge. Piaget's studies were concerned with how children attain knowledge into adulthood. He was concerned with how *cognitive structures, schemata,* are developed through individuals' environmental interactions. Typically, the term "genetic" refers to inheritance. However, in this instance, the term "genetic" refers to the developmental processes of individuals. In total, genetic epistemology is the study of how individuals attain knowledge through intellectual development and experience. In Jean Piaget's genetic epistemology, the cognitive structure of the organism is modified through the dual processes of assimilation and accommodation. As the organisms interact with the environment, as they develop, the schemata themselves are modified in order to allow the individuals to deal with the changes occurring as a result of interactions with the environment through the process of development. Those who focus on Piaget's process of accommodation over assimilation tend to regard him as a cognitivist and those who focus on Piaget's process of assimilation over accommodation tend to regard him as a constructivist, but it could be easily argued that Piaget's theories fall under both categories.

Gestalt theory (humanism)

In 1912, Max Wertheimer, along with his colleagues Wolfgang Kohler and Kurt Koffka of Germany, began the movement that opposed *behaviorism* and favored a *holistic* approach to how humans learn. In contrast to behaviorism, which focused on objective, *molecular* behavior that could be broken apart and analyzed, Gestalt theory focused on subjective, *molar* behavior that could not be separated from the individual's shaping influence of human perception. As the behaviorists looked back to a radical form of *empiricism* as their philosophical foundation, the Gestaltists looked back to Kant's theory of *innate categories of thought* and of the shaping influence of the individual's perceptions of his or her experiences in the environment. In Kant's *epistemology,* the mind itself is the source of human knowledge. Gestalt, the German word for configuration, is a way of describing how humans perceive the world, as a meaningful whole rather than as isolated stimuli. Humans see complete shapes (i.e., mountains, houses, trees, and rivers). Humans do not see merely lines, incomplete shapes, and bits of color. To adherents of Gestalt theory, dissection and analysis of individual parts is a distortion of reality. To Gestaltists, the whole is greater than the sum of the parts.

Because the focus of study for Gestaltists is often human perceptual phenomena, Gestalt psychology is also referred to as *phenomenology*. To Gestaltists, the phenomenological experience that each human has is greater than the multitude of individual parts that make up the experiences. All of these experiences make up what Kurt Lewin refers to as *life space*. As such, Gestalt theory is an application of field theory from physics. Field theory, in brief, is the study of dynamic, interrelated systems, where nothing exists in isolation. In Gestalt theory, no event, no single part can be separated from the whole. Whatever occurs to an individual human shapes that individual and influences all aspects of that person. In Gestalt theory, the focus is on the totality, not on the individual parts. *Consciousness* determines behavior. Human values, beliefs, and attitudes influence tremendously human conscious experience. Learning occurs through insight. After pondering a problem for a while, after considering all of the ramifications of it, a human reaches a solution all at once.

In his book, "Productive Thinking," Max Wertheimer lays out how humans learn and solve problems. He states that humans do not learn by memorization of facts, by learning rules which are quickly and easily forgotten, or by using logic. Instead, learning occurs according to Gestalt principles through an understanding of the entire problem that the individual considers without having an answer imposed by someone else. The answer comes to the individual as a sudden insight, after pondering all of the ramifications, possibilities, and effects.

goal-based scenarios (cognitivism)

According to Roger Schank, goal-based scenarios, sometimes referred to as GBS, are important for *curriculum design* reform, in which the emphasis is on learners obtaining

new knowledge through cases and simulations of how to do things, how to learn new sets of skills. By emphasizing skill sets, the curriculum changes from a focus on the replay of facts and theories to a focus on the completion of action items required by professionals in a particular discipline. For example, a professional biologist's skill set would include developing technical reports and papers, using and creating tables and graphs, formulating hypotheses, testing hypotheses through various experiments, and obtaining relevant information from technical reports and papers. Within an undergraduate biology curriculum, students would need to learn these skills. They would also need to learn to perform a basic set of skills that include being able to solve Mendelian genetics problems; understand gene splicing; distinguish cellular organelles; identify major groups of organisms; use a pH meter; perform sterile transfer techniques; and use balances, centrifuges, and microscopes in experiments.

Goal-based scenarios are cases or situations that the instructor provides within the curriculum in which the learner plays a particular role or set of roles, performs a set of actions that develop skill sets to accomplish a particular mission set out at the beginning of the course through the case. In Roger Schank's *script theory* of learning, human beings follow a similar case-based learning approach. They learn to perform new activities by creating scripts that contain sequential procedures for given goal-based scenarios. Humans store these in memory and pull out specific scripts for situations that are similar to previous scenarios we have encountered and adapt them to the new situation. Through this method, repeated over and over through various simulations and cases, humans learn a body of skill sets required by a given profession.

goal gradient (behaviorism)

A term related to Clark Leonard Hull's concept of *habit strength*, goal gradient refers to a measure of the time length between a response and the *reinforcement* of that response. The shorter the goal gradient, the higher the habit strength. In Hull's *drive reduction theory*, habit strength is the measure of a bond formed between a particular stimulus and a given response. The more the stimulus leads to obtaining a basic need (such as water), the greater the habit strength exists. Also, the more quickly (i.e., the shorter the goal gradient) that the need is fulfilled and met with a positive reward, the more likely that the habit strength will be regarded as high. The higher the habit strength, the more likely that the response will be repeated successfully by the organism. Goal gradient is also related to Hull's concept of *habit family hierarchy*, since the response that the organism responds to first is likely to be the one that it has been reinforced with the most quickly. Animal trainers seeking increased and repeated performance of particular tasks seek stimuli and responses that can be combined for a high habit strength to ensure successful learning of the desired act.

goal reconstruction (cognitivism)

For *artificial intelligence* systems, goal reconstruction refers to the ability of an *agent* to use procedural shortcuts to go back to a problem it was trying to resolve, but was interrupted before completing. Though interrupted in the midst of the *problem-solving* activity, the agent is able to mimic what humans do in restarting a problem after being interrupted and retracing their mental steps. Related to Kurt VanLehn's *repair theory*, which looks at how humans learn procedures inductively and by fixing "bugs" along the way, goal reconstruction involves overcoming impasses that stop temporarily the process of problem resolution.

Godel's theory of incompleteness (constructivism)

Within *metamathematics* (i.e., the study of what is mathematics and what is the nature of mathematical reasoning), Godel's theory of incompleteness is an example of a current metamathematical proposition. Godel's theory sought to dispute over 3,000 years of proofs by mathematicians that a mathematical system, such as the number system, can be complete and consistent. Godel's theory said that the number system is not complete and is not consistent. This new metamathematics postulate declares that math is not about proving certainties, but about discovery patterns amid much that appears at first to be without a pattern in the real world. As such, Godel's theory follows that of *chaos theory*. Partially as a result of Godel's theory, since mathematics cannot prove what is not provable, new emphasis has been placed on the cultural, social, and collaborative aspects of mathematics learning and its effective usage in solving-real world problems.

GOMS (cognitivism)

A later enhancement to the *logic theorist* and GPS, *General Problem Solve*r, GOMS is a *cognitive architecture* (i.e., a model of mental processing for human *problem solving*, learning, and task completion) developed originally in the mid–1980s by Newell, Card, and Moran. GOMS is an acronym for Goals, Operators, Methods, and Selection. GOMS has developed into a family of techniques that includes *keystroke level model, CMN-GOMS, natural GOMS language,* and *CPM-GOMS*. The GOMS family is a prominent model for *human-computer interaction* and human learning used today to measure the usefulness of computer user interface designs and human task performance. Through the observation of human task performance with computers, GOMS seeks to model human *cognitive processing* and *memory* that occur in defined stages (i.e., *sensory memory, working memory,* and *long-term memory*). All cognitive activities in GOMS are described in terms of the learner searching a *problem space*.

Almost all of the current GOMS techniques are built upon the *Model Human Processor*, which is a basic map and representation of human cognitive processing in GOMS. Thus, at the core of GOMS is the Model Human Processor, which consists of separate components for cognitive, perceptual, motor, memory, and control processes. An important GOMS mission is to determine task completion times and error rates of tasks to be performed by the learner to accomplish a particular goal. Goals refer to the desired result that the learner seeks to achieve. Operators are sets of operations that the learner constructs to meet the goal. Methods are operator sequences grouped together to achieve goal completion. And selection rules are decision points for particular methods to be used for particular situations that come up during the goal-seeking activity.

H

Laws are never as effective as habits.
—Adlai E. Stevenson, twentieth-century
American statesman

habit family hierarchy (behaviorism)

Within Clark Leonard Hull's *drive reduction theory*, the habit family hierarchy refers to the fact that there are a number of given responses that an organism may take with regard to a particular stimulus. However, one response that typically involves the least amount of effort is the one chosen because it is most likely to provide the quickest *reinforcement*. If this first response is blocked, the second and third responses (and so on), are selected according to what takes the next least amount of effort to draw the next quickest *reinforcement*. These multiple responses that follow a particular order, based upon their effectiveness in achieving the desired reinforcement, are known as the habit family hierarchy.

habit strength (behaviorism)

In Clark Leonard Hull's *drive reduction theory*, habit strength is the measure of a bond formed between a particular stimulus and a given response. The more the stimulus leads to obtaining a basic need (such as water), the greater the habit strength exists. Also, the more quickly the need is fulfilled (i.e., the shorter the *goal gradient*) and met with a

positive reward, the more likely that the habit strength will be regarded as high. Also, the higher the habit strength, the more likely the response will be repeated successfully by the organism. Animal trainers seeking increased and repeated performance of particular tasks seek stimuli and responses that can be combined for a high habit strength to ensure successful learning of the desired act.

handle (educational technology)

In its simplest definition, a handle is a name that identifies a *digital object* in a *digital library*. A digital library is a library of information provided in various electronic forms (text, audio, video, graphics) and available to a geographically dispersed group of users by means of a *distributed network system*. Various types of digital forms of information within the digital library are referred to as *digital objects*. Digital objects contain *digitized* information along with a unique identifier that provides a means for cataloging the object. These unique identifiers are referred to as handles. The primary goal of the digital library is to provide users with universal access to a network of libraries and information servers that includes a wide array of *knowledge objects* and *metadata* that define what the objects are. Metadata is information about the information, such as title, subject, author, date, and summary. A handle is the mechanism that provides the digital objects with metadata. Basic naming and storage conventions for digital objects are used to identify the digital object, register intellectual property, and link digital objects together within the digital library.

haptic memory (cognitivism)

Coined by Ulric Neisser in 1967, currently professor of *cognitive psychology* at Cornell University, haptic memory is the aspect of human cognitive processing that deals with touch stimuli from the outside world. Once the touch is perceived and enters the *sensory memory* (also known as the sensory store or the sensory registry), haptic memory information then moves from *short-term memory* to *long-term memory*. *Memory* itself is an important aspect of learning theory, for it is generally regarded that learning takes place through memory as sensations and other information pass from the sensory store to short-term memory to long-term memory. The important thing to note about haptic memory is that it is not generally under conscious control and that the sensation remembered is very brief in duration.

Hebb's rule (cognitivism)

This is a postulate of Donald O. Hebb, a cognitive psychologist who studied how human brains process information through the firing of *neurons, cell assemblies* of neurons, and *phase sequences* of cell assemblies. Hebb's rule is a learning law used for determining learning within a *neural network*. Neural networks are an important area of study within *artificial intelligence* that is sometimes referred to as artificial neural networks. Neural networks are an attempt to simulate the neural functions of the human brain. The primary element of the human brain is a cell called a neuron. Neurons are the means by which humans remember, think, learn, and perform *problem-solving* activities. The power of the human brain is the result of all of the multiple connections that neurons make between each other. In fact, each neuron can connect with up to 200,000 other neurons. Each and every neuron has four components: (1) dendrites, which accept inputs; (2) soma, which process the inputs; (3) axon, which turn the processed inputs into outputs; and (4) synapses, which are the electrical chemical contacts between each neuron.

The basic unit of the neural network is the artificial neuron, which simulates the four functions of the biological neuron. The human brain learns through experiences and inputs provided through the environment. Neural networks, sometimes called *machine learning*, learn through the manipulation of algorithms, through the change in the connection weights, which causes the network to "learn" the solution to a posed problem. The connection strength is stored as a weight value for that connection. The neural network obtains new knowledge through the adjustment of these connection weights. The network's learning ability is a result of its *cognitive architecture* and the algorithmic method selected for learning, based upon learning laws. Learning laws are mathematical algorithms used to change connection weights. The first and the best-known learning law is that of Donald O. Hebb. Hebb's rule states that if a neuron receives an input from another neuron, and if both are highly active (i.e., mathematically they have the same number), the weight between the neurons should be strengthened.

hierarchy of needs theory (organizational learning)

Espoused by Abraham Maslow in the mid–1950s, the hierarchy of needs theory can be regarded within the *learning paradigm* of *humanism,* as its focus is upon human motivation through the satisfaction of certain basic human needs. From an *organizational learning* perspective, Maslow's theory postulates that the leader of an organization must satisfy the human needs of his or her employees. Human needs range from lower-order needs (e.g., food, shelter, and safety) to higher-order needs (e.g., belongingness, esteem, and self-actualization). All of these needs are important factors for motivating humans to learn and perform well within the enterprise.

Douglas McGregor's *Theory X / Theory Y* (first espoused in the early 1960s) is based to a great extent upon Maslow's hierarchy of needs theory from the mid–1950s. Theory X workers who are not well motivated and who are regarded by management as lazy and unproductive are dominated by satisfying lower-order needs. Management's strategy is to control Theory X workers by strict discipline, threats of punishment within a rigid environment. Theory Y workers, on the other hand, are regarded by management as more creative and productive employees who enjoy learning and performing on the job. They wish to participate in management and in the *decision making* that occurs within the organization. They are dominated by satisfying higher-order needs, such as belongingness, esteem, and self-actualization. McGregor postulates that Theory Y is a better approach toward motivating employees (who are Theory Y types) in organizations than Theory X. It is interesting to note that McGregor perceived schools as following Theory X from the 1930s through the 1950s, and Theory Y from the 1960s on.

holistic learning (humanism)

Going back to the Greeks and Romans who believed that individuals had an innate excellence or genius that needs to be brought forth from within to transform the individual and the society, holistic learning emphasizes the interconnectedness of the individual's body, mind, emotions, and spirit. The goal of holistic education is to bring out the whole individual, to bring out his or her innate excellence or genius. Holistic learning draws upon the life experiences of the learner and the unique qualities that the learner wishes to develop in order to link the learning experience to personal growth and development. Holistic learning seeks to tie the learning process to the learner's everyday life and experience in order to enrich the learning process and make it more meaningful. Holistic learning is thus regarded as experiential, experi-

mental, and organic, wherein the key concept to be taught is the interconnectedness of all things.

Hull's law (behaviorism)

Hull's law states that learning occurs as a result of an organism seeking to fulfill a physical need. Clark Leonard Hull's *drive reduction the*ory (i.e. organisms, including humans, learn to perform behaviors that have the effect of reducing their biological drives) is based upon Hull's mathematical formulation known as Hull's law. The equation of Hull's Law reads as follows:

$E = H \times D,$ where

D = **Drive:** the strength of a biologically-based homeostatic need.

H = **Habit:** the strength of a particular stimulus-response association.

E = **Energy or Response Potential:** the energy for performing the behavior, which is directly related to the probability of the behavior being completed.

Hull's law helps to explain *behaviorism* in humans better than earlier theories of Skinner and Thorndike, which were able to look fairly accurately at the *stimulus-response association* of animals. By means of the equation of Hull's law, Hull was able to consider the drive and motivation of humans more explicitly by taking in such factors as environment, emotion, and prior training (*habit strength*) that would affect the stimulus-response association.

human-computer interaction (educational technology)

A discipline primarily within computer science and data processing, human-computer interaction (sometimes simply referred to as HCI) considers the analysis, design, development, implementation, and evaluation of interactive computer systems that are used by humans for various work, learning, and other tasks. It is primarily focused on the design of computer systems that are usable, friendly, and able to support people using them efficiently and effectively.

Human computer interaction is an important factor in the development of *computer-based training, Web-based training, electronic performance support systems, multimedia applications,* and *hypermedia applications.* It is an important discipline for *organizational learning* and the *learning organization.* It is a critical success factor as well to the *digital age educational paradigm,* to *virtual learning environments,* the *electronic campus,* and the *universal campus network.* Though it often exists in academic departments of computer science, human-computer interaction is an important research area among cognitive psychologists who study *cognition* in relation to how humans use computers.

humanism

One of the four major learning paradigms, humanism is the belief that human thinking and learning are not driven by *information processing theory* (as some cognitivists believe), nor by the enhancement of *schemas* through the creation of new knowledge structures (as other cognitivists believe) nor by conditioned responses to various stimuli (as many behaviorists believe). Rather human thinking and learning are driven by the growth of the self as a whole, mature, and complete human being, who has a strong character and an ability to make decisions that positively influence others.

Though many behaviorists and some cognitivists often dismiss humanism as not being a major learning theory school (due to their having such opposite philosophies), modern humanistic learning theory has very ancient philosophical roots. The roots of humanism go back to the Chinese philosopher, Confucius; the Greek philosopher, Aristotle; and the continental Renaissance philosophers, Erasmus and Montaine; as well as others after them. As a philosophy, humanism is the belief that human beings have the freedom and autonomy to make choices that positively affect others as well as the ability to advance themselves morally, spiritually, emotionally, physically, and mentally. Humanistic assumptions are that man is basically good, that individuals are free to make personal choices, that the growth of the individual and the race is unlimited, that self-concept development is critical to the maturation of the individual, that individuals are inherently driven toward self-actualization, that reality is influenced greatly by the individual's perception of reality, and that individuals have responsibilities to self and society.

In the twentieth century, humanistic theories of psychology and education originated primarily from the work of Abraham Maslow and Carl Rogers (though many others could also be mentioned). Maslow's *hierarchy of needs* described seven levels that humans seek to achieve, beginning with basic physiological needs (food, water, sleep, etc.) to self-actualization, a state of "full use and exploitation of talents, capacities, potentialities, etc." of the individual. Carl Rogers's client-centered therapy and *experiential learning* theory both focus on the goal of achieving self-direction and personal choice that lead to individual growth and maturation.

Within this humanistic context, individual human knowledge centers upon the personal learning experiences of the learner, all leading toward a state of self-actualization. Human thinking is a growth process that leads to a greater tolerance for ambiguity, a greater acceptance of self and of other people, and a personal transformation through new insights that result from peak life and learning experiences. In education, humanism focuses on the instructor's ability to foster the student's self-concept, autonomy, and ability to make personal decisions, as well as to be self-directed and ultimately self-learned. As such, humanism as an educational theory is allied to Lindeman's views of *adult education,* Anderson's views of *andragogy,* and the *discovery learning* theory of Bruner, all of whom are constructivists.

Unlike *behaviorism,* which does not involve the humanistic learning concerns of personal growth and personal change through self-direction, but rather involves external outputs, learning products, and outward behavioral change, humanism is completely concerned with inner self-actualization and individual transformation that occurs as a result of emotional and aesthetic responses to learning experiences. With *cognitivism*, the focus of research is on how the brain receives, internalizes, and recalls information. Humanism is not concerned with these internal mental states (from a mechanistic perspective) that are the result of various inputs, outputs, and knowledge transfers that occur according to *information processing theory* principles. Humanism is concerned with the learner's self-direction, inner motivation, self-reflection, and personal growth that result from the learning process. Like *constructivism*, humanism is concerned with the willfulness, *creativity*, and autonomy of the learners.

With constructivism and humanism, the focus is on how to help learners construct content that is highly iterative, subjective, and not fixed according to a single symbol system or mental construct (that the cognitivists seek). But where constructivists are concerned with the act of *knowledge construction* and the development of these knowledge constructs in the learner, humanists are concerned with the constructor, the attainment of psychological balance, and the growth of the individual that occurs through the learning process.

Despite its detractors and opposing schools of learning (primarily behaviorism and cognitivism), humanism is still a powerful force in defining how humans learn, develop, and grow.

hypermedia (educational technology)

A technology that permeates the *Internet*, hypermedia is a design type that incorporates other media besides text. A favored design incorporated within many current *hypermedia applications* and *multimedia applications*, hypermedia is a widely and deeply interconnected body of content linked together in a vast Web that includes text, graphics, animations, video, audio, sound, music, etc. One could say that the Internet itself is a vast hypermedia *digital library* of information available globally. The term was originally derived from *hypertext*, which is text-based-only linked content.

hypermedia applications (educational technology)

These are exploratory applications available on CD-ROM titles as well as on the Internet. The design model of hypermedia applications emphasizes the user's navigation through a visually coherent set of information all linked together. Examples of hypermedia applications are as follows:

1. Electronic encyclopedias, such as *Compton's Interactive Encyclopedia* Compton's New Media and the *Encyclopaedia Britannica*, founded in 1768 in Edinburgh, Scotland, by Colin Macfarquhar, a printer, and Andrew Bell, an engraver, are now available globally on the Internet at Britannica.com. These applications provide a visually-oriented, vast body of interconnected content that uses text, graphical images, audio, and video to render obsolete the physical encyclopedia volumes that people formerly used in school.

2. Virtual museums, which provide an online gallery of content available on the Internet of graphical images and information that rival and sometimes better the gallery and exhibit content available in the physical museum. By going to the Virtual Smithsonian (http://2k.si.edu/), for example, one can click on Discovery, then Space Exploration, and then go to various exhibits available online that include Apollo mission artifacts, such as the Columbia and Kitty Hawk command modules, space suits, lunar boots, and lunar maps.

3. Electronic marketing brochures, which provide a complete set of information on the corporation, organization, or school with information on products, services, people, locations, etc. In essence, the main design features of hypermedia applications have been transferred to the Internet, where they are used to structure a majority of Web sites, whether they are for information, instruction, or marketing.

hypertext (educational technology)

A term coined by Ted Nelson in the 1960s, hypertext is nonsequential writing that allows its developers to link together content, create a vast Web of paths through the content, annotate the content, and refer the reader of the content to other linked information on similar topics from other online sources. Hypertext allows for the creation of associative trains of thought through a body of content. It is highly useful for the exploration of a large body of content. The design of both hypertext and *hypermedia* is at the center of the design construction of the *Internet*, a vast *digital library* of globally linked information, loosely organized in a nonhierarchical, nonsequential fashion.

hypothetical deductive theory (behaviorism)

This is a reference to how Clark Leonard Hull developed his learning theories, including *drive reduction theory* and *drive stimulus reduction theory*. This method is also sometimes referred to as logical deductive. It generally follows four steps, as follows: (1) Create a set of postulates, which are assumptions that the behavioral scientist makes that cannot be directly verified. (2) Deduce from the postulates a set of theories, which can be directly verified through a series of experiments. (3) Test the theories in the experiments. (4) If the experiments produce what is predicted, then the postulate is indirectly verified and the theory strengthened. If the experiment does not come out as predicted, then the theory loses strength and a new or modified theory is needed. Thus, all hypothetical deductive theories are dynamic in the light of new experiments and new evidence arising from each succeeding experiment. Hull recommended that all learning theories follow this method of theorizing and testing to prove validity.

I

Enough shovels of earth—a mountain.
Enough pails of water—a river.
                    —Chinese Proverb

iconic memory (cognitivism)

Coined in 1967 by Ulric Neisser, currently professor of *cognitive psychology* at Cornell University, iconic memory is one of three *sensory memories* along with *echoic memory* and *haptic memory*. Ironic memory is the aspect of human cognitive processing that deals with sight stimuli from the outside world. Once the visual image is perceived and enters the sensory memory (also known as the sensory store or the sensory registry), iconic memory information then moves from *short-term memory* to *long-term memory*.

According to Nelson Cowan of the University of Missouri, iconic memory has two phases: one at the sensory memory level and one at the central nervous system level, where higher level brain processing occurs. *Memory* itself is an important aspect of learning theory, for it is generally regarded that learning takes place through memory as sensations and other information pass from the sensory store to short-term memory to long-term memory. The important thing to note about iconic memory is that it is not generally under conscious control and that the sensation remembered is very brief (200 to 400 milliseconds) in duration.

identical elements theory of transfer (behaviorism)

Opposing the *formal discipline theory of transfer*, which regards the human mind as composed of specific faculties that must be exercised, Edward Thorndike's identical elements theory of transfer states that as an increasing number of common elements applied in one learning situation are applied to another learning situation, the likelihood of transfer (i.e., learning) will also increase. In other words, the more elements there are in common between two learning situations, the more likely learning will take place and be remembered. The contrary position (i.e., formal discipline theory of transfer) states, as an example, that the act of learning mathematics automatically should improve one's reasoning faculty. Thorndike felt that this general transfer was not applicable, that learning must take place in terms of very specific skills.

Thus, according to Thorndike, a good mathematician may not necessarily have other types of *intelligence* beyond mathematics. To Thorndike, schools must focus their efforts on direct training of specific skills that can be applied outside of school. For example, teaching children to use the dictionary is an important activity that will aid learning on one's own outside of school. Ultimately, Thorndike's identical elements theory of transfer was his explanation of how we learn when confronted with new situations.

imitative learning (behaviorism)

In the 1940s, N.E. Miller and J.C. Dollard, influenced by *Hull's law* and Thorndike's *instrumental conditioning*, developed a theory of imitative learning. Their postulate was that if an organism observes another performing an action, and if the observer repeats the action and is reinforced, the organism will learn from the observation. The assumption Miller and Dollard made is that if the imitative behavior is reinforced, it will be learned like any other behavior. This opposed the belief of Thorndike and the other behaviorists who believed that an organism can only learn through direct rather than vicarious experience. Later, Albert Bandura in the 1960s developed his *observational learning* theory, which challenged the *reinforcement theory* assumptions of *behaviorism* regarding imitative learning.

immediate feedback (behaviorism)

This term refers to the third of a set of learner behaviors that are to be followed within *programmed learning*, also more popularly known as *self-paced instruction*. Though first developed by Sidney L. Pressey in the 1920s, and modeled after the *reinforcement theory* implicit within the *learning paradigm* of *behaviorism*, programmed learning was rediscovered and popularized by B.F. Skinner.

Skinner's programmed learning involves the following learner behaviors: (1) Small Steps. Learners obtain small amounts of information and proceed from one task to the next in an orderly, step-by-step fashion. (2) *Overt Responding*. Learners must provide an overt response to a problem or step so that correct responses are reinforced and incorrect responses corrected. (3) *Immediate Feedback*. Learners are provided with an immediate response to let them know whether they have answered or performed correctly or incorrectly. (4) *Self-Pacing*. Learners are to work through the programmed learning activity at their own pace. Programmed learn-

ing techniques have been employed and re-used in many current *computer-based training, Web-based training, multimedia applications,* and *electronic performance support systems.* Programmed learning has been proven to be an effective technique for *skills management* and *organizational learning.*

implicit memory (cognitivism)

In the mid–1980s, Peter Graf and Daniel L. Schacter defined implicit memory as the effects of a previous event on a particular task not requiring conscious recall. This is opposed to *explicit memory*, which Graft and Schacter regard as the mind's conscious recall of a past event. Data stored in explicit memory relates to a specific event that occurred at a particular place and time. Unlike explict memories, implicit memories cannot be recalled and used for actions and reasoning. Examples of tasks in which implicit memory is involved are driving an automobile or hitting a baseball. Learning the rules and techniques of driving a car or hitting a baseball involve explicit memory. Explicit and implicit memory can be dissociated. For example, patients suffering from amnesia typically have greatly impaired explicit memory, while their implicit memory remains relatively intact.

incremental learning (behaviorism)

As espoused by Edward Thorndike, incremental learning is learning that occurs in small steps over time rather than in large leaps (e.g., *insightful learning*). In Edward Thorndike's *puzzle box* experiments, a cat is placed in a very confining box with a pole sticking up in the middle or a chain hanging from the top of the box. The cat seeks to get out of the box by pushing against the pole or pulling on the chain. In the puzzle box experiments, Thorndike sought to keep track of the time it took for the cat to get out of the box, as well as how many times the cat tried, using various means, to get out before being successful. Thorndike observed that the time it took for the cat to get out of the box decreased as the number of attempts increased.

He concluded from these experiments that learning occurs in small, incremental steps rather than in huge jumps. He referred to this as *incremental learning* as opposed to *insightful learning.* Thorndike also concluded that the most basic, yet most successful type of learning was *trial-and-error learning,* in which the animal tries different means and methods to get out of the puzzle box.

inductive learning (cognitivism)

A much sought-after form of *machine learning* in *artificial intelligence* systems, inductive learning involves the acquisition of new concepts and methods without direct external input from an outside source. Inductive learning is opposed to *deductive learning,* which is rote learning that does not result in the gain of any new knowledge. Generally speaking, inductive learning is more difficult for *machine learning* because it involves the addition of new information and concepts based upon educated inferences, which may in fact be incorrect. In most *artificial intelligence* systems, such as *Soar,* the *cognitive architecture* employs both inductive and deductive learning attributes as a model for mental processing.

industrial age educational paradigm (organizational learning)

This is the name given to an educational paradigm now considered outmoded in today's digital age. The industrial age modeled its schools after the factory. The administrators managed the buildings, the teachers, and the staff. As overseers in this factory, the teachers made sure that the workers, i.e., the students, produced and were tested to meet certain educational objectives. The staff supported the administration by taking care of the buildings and the administrative infrastructure. Following this paradigm, a successful school administrator built more buildings, brought in more students, hired more teachers—and more administrators and staff to manage the process. In the industrial age educational paradigm, instruction was often limited to teaching basic facts and theories, in which conceptual knowledge predominated over putting ideas into action. The predominant method of knowledge transfer was the instructor using chalk and chalkboard, reciting ideas taken down by students using pen or pencil and notepad.

In the factory and in the schoolhouse, the industrial age educational paradigm provided a great social conditioning process for lower-level managers and workers who needed to process atoms instead of bits now handled for the most part by the computer. In the work environment of the industrial age, most tasks were relatively rote and repetitive. More creative activities were the domain of the middle- and upper-level managers who directed the workers on the factory and data processing floors. The need did not exist then as it does now in the digital age for workers to share knowledge, think critically, and exercise creative *problem solving.*

inert knowledge (organizational learning)

Coined in 1929 in his book, *The Aims of Education,* Alfred North Whitehead referred to inert knowledge as knowledge gained in traditional schools that is not useful, not applicable to work. It is knowledge that is learned in an artificial, static environment but not applied to performance in a real-world dynamic situation. As such, inert knowledge is a useless tool, as opposed to useful knowledge that is learned and actively applied to life and work situations. As noted by Whitehead, it is quite possible to gain knowledge about a tool but be wholly unable to use it.

infoglut (organizational learning)

One of the chief impediments to the implementation of *organizational learning* and the establishment of the *learning organization* is infoglut, too much information that is unusable because it cannot be accessed and used easily by employees. Through the development of *Web-based knowledge transfer, taxonomy, data mining,* and *electronic performance support systems* and technologies, organizations seek to reduce infoglut and make useful and usable knowledge available to all employees to encourage *knowledge sharing* and better *decision making* within and outside of the twenty-first century enterprise.

An important goal that facilitates the reduction of infoglut in both industry and our schools is to build the *digital library*, the active storehouse of knowledge that comprises the electronic corporate memory in industry and the *electronic campus* curriculum and content in education. Through *natural language processing* and *artificial intelligence* programs such as the *machine tractable dictionary*, organizations and schools are actively engaged in attempting to overcome the current mind-numbing situation in our businesses and schools in which employees and learners are overwhelmed by a wealth of information, by infoglut. From a *knowledge management* perspective, the four steps needed to alleviate infoglut within organizations are as follows: Step 1. Capture and collect the knowledge. Step 2. Organize, categorize, and catalogue it. Step 3. Provide a vehicle to distribute and disseminate it. Step 4. Share it and use it within and outside of the organization.

informatics (cognitivism)

A discipline within the world of *cognition* and *artificial intelligence,* informatics is the study of information in all of its forms (text, graphics, audio, video, etc.) and how this relates to human knowledge and the simulation of human thinking through *artificial intelligence* models such as *Soar* and *GOMS.* In terms of *cognition,* informatics is the study of how humans input, process, generate, and communicate information. From a *knowledge management* perspective, informatics looks at how we acquire, represent, store, and retrieve knowledge. Informatics considers as well the design of artificial intelligence systems as they seek to match with human brain functions and higher-order thinking.

information architecture (organizational learning)

Sometimes called *information design*, information architecture is the discipline whereby knowledge is written, organized, and structured in a fashion that makes it easy for the user to access, understand, and use. Information architects are often concerned with the visual presentation of information. It is an important area of expertise for *knowledge management*, the development of *digital libraries*, and the creation of *Web-based knowledge transfer* applications to support the *learning organization*.

information design (organizational learning)

The discipline of information design is sometimes called technical communication. Information design exploits the online reference and presentation power of *computer-mediated communication* to access and show information to the user or learner in discrete, defined units visually segmented and structured to make the information easy to understand and use. This area of specialization employs experts in information design who help to create *electronic performance support systems, computer-based training, Web-based training,* and *Web-based knowledge transfer* systems. Information design is an important element to the development within enterprises of *knowledge management, organizational learning*, and the creation and structuring of *digital libraries* in organizations.

information pickup theory (humanism)

Developed by James J. Gibson from the 1950s through the1970s, information pickup theory is a Gestalt approach to perception and learning (i.e., *perceptual learning*). Gestalt, the German word for shape, or configuration, is a way of describing how humans perceive the world, as a meaningful whole rather than as isolated stimuli. Humans see complete shapes (e.g., mountains, buildings, or trees). Humans do not see merely lines, incomplete shapes, and patches of color. To adherents of Gestalt theory, dissection and analysis of individual parts is a distortion of reality.

To Gestaltists, the whole is greater than the sum of the parts. Thus, given this philosophical background, Gestaltists study *molar behavior* (i.e., the whole) versus *molecular behavior* (i.e., the parts). In his information pickup theory, Gibson proposes that there exists in the environment a set of *affordances*, which includes the physical landscape, land, sky, and water that make up the *stimulus array*. Also within the stimulus array are *invariants*, such as shadow, texture, color, and layout that help determine what we perceive. To Gibson, the act of perception is a dynamic between the organism and the physical environment. In terms of perceptual learning, Gibson postulates that the learner must have a rich, complex *learning environment* within which to interact. Perceptual learning should be based upon visual cues that the learner obtains from interacting with the environment. To increase perceptual learning, the instructor must provide realistic settings within which the learners can learn and perform a series of activities.

information processing theory (cognitivism)

In terms of *cognition*, information processing theory is an approach toward understanding how the human brain operates. By analogy, the human brain is thought to operate like a central processing unit of a computer, with environmental inputs, outputs, and an internal processing unit that performs *cognitive processes* on these inputs and outputs. An object of focus among *artificial intelligence* experts, information processing theory is at the core of the study and development of *neural networks*. It is also closely tied to the development of *unified theories of cognition*. In the mid–1990s, Allen Newell postulated in his book *Unified Theories of Cognition* that *cognitive psychology* has reached a point in its evolutionary development that it is now able to design a *cognitive*

architecture and a working model of human learning and *intelligence*. This working model is based to a large extent on information processing theory. Cognitive psychologists use computer programs to replicate how they believe the human brain operates. Allen Newell asserts in his book that the cognitive processing that occurs in human brains can be replicated in computer models with *agents* acting as human learners seeking to complete goals.

Newell is at the center of several cognitive architectures and *artificial intelligence* programming languages, including the *logic theorist, GPS, GOMS,* and *Soar*. This unified theory that Newell proposes embodies subcategories of cognitive behavior, such as the ability to process language, the ability to do mathematical problems, and the ability to memorize information. An important goal for all of the artificial intelligence applications is the program's ability to measure agent and human learner performance toward the attainment of a goal. At its center is the belief that information processing theory is central to an understanding of how human brains and simulated human brains operate.

information theory

Not really associated with any individual *learning paradigm*, Claude Shannon's *information theory* was an attempt in the late 1940s to solve the problem of communicating information efficiently over noisy data and communication lines by using probability and statistics, as well as by having various types of feedback and control mechanisms. It is important from a learning theory perspective in that it was a precursor to *cybernetics*, which postulates that no matter how complex and disordered our world appears to be, there lies an inherent self-organizing order that is self-adapting, self-regulating, and based upon mathematical principles and statistical calculations. As such, information theory is also an important precursor of *chaos theory* and *artificial life*.

inhibitory potential (behaviorism)

An aspect of Clark Leonard Hull's *drive stimulus reduction theory*, inhibitory potential refers to the resistance of a subject to repeating a response to a stimulus. The more often the stimulus is repeated, the more likely the individual will resist making the intended response. Also known as a "wild card" in Hull's theory, the inhibitory potential is a mental factor of sorts in which the animal or human has a choice either to respond or not to respond. It also affects the *reaction potential* of the behavior, which is the likelihood of a particular response being performed at a particular time by the subject.

innate categories of thought (cognitivism)

In the eighteenth century, Immanuel Kant, opposing David Hume's radical view of *empiricism*, stated that there are innate categories of thought or mental faculties that are not derived from sensory experience. These innate categories of thought shape completely all of our cognitive experiences and provide a *cognitive structure* to human thinking and learning. These mental faculties influence and provide meaning to all of our sensory experiences, in other words, to all life and learning experiences. In Kant's *epistemology*, the mind itself is the source of human knowledge. Immanuel Kant with his philosophy of innate knowledge, with his postulate of innate categories of thought, can be regarded from a philosophical perspective as the father of *cognitivism*.

inquiry-based learning (constructivism)

Somewhat in the same vein as Jerome Bruner's *discovery learning*, inquiry-based learning is an *instructional design* method of the University of Michigan *Digital Library* (UMDL) Project. The focus of inquiry-based learning is to use online resources from the *Internet* to enhance the science learning activity of middle school students. As developed by Phyllis C. Blumenfeld, Elliot Soloway, Ronald W. Marx, Joseph S. Krajcik, Mark Gudzial, and Annemarie Palincsar, inquiry-based learning is based upon five basic principles: (1) Provide a driving question in which learners must investigate authentic problems that occur in the scientific *community of practice*. (2) Learners in *collaboration* with one another investigate the driving question by asking additional, follow-on questions, planning and designing experiments, debating basic concepts, collecting and analyzing information, outlining conclusions, and communicating their findings to the group. (3) Learners create deliverables to demonstrate that they understand the issues underlying the driving question. (4) Learners expand their community of practice to include scientists exploring the issue in the outside scientific community. (5) *Computer-mediated communication* is used for *knowledge sharing* among the community of practice. The goal is that through the specific *curriculum design* approach outlined above for inquiry-based learning and through the use of the digital library of online materials available to the students throughout the activity, students' learning in middle grade science will be greatly enhanced.

insightful learning (constructivism)

Similar to Bandura's *observational learning*, insightful learning involves the learner actively observing the behavior of others performing a task, incorporating the behavior within his or her own *behavioral repertoire*, and applying the insight to another different activity. Insightful learning involves a recognition by the learner of an "aha," a realization or a piece of information that allows the learner to capture the essence of the activity and apply it to other life situations.

instructional design (cognitivism)

The primary purpose of instructional design is to exploit the computer, to exploit the usage of various types of *instructional technologies*, and especially of late to exploit the usage of the *Internet* in order to enhance the learning experience of the learner or user. Instructional design is a process that developers of instructional content follow to create effective learning applications, such as *multimedia applications, hypermedia applications, computer-based training, Web-based training*, etc.

Typically, there are four phases to the instructional design process: (1) Analysis Phase. The instructional design team analyzes the audience and its needs and analyzes the tasks to be performed within the learning activity. (2) Design Phase. The instructional design team defines learning goals, objectives, and strategies. (3) Development Phase. The instructional design team develops the instructional content. (4) Implementation/ Evaluation Phase. The content or course is delivered to the learners and feedback is obtained on the effectiveness of the product. It should be noted that the instructional design process follows very much the process used by computer software developers as they follow a software development process to create computer software applications. Though not always the case, most instructional designers tend to follow the *learning paradigm* of *cognitivism*.

instructional events (cognitivism)

Instructional events are an important aspect of Robert Gagne's *conditions of learning theory*. This theory describes a hierarchy of different types of learning, which require different instructional strategies and *instructional designs* based upon specific *learning outcomes*. As delineated in the conditions of learning theory, there exists a hierarchical set of *cognitive processes* that occur in relation to nine *instructional events*. The nine instructional events and their respective cognitive processes (in parentheses) are: (1) Gain attention (reception) in order to focus upon the task at hand. (2) Inform learners of the objective (expectancy) in order to provide up front what are the projected *learning outcomes* for the course or module. (3) Stimulate recall of prior learning (retrieval) in order to stimulate prior knowledge previously remembered and gained. (4) Present the stimu-

lus (selective perception) in order to initiate new information. (5) Provide learning guidance (*semantic encoding*) in order to structure the new information in a form that can be stored and remembered. (6) Elicit performance (responding) in order to stimulate learner recall through learners' active responses. (7) Provide feedback (reinforcement) in order to ensure that learning has occurred. (8) Assess performance (retrieval) in order to determine if the learners' performance is appropriate, correct, and in line with the projected learning outcomes. (9) Enhance retention and transfer (generalization) in order to place the new knowledge gained into *long-term memory*. For Gagne, these hierarchies provide a rationale for *sequencing of instruction*.

instructional sequence (cognitivism)

Sometimes referred to as *sequencing of instruction*, instructional sequences are an important aspect of many cognitivist learning theories, including but not limited to Gagne's *conditions of learning* and Merrill's *component display theory* and *instructional transaction theory*. In Gagne's conditions of learning theory, as an example, he describes a hierarchy of different types of learning, which require different instructional strategies and *instructional designs* based upon specific learning outcomes. For Gagne, these hierarchies provide a rationale for the instructional sequences to occur within the learning activity. For Merrill, the instructional sequences are then arranged on the basis of the specific type of instructional transactions (e.g., Merrill's *instructional transaction theory*) that are to occur and *knowledge objects* to be manipulated by the learner. Thus, instructional sequences are determined by the type of learning to occur, the goals and objectives of the learning activity, the state and *knowledge base* of the learner at the start of and during the course of the learning activity, and the *knowledge objects* to be manipulated by the learner.

instructional technology (educational technology)

Within the world of education and business and in support of all of the *learning paradigms* discussed in this book, especially as it relates to the *digital age educational paradigm*, instructional technology, also called *educational technology*, is an umbrella term that refers currently to any form of computer products or *computer-mediated communication* tools that support or are intrinsic to the learning process. Using a plethora of currently available computer hardware and software solutions that make up a school's instructional technology mix (including *multimedia* and *hypermedia*), learners can create, exchange, enhance, and access information through the computer, and increasingly in this digital age through the *Internet,* to enhance their learning activities. A current goal of many instructional technology products and solutions is the creation of the *virtual learning community*, the *electronic campus*, and the *universal campus network*.

instructional transaction theory (cognitivism)

In David Merrill's *instructional transaction theory*, which is an enhancement of his *component display theory,* the central aspect is the learner's interactions with a set of *knowledge objects*. Also referred to as *learning objects*, knowledge objects are containers of information, often presented in *multimedia* form, regarding a particular learning topic or subject. The container could include multiple files on the topic that are in the form of text, graphics, audio, and video. The knowledge object may be a *knowledge representation* of any particular topic or subject, though the object is usually focused on acquiring a set of information to perform a job. As such, the knowledge object is built to be a set of highly interactive *instructional sequences.*

Merrill's original component display theory sought to identify the components from which instructional sequences could be constructed. His instructional transaction theory seeks to integrate the components into what he calls instructional transactions. An instructional transaction is composed of each and every interaction required for the learner to obtain knowledge on a particular set of job tasks. Within instructional transaction theory, knowledge objects, with all of their multimedia elements, provide the components of the subject matter content (i.e., the job task knowledge to be acquired). Merrill's goal of instructional transaction theory—his goal for describing instructional strategies and sequences as transactions or algorithms of knowledge objects—is to attain a much more precise definition and description of the different types of instructional activities useful for a specified set of job tasks.

instructionism (constructivism)

Coined by Seymour Papert, developer of the Logo programming language for *computer-aided instruction* (CAI) applications that are created by children, instructionism is the opposite of *constructionism*, a minimalist approach to teaching, whose goal is to produce in learners the most learning for the least teaching. Instructionism, according to Papert, who is currently a professor at MIT, takes us back to the traditional methodology of too much instruction, too little learning. To Papert, instructionism is well represented by the *instructor-centric*-oriented approaches toward teaching that focus on how the teacher should utilize *instructional design* methods, *curriculum design* development strategies, and *instructional technology* in order to construct the knowledge for the learners. Also according to Papert, there is too much emphasis in instructionism on the teacher constructing content, too little on the student constructing his or her own world using tools and technology made available via computers and the Internet. Papert believes that the content of the average traditional school curriculum represents a small fraction of human knowledge that is now available to children via the *Internet* and through computers. Merely putting a computer in front of a child is not a solution to the problems facing schools still caught up in the *industrial age educational paradigm,* still caught up in instructionism. To move to the *digital age educational paradigm,* schools must embrace *constructivism,* the larger *learning paradigm* within which constructionism fits. Constructionism, related to Bruner's *discovery learning* approach with its emphasis on a *learner-centric* orientation, in which the learner is actively engaged in constructing knowledge, focuses on a *curriculum design* that is expansive, that allows the learner to reach out beyond the limits of the traditional classroom environment to construct his or her own learning environment, to construct a little school of discovery within a school.

In short, Papert's constructionism is a process that encourages the students to fish by giving them the rod, the reel, and taking them to the lake where the fish are, rather than merely telling them how to fish or reading them a fishing story in the classroom. In contrast, the goal of instructionism is to perpetuate the outdated model of the teacher being center stage, lecturing and organizing the curriculum while the students passively observe the construction of knowledge by the expert, by the instructor.

instructor-centric (cognitivism)

Many theories within the *learning paradigm* of *cognitivism* tend to be instructor-centric, in that the focus is on the instructor as the primary content provider who organizes and presents the information to the student. A clear-cut example of a *cognitivist,* instructor-centric learning approach is David Ausubel's subsumption theory. Opposing somewhat Jerome Bruner's *discovery learning* process, a *learner-centric* approach in which the student discovers and shapes content on his or her own, Ausubel believes that instructors must provide to the students contextual information and must shape and organize the content for the students. Ausubel's cognitivist *learning paradigm* is thus more instructor-centric than *learner-centric.*

Ausubel refers to the instructional aspects of the subsumption process as *expository teaching.* Ausubel further defines, from the learner's perspective, the subsumption process (new ideas placed by the instructor in the context of old ideas within some sort of conceptual structure) as *reception learning.* This opposes Bruner's learner-centric *active learning, discovery learning* approach, in which the students, not the teacher, construct and organize the content. Instructor-centric approaches tend to fall into the *industrial age educational paradigm* versus the *digital age educational paradigm.* Most theories within the *learning paradigm* of cognitivism tend to be instructor-centric. Most theories within the learning paradigm of *constructivism* tend to be learner-centric.

instrumental conditioning (behaviorism)

Edward Thorndike's instrumental conditioning is a behavioral learning theory in which an organism must act in a certain way (i.e., must perform a specific action) before it is reinforced. The organism's behavior is thus "instrumental" to the attainment of a specific reward. Thorndike's instrumental conditioning is quite similar to B.F. Skinner's *operant conditioning.* Operant conditioning is a behavioral learning theory in which a stimulus (e.g., food for the pigeon or rat) and a *reinforcer* (e.g., a light) are used by the experimenter to generate a specific response (e.g., pressing a lever). The goal of B.F. Skinner's *operant conditioning* is to achieve behavior shaping, or *behavior modeling,* so that the animal is rewarded for following a particular path or set of actions that is desired by the behavioral scientist.

Typically, animal training has as its basis operant conditioning. The animal is provided immediately with a reward (i.e., a *reinforcement*) following a particular action. By using operant conditioning, the experimenter alters the behavior of the animal to perform along a desired path or result. When the animal is provided with a reward for performing the behavior, it is likely to repeat the *elicited behavior* on subsequent occasions. The experiment is performed in an *operant chamber,* often an enclosed cage, sometimes called a *Skinner box* (for dogs and cats), where the animal can obtain food by pressing a lever. The two general principles of both instrumental conditioning and operant conditioning are as follows: (1) The organism's response that is followed by a reward is often repeated. (2) The reward or reinforcement is anything that increases the probability of the behavior recurring due to the animal repeating the action (e.g., pressing a lever) to obtain the reward. With both instrumental and operant conditioning, the key postulate is that, by controlling reinforcement, one can control behavior.

instrumentalism (humanism)

As the basis of his progressive, pragmatic, and humanistic philosophy of education of the 1920s, the instrumentalism of John Dewey (also referred to as *progressive education*) postulates that learning is developing and that developing is learning. Instrumentalism regarded truth as an instrument that humans utilize to solve problems and promote changes in a global society. Rejecting authoritarian teaching methods, Dewey regarded education as a tool to be used to integrate the citizen into the democratic culture and to change that culture to make it more democratic, more progressive. Thus, the individual human becomes an instrument to the progress of a democratic society. Dewey's instrumentalism has had a profound and lasting impact on education to this day. His philosophy was regarded globally as radical and influential.

intellectual capital (organizational learning)

According to Leif Edvinsson and Michael S. Malone in the book with the same title, intellectual capital, a key ingredient for *knowledge management* in *learning organizations*, is knowledge that is of economic value to the business enterprise. Intellectual capital is made up of human capital, structural capital, and customer capital. Human capital refers to the knowledge, skills, and competencies of employees within the orga-

nization. As knowledge workers walk out the door each evening from work, the human capital of the enterprise goes with them. Structural capital is the procedures, processes, business structures, patents, and information systems that remain with the organization, even if and when employees leave. Customer capital is the relationships that the organization has with its customers, including their purchasing patterns, ability to pay, and the loyalty to the enterprise's organization and product line. All three types of intellectual capital are secured by the development and enhancement of a *distributed network system* that promotes cooperation, *collaboration,* and *knowledge sharing* within and outside of the organization.

intelligence (cognitivism)

Typically, intelligence for humans is regarded as the ability to perform *problem-solving* activities, to use logic and mathematics, and to think and read critically. Traditionally, intelligence has been measured through intelligence tests or scales. Sometimes referred to by the acronym WAIS, the *Wechsler Adult Intelligence Scale* is used as a measure of cognitive ability and intellectual aptitude for adults.

Over a century ago, Sir Frances Galton of Great Britain sought to determine a measurement for human intelligence. Taking up Galton's drive to come up with an intelligence measure, Alfred Binet in Paris developed a series of questions for schoolchildren to measure aptitude and to predict future performance in school. Lewis Terman of Stanford University incorporated Binet's questions and enhanced the test to create the *Stanford-Binet Intelligence Scale*.

The WAIS-R, the 1981 revision of the original Wechsler Adult Intelligence Scale, is an intelligence test developed for adults who are between the ages of 16 and 74. The test is subdivided into 11 modules, which include information, digit span, vocabulary, arithmetic, comprehension, similarities, picture completion, picture arrangement, block design, object assembly, and digit symbol. Using the test, a full scale IQ is scored, with 100 being an average or mean score. The standard deviation for the WAIS is an indicator of how far above or below an individual is from the average score.

A modified version of the WAIS is provided to very young children between the ages of four and six-and-a-half years. Another modified version of the WAIS is used for children between six-and-a-half and fifteen years. The test is used for school placement, giftedness, learning disabilities, brain disorders, and for tracking individual development over time. Along with the Stanford-Binet Intelligence Scale, the WAIS is an important tool used by experts in *cognition* who seek to determine and measure *cognitive processes* of humans.

Another example of a more contemporary intelligence measure is Howard Gardner's *multiple intelligences*. Howard Gardner's theory regarding human *intelligence*, multiple intelligences, states that our culture and school systems focus far too much attention as a measure of success on *verbal-linguistic intelligence* and *logical-mathematical intelligence*. Gardner's theory includes at least eight other types of human intelligence that are just as significant and that need to be considered within our culture and schools. Gardner's eight intelligences are as follows: (1) verbal-linguistic intelligence (e.g., a poet's mind); (2) logical-mathematical intelligence (e.g., a scientist's mind); (3) *musical intelligence* (e.g., a composer's mind); (4) *spatial intelligence* (e.g., a sculptor's mind); (5) *bodily kinesthetic intelligence* (e.g., an athlete's or a dancer's mind); (6) *interpersonal intelligence* (e.g., a salesperson's or an instructor's mind); (7) *intrapersonal intelligence* (e.g., those with accurate views of themselves); and (8) *naturalist intelligence* (e.g., the mind of a biologist or an explorer who observes and recognizes patterns in the natural environment).

As an adherent of *constructivism*, especially Vygotsky's *social development theory*, Gardner believes strongly that intelligence cannot be defined or measured without consideration of the individual's cultural and social context. In fact, critics of the Wechsler Adult Intelligence Scale and the Stanford-Binet Intelligence Scale feel that these tests are culturally biased because they measure math and verbal ability primarily and simply reflect the values and focus of traditional school systems rather than the intelligence of the individual being measured.

intelligence augmentation (cognitivism)

Intelligence for humans is regarded as the ability to perform *problem-solving* activities, to use logic and mathematics, and to think and read critically. Intelligence augmentation is a discipline within *artificial intelligence* in which the goal is to use various forms of *agents* and *computer-mediated communication* to help make humans perform intelligence tasks more creatively and effectively. Humans are generally good at using judgment, understanding, reasoning, and creativity to solve problems. Computers are generally good at remembering a great deal of information, searching through information, and performing multiple tasks at once. By combining forces (computers and humans), experts in intelligence augmentation believe that we can augment or increase human intelligence, especially with regard to solving problems related to intelligence that occur in our personal and professional lives, by using the computer. Examples of intelligence augmentation in use are *expert systems, intelligent tutoring systems,* and *electronic performance support systems*.

intelligent tutoring systems (educational technology)

A type of *artificial intelligence* application, intelligent tutoring systems are computer programs embedded into *computer-aided instruction, computer-based training*, or *Web-based training* that provide *cognitive coaching* and guidance to the learner as he or she goes through each exercise within the program. These systems presuppose a knowledge of the learner's ever-increasing abilities and progress through the application. They involve tracking mechanisms (i.e., *performance tracking*) that determine the learner's knowledge and experience level (i.e., *level of competence*) at each stage within the learning application. Intelligent tutoring systems provide helpful hints and support as the learning exercises become more difficult and the learning path more arduous for the user. The ultimate goal of these systems is to simulate human tutoring and coaching strategies.

interiorization (constructivism)

An important concept to Jean Piaget, interiorization is a development process that occurs in children as they move from being directly influenced by environmental factors to being more influenced by their own cognitive structures and interior thoughts. During the growth process, individuals go through the dual developmental processes of *accommodation* and *assimilation*. Accommodation involves the process of changing the child's *cognitive structures* to make sense of the new events occurring in the environment. Assimilation involves the child interpreting environmental events within the context of already existing cognitive structures. Accommodation and assimilation work together as the child develops and interacts with the environment in order to achieve a state of *equilibration*.

However, as the child grows older, as the child develops a more developed cognitive structure, he or she becomes less dependent on the environment as the developed cognitive structures are used for adaptation to new situations. Thus, as more and more experiences are interiorized, the process of thinking becomes of paramount importance for complex problem solving and environmental adaptation. Strongly influenced by laws of biological development, Jean Piaget, the father of *genetic epistemology*, observed that as the child grows older and becomes an adult, the combined processes of assimilation and accommodation increase cognitive growth, interiorization, and maturation.

Internet (educational technology)

The successor of an experimental *distributed network system* of computers by the U.S. Department of Defense in the 1960s, the Internet is a vast communications system that links millions of computers worldwide. The majority of connections on the Internet originally belonged to universities and research and development organizations, but currently its use has expanded to a vast array of large and small businesses as well as individuals. Important to note is that the Internet is not a centrally managed or controlled organization. It is instead a huge, decentralized collection of computers and networks spread out worldwide. Nevertheless, the Internet is extremely important as a distribution method for *distance learning*, and as such, is used by universities to create *electronic campuses* for their students as well as by businesses to create *electronic learning environments* for their employees.

interpersonal intelligence (constructivism)

One of Howard Gardner's eight *multiple intelligences*, interpersonal intelligence is the ability to cultivate positive relationships with others by understanding and empathizing with people while being particularly adept at appreciating and acting with others' moods, intentions, motivations, attitudes, and personality. Individuals who possess interpersonal intelligence are able to sense and understand others' feelings and positions and, concomitantly, to define well and communicate their feelings and positions to others. Examples of interpersonal intelligence activities are leading group projects, providing and receiving feedback from the group, collaborating with others in work and learning activities, and being able to assign activities and monitor group activities. Individuals who possess interpersonal intelligence, and who are provided with the right cultural and educational background in interpersonal skills, are apt to pursue careers as marketers, managers, and teachers. Gardner believes that interpersonal intelligence needs to be developed in the individual. It must not be undervalued or underemphasized in schools in favor of *verbal-linguistic intelligence* and *logical-mathematical intelligence*.

intervening variable (behaviorism)

In Clark Leonard Hull's *drive reduction theory*, the intervening variable is anything that can come between a stimulus and a response, or anything that can inhibit a response. The variable could be an external event, an inhibiting factor in the test environment, or a physical factor with the organism, such as boredom or fatigue. No matter what the cause, an intervening variable has a negative effect on *habit strength*. Habit strength is the measure of a bond formed between a particular stimulus and a given response. The more the stimulus leads to obtaining a basic need (such as water), the greater the habit strength exists. Also, the more quickly that the need is fulfilled (i.e., the shorter the *goal gradient*) and met with a positive reward, the more likely that the habit strength will be regarded as high. Also, the higher the habit strength, the more likely that the response will be repeated successfully by the organism. Animal trainers seeking increased and repeated performance of particular tasks seek stimuli and responses that can be combined for a high habit strength to ensure successful learning of the desired act. Animal trainers seeking high habit strength strive to control as much as possible, and even eliminate, all intervening variables that can greatly reduce success rate and predictability of the outcome of the experiment.

intrapersonal intelligence (constructivism)

One of Howard Gardner's eight *multiple intelligences,* intrapersonal intelligence is the ability to have self-knowledge about one's beliefs, feelings, motives, attitudes, and personality, including one's personal strengths and weaknesses, and to draw upon this knowledge to guide one's actions and behaviors in life situations. Individuals who possess intrapersonal intelligence have a usable and strong self-knowledge and are adept at *metacognition*. Examples of intrapersonal intelligence activities are self-reflection, creativity, concentration, higher-order reasoning, and analysis of situations and people. Individuals who possess intrapersonal intelligence, and who are provided with the right cultural and educational background in these skills, are apt to pursue careers as social scientists, business consultants, and ministers. As with interpersonal intelligence, Gardner believes that intrapersonal intelligence skills need to be developed in school systems' *curriculum design*, where greater emphasis has been placed traditionally on *verbal-linguistic intelligence* and *logical-mathematical intelligence.*

invariants (humanism)

Within James J. Gibson's *information pickup theory*, affordances refer to the physical environment (i.e., the physical landscape, the land, sky, and water) that we perceive and which make up the *stimulus array*. Also within the stimulus array are invariants, such as shadow, texture, color, and layout that help determine what we perceive in relation to the afforadances. As espoused in Gibson's information pickup theory, the act of perception is a dynamic between the organism and the physical environment. Developed by James J. Gibson from the 1950s through the 1970s, information pickup theory is a *Gestalt theory* and approach to perception and learning. In terms of *learning and performance*, Gibson postulates that the learner must have a rich, complex *learning environment* within which to interact. Learning should be based upon visual cues that the learner obtains from interacting in the environment. To increase learning, the instructor must provide environmental affordances replete with all of the shadows, textures, and colors (i.e., the invariants) of the stimulus array within which the learners can learn and perform a series of activities.

J

The commonest error of the gifted scholar, inexperienced in teaching, is to expect pupils to know what they have been told. But telling is not teaching.
— Edward Lee Thorndike, twentieth-century American psychologist

just-in-time training (organizational learning)

An important theory within *organizational learning*, just-in-time training is a key aspect of current thinking in *instructional design* with regard to *embedded training* in corporations. Embedded training involves learning information provided in either *computer-based training* or *Web-based training* modules in a *just-in-time* fashion to working adults in a business organization. Just-in-time training typically employs a *learner-centric* versus *instructor-centric* approach to learning. For that reason, it is often called just-in-time learning. Just-in-time training is an important aspect of *electronic performance support systems*. It is regarded as a far better training method than classroom-type training which is provided all at once in a more traditional lecture manner. Coined by Gloria Gery, and also referred to by the acronym EPSS, an electronic performance support system is a *computer-based training* or *Web-based training* system designed to provide employees learning information just when they need it at the moment of need. Just-in-time training is an important aspect of the *digital age educational paradigm*.

K

Knowledge is of two kinds: We know a subject ourselves, or we know where we can find information about it.
> —Samuel Johnson, eighteenth-century
> English writer

Keystroke level model (cognitivism)

The most elementary GOMS technique, the keystroke level model (sometimes simply referred to as KLM) focuses on the measurement of discrete observable events and task times. KLM gets down to the keystroke level of measurement regarding the users or agents performing particular tasks to meet the goals of the GOMS program. A later enhancement to the *logic theorist* and GPS, *General Problem Solver*, GOMS is a *cognitive architecture* (i.e., a model of mental processing for human *problem solving*, learning, and task completion) developed originally in the mid–1980s by Newell, Card, and Moran. GOMS is an acronym for Goals, Operators, Methods, and Selection.

GOMS has developed into a family of techniques that includes keystroke level model, *CMN-GOMS, natural GOMS language,* and *CPM-GOMS*. The GOMS family is a prominent model for *human-computer interaction* and human learning used today to measure the usefulness of computer user interface designs and human task performance. Through the observation of human task performance with computers, GOMS seeks to model human *cognitive processing* and *memory* that occur in defined stages (i.e., *sensory memory, working memory, long-term memory*).

kinematics (cognitivism)

With regard to the creation of robots (e.g., cognitive robotics) and other *artificial intelligence* systems that can move and manipulate objects, kinematics is the research, study, and science of motion and movement. Regarding *cognition* and the creation of *neural networks*, kinematics refers to the generation of intelligent computer models that can simulate motion and movement.

knowledge acquisition (organizational learning)

From a *brain-based learning* perspective, knowledge acquisition involves the *active processing* that learners go through as they capture knowledge and learn new information. From an *organizational learning* perspective, knowledge acquisition involves the capture of all *explicit knowledge* and *tacit knowledge* extant within the business enterprise in order to create a *digital library*, a *knowledge base* that facilitates *knowledge sharing* among the employees of the organization by means of a *distributed network system*.

knowledge assets (organizational learning)

From a *knowledge management* perspective, knowledge assets are *knowledge objects* that the organization seeks to capture through a *knowledge acquisition* process and to place within its *knowledge base* or *digital library*. In the recent past, data processing primarily handled structured information to run the financial and accounting aspects of the business. With the rise of the Web and the digitization of rich data types (e.g., image, audio, video, and animation) extant within digital knowledge objects (e.g., white papers, design documents, policies and procedures, and technical specifications), enterprises are shifting their focus from the development of physical assets to knowledge assets. Knowledge assets currently are regarded as having a tangible value for the corporation, more valuable in the digital age than brick-and-mortar infrastructure or physical products. Knowledge assets that are shared by employees within the organization give the enterprise a competitive business advantage over firms that lack a *distributed network system* which promotes *knowledge sharing* within the *learning organization*.

knowledge base (organizational learning)

Knowledge base is closely associated currently with *Web-based knowledge transfer,* a process that involves sharing information within an organization via the Web to promote and facilitate *knowledge management* and *organizational learning* for the enterprise. A knowledge base is a database of information (available in various formats such as video, audio, text, and graphics) available across a *distributed network system*. A distributed network system is a computer network or series of networks in which *knowledge objects* are distributed across many computers that work together to provide information within a *digital library* to geographically dispersed users and learners. In education, an example of a knowledge base is Roger Schank's *ASK systems*.

With the rise of the digital economy and the Web, organizations are better able to disseminate and share information within and outside of the corporation on a global scale by means of the knowledge base. In so doing, these organizations become more cognizant of who they are and who their customers are. They achieve a state of *metacognition*. Knowledge managers, industry trainers, and school educators are focusing more and more of their attention on the evolution of *knowledge objects* from analog to digital, from paper-based information to electronic information that is indexed and cataloged in order to facilitate *knowledge sharing* by means of the corporate *knowledge base*. An important goal in industry and in schools is to build the digital library, the active storehouse of knowledge that comprises the *electronic learning environment* in industry and the *electronic campus* curriculum and content in education.

knowledge construction (organizational learning)

Often using techniques such as *concept mapping* and *mind mapping*, knowledge construction is an important creative learning activity within knowledge workers' jobs in the digital age. The overall assumption of knowledge construction is that knowledge for performing various work processes is "not out there" and not hidden "inside people's heads." In fact, knowledge needs to be created by the employees and shared. The act of creating and sharing information, sharing *knowledge objects*, leads to the creation of new knowledge, especially in regard to work processes.

An important aspect of the *learning organization*, knowledge construction is key to the success of the business enterprise in the digital age. The creation of a learning organization is a result of a business enterprise reaching a point of *metacognition*, of becoming conscious of its own processes and decisions and aware of the skills of its knowledge workers. In order to reach a point of metacognition, knowledge workers must begin by performing various shared knowledge construction activities, by using techniques such as mind mapping, *concept mapping*, and *knowledge mapping*. An organization creates and maintains a business culture for knowledge construction when it learns by collecting knowledge constructed by its employees in the course of their day-to-day work activities. The individual employees concomitantly learn in the course of their day-to-day work, share information, and in turn benefit from the innovations and novel solutions of their peers. Knowledge construction is an important part of the *knowledge management* process.

knowledge management (organizational learning)

This is a new perspective on information and communication in the business organization and the school that focuses on knowledge as dynamic, ever-changing, socially based, and shared via computer technology. The current goal of knowledge management is to capture the organization's *explicit knowledge* (i.e., knowledge extant in corporate memos, reports, policies, and procedures) and individuals' *tacit knowledge* (i.e., knowledge stored in individuals' heads and shared among immediate colleagues), and then store it, spread it, and reuse it. A key element of knowledge management is *collaboration*. An important goal of educators in the digital age is to teach students how to be effective knowledge managers in this new digital environment. In the current *digital age educational paradigm*, knowledge management involves primarily three areas: (1) *business transformation*, (2) *organizational learning*, and (3) *Web-based knowledge transfer*.

Business transformation involves using technology, especially communications and *collaboration* technology, to enhance every aspect of how the business enterprise operates. Business transformation is different from reengineering because it is less concerned with departmental cost reductions and more concerned with spearheading enterprise-wide *organizational learning*, innovation, and the application of breakthrough

digital age technologies to create new products and services. In the recent past, data processing primarily handled structured information to run the financial and accounting aspects of the business. With the rise of the Web and the digitization of rich data types (e.g., image, audio, video, and animation) within digital *knowledge objects* (e.g., white papers, design documents, policies and procedures, and technical specifications), enterprises can now shift their product focus from physical assets to *knowledge assets*.

Organizational learning, which is the learning that occurs among individuals, groups, and teams within the enterprise, allows for the creation of the *learning organization*, which is learning by the organization as a total entity or system. The creation of a learning organization is a result of a business enterprise reaching a point of *metacognition*, of becoming conscious of its own processes and decisions and aware of the skills of its knowledge workers. In the recent past, many pre-digital companies were not consciously able to identify how they satisfy their customers. Vannevar Bush's vision of a global, research-oriented *digital library* is closer to being a reality today with the rise of the Web as an information-sharing and distribution "collaboratorium" (Bush's term) that helps the enterprise better understand itself and transform itself.

Educational institutions have the same potential to build an *electronic campus* infrastructure and to build their own *distributed network system* so that their customers—their students—can share information electronically with instructors and peers alike, whether they are on-campus students or distance learners. Educational institutions need to be learning organizations. They need to be more conscious of how they transfer and share knowledge and how effectively they use technology to do so.

With the rise of the digital economy and the Web, enterprises are better able to disseminate and share information within and outside of the corporation on a global scale through Web-based knowledge transfer. In so doing, these organizations become more cognizant of who they are and who their customers are. In the world of electronic work teams, knowledge workers are manipulating bits more and atoms less. Knowledge managers, industry trainers, and school educators are focusing more and more of their attention on the evolution of *knowledge objects* from analog to digital, from paper-based information to electronic information that is indexed and cataloged. Thus, an important goal in both industry and our schools is to build the *digital library*, the active storehouse of knowledge that comprises the electronic corporate memory in industry and the *electronic campus* curriculum and content in education.

The four basic steps that organizations must perform to manage knowledge successfully are the following: Step 1. Capture and collect the knowledge. Step 2. Organize, categorize, and catalogue it. Step 3. Provide a vehicle to distribute and disseminate it. Step 4. Share it and use it within and outside of the organization.

knowledge mapping (organizational learning)

In the same vein as *concept mapping* and *mind mapping*, knowledge mapping has been espoused by Edward W. Rogers of Cornell University's School of Industrial and Labor Relations. Knowledge mapping is a learning process utilized in organizations to bring out *tacit knowledge* that often is stored in employees' heads, but not shared among them. *Explicit knowledge* in organizations, that is, knowledge represented formally in memos, reports, policies, and procedures (even though they may be *digitized* and stored in a *digital library*) often block out creative, innovative solutions to new problems that arise in the workplace. Knowledge mapping is a *collaboration* technique that has employees brainstorm and create (using simple lines and circles) a visual map of their thoughts, a graphical representation that describes concepts and processes that are the result of previous work activities and attempts at solutions to problems. The goal of knowledge map-

ping is for the participants to create something together that can be depicted visually, to come up with a solution that is more than what each one would be able to achieve alone. It is a less formal technique than that of concept mapping and mind mapping.

knowledge media design (constructivism)

A coined term from Ron Baecker of the Knowledge Media Design Institute at the University of Toronto, knowledge media design refers to the analysis, design, development and evaluation of media (e.g., *multimedia, hypermedia*, and *Internet* content) utilized to support human thinking, learning, communicating, and *knowledge sharing*. Besides looking at digital technologies, knowledge media design considers also the role of traditional knowledge media (e.g., books, films, and lectures) in the design of *learning environments*. The current research focus of the Knowledge Media Design Institute is to investigate the uses of new computer application technologies to *knowledge management*, education, training, and human *problem solving* that facilitates *collaborative learning* and *distance learning*.

knowledge objects (cognitivism)

Sometimes referred to as *learning objects*, knowledge objects are containers of information, often presented in *multimedia* form, regarding a particular learning topic or subject. The container could include multiple files on the topic that are in the form of text, graphics, audio, and video. The knowledge object may be a *knowledge representation* of any particular topic or subject, though the object is usually focused on acquiring a set of information to perform a job. As such, the knowledge object is built to be a set of highly interactive *instructional sequences*.

In David Merrill's *instructional transaction theory*, which is an enhancement of his *component display theory,* knowledge objects play a prominent role. Merrill's original component display theory sought to identify the components from which instructional sequences could be constructed. His instructional transaction theory sought to integrate the components into what he calls instructional transactions. An instructional transaction is composed of each and every interaction required for the learner to obtain knowledge on a particular set of job skills. Knowledge objects, with all of their multimedia elements, provide the components of the subject matter content (i.e., the job task knowledge to be acquired). With regard to *artificial intelligence* development of *machine tractable dictionaries* that facilitate computer-based *natural language processing*, knowledge objects are a library of dictionary or encyclopedic entries that are tractable (i.e., able to be "read" and understood by computers) on a particular subject area or a set of subject areas.

knowledge representation (cognitivism)

An aspect of *machine learning* and the development of *artificial intelligence* applications, knowledge representation is a process by which information within a given domain is acquired, usually extracted from databases or *knowledge bases* through *data mining,* and made explicit and usable in the form of *knowledge objects.* Knowledge representation allows computers to reconfigure and reuse information stored in the computer's data base in ways that have not been previously anticipated or specified by the computer program. Within David Merrill's *instructional transaction theory*, these knowledge representations in the form of knowledge objects are sequenced into a set of instructional transactions, which include all of the content and all of the interactions necessary for a learner to obtain a needed set of knowledge to accomplish sets of job tasks.

knowledge sharing (organizational learning)

Very closely related to *Web-based knowledge transfer* and an important goal of corporate *knowledge management* initiatives, knowl-

edge sharing is a process that involves sharing information within an organization, most typically via the Web, to promote and facilitate *organizational learning* for the enterprise. With the rise of the digital economy and the Web, enterprises can disseminate and share information within and outside of the corporation on a global scale through *Internet*-based knowledge sharing. In so doing, these organizations become more cognizant of who they are and who their customers are. They achieve a state of corporate *metacognition.* In the academic arena, knowledge sharing is an important activity within an *electronic learning environment,* a *universal campus network.* In both business and academic circles, the key to knowledge sharing is *collaboration* and *collaborative learning.*

knowledge sources (organizational learning)

From a *knowledge management* perspective, knowledge sources that *learning organizations* seek to capture are of two kinds: internal knowledge sources and external knowledge sources. Internal knowledge sources involve either *tacit knowledge* or *explicit knowledge.* Explicit knowledge is knowledge that is extant in the form of corporate memos, reports, policies and procedures within the business enterprise. Explicit knowledge resides in formal documents of the organization. Even though these documents may be *digitized* and provided to employees within a *digital library,* they are often less important than *tacit knowledge.* Tacit knowledge is knowledge that is stored in people's heads and shared among immediate colleagues within the organization. It is often harder to capture, yet contains more valuable information that needs to be disseminated throughout the organization. Common external knowledge sources are external publications, university research information, government agency research, professional associations, consultants, customers, as well as vendors with whom the organization works and shares information. Companies that seek to integrate their internal and external knowledge sources within a knowledge management system are at the forefront of the *digital age educational paradigm*.

knowledge space (educational technology)

This is a computer modeling approach that represents information flow across a *distributed network* system as the physical movement of *knowledge objects* from one location to another location. A distributed network system is a computer network or series of networks in which knowledge objects are distributed across many computers that work together to provide information to geographically dispersed users and learners. The *Internet* itself is a vast array of distributed network systems that essentially represent a huge distributed computing environment spread globally. The distributed network system that schools and businesses build for *distance learning* is a crucial infrastructure for the *digital library*, the *electronic campus*, and the *universal campus network*. By using a spatial model (i.e., the knowledge space) to describe physically the flow of knowledge across the network, researchers can analyze the results of how people do *knowledge sharing* and *collaborative learning* within a *virtual learning environment*.

knowledge structure (cognitivism)

An important aspect of Roger Schank's theories of learning, including *conceptual dependency theory*, *contextual dependency theory*, and *script theory*, a knowledge structure, more commonly called a schema, is created in the mind as we experience new things in the environment and from which we create scripts. The concept of a knowledge structure, or schema, is important to an understanding of how language processing and higher thinking works within Schank's script theory. Script theory postulates that human memory, which Schank regards as *episodic memory*, is based upon personally remembered episodes and experiences (i.e., *scripts*) that we call upon and apply to the new problem-solving situations. Scripts allow human beings to make inferences. The schema, the knowledge structure that is created through the development of scripts, is highly dynamic and continually enhanced over time. As new experiences occur, new scripts get written, and the knowledge structure becomes further enhanced as a result of an ever-growing set of personal life episodes and experiences. Roger Schank's concept of a knowledge structure, or a schema, is an elaboration and enhancement of Jean Piaget's *schemata* discussed within his theory of *genetic epistemology*.

L

latent learning (behaviorism)

According to Edward Chace Tolman, latent learning is learning that occurs in organisms independent of any sort of behavioral *reinforcement* or reward. Latent learning can remain dormant and completely unused for a fairly lengthy period of time. The learning is only made manifest as overt behavior, overt performance when the organism needs to use it and is provided with an incentive to use it. To Tolman, *reinforcement* is a performance variable, not a learning variable. Most learning theorists, while not necessarily agreeing with all or even a few aspects of *behaviorism*, tend to agree that learning involves a change of behavior in the learner as a result of experience. In other words, learning is tied to observable performance. Tolman, an adherent of *cognitive behaviorism*, noted that learning involves the learner's creation of *cognitive maps* (i.e., *internal schemas*) that are not specifically, directly, and immediately tied to performance. New concepts are learned, but they are not necessarily observable or put into action immediately. This is the basic principle of latent learning, a theory which moves Tolman away from strict behaviorism and toward *cognitivism*.

lateral thinking (organizational learning)

In the late 1960s and early 1970s, Edward de Bono developed his theory of lateral thinking, the generation of creative and innovative solutions to business problems. In lateral thinking, there are four steps to innovation: (1) Focus on dominant ideas that come to mind and polarize perception of a problem. (2) Look at multiple perspectives of the problem. (3) Relax the logical thinking process typically taught in schools as part of the scientific method. (4) Allow "outside of the box" ideas to come to mind and be considered even though they do not fit into the logical, scientific thinking pattern.

Lateral thinking is moving sideways and looking at problems from multiple angles and perspectives. It is a method for brainstorming and idea generation. This theory was later incorporated in Edward de Bono's *CoRT thinking* and *Six Thinking Hats*, both of which emphasize the importance of creativity to *problem solving* and *decision making*. Edward de Bono's CoRT thinking provides sixty thinking lessons to help motivate learners to develop creative solutions to problems, write more creatively, and become more active, self-confident, and effective thinkers. Six Thinking Hats is a method for incorporating *lateral thinking* (i.e., the generation of novel solutions to problems) into organizations. The six hats represent six modes of thinking. They are not as much labels as they are directions that thinking can take, especially within corporate meetings when decisions need to be made. During a meeting, there are literally six color hats. Each participant dons a hat as each tries to take on the perspective of a "green hat" (creative) thinker, for example. The Six Thinking Hats are: white (objective, data, facts); red (feelings, emotions, intuitions); purple (logical, negative, cautious); yellow (logical positive, optimistic); green (creative, innovative); and blue (*metacognition*, thinking process).

law of effect (behaviorism)

One of the three laws of Edward Thorndike's behaviorist theory of *connectionism*, the law of effect states that an organism's response that is immediately followed by a positive *reinforcement* is much more likely to be repeated than having the organism respond to a negative reinforcement. In other words, responses that occur just before a positive reinforcement (a pleasant event, such as obtaining food) are likely to recur. Responses that occur just before a negative reinforcement (such as an electrical shock) are likely to diminish. As a result of Thorndike's law of effect, educators came to believe that reinforcing good behavior is effective, but punishing bad behavior is ineffective. The law of effect also states that the degree of the pleasantness of the event is not as much a factor to the effectiveness of the learned behavior as simply offering the reward itself. This law is closely related to Hull's postulate regarding *habit strength*. This law and the other two laws of connectionism bring Thorndike to conclude that *intelligence* can be measured by how many connections have been learned by the organism.

law of exercise (behaviorism)

One of the three laws of Edward Thorndike's behaviorist theory of *connectionism*, the law of exercise states that an organism's repeating a response several times will in all likelihood increase the speed and ability of the organism to perform the learned behavior in the future. In other words, learning is strengthened the more often the particular learned activity is repeated by the organism. Performing experiments with cats in *puzzle boxes*, Thorndike was able to calculate a learning curve that resulted from repeated learned behavior. The more often the task was completed by the organism, the quicker the task could be done with fewer errors. This law is also closely related to Hull's postulate regarding *habit strength*. This law and the other two laws of connectionism bring Thorndike to conclude that *intelligence* can be measured by how many connections have been learned by the organism.

law of frequency (behaviorism)

In the mid-to-late nineteenth century, Hermann Ebbinghaus sought to separate the study of human learning and memory from philosophy by performing a series of behavioral experiments that followed Aristotle *laws of association*, in particular by studying the effects of the *law of frequency*. Aristotle's postulate regarding frequency is that the more often two events occur together, the stronger will be the association between them. Or, from a learning theory perspective, the more often two objects are experienced by an organism simultaneously, the more likely they will be remembered and learned.

For Ebbinghaus, the greater the number of trials one experienced (e.g., the greater the number of successive exposures to a list or a group of syllables), the better was the association, as well as the rate of learning and remembering. Later, Edwin Guthrie rejected this notion. With Guthrie, one trial, one successful pairing of a stimulus with a response, is sufficient for learning to occur by the organism. This is known as *one-trial learning*. Nevertheless, Ebbinghaus's experiments demonstrating the law of frequency dramatically changed the study of the associative process and led the way toward later empirical studies by the behaviorists. Rather than make theoretical assumptions about the law of frequency, Ebbinghaus used experiments to chart how the law of frequency functioned, especially in relation to what Skinner would later refer to as *verbal behavior*.

law of Pragnanz (humanism)

An important corollary to the *principle of closure* within *Gestalt theory*, the law of Pragnanz refers to the strong human tendency to provide meaning to all experiences. The principle of closure states that as humans, we seek to complete incomplete perceptions and experiences. The principle of closure follows completely the *law of Pragnanz*, which states that humans respond to the world of phenomena to make it as meaningful as possible given the current conditions and situation. In German, pragnanz means "essence." A constant human goal is thus to provide meaning, essence, structure, and form to all of life's experiences. Thus, the individual provides a *perceptual organization* to that which is perceived or experienced. This perceptual organization is applied to all life experiences as one grows and learns, and as one's *perceptual field* expands.

law of readiness (behaviorism)

One of the three laws of Edward Thorndike's behaviorist theory of *connectionism*, the law of readiness states that the organism follows a chain of responses as it pursues an externally rewarded goal. If the organism is blocked at any point in the chain, it undergoes frustration and annoyance as it seeks other means to achieving the goal. This law is also closely related to Hull's postulate regarding *habit family hierarchy*. This law and the other two laws of connectionism bring Thorndike to conclude that *intelligence* can be measured by how many connections have been learned by the organism.

laws of association (behaviorism)

The laws of association are an important part of Aristotle's *empiricist* view of knowledge that all we learn in life is gained through sensory experience and reasoning. According to Aristotle, experiencing one object recalls either similar objects (similarity), opposite objects (contrast), or objects experienced along with the object (contiguity). To Aristotle, the more often two objects are experienced simultaneously, the more likely they will be remembered and learned (frequency). These laws of association are important to many later modern learning theories, including, for example, Thorndike's *connectionism* and Guthrie's *contiguity theory*. Aristotle's laws of association were a tremendous influence on *behaviorism*, given its stress on observable behavior of organisms that learn via sensory experiences and external stimuli that can be measured and tracked by the experimenter.

layers of necessity (cognitivism)

Developed by J.F. Wedman and M. Tessmer in the early 1990s, layers of necessity is an *instructional design* model for *curriculum design* of *computer-based training, Web-based training,* and *multimedia applications* that emphasize the development of content by utilizing whatever resources are available. The assumption is that time, resources, and money are limited. Given this context, instead of following the complete instructional design process, one follows a streamlined top layer (and then additional layers as time allows) that focuses initially on the basic steps to completing the job. Typically, there are four phases to the instructional design process: (1) Analysis Phase. The instructional design team analyzes the audience and its needs and analyzes the tasks to be performed within the learning activity. (2) Design Phase. The instructional design team defines learning goals, objectives, and strategies. (3) Development Phase. The instructional design team develops the instructional content. (4) Implementation/Evaluation Phase. The content or course is delivered to the learners and feedback is obtained on the effectiveness of the product.

To Wedman and Tessmer, this process is all well and good but not realistic in a dynamic, deadline-oriented *instructional technology* environment. The main point of the layers of necessity model is that the standard instructional design model can be broken down into components based on their necessity. Using this model, the instructional designer only does those things necessary to get the job done. With more time and resources, additional layers can be added to the development project. As time allows and as layers are added, enhancements and changes to the original design can be made to the content and product.

learner-centric (constructivism)

Most learning theories within the *learning paradigm* of *constructivism* tend to be learner-centric, where the focus is on the learner as the primary content organizer and builder of the information learned in a course. This is opposed to the *instructor-centric* learning theories within the *learning paradigm* of *cognitivism*, in which the instructor is the primary content provider who organizes and presents the information to the student. A clear-cut example of a constructivist, *learner-centric* learning approach is Jerome Bruner's *discovery learning* process, in which the student discovers and shapes course content on his or her own, with the instructor acting as a coach or facilitator, rather than as an information organizer and disseminator. Learner-centric approaches tend to fall into the *digital age educational paradigm* versus the *industrial age educational paradigm*.

learner control (educational technology)

For *hypermedia* and *hypermedia applications*, learner control refers to the ability of the learners to make their own decisions regarding what to learn, what *navigation* paths to take within the system, and how to learn with the system. In other words, learner control means that the users of the system determine what links to take, in what order to take the links, and at what pace to navigate through the links to absorb the content. An example of less learner control would be learners following through a structured path, a *multimedia application*, in which the system developer has already predetermined the content structure, the paths the learners are sup-

posed to take through the content, and even the pace of going through the content. A greater degree of learner control translates into a *learner-centric* design of the hypermedia content. A lesser degree of learner control translates into an *instructor-centric* design of the multimedia content.

learning and performance (behaviorism)

Most learning theorists, while not necessarily agreeing with all or even a few aspects of *behaviorism*, tend to agree that learning involves a change of behavior in the learner as a result of experience. In other words, learning is tied to observable performance. Edward Chace Tolman, an adherent of *cognitive behaviorism*, noted that learning involves the learner's creation of *cognitive maps* (i.e., *schemas*) that are not specifically, directly, and immediately tied to performance. This he referred to as *latent learning*, which is learning that remains dormant for a length of time before it is utilized by the learner and made manifest in specific observable behaviors. In this case, learning is not tied to performance. New concepts are learned, but they are not necessarily observable or put into action immediately.

learning by being told (cognitivism)

Within the field of *artificial intelligence* and *machine learning*, learning by being told is learning that occurs when the system is specifically provided with external input and knowledge from an outside source. Closely related to *deductive learning*, it is not as high an order of *machine learning* as *inductive learning*. Inductive learning occurs in a system that acquires new knowledge not explicitly or implicitly provided previously from an outside source. Learning by being told is a function of many *artificial intelligence* applications and *neural networks* that simulate how the mind works with regard to retrieving, sifting through, and processing information.

learning environment (educational technology)

This term refers to the place or setting within which the learning activity takes place. Within the *industrial age educational paradigm*, the learning environment was typically a classroom, with the instructor providing content primarily through lecture. Currently, within the *digital age educational paradigm*, the learning environment often involves *educational technology* that includes *computer-mediated communication*. Examples of the latter type of learning environments are *electronic learning environments*, *constructivist learning environments*, and *virtual learning environments*.

learning objectives (cognitivism)

The mantra of most *instructional design* practitioners, who are more often than not adherents of *cognitivism*, is that learning objectives must be tied to learning outcomes. Several cognitivist theories of instruction focus on tying the *curriculum design* and the *sequence of instruction* to the learning objectives and learning outcomes of the students. These include, but are not limited to, Gagne's *conditions of learning*, Merrill's *component display theory*, and Mager's *criterion-referenced instruction*. All emphasize the importance of structuring the instruction to meet the individual needs of the learners who seek to complete a set of learning objectives spelled out at the beginning of the learning activity. Most important, these learning objectives must be tied to performance, that is, to *learning outcomes*, as the student learns to perform a specific activity or set of activities delineated at the outset of the instruction.

learning objects (cognitivism)

More often referred to as *knowledge objects*, learning objects are containers of information, often presented in *multimedia* form, regarding a particular learning topic or subject. The container could include multiple files on the topic that are in the form of text, graphics, audio, and video. The learning object may be a *knowledge representation* of any particular topic or subject, though the object is usually focused on acquiring a set of information to perform a job. The learning object is built to be a set of highly interactive *instructional sequences*. In David Merrill's *instructional transaction theory*, which is an enhancement of his *component display theory*, learning objects, which he refers to as knowledge objects, play a prominent role. Merrill's original component display theory sought to identify the components from which instructional sequences could be constructed. His instructional transaction theory sought to integrate the components into what he calls instructional transactions. An instructional transaction is composed of each and every interaction required for the learner to obtain knowledge on a particular set of job skills. Learning objects, with all of their multimedia elements, provide the components of the subject matter content (i.e., the job task knowledge to be acquired).

learning organization (organizational learning)

This important organizational *learning paradigm*, spearheaded by the work of Peter Senge, is a result of business enterprises reaching a point of *metacognition*, of becoming conscious of their own processes and decisions and aware of the skills of the knowledge workers they employ. In the recent past, many pre-digital companies were not consciously able to identify how they satisfy their customers. They did not achieve a state of metacognition. Given the advent of the *Internet*, Vannevar Bush's early vision of a global research-oriented *digital library*, espoused in his now famous 1945 article "As We May Think," is close to being a reality today. As a result of the rise of the Web as an information-sharing and distribution "collaboratorium" (Bush's term), enterprises have the opportunity to better understand themselves and transform themselves into a learning organization now more than ever.

Educational institutions have the same potential to build an *electronic campus* infrastructure and to build their own *distributed network learning framework* so that their customers—their students—can share information electronically with instructors and peers alike, whether they are on-campus students or distance learners. Educational institutions thus need to be learning organizations as well businesses. They need to be more conscious of how they share knowledge and how effectively they use technology to do so.

Before Gutenberg, information was shared primarily by monks in medieval monasteries. Retrieval of this information was difficult, copying was laboriously slow, and cataloging of information was virtually nonexistent. After Gutenberg, information was published and disseminated more readily, but the cataloging and indexing of information was still slow and laborious, making information retrieval difficult at best. In more recent pre-digital times—the era of print publishing, analog media, and manual cataloging—information is still not easily cataloged, indexed, and shared.

In this early digital age in which we are working and learning, a vast array of unstructured digital information (i.e., *knowledge objects*) is available via the computer. The problem is that most high-tech organizations that seek to be learning organizations are choking on *infoglut*—too much information that is not easily indexed, cataloged, retrieved, or shared by the knowledge workers. And unfortunately, in education, many institutions are still in the pre-Gutenberg stage, wherein information is not yet in digital form. In the more mature phase of the digital age (a state that no one in industry or education has quite reached yet), infoglut will be alleviated as media objects are cataloged and indexed, and become more accessible to the knowledge worker (and student) to facilitate the development of the learning organization.

learning outcomes (cognitivism)

From a general *instructional design* perspective, learning outcomes are what the instructor intends to have the learner master as a result of the learning activity. More often than not these learning outcomes are tied to performance, to performing specific actions, such as finding the square root of any number in mathematics. Learning outcomes are tied to the *learning objectives* that the instructor lays out at the beginning of the course. Several cognitivist theories of instruction focus on tying the *curriculum design* and the *sequence of instruction* to the learning outcomes of the students. These include, but are not limited to, Gagne's *conditions of learning*, Merrill's *component display theory*, and Mager's *criterion-referenced instruction*. All emphasize the importance of structuring the instruction to meet the individual needs of the learners who seek to complete a set of learning objectives spelled out at the beginning of the learning activity.

For example, Gagne's conditions of learning theory describes a hierarchy of different types of learning, which require different instructional strategies and *instructional designs* based upon specific *learning outcomes*. As delineated in the conditions of learning theory, there exists a hierarchical set of *cognitive processes* that occur in relation to nine *instructional events*. The nine instructional events and their respective cognitive processes (in parentheses) are: (1) Gain attention (reception) in order to focus upon the task at hand. (2) Inform learners of the objective (expectancy) in order to provide up front what are the projected *learning outcomes* for the course or module. (3) Stimulate recall of prior learning (retrieval) in order to stimulate prior knowledge previously remembered and gained. (4) Present the stimulus (selective perception) in order to initiate new information. (5) Provide learning guidance (*semantic encoding*) in order to structure the new information in a form that can be stored and remembered. (6) Elicit performance (responding) in order to stimulate learner recall through learners' active responses. (7) Provide feedback (reinforcement) in order to ensure that learning has occurred. (8) Assess performance (retrieval) in order to determine if the learners' performance is appropriate, correct, and in line with the projected learning outcomes. (9) Enhance retention and transfer (generalization) in order to place the new knowledge gained into *long-term memory*. For Gagne, these hierarchies provide a rationale for *sequencing of instruction*. The key point is that different types of instructional events promote the learner's development in regard to specific types of cognitive processes, which result in specific sets of learning outcomes.

learning paradigm

In general, learning paradigms are classifications of learning theories into schools based upon their most dominant traits. Though there is not universal agreement on what constitutes the learning schools, learning theories defined in this book are categorized under the following learning paradigms: *behaviorism, cognitivism, constructivism,* and *organizational learning.* By classifying the theories into these learning paradigms, the book seeks to provide a context and framework for the theories. The goal is to give the reader a point of reference for comparison and contrast.

Though some learning theories, such as Jean Piaget's *genetic epistemology* and Jerome Bruner's *discovery learning*, could easily fall under the two schools of cognitivism and constructivism, those theories are categorized herein as primarily constructivist. The approach taken is to categorize a particular theory within what is regarded by the author as the most dominant school or learning paradigm for that theory. Argument could be made that several theories may fall under a different category or multiple categories than the ones noted in this book. Cognitivists (as well as behaviorists, humanists, and constructivists) often classify a theory and place it within their own learning paradigm because they see traits that apply to their own view and perspective. Some adherents of learning theory schools or learning paradigms even deny the existence of other learning paradigms.

Nevertheless, an attempt has been made here to provide a classification to the theories based upon what the author regards as their most dominant traits in order to provide the reader with a contextual definition of the term. This attempt at providing a framework, a point of reference is also complicated by the fact that the theories themselves are often confusing and not easily differentiated from one another. For example, *cooperative learning* and *collaborative learning* are often confused, yet they both fall clearly under the learning paradigm of constructivism based upon their most dominant traits. The hope is that the reader will be able to see patterns and trends to the theories that match with the general characteristics of the learning paradigms under which they are classified.

learning styles (cognitivism)

In his book *Experiential Learning: Experience as the Source of Learning and Development,* David Kolb creates a model for experiential learning by matching types of *cognitive processes* with specific types of *instructional design* strategies that are based upon his four learning styles. These four learning styles are tied to four types of learners: reflectors, theorists, pragmatists, and activists. (1) Reflectors observe, watch, and take in information from the environment and reflect upon these experiences often in a visual manner. They are characterized as imaginative types. (2) Theorists also observe, watch, and take in information from the environment, but they process these experiences abstractly and play with the idea of the environment in an analytical fashion. They are thus characterized as analytical types. (3) Pragmatists take in the experiences from the external environment and process them by testing them out in an active fashion. They are characterized as practical, common sense types. (4) Activists are intimately tied to their senses and sensory experiences. They process what they see, hear, touch, and feel. They are characterized as dynamic, intuitive types.

From an instructional design perspective, the following learning strategies should be employed for each learning style type. (1) Reflectors need instruction that is discussion- or simulation-oriented. They need to see patterns, to probe, question, and reflect. They seek to answer the question, "Why." The instructor's role for reflectors is to motivate and witness. (2) Theorists need instruction that is structured, factual, and challenging. They need to analyze, organize, classify, and use logic to see the interrelationships between concepts. They seek to answer the question, "What." The instructor's role is to give them the facts. (3) Pragmatists need instruction that is practical, involving *problem-solving* activities, with the instructor acting as a facilitator and a coach. They seek to answer the question, "How." And they desire to discover on their own links between content and opportunities to solve real-life problems. (4) Activists need instruction that focuses on self-discovery with the instructor being an assessor of process and product. Activists prefer to focus on evaluations, summaries, syntheses; they enjoy role-playing and competitive tasks. They seek to answer the question, "What if."

In more recent years, Kolb has applied his perspectives on experiential learning and learning styles to organizational behavior and *organization learning*. In *Organizational Behavior: An Experiential Approach* published in the mid–1990s, Kolb provides group learning exercises and *problem-solving* situations and simulations to promote experiential learning for the various types of learning styles of the employee audiences he addresses. The twin goals are to have employees learn specific, new work-related content and, through that experience, to learn more about oneself, one's learning style, as well as one's learning strengths and weaknesses.

learning web (constructivism)

A way of achieving deschooling is through Ivan Illich's learning web, which is a precursor of the *Internet* and a way out of the traditional learning environments of brick-and-mortar schools that are thoroughly enmeshed in the *industrial age educational paradigm*. Deschooling's primary emphasis is on the individual's pursuit of knowledge. In the 1970s, Illich argued that education's

top-down management style was robbing students of their *creativity* and personal *decision-making* abilities. Learners, in effect, needed to be deschooled, that is, to be deprogrammed from the industrial age educational paradigm whose principles and policies get in the way of the natural curiosity and self-motivation of the learner.

The primary way to achieve deschooling is through Illich's learning web, which had the following four objectives: (1) Provide learners with online reference information and *learning objects*. (2) Allow for learner exchanges of information and skills. (3) Provide peer *collaboration* and matching. (4) Provide reference information for educators at large. Both the concepts of the learning web and deschooling are definite precursors to the *virtual learning environments* in institutions that have embraced the *digital age educational paradigm*, along with Bruner's *discovery learning* approach, wherein the focus is on the learner and the learner's construction of content and meaning.

legitimate peripheral participation (constructivism)

In Jean Lave's *situated learning* theory, the social interaction process that occurs between newcomers and old-timers within the *community of practice* is called *legitimate peripheral participation*. All learners, new and seasoned, participate in a community of practice, which is a social, interactive group that has at its center seasoned practitioners who provide *cognitive coaching* and *apprentice learning* to novices who are in the process of learning a particular skilled craft or trade. Lave made observations based upon her anthropological studies of cross-cultural knowledge transfer of skilled tradespeople, including midwives, meat cutters, tailors, and others. Laves observations became the basis of her *situated learning* theory. In her observations, she noted that as the novice gains knowledge and moves closer to the community's center, he or she begins to take on the role of mentoring new, uninitiated individuals into the community of practice.

Through this participation process, otherwise known as legitimate peripheral participation, knowledge and skills are transferred amongst the members of the society.

Lave's conclusion is that knowledge transfer is closely tied to the social situation in which the knowledge is learned. Out of the social context, the knowledge itself is meaningless. Lave's further conclusion is that classroom learning, by its very nature, is out of context and irrelevant, and that knowledge gained through legitimate peripheral participation within the work setting, within the community of practice, is in context and relevant.

level of competence (educational technology)

An important aspect of *intelligent tutoring systems*, level of competence refers to the knowledge and skill level of a given learner as he or she is going through the learning application. It is based upon a set of *performance objectives* predetermined by the *instructional design* specialist. In order to determine human performance for specific sets of tasks being attempted by the learner, most intelligent tutoring systems employ *performance tracking* mechanisms to determine the user's level of competence per task. A type of *artificial intelligence* application, intelligent tutoring systems are computer programs embedded into *computer-aided instruction, computer-based training,* or *Web-based training* that provide *cognitive coaching* and guidance to the learner as he or she goes through each exercise within the program. These systems presuppose a knowledge of the learner's ever-increasing abilities and progress through the application. They involve tracking mechanisms (i.e., *performance tracking*) that determine the learner's knowledge and experience level (i.e., level of competence) at each stage within the learning application. Intelligent tutoring systems provide helpful hints and support as the learning exercises become more difficult and the learning path more arduous for the user. The ultimate goal of these systems is to simulate human tutoring and coaching strategies as the user's level of competence increases.

levels of processing (cognitivism)

Craik and Lockhart's level of processing theory postulates that the human mind processes information and learns at a number of different levels simultaneously. The more levels experienced, the deeper the processing that occurs. Rote memorization (as experienced in the *industrial age educational paradigm*) is ultimately unsuccessful for long-term memory because deep processing does not occur and the information remains (only temporarily) in short-term memory. When information is given a context, the information can be processed and fixed in long-term memory. Though still following the *Atkinson-Shiffrin memory model*, in which there are three processing levels (*sensory memory, short-term memory,* and *long-term memory*), Craik and Lockhart improved on the model by defining how some information can be processed more deeply.

They define two means of committing information to *memory: maintenance rehearsal* and *elaborative rehearsal*. Maintenance rehearsal is simply a means of keeping short-term stimuli and knowledge in short-term memory by using rote repetition. An example of this would be memorizing a word list. Elaborative rehearsal is a means of committing information to long-term memory by putting information in context through *chunking, cognitive coaching,* and *analogical learning* activities. Craik and Lockhart's levels of processing model matches cognitivist approaches, such as Bransford's *anchored instruction* and the Caines's *brain-based learning* as well as constructivist approaches, such as Vygotsky's *social development theory* and the Johnsons' *cooperative learning*. Examples of ways to process information more deeply through elaborative rehearsal are creating summaries of information, linking the content to one's life while providing personal examples that are discussed out loud with fellow students, and generating questions for discussion with colleagues who are also studying the information.

lifelong learning (humanism)

Based upon *Instrumentalism*, in which John Dewey postulates that learning is developing and developing is learning, lifelong learning is the concept, much touted over the last decade, that the process of learning continues throughout all phases of human life. Therefore, opportunities for education and enrichment should be available to all who desire it regardless of age, status, and location. In 1970, UNESCO (United Nations Educational, Scientific and Cultural Organization) declared that there needs to be a unifying principle for all nations in which all aspects of education are coherently organized and available on a lifelong basis, and on a global scale, to all individuals. Lifelong learning goes beyond the walls of the traditional educational classroom. Lifelong learning includes personal improvement and enrichment as well as knowledge, skills, and job development education. With its emphasis on personal improvement and enrichment, lifelong learning is also closely allied to *holistic learning*.

life space (humanism)

Kurt Lewin, an adherent of *Gestalt theory*, developed a sub-theory of how humans are motivated to learn and act. He stated that human behavior is influenced by the total set of psychological facts experienced. Psychological facts are anything that exists in a human's *consciousness*, including being thirsty, having a toothache, a past memory, a present experience, etc. The total of these psychological facts make up what Lewin calls a human's life space. Lewin's life space is an important concept to describe an individual's Gestalt, or total set of experiences that determine his or her consciousness.

Gestalt, the German word for shape or configuration, is a way of describing how humans perceive the world as a meaningful whole rather than as isolated stimuli. Humans see complete shapes, for example, not merely lines, incomplete shapes, and bits of color.

To adherents of Gestalt theory, dissection and analysis of individual parts present a distortion of reality. The whole is greater than the sum of the parts. Because the focus of study for Gestaltists is often human perceptual phenomena, Gestalt psychology is also referred to as *phenomenology*. To Gestaltists, the phenomenological experience that each human has in life is greater than the multitude of individual parts that make up the experiences.

All of one's life experiences make up what Kurt Lewin refers to as life space. Lewin's interpretation of Gestalt theory is an application of field theory from physics. Field theory, in brief, is the study of dynamic, interrelated systems, wherein nothing exists in isolation. From Lewin's perspective, no single human event, no single part can be separated from the whole. Whatever occurs to an individual in life shapes and influences all aspects of that individual.

Logic Theorist (cognitivism)

Allen Newell and Herb Simon's *logic theorist* is considered by some to be the first *artificial intelligence* program. It was developed in the mid–1950s. The program depicted each problem to be resolved in a tree model, in which particular paths were selected that would most likely yield a desired conclusion. The importance today of the logic theorist is that it was a first step in the new field of artificial intelligence. It was later enhanced in GPS, the *General Problem Solver*.

The goal of GPS was twofold: (1) to solve problems that require *intelligence,* and (2) to understand better how humans perform *problem-solving* activities. GPS made a clear-cut differentiation between problem solving (people solve problems in relation to knowledge) and domain knowledge (the collection of knowledge people need to solve generic tasks). GPS also introduced *means-ends analysis,* which is a method for problem solving that involves comparing the current state to a goal state, with subgoals noted in between the two that are needed to meet the overall goal.

GPS is an important foundation for *GOMS,* which was developed in the mid–1980s by Newell, Card, and Moran. GOMS is an acronym for Goals, Operators, Methods, and Selection. It is a prominent model for *human-computer interaction* still employed today to measure the usefulness of computer user interface designs. Without the logic theorist, there would have been no GPS, no GOMS, and no other artificial intelligence applications like *Soar.*

logical deductive (behaviorism)

This is a reference to how Clark Leonard Hull developed his learning theories, including *drive reduction theory* and *drive stimulus reduction theory.* This method is more often referred to as *hypothetical deductive theory.* It generally follows four steps: (1) Create a set of postulates, which are assumptions the behavioral scientist makes that cannot be directly verified. (2) Deduce from the postulates a set of theories, which can be directly verified through a series of experiments. (3) Test the theories in the experiments. If the experiment produces what is predicted, the postulate is indirectly verified and the theory strengthened. If the experiment does not come out as predicted, the theory loses strength and a new or modified theory is needed. Thus, all logical deductive theories are dynamic in the light of new experiments and new evidence arising from each succeeding experiment. Hull recommended that all learning theories follow this method of theorizing and testing to prove validity.

logical-mathematical intelligence (constructivism)

Howard Gardner's theory regarding human *intelligence.* Multiple intelligences posits that our culture and school systems focus far too much attention as a measure of success on *verbal-linguistic intelligence* and logical-mathematical intelligence. Gardner's theory suggests that at least eight other types of human intelligence are just as significant, and that they need to be considered within our culture and schools. Gardner's eight intelligences include verbal-lin-

guistic intelligence, logical-mathematical intelligence, *musical intelligence, spatial intelligence* (e.g., a sculptor's mind), *bodily kinesthetic intelligence, interpersonal intelligence, intrapersonal intelligence,* and *naturalist intelligence.*

Examples of logical-mathematical intelligence activities are deciphering codes, creating outlines, creating graphical organizers of information, calculating, learning number sequences, learning abstract symbols and mathematical formulas, *problem-solving,* and pattern recognition. As an adherent of *constructivism,* especially Vygotsky's *social development theory,* Gardner believes strongly that intelligence cannot be defined or measured without consideration of the individual's cultural and social context. Each individual's development of particular types of intelligence is partially inherent but also shaped very much by environment, culture, and upbringing.

long-term memory (cognitivism)

A concept of great importance to the understanding of how we learn, long-term memory is a key element of several brain-processing models of human cognition and *artificial intelligence,* including the *logic theorist,* the *General Problem Solver, GOMS, Soar,* and *ACT theory.* John Anderson's Act Theory, a *cognitive architecture* that pays particular attention to the workings of long-term memory, postulates that human cognition is an interplay of procedural, declarative, and working memory. *Declarative memory* is a type of long-term memory that stores facts and ideas in a semantic network structure (i.e., a *network model*). *Procedural memory,* another type of long-term memory, takes sequences of declarative knowledge in the form of *productions* and makes further logical inferences about them. Each production contains a set of conditions and actions found within declarative memory. *Working memory,* or short-term conscious thought, retrieves declarative information of facts and ideas, carries out task sequences found in long-term procedural memory, and adds new information gathered from the environment, forming new sequences that are then stored again in long-term procedural memory.

Also important to constructivists, such as Piaget and Bruner, long-term memory is the place in the mind where a combination of factual memory, individual and group perceptions, and interpretations are stored. In the constructivist framework, learning takes place when the learner builds meaning (not always objective) and constructs content based upon past knowledge and experiences residing in long-term memory. Without long-term memory, human learning of any sort would become an unlikely scenario. Generally speaking, learning takes place when knowledge moves from short-term memory to long-term memory.

M

You are told a lot about your education, but some beautiful, sacred memory, preserved since childhood, is perhaps the best education of all. If a man carries many such memories into life with him, he is saved for the rest of his days. And even if only one good memory is left in our hearts, it may also be the instrument of our salvation one day.
—Fyodor Dostoevski, nineteenth-century Russian writer

machine learning (cognitivism)

Within the field of *artificial intelligence* and closely related to *data mining*, machine learning is a process by which a system can extract knowledge from databases to simulate how knowledge is acquired by humans and by *agents*. Machine learning is a process in which a system can learn from its repeated experiences, from analytical observation, and from *inductive learning* as a means of *knowledge acquisition*. There are three types of learning that a system can simulate: (1) *speed up learning*, which is learning that occurs in the system that allows it to complete tasks more quickly and efficiently over time without external input; (2) *learning by being told*, which is learning that occurs when the system is specifically provided with external input and knowledge from an outside source; and (3) *inductive learning*, which is learning that occurs in a system that acquires new knowledge that is not explicitly or implicitly provided previously from an outside source. Machine learning is an important function of many *artificial intelligence* applications and *neural networks* that simulate how the mind works with regard to retrieving, sifting through, and processing information.

machine tractable dictionary (cognitivism)

A machine tractable dictionary is one that a computer can use to communicate with humans in their *natural language*. An important *artificial intelligence* research focus, *natural language processing* is an attempt to make computer programs able to understand spoken or written natural languages. This would mean that computers would be able to understand meaning. Research is currently being conducted into compiling dictionaries of words and their meanings that are *tractable* (that a computer can "read" and "understand"). Thus, an objective of *computer lexicography* is the development of *machine tractable dictionaries* to facilitate computer-based natural language processing.

This area of AI research is also closely associated with *computational linguistics*, which involves the use of statistics and statistical programs to identify word patterns and recurrences. *Voice recognition* is also related to natural language processing, which is the "holy grail" of AI research. The computer will be able to understand meanings of human words and communicate with humans, and vice versa. The path to that holy grail in the minds of more than a few AI researchers is through the creation of the machine tractable dictionary.

magical number seven (cognitivism)

In the now famous article published in 1956 in *The Psychological Review* entitled "The Magical Number Seven, Plus or Minus Two: Some Limits on Our Capacity for Processing Information," George A. Miller of Harvard University argued that the human brain's capacity to retain information in *working memory* is very, very limited. In fact, he postulated that the human brain only processes from five to nine information items at a time. Also, the time limit for retaining this small set of information is no more than twenty seconds. Working within the tradition of *information processing theory*, in which the mind processes information similar to the way a computer processes data, Miller theorized that humans are very limited with regard to initially retaining new information, much more so than was previously thought.

The implication of this finding from a *curriculum design* and an *instructional design* perspective is that information must be provided to learners in small units. Otherwise, the learners will be overloaded with data that is not retained. They will be overloaded with *infoglut*. If humans are faced with a large volume of information, the only way that they can process it is by breaking it up into manageable chunks. In short, the human brain's hardware specifications for working memory do not extend beyond that of the magical number seven.

mail list (educational technology)

An *asynchronous learning* technology, a mail list is a type of group-oriented e-mail, or electronic mail, that fosters group interactions and *collaboration*. It is a catalyst for the development of the *digital age educational paradigm* as well as an important means of *computer-mediated communication* for *distance learning,* in which the learners and the

instructor communicate with each other very quickly over the *Internet* as part of their class activities. With a mail list, the instructor, or any individual student in the class, can send messages over computer networks or over the *Internet,* as well as attach *multimedia* files that can be perused by the recipients of the message (i.e., all of the members of the class). These files can contain audio, video, and graphical files that the recipients can open up and read at will. With the mail list, communications are occurring nonsimultaneously.

Another example of an asynchronous learning tool is the *class Web site.* Asynchronous learning derives its meaning from the data processing world, in which the term asynchronous refers to computer interactions or processes that occur at various points in time, rather than at the same time. Asynchronous learning is opposed to *synchronous learning.* Synchronous learning is computer-mediated communication in which the learners and the instructor are communicating over the *Internet* at the same time as part of their course activities. With synchronous learning, interactions and communications are occurring simultaneously through the use of *videoconferencing*, voice or text *chats, or audio-conferencing.* Typically, most Internet-based distance learning courses employ both asynchronous learning and synchronous learning methods and techniques. Both are of value for the creation of *virtual learning communities*, the *electronic campus*, and the *universal campus network.*

maintenance rehearsal (cognitivism)

An aspect of Craik and Lockhart's *level of processing* theory, maintenance rehearsal is a means of keeping short-term stimuli and knowledge in *short-term memory* by using rote repetition. An example of maintenance rehearsal would be memorizing a word list. *Elaborative rehearsal*, in contrast, is a means of committing information to *long-term* memory by putting information in context. Examples of ways to process information more deeply through elaborative rehearsal are creating summaries of information, linking the content to one's personal life while providing examples that are discussed with fellow students, as well as generating questions for discussion with colleagues who are also studying the information. Opposing the *industrial age educational paradigm*, Craik and Lockhart maintain that deep processing of information (i.e., true learning) can be obtained not by memorization (i.e., maintenance rehearsal) but only by placing information in conceptual, personal, and social context (i.e., elaborative rehearsal).

management thinking (organizational learning)

Management thinking utilizes *social learning* skills and *creativity* for corporate *problem solving* and *decision making*. Edward de Bono's book and software application, *Atlas of Management Thinking*, is a descriptive explication using graphic images of how managers can be more effective, creative, and innovative thinkers and change agents. From a de Bono perspective, management thinking is using the right side, the creative side of the brain, to solve business problems. By contrast, management "not thinking" is being too analytical, logical, and cautious while stifling creativity, innovation, and corporate change. Management thinking is in line with many of the principles embodied in de Bono's *lateral thinking*, *CoRT thinking*, and *Six Thinking Hats*.

mands (behaviorism)

This term refers to the first of four categories of human *verbal behavior* delineated by B.F. Skinner. According to Skinner, verbal behavior (i.e., language) of humans can be entirely defined and explained within the context of *reinforcement theory*. For Skinner, both human talking and listening are actions that are directly influenced, just like any other behavior, by reinforcement from the environment. Skinner classified verbal behaviors that are responses to reinforcement as follows: (1) *Mands*. These are commands and utterances that require an immediate response. An example of a mand is, "Watch out for the baseball." (2) *Tact*. These are words that represent specific objects recognized by the human in the environment, expressed out loud, and reinforced not only by the sound of the word but also by an observer's recognition that the word corresponds to the object and to the sound of the word itself. (3) *Echoic Behavior*. When the human repeats exactly same the set of words stated verbatim by another, this action is known as echoic behavior. It is a first step toward learning more complex verbal behavior beyond repeating what another has said. (4) *Autoclitic Behavior*. This behavior is entirely dependent upon other verbal behavior to qualify responses, to express relationships, and to provide a grammatical frame to the verbal behavior. Overall, Skinner's view of human verbal behavior is that it is based entirely upon the environment and environmental responses. He rejects the cognitive processes that are delineated by cognitivists as they seek to define natural language processing of humans.

mastery learning (cognitivism)

Developed by John M. Carroll in 1963, mastery learning shifts the focus from the teacher to the learner in terms of the student being able to master certain content and skills within the instruction specified by the instructor. In the more classical tradition, in which all students are given the same amount of time to learn and to complete tasks, mastery learning emphasizes the individual needs and pace of each learner. According to Carroll, aptitude should be measured in terms of time required to complete successfully the learning task. Some individuals take longer than others to finish a particular exercise. With the master learning method, teachers must provide an instructional strategy within the *curriculum design* that permits all learners to be successful. This is done by the following four activities: (1) Specify to the learner the goal of the learning in terms of what is to be learned and how the learning activity will be evaluated. (2) Permit learner self-pacing whereby each student can learn at his or her own rate. (3) Monitor student progress and provide immediate feedback to keep the students on the learning path. (4) Evaluate to ensure that the final goal of the learning activity is achieved by each student. Mastery learning is in the same tradition as Gagne's *conditions of learning*, Merrill's *component display theory*, and Mager's *criterion-referenced instruction*. All emphasize the importance of structuring the instruction to meet the individual needs of the learners who seek to complete a set of objectives spelled out at the beginning of the learning activity.

mathematical metacognition (cognitivism)

From Allen Schoenfeld's perspective, mathematical metacognition is a critical element to performing *mathematical problem solving*. By using techniques such as the *think aloud protocol*, learners can achieve a degree of *self-regulation*, which allows them to understand their own cognitive processes while in the act of achieving a learning goal. Mathematical metacognition is the ability to think about the process of thinking and problem solving, to be consciously aware of one's actions within the problem-solving activity, and to be able to monitor and control one's cognitive processes to become a better mathematics problem solver. Being able to assess one's status and progress, make adjustments to strategy, and adjust actions and procedures to meet task goals while the task is in process are essential to the self-regulation process and to achieving a high degree of mathematical metacognition.

mathematical problem solving (cognitivism)

This term refers to Alan Schoenfeld's theory of mathematical problem solving, his theory for teaching and understanding mathematics first elaborated upon in the mid–1980s in his book of the same title. To Schoenfield, mathematics is a problem-solving activity in which four sets of skills are needed: (1) Resources, which involve knowledge of mathematical propositions and procedures; (2) Heuristics, which are techniques for mathematical problem solving, such as the *think aloud protocol*; (3) Control, which involves *decision making* as to when and how to use resources and problem-solving techniques; and (4) Beliefs, which involve *thinking mathematically* (i.e., being able to look at the world from a mathematical point of view). Implementing these skills places learners squarely within a *culture of mathematics*, which is achieving over time a level of competence with the mathematical theorems and postulates, and their applications, while using them to better understand our world and our society. Though classified here as a cognitivist approach, mathematical problem solving is also tied to the social and cultural aspects implicit in the *learning paradigm* of *constructivism*.

maximum rationality hypothesis (cognitivism)

Allen Newell's maximum rationality hypothesis is his theory regarding *cognition* that describes the principles of *bounded rationality* to an *agent* seeking to perform an action and reach a specified goal. According to Newell, if an agent in an *artificial intelligence* system obtains knowledge that one of its actions will lead to one of its goals, it will select that action in order to successfully attain the goal. Thus, within Newell's vision of a *cognitive architecture* for human thinking, there is a direct relationship between goals, knowledge, and actions. Closely related to a *unified theory of cognition*, cognitive architecture refers to a model of mental processing for human *problem solving*, learning, and task completion. An example of a cognitive architecture is Newell's *Soar*, which is a framework for understanding how humans and *artificial intelligence* computer systems use knowledge to take actions that will lead to a set of predetermined goals. In short, Newell's research focus is the use of artificial intelligence models to determine how humans learn.

means-ends analysis (cognitivism)

From Allen Newell and Herb Simon's GPS, the *General Problem Solver*, means-ends analysis is a method for *problem solving* that involves comparing the current state to a goal state, with subgoals noted in between the two that are needed to meet the overall goal. Means-ends analysis, which is an important aspect of GPS, focuses in particular on the problem-solving aspect of cognitive processing in the human brain. Means-ends analysis involves moving back from the final goal and considering what specific subgoal activities are needed to move the individual from the current state to the desired result.

Memex (educational technology)

In 1945 in the *Atlantic Monthly*, Vannevar Bush wrote an article entitled, "As We May Think," in which he envisioned a mechanical device called the Memex that could be utilized to browse through a vast array of content available on microfilm. Users of the Memex could follow paths through the information and go back at another time to follow the same paths again, as well as take to take variant paths and offshoots from their original ones. Bush envisioned that any type of information could be stored in the Memex, whether text, photographs, or drawings. In essence, Bush envisioned a *digital library* of information that very much resembles what we have today with the *Internet*. The only difference is that Memex, is *multimedia* and *hypermedia* content stored on a vast array of networks of computers rather than on microfilm.

memory (cognitivism)

Following the *Atkinson-Shiffrin memory model* as well as Craik and Lockhart's *levels of processing* model, among others, memory in humans is generally regarded as being divided into three types: *sensory memory, short-term memory,* and *long-term memory*. According to most learning theories, the goal of learning is to have knowledge progress from sensory memory to short-term memory to long-term memory. Memory is an impor-

tant area of study within *cognitive psychology*, it is an important area of focus within *artificial intelligence* models of cognition, including the *Logic Theorist, GPS, GOMS,* and *Soar*.

Memory is central to most cognitivist theories of learning for both human thinking and computer simulations of how humans think. An important example of how memory plays a prominent role in cognitivist thought is John Anderson's *ACT theory*, which is a *cognitive architecture* that regards human cognition as an interplay of procedural, declarative, and working memory. *Declarative memory* is a type of *long-term memory* that stores facts and ideas in a semantic network structure (i.e., a *network model*). *Procedural memory*, another type of *long-term memory*, takes sequences of declarative knowledge in the form of *productions* and makes further logical inferences about them. Each production contains a set of conditions and actions found within declarative memory. *Working memory*, or short-term conscious thought, retrieves declarative information of facts and ideas, carries out task sequences found in procedural memory, and adds new information gathered from the environment, forming new sequences that are then stored in procedural memory.

Constructivists, like Jerome Bruner (*discovery learning*) and Jean Piaget (*developmental learning*), regard memory as a critical component to their learning theories, in which the learner's past experiences, committed to long-term memory, help the learner provide a context to the content as well as help to shape the learner's construction of that content within the learning activity. Memory is also a significant aspect to Roger Schank's learning theories that focus on *case-based reasoning* and human *problem solving*. A case-based reasoning system stores previous experiences categorized in long-term memory, retrieves them as it applies a new situation, reuses the experiences in the new situation, and then categorizes and records the new result in memory.

In Roger Schank's *script theory* of learning, human beings follow a similar case-based reasoning approach. Humans learn to perform new activities by creating scripts that contain sequential procedures for given situations. The learners store these in memory and "pull out" specific scripts for situations that are similar to previous scenarios encountered, and then adapt them to the new situation. In Roger Schank's world, scripts govern our memories, learning, and actions. Through *active learning*, humans build scripts and develop a *dynamic memory* system that helps them to act again in similar situations. By creating scripts, the learners integrate what has been previously learned with new situations that demand new solutions to problems. From a case-based reasoning perspective, humans store and categorize a series of cases in long-term memory from previous situations, and recall and reuse them for new problem situations that require a solution.

In fact, all learning theorists studying human thinking and learning regard memory as a critical element to the learner's achieving success in the learning experience. Without memory, no long-lasting learning can occur.

mental constructs (constructivism)

Related to *cognitive architecture*, but from a constructivist learning perspective, mental constructs refer to models of mental processing for human *problem solving*, learning, and task completion typically occurring through a *collaborative learning* set of activities. By transferring and sharing mental constructs between and among instructor and learners, *knowledge sharing, discovery learning,* and *active learning* activities are allowed to occur to enhance the entire learning process. In so doing, the instructor moves from the center stage to allow for more *learner-centric* versus *instructor-centric* experiences on behalf of the learner.

mental models (organizational learning)

One of the disciplines for the *learning organization* in Peter Senge's *The Fifth Discipline*, mental models are deeply ingrained assump-

tions, ideas, and mental images we have of ourselves and others. These mental models influence greatly how we perceive ourselves and the world and how we interact with it. The activity involved in this discipline is reassessing our own mental models and how they came to be in order to gain a better understanding of how they influence our sense of self and our world vision. It involves a process that Senge defines as turning the mirror inward to better understand our shortcomings with regard to our own perceptions and notions in order to allow us to make better judgments and decisions that are more objective and in line with outward reality.

metacognition (organizational learning)

In the 1990s, Peter Senge's book entitled *The Fifth Discipline*, elaborated upon a new way for companies to perceive themselves, grow, and develop a sense of self-awareness, a state of *metacognition*. To Senge, metacognition is a state in which the organization becomes conscious of its own processes and decisions and more acutely aware of the skills of its knowledge workers. In Peter Senge's paradigm for the *learning organization,* a key way to achieve a state of metacognition is through the development of *systems thinking*, the *Fifth Discipline*. This is a mode of thinking, a process in which one not only analyzes the entire organization and breaks it down into its constituent parts, but also considers carefully the relationships between all of the parts. With systems thinking, one must focus on all or almost all of the interactions and interrelations that occur within the organization being studied. Systems thinking is an important and necessary milestone to be achieved for the enterprise to become a learning organization. It allows one to look more carefully at the overall corporate situation and make informed decisions that are based upon an understanding of how the entire organization operates within a social context. In short, with systems thinking, one looks at all of the aspects and interrelations occurring within the system (i.e., the enterprise) before making judgments about the direction that the organization should take to be effective as a whole and within the society at large.

Metacognition also plays a prominent role in Edward de Bono's *Six Thinking Hats*. The overall purpose of using six thinking hats is to make for more effective, corporate-wide problem solving and *decision making*. One of the six hats is blue, the hat that focuses on the process itself. This hat for de Bono is the hat of *metacognition*, of thinking about the thinking process over and above the facts and feelings of the proposals on the table. Blue hat thinking is that of the observer. It is done by someone who is viewing the process from an objective, outsider's perspective. Blue hat thinking helps the group move toward a solution that is helpful to the entire enterprise.

Metacognition is also closely related to the concept of *critical thinking*. Critical thinking is the process of collecting information, processing it, and using the information for wise *decision making* and informed *problem solving*. It is the ability to exercise control over one's *cognitive processes* as well as the ability to communicate effectively what one has learned. In exercising critical thinking, one reviews the situation, asks pertinent questions, weighs the facts, interprets the data, and makes clear judgments. Similar to reading and writing, it is a skill that can be developed with time and practice. From an organizational learning perspective, critical thinking is allied to *management thinking*. In his book published shortly after the turn of the twentieth century, *How We Think*, John Dewey defined critical thinking as "reflective thought." Reflective thought is achieved when one withholds judgment, remains skeptical and questions assumptions, yet keeps an open mind to solutions that will surface through a close intellectual and emotional examination of the problem and its social context.

The concept of metacognition plays a prominent role in the Caines's *active processing*, as well as in the constructivist learning theories of *cognitive coaching, cognitive apprenticeship, apprenticeship learning,* and *collaborative learning*. Achieving a state of corporate metacognition is a key goal for

knowledge sharing and *enterprise-wide learning*. Within current *knowledge management* circles, achieving a state of metacognition through enterprise-wide learning is a much-touted, much-repeated reference to building a *Web-based knowledge transfer* system, building an *electronic learning environment* that promotes *business transformation* and organizational learning.

Through *agents, electronic performance support systems,* and other *just-in-time training* approaches, organizations achieve a state of metacognition as they move from the *industrial age educational paradigm* to the *digital age educational paradigm*. As a result of the *Internet*, organizations can build and maintain a *knowledge construction* factory (vs. the old industrial-age factory that produced widgets). Organizations can create an infrastructure for enterprise-wide learning via a *virtual learning environment* (including both *Web-based education* and *Web-based training components*) that is all-encompassing and used by internal employees, as well as outside customers and even the public. In this sense, achieving a state of metacognition extends the concept from a corporate *consciousness* of employees within the organization to external entities outside the organization to achieve a *universal campus network* that is an extension of what Vannevar Bush envisioned with his *Memex* in the 1940s.

metadata (educational technology)

Used originally in the data processing community to describe data dictionaries that identify the information contents of corporate databases, metadata now refers to the identifying information that defines, catalogs, and indexes the entire set of information extant in digital form within a *digital library*. The objective of the creation of metadata is to identify the type of *digital objects* that exist within the digital library through a system of electronic cataloging and indexing. The goal of the digital library is to provide users with universal access to a network of libraries and information servers that includes a wide array of *digital objects* and metadata that define what the objects are.

Simply stated, metadata is information about the information. Metadata includes information like title, subject, file formats, author(s), date, summary or abstract, etc. A *handle* is the mechanism that provides the digital objects with metadata. Basic naming and storage conventions for *digital objects* are used to identify the object, register intellectual property, and link objects together within the digital library. In its simplest definition, a handle is a name that identifies a *knowledge object* in a *digital library*.

A digital library is a library of information provided in various electronic forms (text, audio, video, graphics) and made available to a geographically dispersed group of users by means of a *distributed network system*. Various types of digital forms of information within the digital library are referred to as *digital objects*. Digital objects contain *digitized* information along with a unique identifier that provides a means for cataloging the object. These unique identifiers are referred to as *handles*. Handles are the means by which metadata are indexed and cataloged in the digital library.

metamathematics (constructivism)

This term refers to the study of what is mathematics and what is the nature of mathematical reasoning. An example of a metamathematical proposition is *Godel's Theory of Incompleteness*. Godel's theory sought to dispute over 3,000 years of proofs by mathematicians that a mathematical system, such as the number system, can be complete and consistent. Godel's theory said that the number system is not complete and is not consistent. Current thinking about what is mathematics has been greatly influenced by research in *mathematical metacognition* and *self-regulation*. This new metamathematical thinking declares that math is not about proving certainties but about discovering patterns amid much that appears at first to be without a pattern in the real world. As such, the new metamathematics thinking follows that of

chaos theory. Since mathematics cannot prove what is not provable, new emphasis has been placed on the cultural, social, and collaborative aspects of mathematics learning and its effective usage in solving real-world problems. This emphasis on the social, cultural, and creative aspects of metamathematics places it under the *learning paradigm of constructivism*.

mind mapping (cognitivism)

A learning process similar to that of *concept mapping*, mind mapping is a visualization activity that learners use to organize information, often as a *collaboration* activity. Originally developed by Tony Buzan of the United Kingdom, mind mapping is also a software product of The Bosley Group, entitled MindMapper. The mind mapping process is as follows: (1) The topic being focused upon is represented by a central image or graphic. (2) The main themes of the topic radiate out from the central image as primary branches. (3) In a tree-like structure, the minor themes of each main theme radiate out further from the primary branches. (4) All branches are interconnected to form a series of links.

Mind mapping is, in a sense, a two-dimensional word picture. Its use is to take complex topics and to organize all of their related subtopics in a structured, associated, graphical manner. This pictorial representation, once created, is theoretically easier to recall than words and concepts presented in a traditional outline format. It is used often in organizations to enhance *creativity* and to capture knowledge as an initial step in the *knowledge construction* process. Though its learning theory roots are that of cognitivism and David Ausubel's *subsumption theory* (i.e., new material is processed from existing *cognitive structures* previously created), it is allied as well to the *learning paradigms* of *constructivism* and *organizational learning*.

mindtools (constructivism)

In his book published in the late 1990s, *Computers as Mindtools for Schools: Engaging*

Critical Thinking, 2nd edition, David H. Jonassen of Penn State University develops his thesis that computers, *multimedia, hypermedia,* the *Internet,* and other educational technologies (i.e., mindtools) should be used to actively engage learners in constructivist, higher-order thinking and reasoning. *Instructional design* too often focuses first on technology. It is too often concerned with a highly structured *curriculum design* that is developed at the expense of a *learner-centric, active learning* approach to education. To Jonassen, mindtools are catalysts to facilitate, support, guide, and extend human *cognitive processes, knowledge acquisition,* and *knowledge sharing.* When learners actively create their own *knowledge bases* through the use of *expert systems,* they learn much more and much better. They construct their own *learning environment,* rather than have a learning environment constructed on their behalf.

Instructional designers learn the most about a given topic when they construct their *multimedia applications* and other learning systems that they provide to the learners. But in so doing, they rob the learners of the opportunity to achieve this deeper level of learning through the use of technology as a constructivist tool, a mindtool. It is the learners who must become the instructional designers. It is they who should use the technologies, not the traditional developers of content, to create their own content, their own meanings, their own *digital library* of information that supports and enhances their learning activities.

minimalism (contructivism)

An *instructional design* approach of John M. Carroll, minimalism is a strategy that focuses on how to create effective training and user materials to support computer applications. Minimalism is sometimes referred to as the *minimalist model.* Following in the tradition of Malcolm Knowles's *andragogy* with its emphasis on learner background, Carroll's minimalism focuses on the need to create content that builds upon the learner's past

knowledge and experience. Carroll believes that the learner is not a "blank slate," nor is his or her brain a container in which knowledge is to be poured by the instructor through a funnel (i.e., the *Nurnberg Funnel*).

Carroll's minimalism is *learner-centric* as opposed to *instructor-centric.* It is in the constructivist tradition of Jerome Bruner's *discovery learning* and Jean Piaget's *genetic epistemology.* Its five postulates are as follows: (1) Have learners begin performing meaningful tasks as soon as possible. (2) Minimize the amount of background materials as much as possible and allow the learners to fill in the gaps themselves with information that they will need to perform the tasks. (3) Allow the learners to make errors and recover from errors in the learning module. (4) Have all learning activities per module self-contained and independent of a particular sequence preordained by the instructor. (5) Have all learning modules be directly tied to real tasks that the learners would perform on the job. In short, don't let the instructor or the instructional materials get in the way of the learner's natural ability to learn. Instead, focus on activities that are learner-directed and applicable to the actual activities that the learners perform on the job.

Minimalism has also been incorporated into *GOMS. GOMS* is a *cognitive architecture* (i.e., a model of mental processing for human *problem solving,* learning, and task completion) developed originally in the mid–1980s by Newell, Card, and Moran. *GOMS* is an acronym for Goals, Operators, Methods, and Selection. In 1990, Gong and Elkerton wrote a paper in *CHI90* entitled "Designing Minimal Documentation Using the GOMS Model," in which they sought to prove that the minimalist model is an effective strategy and paradigm for creating instruction on how to teach novice users to use word processing applications.

minimalist model (constructivism)

Also referred to as *minimalism,* the minimalist model as a term is most often used in reference to testing out the theory of minimalism on new learners and users who seek to understand and use computer applications for job activities. By observing in a controlled environment the problems that new users encountered trying to work with the instructional and user materials that supported computer applications, John Carroll derived his minimalist model. His basic assumption was that adult learners are not stupid. They have a low tolerance for being guided through a process in detail and for having to read through a great deal of content before performing a set of tasks. Thus, developing content within the minimalist model means creating a concise set of task-oriented information that allows the learners to get up and running quickly on the activity that they need to perform on the job with the computer. Carroll and his colleagues have subsequently tested out instructional materials that follow the minimalist model on new learners and users of computer applications to prove that his model has validity.

Model Human Processor (cognitivism)

Most all of the *GOMS* techniques currently extant are built upon the Model Human Processor, which is a basic map and representation of human *cognitive processing* in GOMs. At the core of GOMS is the Model Human Processor, which consists of separate components for cognitive, perceptual, motor, memory, and control processes. A later enhancement to the *logic theorist* and GPS, *General Problem Solver*, GOMS is itself a *cognitive architecture* (i.e., a model of mental processing for human *problem solving*, learning, and task completion) developed originally in the mid–1980s by Newell, Card, and Moran. GOMS is an acronym for Goals, Operators, Methods, and Selection.

GOMS has developed into a family of techniques that includes *keystroke level model* (i.e., KLM), *CMN-GOMS, natural GOMS language,* and *CPM-GOMS.* The GOMS family is a prominent model for *human-computer interaction* and human learning used today to measure the usefulness of computer

user interface designs and human task performance. Through the observation of human task performance with computers, GOMS seeks to model human *cognitive processing* and *memory* that occur in defined stages (i.e., *sensory memory, working memory, long-term memory*). All cognitive activities that occur in GOMS are described in terms of the learner searching a *problem space*.

modes of learning (cognitivism)

This is one of three *modes of learning* (a general human learning model) delineated by D.E. Rumelhart and Donald A. Norman in the late 1970s and early 1980s. The main point of modes of learning is that *instructional design* and *curriculum design* should match with these three learning modes: *accretion, structuring,* and *tuning.* Accretion, the most common mode, is a process of *knowledge acquisition,* whereby new knowledge enters into human *memory.* Structuring (and restructuring), the most difficult mode, involves the creation of new *schema* or *knowledge structures* that include reflection that leads to a state of *metacognition.* Tuning, the most time-consuming mode, is the process of taking the new knowledge and using it to perform tasks to facilitate expert human performance.

molar behavior (humanism)

In 1912 Max Wertheimer, along with his colleagues Wolfgang Kohler and Kurt Koffka of Germany, began the movement that opposed *behaviorism* and favored a *holistic* approach to how humans learn. In contrast to behaviorism, which focused on objective, *molecular* behavior that could be broken apart and analyzed, Gestalt theory focused on subjective, *molar* behavior that could not be separated from the individual's shaping influence of human perception. Thus, molar behavior is, in short, the large segment of actions humans perform that can be characterized as goal-directed, purposive behavior. Purposive behavior as a field of study links the Gestaltists to the cognitive behaviorists.

Later called *cognitive behaviorism*, Edward Chace Tolman's *purposive behaviorism* postulates that there is a purpose for all behaviors of organisms. Like the Gestaltists, Tolman believed that looking at stimuli and responses alone is not an effective way of studying animal and human behavior. Unlike many other behaviorists, such as Skinner with his *operant conditioning*, Tolman began to theorize about internal mental aspects of behavior. For example, as rats go through mazes, they create a *cognitive map* that they rely upon to successfully perform the task of getting through the maze and obtaining the reward (i.e., food). Tolman referred to this purposeful behavior as *molar behavior*.

As the behaviorists looked back to a radical form of *empiricism* for their philosophical foundation, the Gestaltists (as well as the cognitivists) looked back to Kant's theory of *innate categories of thought* and of the shaping influence of the individual's perceptions of personal experiences in the environment. In Kant's *epistemology*, the mind itself is the source of human knowledge.

Gestalt, the German word for shape or configuration, is a way of describing how humans perceive the world as a meaningful whole rather than as isolated stimuli. In other words, humans see shapes such as buildings, houses, and lakes, instead of just lines, incomplete shapes, and patches of color. To adherents of Gestalt theory, dissection and analysis of individual parts is a distortion of reality. To Gestaltists, the whole is greater than the sum of the parts. Thus, Gestaltists study molar behavior (i.e., the whole) versus molecular behavior (i.e., the parts).

molecular behavior (humanism)

In contrast to *molar behavior*, which is regarded as the large segment of actions humans perform that can be characterized as goal-directed, *purposive behavior*, molecular behavior (as viewed by Gestaltists) is the small segment of behaviors (e.g., conditioned reflexes) studied by behaviorists in their work. From a *Gestalt theory* perspective, molecular behavior is that small set of stimuli and responses which is dissected and overanalyzed by behaviorists as they perform experiments on organisms in *operant chambers* and *puzzle boxes*.

motivation (behaviorism)

Within this corpus, the term, "motivation" is referenced over fifty times. A simple, single definition of the term would not do it much justice within the confines of a single entry. Nevertheless, from a behaviorist perspective, motivation is tied to the organism's need or drive that is an essential part of Hull's *drive reduction theory*. Edward Tolman's *purposive behaviorism* ascribes a purpose, a goal-directed behavior of the organism to a set of actions tied to the *stimulus-response association*. Within the *learning paradigm* of *constructivism*, motivation is closely related to the *active learning* of the learner, who is by nature instrinsically self-motivated to learn. Within the realm of Malcolm Knowles's *andragogy*, motivation that is *learner-centric* is central to the success of the adult learning activity. Within the traditional assumptions and methodology of *pedagogy*, learner motivation is *teacher-centric*. The student is driven to complete successfully the learning activity typically because of a desire to please the teacher and to receive a good grade.

From the Gestalt perspective, motivation is tied to *molar behavior*, that is, behavior that is purposive, directed toward a goal. Within the *learning paradigm* of *cognitivism*, goals are a central ingredient to the systems that seek to model human *cognitive processes*. An example of such a model is that of *GOMS*. GOMS is a *cognitive architecture* (i.e., a model of mental processing for human *problem solving*, learning, and task completion) developed originally in the mid–1980s by Newell, Card, and Moran. GOMS is an acronym for Goals, Operators, Methods, and Selection. Goals refer to the desired result that the learner seeks to achieve. Operators are sets of operations that the learner constructs to meet the goal. Methods are operator sequences grouped together to achieve goal completion. And selection rules are decision points for particular methods to be used for particular situations that come up during the goal-seeking activity. Most all *learning and performance* activities are goal-oriented and influenced directly by the motivation of the learner to achieve the goal.

multimedia (educational technology)

This is an umbrella term for the use of mixed media, including text, voice music, graphics, video, and other data forms in *multimedia applications*. Multimedia as a design type is ubiquitous in online and CD-ROM form. The amount of extant multimedia titles is huge and extends into the domains of business, government, and educational institutions and their corresponding *Internet* Web sites. The primary purpose is to enhance the use of the computer as a communications medium beyond text.

multimedia applications (educational technology)

These are varying forms of mixed media applications available in CD-ROM titles as well as on the Internet. The design model for multimedia applications falls into three categories, which are as follows: (1) Structured pathways are largely instructional applications designed as online tutorials that guide the learner through a series of interactive instructional sequences with the goal of meeting a detailed set of learning objectives. Examples of multimedia applications that follow the structured pathways approach are drill and practices for mathematics as well as foreign language instruction. Structured pathways are most often utilized in an *instructor-centric* orientation, wherein the learner has little knowledge brought to bear on the topic to be learned. As a result, the structure and sequence of instructional content is laid out by the developer (i.e., the instructor) versus the learner. The roots of structured pathways are *computer-based training* modules. (2) Exploratory applications represent the most common type of multimedia applications, and in fact, are often called (more accurately)

hypermedia applications. Examples of exploratory titles are electronic encyclopedias, virtual museums, and electronic marketing brochures. They are nonlinear and nonsequential in structure and are either contained in structured pathway applications or have structured pathway sequences designed at points within the exploratory application. They are *learner centric* in orientation, whereby, in effect, each learner structures the content as he or she follows a particular path through a nonsequential set of information. The roots of exploratory applications are early *digital libraries* of content, such as Vannevar Bush's *Memex*. (3) Gaming applications are the most demanding and difficult to create multimedia application. The learner becomes engaged in the interactive content by going through a series of challenges with a very specific set of objectives (finding treasure, slaying villains, earning sums of money). The design of gaming is highly interactive. Gaming applications employ a great deal of feedback provided by the developers of the content to let the learners know how they are performing within the application. The roots of gaming applications are early electronic video arcade games. In all of its various forms, multimedia is a ubiquitous design form seen in CD-ROM title as well as on the Internet.

multiple intelligences (constructivism)

Howard Gardner's theory regarding human *intelligence*, multiple intelligences posits that our culture and school systems focus far too much attention as a measure of success on *verbal-linguistic intelligence* and *logical-mathematical intelligence*. Gardner's theory suggests that at least eight other types of human intelligence are just as significant and that they need to be considered within our culture and schools. Gardner's eight intelligences are:

1. *Verbal-linguistic intelligence* (e.g., a poet's mind);
2. *Logical-mathematical intelligence* (e.g., a scientist's mind);

3. *Musical intelligence* (e.g., a composer's mind);
4. *Spatial intelligence* (e.g., a sculptor's mind);
5. *Bodily kinesthetic intelligence* (e.g., an athlete's or a dancer's mind);
6. *Interpersonal intelligence* (e.g., a salesperson's or an instructor's mind);
7. *Intrapersonal intelligence* (e.g., those with accurate views of themselves);
8. *Naturalist intelligence* (e.g., the mind of a biologist or an explorer who observes and recognizes patterns in the natural environment).

As an adherent of *constructivism*, especially Vygotsky's *social development theory*, Gardner believes strongly that intelligence cannot be defined or measured without consideration of the individual's cultural and social context. Each individual's development of particular types of intelligence is partially inherent but also shaped very much by environment, culture, and upbringing. Greg Maddux of the Atlanta Braves major league team is regarded by many currrent sportswriters as a great pitcher in the sport of baseball, but had he been brought up in a culture without baseball, he may have wound up as an accountant or a teacher. Thus the development of intelligence is an interaction between inherent biological tendencies and the opportunities for learning within the culture.

Like Cronbach and Snow's *aptitude-treatment interaction* (ATI), Gardner's theory of multiple intelligences emphasizes the individual differences and *learning styles* of students and how learning content should be tailored to take into consideration these differences. As one of the co-directors of *Project Zero* at Harvard University, Gardner and his colleagues have sought to put his and similar theories into practice. Project Zero's mission is to enhance thinking, *learning*, and *creativity* in all disciplines at the individual and institutional levels.

musical intelligence (constructivism)

One of Howard Gardner's eight *multiple intelligences,* musical intelligence is the ability to recognize rhythm, tone, and musical segments. One who possesses musical intelligence can recognize and repeat melodies and keep time. Examples of musical intelligence activities are singing, humming, musical composition, and recognizing instrumental and environmental sounds, tone patterns, and percussion. Individuals who possess musical intelligence and are provided with the right cultural and educational background in music are apt to pursue careers as singers, songwriters, musicians, and composers. Gardner believes that musical intelligence needs to be developed in the individual and must not be given less focus in favor of *verbal-linguistic intelligence* and *logical-mathematical intelligence*, which most schools tend to emphasize in their *curriculum designs*.

N

natural GOMS language (cognitivism)

Developed by David Kieras in the late 1980s, natural GOMS language is a high-level syntax and technique for *GOMS* that helps to define and evaluate GOMS applications. In this technique, the goals of the users are broken down into a hierarchy that becomes increasingly more detailed and delineated down to the operator level to represent better all sets of tasks occurring in a GOMS application. The overall, the usefulness of this technique is to understand better how humans perform computer-related tasks. The technique is an enhancement of both GOMS and *cognitive complexity theory*. GOMS is a *cognitive architecture* (i.e., a model of mental processing for human *problem solving*, learning, and task completion) developed originally in the mid–1980s by Newell, Card, and Moran.

GOMS is an acronym for Goals, Operators, Methods, and Selection. GOMS has developed into a family of techniques that includes *keystroke level model* (KLM), *CMN-GOMS,* natural GOMS language, and *CPM-GOMS*. The GOMS family is a prominent model for *human-computer interaction* and human learning used today to measure the usefulness of computer user interface designs and human task performance. Through the observation of human task performance with computers, GOMS seeks to model human *cognitive processing* and *memory* that occur in defined stages (i.e., *sensory memory, working memory,* and *long-term memory*). Cognitive complexity theory seeks to decompose user goals for completing computer tasks to obtain more accurate predictions of how long it will take users to learn to complete tasks online with fewer errors.

natural language (cognitivism)

An important goal of *artificial intelligence* research and development is to make computers able to understand, process, and even speak natural languages. Natural languages are the variety of human languages in the world. Examples of natural languages are English, Spanish, French, German, Italian, Japanese, Chinese, Russian, Arabic, etc. Computer languages are typically classified in terms of generations. First-generation computer languages are called machine languages. These are languages easily understood by machines, but not easily understood by humans. They consist of numbers.

Second-generation computer languages are called assembly languages. Assembly language programs are translated into machine language that the computer can understand through a program called an assembler. Assembly languages have the same numerical structure as machine languages, with the exception that humans (e.g., programmers) are able to assign names in natural language to the computer instructions and operations. Third-generation computer languages are called high-level languages. These are closer to English (e.g., a natural language) and are written in highly structured English terms. Through the use of a compiler, a high-level language (e.g., Java, C++, etc.), is translated into machine language that the computer can understand and process. An important goal in AI research is to have computers understand natural languages directly, without going through the processes involved with high level languages, assembly languages, and machine languages with regard to human and computer communication.

natural language processing (cognitivism)

An important *artificial intelligence* research focus, natural language processing is an attempt to make computer programs able to understand spoken or written natural languages. This would also mean that computers would be able to understand meaning. Research is currently being conducted into compiling dictionaries of words and their meanings that are *tractable* (that a computer can "read" and "understand"). Thus, an objective of *computer lexicography* is the development of *machine tractable dictionaries*. This area of AI research is closely associated with *computational linguistics,* which involves the use of statistics and statistical programs to identify word patterns and recurrences. Closely associated with *voice recognition*, which is sometimes referred to as natural language recognition, natural language processing is a "holy grail" of AI research that has as its ultimate goal making the computer able to understand meanings of human words and to allow computers to communicate with humans, and vice versa.

naturalist intelligence (constructivism)

A recent addition to Howard Gardner's original set of multiple intelligences, naturalist intelligence, the eighth intelligence, involves an individual's ability to identify and classify patterns that exist in nature. For the nonnaturalist type of thinker, these patterns are not at all apparent. However, the naturalist exhibits a heightened sensitivity to the environment, to nature, to organisms in nature, as well as to the weather and its changes. Individuals who have developed their naturalist intelligence capabilities may tend toward the disciplines of biology, botany, ecology, and meteorology. Gardner believes that naturalist intelligence needs to be developed in the individual and must not be given less focus in favor of *verbal-linguistic intelligence* and *logical-mathematical intelligence*, which most schools tend to emphasize in their *curriculum designs*.

navigation (educational technology)

The path that users or learners take through *hypermedia applications* or *multimedia applications*, the ability to travel through the path and not get easily lost despite the nonlinearity of the application, is referred to as navigation. Most hypermedia applications have a very *learner-centric*, nonlinear orientation that gives the learners a great deal of *learner control* over the navigational paths they choose to take. Most structured-path multimedia applications have a more *instructor-centric*, linear path that the learners follow (i.e., with less learner control).

The problem with systems that have a high degree of *nonlinearity* is that they often lead to learner or user *disorientation*. In a hypermedia application, disorientation refers to the act of getting lost within cyberspace. By its very nature, *hypermedia,* as noted above, has a high degree of nonlinearity that can easily cause user disorientation. To reduce the effects of disorientation, authors typically include in the application an important navigational feature, a textual or graphical table of contents, a *cognitive map* which provides an overview of the landscape of the nonlinear environment. This helps the learners so that they will not get lost between all of the various links in cyberspace. Otherwise, user disorientation will result, which can have a detrimental effect on the learning experience. The learners spend so much time selecting and attempting to navigate through the application that they have little energy left for absorbing the information. However, disorientation can also be regarded as a positive effect, in which the act of trying to recover from being lost along the navigational path is a catalyst for the users to learn and structure the content.

negotiated belief structures (organizational learning)

According to James Walsh and Liam Fahey in 1986, negotiated belief structures are the configurations of power and beliefs within an organization that are at the root of work group *decision making*. Walsh and Fahey research on negotiated belief structures built on the *organizational cognition* research of Linda Smircich. In a study of cultural, learning, and communication aspects of organizations, Smircich in 1983 defined organizational cognition as a system of shared knowledge and beliefs of individuals within the organization that are based upon common *knowledge structures* (*shared cognitive maps*) and *communication rules*. According to Kim Langfield-Smith in 1992, shared cognitive maps are based upon the shared knowledge and belief systems of the entire organization as well as those of specific subcultural groups used for daily interactions and group *decision making*.

Ultimately, according to both Walsh and Fahey and Langfield-Smith, organizations share knowledge, share cognitive maps that are primarily domain-specific and transitory (i.e., not of long duration). Some shared cognitive maps are thus related to a specific subculture, whereas others span the organization, are shared by all, and tend to be more explicit and of longer duration. For Walsh and

Fahey, negotiated belief structures are based upon a continuum where power is concentrated in one individual or is dispersed among the members of the group; and beliefs are based upon a continuum where members of the work group range from complete agreement to complete disagreement. Decision making is based entirely upon a political process of *negotiation* that occurs between and among the members of the work group.

negotiation (organizational learning)

Many books have been written upon the art and science of negotiation. For our purposes, negotiation is an important aspect of corporate *decision making, problem solving, cooperative learning,* and *organizational learning.* Negotiation involves the process of two or more people or two or more teams working together to resolve problems, utilize resources, handle conflicts, and forge solutions that all participants agree with and buy into. It involves compromise and the use of tact and diplomacy. It involves sorting through facts and knowledge at hand and working together with others in order to come up with a solution that is a correct and ethical one for the organization. Negotiation is not a battle of wills. It is not a win-lose situation. Negotiation involves the exercise of good judgment, cooperation, and sensitivity. It involves mutual agreement along with a great respect for individual differences and perspectives. Its goal is a win-win situation. Negotiation is, in short, an important attribute necessary for the development and maintenance of the *learning organization.*

network model (cognitivism)

In relation to *cognition* and *memory*, *artificial intelligence* experts at times refer to the brain as following a network model that is composed of *knowledge objects* linked together to form *knowledge structures* or *schemas.* As an example, Roger Schank's *conceptual dependency theory* and *script theory* follow a network model with regard to how the brain and, in particular, *episodic memory* work. In Schank's *conceptual depen-*

dency theory and *script theory*, episodic memory is regarded as the sum total of all experiences that an individual has in life and recalls as scripts. Script theory postulates that human memory (which Schank regards as primarily episodic memory) is based upon personally remembered episodes and experiences, i.e., *scripts* (a sequence of events and actions) that humans call upon and apply to a *schema*. Scripts allow humans to make inferences. Schema refers to a *knowledge structure* that gets created as humans experience new things in the environment from which they create more scripts. The knowledge structure or schema is organized in an associative manner in the form of a network model of personal episodes and experiences linked together as scripts. This knowledge structure (schema) is dynamic and continually enhanced over time. As new experiences occur, new scripts get written, and the schema become enhanced as a result of an ever-growing set of personal life episodes and experiences recorded in episodic memory. With both conceptual dependency theory and script theory as their theoretical basis, a number of *natural language processing* computer programs are being tested and developed. Generally speaking, the network model is a reference to the human brain viewed as a memory network of linked pieces of information that are derived from personal life experiences.

neural networks (cognitivism)

An important area of study within *artificial intelligence* is that of neural networks, sometimes referred to as artificial neural networks. Neural networks are an attempt to simulate the neural functions of the human brain. The primary element of the human brain is a cell called a neuron. Neurons are the means by which humans remember, think, learn, and perform *problem-solving* activities. The power of the human brain is the result of all of the multiple connections that neurons make between each other. In fact, each neuron can connect with up to 200,000 other neurons. Each and every neuron has four components:

(1) dendrites, which accept inputs; (2) soma, which process the inputs; (3) axon, which turn the processed inputs into outputs; and (4) synapses, which are the electrical chemical contacts between each neuron.

The basic unit of the neural network is the artificial neuron, which simulates the four functions of the biological neuron. The process that artificial intelligence experts undergo to create an artificial neural network is the following. Step 1. Arrange neurons in layers. Step 2. Decide the types of connections between neurons within a layer and outside of the layer. Step 3. Determine how the neuron will receive input and produce output. Step 4. Determine the strength of the connection between layers through multi-layered clustering of neurons.

The human brain learns through experiences and inputs provided through the environment. Neural networks, sometimes called *machine learning*, learn through the manipulation of algorithms, through the changes in the connection weights which cause the network to "learn" the solution to a posed problem. The connection strength is stored as a weight value for that connection. The neural network obtains new knowledge through the adjustment of these connection weights. The network's learning ability is a result of its architecture and the algorithmic method selected for learning, based upon learning laws. Learning laws are mathematical algorithms used to change connection weights. The well-known learning law is that of Donald O. Hebb, *Hebb's rule,* which states that if a neuron receives an input from another neuron, and if both are highly active (mathematically have the same number), the weight between the neurons should be strengthened.

Thus far, the most successful neural networks are those used for categorization and pattern recognition. For example, a medical diagnosis neural network system would classify an object under investigation (e.g., an illness), recognize a pattern within one of numerous possible categories of illnesses and provide a recommended action (e.g., a prescribed treatment for the illness). Most neural networks predict, classify, associate, conceptualize, or filter data. The development of neural networks is an increasingly important aspect of current *knowledge management* initiatives in corporations today.

neuron (cognitivism)

The primary element of the human brain is the neuron. Our brains have roughly ten billion neurons. Each one performs in a binary fashion similar to a computer. It is either off or on. Neurons are the means by which humans remember, think, learn, and perform *problem-solving* activities. The power of the human brain is the result of all of the multiple connections that neurons make between each other. In fact, each neuron can connect with up to 200,000 other neurons. Each neuron has four components: (1) dendrites, which accept inputs; (2) soma, which process the inputs; (3) axon, which turn the processed inputs into outputs; and (4) synapses, which are the electrical chemical contacts between each neuron. With *neural networks*, artificial intelligence experts seek to simulate the activity of human neurons in our brains through various *machine learning* systems.

nonlinearity (educational technology)

This is a dominating characteristic of *hypertext* and exploratory *hypermedia applications* in which the content is structured in a nonsequential fashion. This allows the user to go through the content according to his or her own desire or choices and follow the links at will, without being constrained by the path that a developer would want taken. Examples of sequentially structured information include most traditional novels, stories, films, as well as structured-path *multimedia applications*. Originally conceived of in Vannevar Bush's *Memex*, this characteristic of nonlinearity is best exemplified with what we know of today as the *Internet*.

Nurnberg Funnel (constructivism)

According to John M. Carroll in books published in the 1990s, *The Nurnberg Funnel: Designing Minimalist Instruction for Practi-cal Computer Skill* and *Minimalism Beyond the Nurnberg Funnel,* the Nurnberg funnel is a legend of an actual funnel used to "pour" instructional content into the learner's brain. Of course, Carroll believes that such a funnel is neither possible nor practical. As an alternative, Carroll posited his theory of *minimalism,* also referred to as the *minimalist model.* Minimalism is an *instructional design* approach of Carroll, a strategy that focuses on how to create effective training and user materials to support computer applications. As such, minimalism is sometimes referred to as the *minimalist model.* Following in the tradition of Malcolm Knowles's *andragogy,* with its emphasis on learner background, Carroll's minimalism focuses on the need to create content that builds upon the learner's past knowledge and experience. Carroll believes that the learner is not a "blank slate" nor is his or her brain a container in which knowledge is to be poured by the instructor through a funnel (i.e., the *Nurnberg funnel*). This sort of instructional strategy is neither effective nor practical.

Carroll's minimalism is *learner-centric* as opposed to *instructor-centric.* It is in the constructivist tradition of Jerome Bruner's *discovery learning* and Jean Piaget's *genetic epistemology.* Its five postulates are as follows: (1) Have learners begin performing meaningful tasks as soon as possible. (2) Minimize the amount of background materials as much as possible and allow the learners to fill in the gaps themselves with information that they will need to perform the tasks. (3) Allow the learners to make errors and recover from errors in the learning module. (4) Have all learning activities per module be self-contained and independent of a particular sequence preordained by the instructor. (5) Have all learning modules be directly tied to real tasks the learners would perform on the job. In short, don't let the instructor or the instructional materials get in the way of the learner's natural ability to learn. Instead, focus on activities that are learner-directed and applicable to the actual activities that the learners perform on the job. While seeking to pour knowledge into the brains of learners who passively sit ready to be enlightened via the Nurnberg funnel, the instructor will become frustrated. The instructor will be unable to accomplish the instructional mis- sion: providing the learners with useful knowledge that they can immediately apply to job tasks.

objects with attributes and values (cognitivism)

An element (along with *problem spaces, search control, data chunking, production rules,* and *automatic subgoaling*) in Allen Newell's *Soar,* a *cognitive architecture* and *artificial intelligence* programming language, objects with attributes and values provide a single representation of temporary knowledge in *sensory memory*. Attributes represent *data chunks*. Within the program, the mission of the operator is to complete a goal. A goal is a result that an operator seeks to achieve from completing a set of tasks (i.e., the operator moving from an initial state to a final state or result). Arguing for a *unified theory of cognition,* Newell developed a set of principles for *cognitive processing* and human *problem solving* with Soar.

Soar stands for State, Operator, and Result. The other elements in Soar, besides objects with attributes and values, are defined as follows: *Problem spaces* are a single framework within which all tasks and subtasks associated with achieving a goal are to be resolved. As such, problem solving in Soar is a search through the problem space in which a learner applies an Operator to a State to

get a Result. Search control is the process of selecting appropriate problem spaces, states, and operators by comparing alternative paths to take. *Data chunking* is the process by which the program recalls information in *working memory* outside of the context in which the information first appeared. Production rules provide a single representation of permanent knowledge in *long-term memory. Automatic subgoaling* is a single mechanism for generating goals. As an attempt to construct a *unified theory of cognition,* Soar focuses on analyzing a task and all related subtasks and developing an effective and efficient means for completing the task and subtasks. Current Soar research is being conducted at Carnegie Mellon University, Ohio State University, University of Michigan, University of Southern California, University of Hertfordshire, and University of Nottingham.

observational learning (constructivism)

Albert Bandura's observational learning, first postulated in the mid–1960s and later enhanced as *social learning theory* in the mid–1970s, states that human learning occurs through the simple process of observing others' activities and imitating that behavior. More specifically, Bandura describes a four-step learning process: Step 1. The learner's attention is drawn to some aspect or activity occurring in the environment. This is known as the attentional process. Step 2. The learner retains a model of the behavior and stores it in long-term memory. This is known as the retention process. Step 3. The learner copies and imitates the behavior (i.e., *behavior modeling*) that he or she has retained. This is known as the behavioral production process. Step 4. The facilitator in the environment (i.e., teacher) attempts to reinforce the behavior through rewards and punishments in the hope that the behavior will be repeated later. This is known as the motivational process.

Though classified here as constructivist, Bandura's obvervational learning has aspects that relate to *cognitivism* and to learning as a *cognitive process*. This is especially evident in Step (2), in which Bandura regards retained information as being stored symbolically through mental images and verbalizations. Once this information is stored, retrieval can occur (in Step [3]) long after the initial observational learning event took place.

olfactory system (behaviorism)

This refers to the sensory cells in the nose and in regions of the brain that allow the organism to have the sense of smell. Because of interest to the *learning paradigm* of *behaviorism*, many experiments have been conducted to see how organisms perform at categorizing various smells. Many experiments have also been conducted on mother and baby monkeys and humans to determine if they are able to recognize each other based on a sense of smell. Adherents of *cognitivism* have also studied the relationship of smell and *memory*. In all cases, the underlying biological process is the same. It involves the conversion of a stimulus from the environment (e.g., smell of bread freshly baked) to an electrochemical nerve impulse that the brain can react to (e.g., the desire to taste the bread).

one-trial learning (behaviorism)

Edwin Ray Guthrie's one-trial learning is a principle closely related to his *contiguity theory* that accepted all of Aristotle's *laws of*

association, except the postulate regarding the *law of frequency*. Aristotle's postulate regarding frequency is that the more often two objects are experienced by an organism simultaneously, the more likely they will be remembered and learned. Guthrie rejected this notion. With Guthrie, one trial, one successful pairing of a stimulus with a response is sufficient for learning to occur by the organism. Given both his contiguity theory and his postulate regarding one-trial learning, Guthrie had to come up with his *recency principle*, which states that whatever the organism did last in the presence of a fixed set of stimuli will be repeated again when those stimuli recur.

To Thorndike and his theory of *connectionism*, learning occurs in small increments. Guthrie disagreed. To prove his point, Guthrie performed a series of experiments with cats in a *puzzle box*. He and his colleagues observed that the very last response that the animal provided (for example, backing into the pole versus hitting the pole with its paw) to get out of the puzzle box was the one repeated the next time the animal was placed in the box. In an attempt to quantify Guthrie's contiguity theory and his postulate regarding one-trial learning, William Kaye Estes's *stimulus sampling theory* used statistics and probabilities to predict the behavior of the organisms, though Estes included both one-trial learning and an incremental approach to learning in his formulation. This debate as to whether learning occurs all at once or in increments is known as the *continuity-noncontinuity controversy*.

on-the-job training (organizational learning)

Sometimes simply referred to as OJT, on-the-job training is the more modern, industry-oriented reference to *apprenticeship learning*. Also referred to as *direct instruction,* on-the-job training is one-on-one training at the job site, in which an expert who already knows how to perform a set of job tasks is directly instructing a novice on how to complete the job. This method of corporate training is still in wide use and is quite popular, for the likelihood of successful skills transfer is quite high. Its downside is that on-the-job training is human resource intensive and expensive, especially if many trainees need to learn the same set of job tasks at a time. Another downside of on-the-job training is that both the trainer and the trainee are, during the training, off the production line or away from the normal course of business activities to be accomplished on the job.

operant chamber (behaviorism)

In B.F. Skinner's experiments, an operant chamber is a controlled learning environment, typically a cage, where an animal (e.g., a pigeon or rat) can obtain food (the stimulus), by performing a particular response (e.g., pressing a lever). The operant chamber keeps track of the number of responses that the animal makes. For learning experiments with dogs and cats, Skinner created a *Skinner box*, which is a type of operant chamber. The main focus of Skinner's experiments is to study *operant conditioning* and the relationship between the stimulus and the response of the animal within a controlled environment, the operant chamber.

operant conditioning (behaviorism)

Operant conditioning is a behavioral learning theory in which a stimulus (e.g., food for the pigeon or rat) and a *reinforcer* (e.g., a light) are used by the experimenter to generate a specific response (e.g., pressing a lever). The goal of B.F. Skinner's *operant conditioning* is to achieve behavior shaping, or *behavior modeling*, so that the animal is rewarded for following a particular path or set of actions that is desired by the behavioral scientist. Typically, animal training has as its basis operant conditioning. The animal is provided immediately with a reward following a particular action. By using operant conditioning, the experimenter alters the behavior of the animal to perform along a desired path or result. When the animal is provided with a reward for performing the behavior, it is likely to repeat the *elicited behavior* on subsequent occasions. The experiment is performed in an *operant chamber*, often an enclosed cage, sometimes called a *Skinner box* (for dogs and cats), where the animal can obtain food by pressing a lever.

operative rules
(organizational learning)

This term refers to a set of communication rules within an organization that are quite similar to the *knowledge management* concept of *tacit knowledge*. In a study of cultural, learning, and communication aspects of organizations, Linda Smircich in 1983 defined organizational cognition as a system of shared knowledge and beliefs of individuals within the organization that are based upon common *knowledge structures* and *communication rules*. According to Maryan Schall in 1983, communication rules are tacit understandings among work groups within an organization that are based primarily on soft and transitory group choices rather than on strict and everlasting corporate laws.

According to Schall, there are two types of communication rules: *operative rules* and *formal rules*. Operative rules are those rules that members of a group agree upon as being relevant and "happening here" within their aspect of the organization. Operative rules are not easily identified and are seldom, if ever, formalized and made available across the organization. They tend to reside within the work group or set of allied work groups working on a project. Formal rules, on the other hand, are more explicit rules found in corporate documents and *knowledge bases*. They are often shared via *Web-based knowledge transfer* systems.

orchestrated immersion (cognitivism)

One of the three types of instructional methods for *brain-based learning*, orchestrated immersion is the process of involving learners in a rich, complex learning environment. It involves developing complex learning environments that immerse the students completely into the learning activity. A complex learning environment is highly interactive, with the students performing at multiple levels as they make connections and construct meaning. Orchestrated immersion may also involve putting the students in a simulated local setting, such as a simulated Prague for an immersion into Czech language and culture. The other two types of brain-based learning methods are *active processing* (when the learner analyzes and becomes aware of the form, meaning, and motivation behind *knowledge acquisition*) and *relaxed alertness* (minimizing learner fear, while retaining a rich educational experience).

In Renate and Geoffrey Caine's book *Making Connections*, the close relationship between the way the brain works and the way people like to learn is explained within a brain-based learning approach. Brain-based learning is closely related to *metacognition*, which is being conscious of and aware of what one has learned. The brain is seen as an immensely powerful processor. Brain-based learning attempts to make the brain work in the way it should work. As long as the brain is not constrained from doing its normal work, learning will take place. Traditional rote learning (from the *industrial age educational paradigm*), however, inhibits learning by punishing the brain's natural processing activity. For brain-based learning to take place, the teacher must create a realistic context for learning (a rich learning environment that facilitates orchestrated immersion). The teacher must let students work in teams and work through mistakes themselves, which allows for continuing assessment of how they learn and why they learn.

organizational cognition (organizational learning)

In a study of cultural, learning, and communication aspects of organizations, Linda Smircich in 1983 defined organizational cognition as a system of shared knowledge and beliefs of individuals within the organization that are based upon common *knowledge structures* and *communication rules*. Other researchers have elaborated upon Smircich's organizational cognition in relation to *shared cognitive maps, negotiated belief structures, transactive memory,* and *organizational memory.*

For proponents of *cognitive behaviorism,* a *cognitive map* is important for studying *learning and performance*. A cognitive map is the body of knowledge that an organism or *agent* has about the surrounding environment. It is a mental picture that allows the organism to navigate through various paths within that environment. A cognitive map is also closely related to Roger Schank's concept of *schema*. An important aspect of Schank's theories of learning, including *conceptual dependency theory, contextual dependency theory* and *script theory*, schema refer to a *knowledge structure* that is created in the mind as humans experience new things in the environment and from which humans create scripts. Schema is important to an understanding of how language processing and higher thinking works within Schank's script theory.

According to Kim Langfield-Smith in 1992, shared cognitive maps are based upon the shared knowledge and belief systems of the entire organization as well as those of specific subcultural groups used for daily interactions and group *decision making*. Ultimately, according to Langfield-Smith, organizations share cognitive maps that are primarily domain specific and transitory (i.e., not of long duration). Some maps are thus related to a specific subculture, whereas others span the organization, are shared by all, and tend to be more explicit and of longer duration. According to James Walsh and Liam Fahey in 1986, negotiated belief structures are the configurations of power and beliefs within an organization that are at the root of corporate *decision making*.

Also related to organizational cognition, Daniel Wegner's theory of transactive memory elaborated upon in 1995 is a network model for describing shared cognitive maps, by which individuals in the organization access shared memory in much the same fashion as a group of networked computers share memory. This theory falls squarely in line with *information processing theory* and *network models* such as the *PDP Memory Model* in which human cognition and memory are described in computer terms and relations. Anand, Manz and Glick in 1998 adapted Wegner's theory of transactive memory and applied it to an *organizational memory* approach to understanding organizational cognition. These researchers define organizational memory as knowledge known by group members through their interactions and communications (i.e., *tacit knowledge*) and knowledge extant and available to individuals in the organization through *knowledge bases* (i.e., *explicit knowledge*).

organizational learning

This reference book uses organizational learning as a broad category for educational and *learning paradigms* that are to be implemented in organizations. Organizational learning as a term itself refers to learning that occurs by individuals and by groups and teams within the business enterprise. A few examples of organizational learning theories are Chris Argyris's *double loop learning*, Reg Reeves's *action learning*, and Edward de Bono's *CoRT thinking* and *Six Thinking Hats*. Organizational learning is slightly different from Peter Senge's *learning organization*, which is learning by the organization as a total entity or system. The distinction is not always easily or clearly made by writers within the *knowledge management* discipline and, as a result, there exists a good deal of confusion among them as they discuss the terms.

Edgar Schein and his colleagues at the MIT Center for Organizational Learning (founded in 1991) at the Sloan School of Management established in 1995 a Society of Organizational Learning, which has a set of guiding principles helpful in understanding what is meant by organizational learning as a paradigm for change in business. These principles are: (1) all humans have a drive to learn, which organizations should try to encourage; (2) learning is a social activity and requires a learning community that should exist within the organization; (3) learning communities are the nucleus and the source of successful organizations; (4) successful organizations are set up to be in harmony with human, social, and natural needs and requirements; (5) organizations must foster individual and collective capabilities to resolve complex, interdependent issues that continually recur within the enterprise; and (6) learning communities that include multiple organizations increase the capacity for organizational change and development. These principles of organizational learning are key drivers for building learning organizations and for creating *business transformation* and organizational change.

organizational memory (organizational learning)

This term refers to an enhancement of Daniel Wegner's theory of transactive memory as it is applied by Anand, Manz and Glick in 1998 to the entire corporate enterprise's organizational memory. Wegner's theory of transactive memory elaborated upon in 1995 is a network model for describing *shared cognitive maps*, in which individuals in the organization access shared memory in much the same fashion as a group of networked computers share memory. This theory falls squarely in line with *information processing theory* and *network models* such as the *PDP Memory Model* in which human cognition and memory are described in computer terms and relations. Anand, Manz and Glick further adapt Wegner's theory of transactive memory and apply it to a *knowledge management* and *organizational memory* approach to understanding *organizational cognition*. These researchers define organizational memory as knowledge known by group members through their interactions and communications (i.e., *tacit knowledge*) and knowledge extant and available to individuals in the organization through *knowledge bases* (i.e., *explicit knowledge*). They recommend that organizations utilize *computer-mediated communication*, including *e-mail, videoconferencing,* and *decision support systems* to facilitate and enhance the enterprise's organizational memory.

originality theory (behaviorism)

Irving Maltzman's originality theory, espoused in the early 1960s, is a behaviorist study of what makes up human creativity. Through a specific set of *behavior modeling* activities, he believed that creativity in humans could be increased. He noted three ways to increase creativity: (1) Present an uncommon stimulus situation in which conventional responses are not available. (2) Evoke different responses to the same stimulus situation. (3) Evoke uncommon responses as text responses. Maltzman's experiments to evoke creativity were through word association tasks. His focus was more on language creativity rather than on other aspects of creativity, such as drawing, sculpting, or musical composition. He concluded that creativity could be increased by means of the practice of evoking uncommon responses in word associations.

overt responding (behaviorism)

This term refers to the second of a set of learner behaviors that are to be followed within *programmed learning*, also more popularly known as *self-paced instruction*. Though first developed by Sidney L. Pressey in the 1920s, and modeled after the *reinforcement theory* implicit within the *learning paradigm* of *behaviorism*, programmed learning was rediscovered and popularized by B.F. Skinner. Skinner's programmed learning involves the following learner behaviors. (1) *Small Steps*. Learners obtain small amounts of information and proceed from one task to the next in an orderly, step-by-step fashion. (2) *Overt Responding*. Learners must provide an overt response to a problem or step so that correct responses are reinforced and incorrect responses corrected. (3) *Immediate Feedback*. Learners are provided with an immediate response to let them know whether they have answered or performed correctly or incorrectly. (4) *Self-Pacing*. Learners are to work through the programmed learning activity at their own pace. Programmed learning techniques have been employed and reused in many current *computer-based training, Web-based training, multimedia applications,* and *electronic performance support systems.* Programmed learning has been proven to be an effective technique for *skills management* and *organizational learning.*

P

pansophism (constructivism)

A precursor to a constructivist approach to education, the seventeenth-century Czech educational reformer, John Comenius, espoused a universal knowledge, or pansophism, that would teach children better and bring global understanding and peace. His goal was to have teachers use children's senses instead of memorization to learn language and new concepts. In 1631, he wrote a book entitled *The Gates of Tongues*. In 1638, he was invited to Sweden to enact his educational theories and reforms. He also published in 1659 an early picture book, "Orbis Sensualium Pictus," that labeled for children objects in both Latin and their native language. Comenius's pansophism was an early response to John Locke's *empiricism* and his philosophy of education, which affirmed that humans obtain knowledge from objects in the real world that are perceived through the senses.

parallel processing (educational technology)

In the world of networked computers, parallel processing refers to an array of computer networks in which many events are considered and acted upon by the systems at once. In other words, with parallel processing, more than one computer processor is devoted to executing the same program or same sets of programs simultaneously, or in parallel. By having many processors working in parallel, more sophisticated, media-rich applications such as *multimedia* and *hypermedia* can be consumed by users. In relation to *artificial intelligence* systems, *agents* that simulate *cognition* utilize parallel processing techniques to perform an array of *problem-solving* activities. The *Internet* itself is an example of the effective usage of parallel processing systems. In contrast, an example of *serial processing* is the single desktop PC that is not attached to a computer network and that performs one particular computer task at a time.

parallel thinking (organizational learning)

Edward de Bono's parallel thinking, based upon his 1994 book of the same name, is a challenge to the Socratic thinking of the Greeks that de Bono regards as adversarial and argumentative. According to de Bono, adversarial thinking does not create anything new. It does not help individuals discover new things or think creatively. Parallel thinking, in contrast, is what de Bono regards as cooperative and coordinated thinking among groups of individuals focused on coming up

146

with practical solutions to real-world problems. De Bono regards utilizing his *Six Thinking Hats* as a method for achieving parallel thinking.

According to de Bono, contradictory statements or thoughts should be laid out in parallel. The approach of dismissing one idea in favor of another is counterproductive and does not produce solutions to today's business problems. By having all ideas brought up by the individuals in the group be considered valid and looked at in parallel, new and creative ideas are allowed to surface and not be easily set aside. Traditional argumentative thinking, in which there are winning and losing ideas, is highly counterproductive. Parallel thinking, on the other hand, keeps all ideas on the table and produces better results.

passive learning (cognitivism)

A term with an obviously negative connotation, passive learning, as opposed to *active learning*, has as its learning focus the instructor over the student. The standard teaching method for passive learning is the traditional lecture, whereby the students are, in effect, bench-bound listeners, passively consuming the content presented by the instructor according to the structure that he or she created. Opposed to passive learning is active learning, also known as *discovery learning*. Active learning emphasizes the intrinsic motivation and self-sponsored curiosity of the learner who fashions content and is actively involved in its formation. Active learning shifts the focus of content structuring from the teacher to the learner. By being actively involved in the shaping of the content, the learners gain a far better understanding than they would otherwise of the information. The opposite of active learning (i.e., passive learning) occurs when the teacher completely shapes the content for the students and provides that information to the passively listening student. The student takes notes, memorizes the content, and feeds it back to the teacher for the test. In the fifth-century B.C., the Chinese philosopher Lao-tse simply defined the essence of active learning when he said: "If you tell me, I will listen. If you show me, I will see. But if you let me experience, I will learn."

PDP memory model (cognitivism)

Related to *information processing theory*, the PDP memory model is in actuality a family of *memory* models that share similar characteristics and define the brain's memory function roughly in relation to computer inputs, outputs, and internal processing activities. PDP stands for parallel distributed processing. In a human brain, parallel distributed processing refers to *cognitive processes* that are occurring simultaneously at multiple locations within the brain. The PDP memory model is a *network model*, composed of a highly interconnected set of units, all of which are reacting to various environmental inputs. Each processing area in turn has output functions connecting to other parts of the brain. As units are activated, pathways in the brain are created. Each new pathway is a new memory. PDP is an attempt to model human *cognition* within a *unified theory of cognition*. From an *artificial intelligence* perspective, the PDP memory model is a *cognitive psychology* theory that is equally applicable to human intelligence as well as computer intelligence. A general *cognitive architecture* for PDP was first and most extensively elaborated upon in the mid–1980s by D.E. Rumelhart, J.L. McClelland, and colleagues at MIT in their book, *Parallel Distributed Processing: Explorations in the Microstructure of Cognition*.

pedagogy (constructivism)

As opposed to Malcom Knowles's *andragogy*, which is the study of how adults learn most efficiently and effectively, pedagogy in general terms is the study of how children learn best. A variety of learning theories within the *learning paradigms* of *cognitivism, constructivism, behaviorism*, and *humanism* have posed methods that enhance pedagogy. Past traditional theories of education have viewed pedagogy from an *instructor-centric* orientation, in which the learner is a passive recipient to the knowledge supplied by the teacher, most typically via a lecture-oriented approach and a highly structured *curriculum design*. More recently, many constructivist theories have taken on Knowles's postulates for adult learning and applied them to pedagogy.

It could be argued that one of the main problems with traditional public education at the K–12 level is the perpetuation of the traditional pedagogic model, with its emphasis on passive, rote, nonsocial, non-contextual learning from an authoritarian type of instructor whose primary means of student motivation is the grade. It could also be argued that at all levels, the use of andragogic elements, including anchors, case studies, role-playing, simulations, self-evaluations, peer evaluations, are most helpful to the pedagogic learning process. Instructors' adoption of the andragogic role of coach and facilitator appears to be an improvement to the learning experience for all levels over that of the role of authoritarian dispenser of information as lecturer, grader, and primary source of knowledge. Current trends are that methods such as Bruner's discovery learning are most effective for enhancing pedagogic learning. Our children today seem far more mature, far more knowledgeable and worldly, than their parents were as children. Students seem to thrive when placed in an andragogic, discovery learning environment.

Many of the reforms being attempted in K–12 schools involve the movement from pedagogy to andragogy for all learning levels. From Knowles's perspective, andragogy was a way to improve education for adults. Thirty years later, andragogic learning methods are being applied on a fairly broad basis to pedagogical learning environments. The success of this approach for all levels of learners is still a subject of debate and discussion. Without Knowles's initial distinction of andragogy and pedagogy, there never would have been a debate. With Knowles, a paradigm shift occurred from *instructor-centric* to *learner-centric* learning.

perceptual field (humanism)

An aspect of Max Wertheimer's *Gestalt theory*, perceptual field is a range of percep-

tions that an individual experiences over a lifetime. As one grows and develops, as one's ability to apply a *perceptual organization* to one's experiences increases, the perceptual field expands as new and repeated experiences are added and included within one's *consciousness*. Perceptual field is also related to Kurt Lewin's concept of *life space*, which is in turn based upon field theory in physics. Field theory, in brief, is the study of dynamic, interrelated systems, wherein nothing exists in isolation. In Gestalt theory, no single event can be separated from the whole life. Whatever occurs to the individual in life shapes that individual and influences all aspects of the life experience. Learning occurs as one's perceptual field expands.

perceptual learning (humanism)

According to James J. Gibson, perceptual learning is an active process of *information pickup*. Developed by Gibson from the 1950s through the 1970s, information pickup theory is a Gestalt approach to perception and learning. Gestalt, the German word for shape or configuration, is one way to describe how humans perceive the world as a meaningful whole, instead of as isolated stimuli. To Gibson, the act of perception is a dynamic between the organism and the physical environment. In terms of perceptual learning, Gibson postulates that the learner must have a rich, complex learning environment within which to interact. Perceptual learning should be based upon visual cues that the learner obtains from interacting in the environment. To increase perceptual learning, the instructor must provide realistic settings within which the learners can learn and perform a series of activities.

perceptual organization (humanism)

Within Max Wertheimer's *Gestalt theory*, perceptual organization is a reference to the structure, form, and meaning that an individual imposes upon his or her perceptions of the phenomenological world. In 1912, Max Wertheimer, along with his colleagues Wolfgang Kohler and Kurt Koffka of Germany, began the movement that opposed *behaviorism* and favored a *holistic* approach to how humans learn. In contrast to behaviorism, which focused on objective, *molecular* behavior that could be broken apart and analyzed, Gestalt theory focused on subjective, *molar* behavior that could not be separated from the individual's shaping influence of human perception.

Gestalt, the German word for shape or configuration, is a way of describing how humans perceive the world as a meaningful whole rather than as isolated stimuli. Humans see complete shapes instead of merely lines, incomplete shapes, and patches of color. To Gestaltists, the phenomenological experience that each human has is greater than the multitude of individual parts that make up the experiences. All of these experiences make up what Kurt Lewin refers to as *life space*. As such, Gestalt theory is an application of field theory from physics. Field theory, in brief, is the study of dynamic, interrelated systems wherein nothing exists in isolation. In Gestalt theory, no event, no single part can be separated from the whole. Whatever occurs to an individual human shapes that individual and influences all aspects of that person.

In Gestalt theory, the focus is on the totality, not on the individual parts. *Consciousness* determines behavior. Human values, beliefs, and attitudes influence tremendously human conscious experience. Learning is a lifelong experience. Learning occurs through insight. After pondering a problem for a while, after considering all of the ramifications of it, a human reaches a solution all at once. Gaps and incongruities are important factors that stimulate learning and ultimately lead to problem resolution. Instruction should be based upon the laws of perceptual organization, which Wertheimer lists as proximity, closure, similarity, and simplicity. As the individual's life and learning experiences evolve, as his or her *perceptual field* expands, so too is one's perceptual organization dynamic, active, and ever-changing.

performance objectives (educational technology)

An important set of planning information for the creation of *intelligent tutoring systems* and other types of learning applications, performance objectives are specific criteria developed by *instructional design* specialists who define what tasks the learners are expected to perform with the application. Performance objectives are typically tied to the learner's *level of competence*. Level of competence refers to the knowledge and skill level of a given learner as he or she is going through the learning application.

In order to determine human performance for specific sets of tasks being attempted by the learner, most intelligent tutoring systems employ *performance tracking* mechanisms to determine the user's level of competence per task. A type of *artificial intelligence* application, intelligent tutoring systems are computer programs embedded into *computer-aided instruction, computer-based training,* or *Web-based training* that provides *cognitive coaching* and guidance to the learner as he or she goes through each exercise within the program. These systems presuppose a knowledge of the learner's ever-increasing abilities and progress through the application and involve tracking mechanisms (i.e., performance tracking) that determine the learner's knowledge and experience levels (i.e., level of competence) at each stage within the learning application.

Intelligent tutoring systems provide helpful hints and support as the learning exercises become more difficult and the learning path more arduous for the user. The ultimate goal of these systems is to simulate human tutoring and coaching strategies as the user's level of competence increases. Performance objectives are thus used to ensure that the learners have met the criteria anticipated by the instructional design specialists who developed the learning application, whether it is in the form of computer-aided instruction, computer-based training, or Web-based training.

performance tracking (educational technology)

As a subsystem within *computer-based training, Web-based training, electronic performance support systems*, or a *multimedia application*, performance tracking records the learner's responses to various queries and problems posed within the learning application. An important component often included within the *instructional design* process, performance tracking allows the developers of the applications to track learner needs, *level of competence*, and performance in relation to a set of *performance objectives*. It is also an important aspect of *intelligent tutoring systems*. These systems presuppose a knowledge of the learner's ever-increasing abilities and progress through the application and involve tracking mechanisms (i.e., performance tracking) that determine the learner's knowledge and experience level at each stage within the learning application.

personal curriculum design (constructivism)

Closely related to Ivan Illich's concept of *deschooling* in the 1970s, personal curriculum design seeks to refocus education on the learners and their own pursuit of knowledge. With personal curriculum design, curriculum choices and methods for completing the curriculum are made by the learners instead of by the instructor. In the 1970s, D. Maley, in his "Maryland Plan," sought to provide an example of a personal curriculum design for industrial arts and technology education. Within this plan, Maley described a program whereby learners chose personally relevant activities and selected their own methods for completing particular industrial arts tasks that were preprogrammed events laid out by the instructor.

personal mastery (organizational learning)

One of the disciplines for the *learning organization* in Peter Senge's *The Fifth Discipline*, personal mastery is a process of understanding better one's personal vision about life in relation to the business organization. It involves the abilities of focusing personal energy, developing patience, and perceiving more objectively things that occur at home and in the workplace. Personal mastery involves the act of determining what is most important in life and how to be of service to our fellow humans.

phase sequence (cognitivism)

According to Donald O. Hebb, all infants are born with a *neural network* that is loosely organized with random *neuron* interconnections. As the child develops, the neural network becomes more organized and better able to interact with the environment, from which the child obtains a multitude of inputs. Each environmental object the child encounters through the senses fires a package of neurons known as a *cell assembly*. Cell assemblies are organized sets of neurons linked together and activated by an environmental object or event. Just as reactions to environmental objects form cell assemblies, so too do cell assemblies interconnect to form phase sequences. Cell assemblies that consistently follow one another sequentially in time form a phase sequence. A phase sequence is a sequence of cell assemblies, a sequence of thought that follows a logical order. Once cell assemblies and phase sequences become more fully developed in the human, a framework for learning is built and the human is able to learn with relative ease and quickness. Once these learning building blocks are fully formed, the adult is able to think and learn with *creativity* and insight.

phenomenonology (humanism)

In 1912, Max Wertheimer, along with his colleagues Wolfgang Kohler and Kurt Koffka of Germany, began the movement that opposed *behaviorism* and favored a *holistic* approach to how humans learn. In contrast to behaviorism, which focused on objective, *molecular* behavior that could be broken apart and analyzed, *Gestalt theory*, also known as phenomenology, focused on subjective, *molar* behavior that could not be separated from the individual's shaping influence of human perception. As the behaviorists looked back to a radical form of *empiricism* as their philosophical foundation, the phenomenologists looked back to Kant's theory of *innate categories of thought* and of the shaping influence of the individual's perceptions of his or her experiences in the environment. In Kant's *epistemology*, the mind itself is the source of human knowledge. Gestalt, the German word for shape or configuration, is a way of describing how humans perceive the world of phenomena as a meaningful whole rather than as isolated stimuli. Humans see complete shapes (i.e., buildings, houses, trees, and lakes). Humans do not see merely lines, incomplete shapes, and patches of color. To adherents of phenomenology, dissection and analysis of individual parts is a distortion of reality. The whole is greater than the sum of the parts. Because the Gestaltist's focus of study is often human perceptual phenomena, Gestalt psychology is thus referred to as *phenomenology*. To Gestaltists, the phenomenological experience that each human has is greater than the multitude of individual parts that make up the experiences. All of these experiences make up what Kurt Lewin refers to as *life space*. As such, phenomenology is an application of field theory from physics. Field theory, in brief, is the study of dynamic, interrelated systems, wherein nothing exists in isolation. In phenomenology, no event, no single part can be separated from the whole. Whatever occurs to an individual human shapes that individual and influences all aspects of that person. In phenomenology, the focus is on the totality, not on the individual parts. Each individual human shapes and influences the world of phenomena through his or her *consciousness*. Consciousness determines behavior. Consciousness determines the phenomenological experience.

physical artifacts (humanism)

These belong to one of two types of artifacts that aid human *cognition*. The other type of artifact is the cognitive artifact. In his book from the mid–1990s, *Things that Make Us Smart: Defending Human Attributes in the Age of the Machine*, Donald A. Norman describes physical artifacts that we interact with, such as pencils, calculators, and computers that are important for the experiential mode of cognition, as well as *cognitive artifacts*, such as reading, math, and language that are important for the *reflective mode of cognition*. The experiential mode of cognition is more of a subconscious mode of thinking that occurs as we experience events and objects in our contemporary work and learning environment. The reflective mode of cognition refers to a higher order thinking, similar to *metacognition*, in which the learner takes in ideas encountered from the world, thinks through them, reflects upon them, and reuses them to construct new ideas and knowledge.

According to Norman, contemporary education focuses on the use of computers, technology, and *multimedia* (the physical artifacts) that help us in regard to the experiential mode of cognition. Yet, he feels that these same physical artifacts can often inhibit learners with regard to thinking creatively and constructively by means of the reflective mode of cognition through reading, math, and language (the cognitive artifacts). Norman's concern about technology and its use in education is that it overemphasizes the experiential mode of cognition and seeks to immerse and entertain students instead of getting them to be thoughtful and reflective, thus strengthening the reflective mode of cognition.

PIGS (constructivism)

An acronym for the essential elements of *cooperative learning* as elaborated by brothers Roger T. Johnson and David W. Johnson of the University of Minnesota, *PIGS* stands for *P*ositive interdependence, *I*ndividual accountability, *G*roup interaction, and *S*ocial skills. Positive interdependence occurs when the learners become aware that they need each other to complete the learning task successfully. Individual accountability refers to the individual effort and instructor assessment required for the individual learner to complete successfully his or her role within the overall group mission. Group interaction is the *cognitive coaching* and sharing of information that the learners engage in during the learning activity. Social skills refer to techniques, methods, and traits that promote group interactions, including but not limited to leadership, *decision making*, trust-building, communication, and conflict management. The fruits of collaborative learning include learners being better able to think for themselves, think with others, investigate topics and share information, and make judgments and assessments about the information learned.

place learning (behaviorism)

Within the *learning paradigm* of *behaviorism*, learning is generally regarded as occurring as a result of *reinforcement* (i.e., reinforcement theory). However, according to Edward Chace Tolman, an adherent of *cognitive behaviorism*, learning is not necessarily a result of reinforcement. Organisms can employ either place learning or response learning to obtain a specific reinforcement. Place learning involves the organism creating a *cognitive map* of its environment. Once the organism has located an object, its creation of a cognitive map of the environment allows it to reach that object again more readily and through multiple paths. *Response learning* occurs when an organism learns a specific set of responses that solve a problem, at which time the experimenter provides a specific reinforcement. Tolman contends that place learners are quicker studies than response learners, and they are not dependent on the reinforcement to perform an action.

power law of practice (cognitivism)

Within John Anderson's postulate for *rational analysis* (human cognition optimizes the behavior adaptation of the organism to accomplish tasks in the environment), the power law of practice is one of three basic *signature* data for studying human *memory*,

thinking, and behavior, which is part of his *ACT theory*. The other two signatures are the *fan effect* and *categorization*. Simply stated, the power law of practice says that the more often one performs a particular task, the less time it takes the system or organism to accomplish it. The power law of practice is quite similar to *speed up learning* or *machine learning*. The fan effect means that the larger and tighter the fan of conceptual links in the brain to the task to be achieved, the more likely the central concept to accomplish that task will be activated in memory. *Categorization* is the Web (fan) of information that is organized in the brain, based upon the feedback obtained from the act of completing the task. The power law of practice states that humans (and systems) adapt their behavior as they acquire skills to accomplish needed tasks. As these skills are practiced repeatedly, the time it takes to complete them efficiently is greatly reduced.

practice field (organizational learning)

According to Peter Senge's *organizational learning* paradigm, a practice field within the *learning organization* is a place where a business coach and a set of learners can practice particular behaviors and skills off the field of play. In other words, they practice useful and positive skills off the field and later apply them on the playing field, i.e., in the live business arena. Utilizing a practice field allows the learners to stop in the midst of the action and examine both positive and negative behaviors that they are displaying on the field. They essentially freeze the action. They look at their performance. After having done a bit of analysis, they make enhancements to improve their level of play on the field.

Premack principle (behaviorism)

Also called the *probability differential hypothesis*, the Premack principle, of David Premack is an elaboration and enhancement of B.F. Skinner's behaviorist notions about *reinforcers*, *operant conditioning*, and the host of *reinforcement theories* within the *learning paradigm* of *behaviorism*. The question that Premack tries to respond to more specifically is, "what is a reinforcer?" In early reinforcement theories, a reinforcer is anything that reinforces behavior. For Hull, a reinforcer is anything that causes *drive reduction* in an organism. Generally speaking, a reinforcer is a stimulus, of which there are two types. A *primary reinforcer* is one that has as its basis the survival of the organism. A *secondary reinforcer* is a stimulus that is paired with a primary reinforcer. David Premack regards all of the organism's responses as potential reinforcers for behavior. According to the Premack principle, an oft-repeated activity of an organism can be utilized to reinforce an activity occurring less frequently.

With regard to reinforcers and their frequency of occurrence, the Premack principle, also known as the *probability-differential hypothesis*, has been questioned by the *disequilibrium hypothesis*. According to William Timberlake, the disequilibrum hypothesis postulates that each and all activities of an organism can be a reinforcer if the experimenter provides a *contingency schedule* whose purpose is to constrain the organism from accessing a particular activity. The contingency schedule creates in the organism a disequilibrium in which the restriction to activity access is itself a reinforcer.

primary reinforcer (behaviorism)

Most advocates of *reinforcement theory* have tried to provide a more specific response to the question, "what is a reinforcer?" In early reinforcement theories, a reinforcer is anything that reinforces behavior. For Hull, a reinforcer is anything that causes *drive reduction* in an organism. Generally speaking, a reinforcer is a stimulus, of which there are two types. A primary reinforcer is one that has as its basis the survival of the organism. A *secondary reinforcer* is a stimulus that is paired with a primary reinforcer. Both are important for understanding animal and human behavior. Pavlov firmly believed, based on his *classical conditioning* method, that

conditioning of the organism is dependent completely upon primary reinforcers.

principle of closure (humanism)

An important aspect of Gestalt theory, the principle of closure states that humans have a strong, universal tendency to complete incomplete perceptions and experiences. For example, if an individual perceives a set of lines that are broken, but nevertheless form a shape such as a rectangle or triangle, he or she will complete the figure and identify it as a rectangle or triangle. Thus, the individual provides a *perceptual organization* to that which is perceived or experienced. This perceptual organization is applied to all life experiences as the individual grows and learns and as the *perceptual field* expands. The principle of closure also follows the *law of Pragnanz*, which states that humans respond to the world of phenomena to make it as meaningful as possible given the current conditions and situation. In German, pragnanz mean "essence." A constant human goal is to provide meaning, essence, structure, and form to all of life's experiences.

probability differential hypothesis (behaviorism)

Also called the *Premack principle*, as elaborated by David Premack, the probability differential hypothesis is an attempt to further refine the definition of what is a *reinforcer*. According to this hypothesis, an oft-repeated activity of an organism can be utilized to reinforce an activity occurring less frequently. Premacks's probability differential hypothesis is an attempt to refine *reinforcement theory* from that of Hull (*drive reduction theory*), Skinner (*operant conditioning*), and Thorndike (*instrumental conditioning*).

problem-based learning (constructivism)

This is a curriculum design approach in which learners are expected to synthesize and construct knowledge to resolve problems based upon objectives and conditions that they themselves establish at the beginning of the class or module. Problem-based learning is developed and maintained by the Center for Problem Based Learning, which was created by the Illinois Mathematics and Science Academy to support *curriculum design* support for K–16 instructors who seek to conduct research, *knowledge sharing*, and training in problem-based learning methods and skills.

The method of problem-based learning is in opposition to the traditional *industrial age educational paradigm*, with its emphasis on a lecture-based, *instructor-centric* curriculum. Problem-based learning advocates regard this traditional approach in the vein of *curriculum as prescription*, as opposed to a more enlightened view of *curriculum as experience*. Curriculum as prescription focuses on the instructor as a transmitter of information with the learners as receivers of information provided linearly within a very structured environment. Curriculum as experience focuses on the learners as constructors of knowledge, with the teacher as a facilitator, with an emphasis on the whole rather than the parts provided within a flexible, informal learning environment. As such, problem-based learning is much in the same family of constructivist methods as that of Jerome Bruner's *discovery learning*, in which the emphasis is on the learner, who sets *learning objectives* and creates and structures the knowledge set to be learned.

problem solving (organizational learning)

In education, problem solving has been explored by a variety of educators and learning theorists going back to John Dewey in the 1920s. From a *discovery learning* perspective, performing problem-solving activities regarding real-life situations is how learners gain knowledge of mathematical and other principles. By applying principles to real-life experiences, learners become effective problem solvers.

From an *organizational learning* perspective, problem solving is closely related to ef-fective *decision making*. Chris Argyris's *action research* and *theory of action* and Edward de Bono's *lateral thinking*, *CoRT thinking*, and *Six Thinking Hats* all address the issue of corporate problem solving and decision making. Indeed, there are a plethora of theorists and researchers who focus on problem solving within academic and business organizations. Their findings tend to focus on the need for *creativity* and the need for *collaboration* in order for managers and other individuals in the organizations to be effective problem solvers and decision makers. Whether problem solving is regarded as a skill, an art, or a context of learning, it will continue to be a focus of theorists in both academe and business.

problem spaces (cognitivism)

In Allen Newell's Soar, a *cognitive architecture* and *artificial intelligence* programming language, problem spaces are represented as collections of tasks. The program begins by selecting a problem space and an initial state within the space. The final goal or end result of completing the set of tasks is a final state within the problem space. This process is repeatedly performed to move the operator from an initial state to a final state (i.e., a result). Arguing for a *unified theory of cognition*, Newell developed a set of principles for *cognitive processing* and human *problem solving* with Soar. Soar stands for State, Operator, And Result. Other Soar elements besides problem spaces are *search control*, *data chunking*, *objects with attributes and values*, *production rules*, and *automatic subgoaling*.

procedural knowledge (cognitivism)

An important component of John Anderson's *Act theory*, which is a *cognitive architecture* describing how humans think, procedural knowledge is the knowledge needed to perform tasks. It is skills knowledge as opposed to *declarative knowledge*, which is conceptual knowledge. Procedural knowledge is stored in *procedural memory*; whereas declarative knowledge is stored in *declarative memory*. Both procedural and declarative memory are types of *long-term memory*, as opposed to *working memory*.

procedural memory (cognitivism)

In John Anderson's *ACT theory*, procedural memory stores *procedural knowledge* that an individual uses to perform tasks, as opposed to *declarative memory*, which stores *declarative knowledge* (i.e., conceptual knowledge) in a particular format that can be further analyzed and broken down. John Anderson's ACT theory, a *cognitive architecture*, states that human *cognition* is an interplay of procedural, declarative, and working memory. *Declarative memory* is a type of *long-term memory* that stores facts and ideas in a semantic network structure (i.e., a *network model*). *Procedural memory*, another type of *long-term memory*, takes sequences of declarative knowledge in the form of *productions* and makes further logical inferences about them. Each production contains a set of conditions and actions found within declarative memory. *Working memory*, or short-term conscious thought, retrieves declarative information of facts and ideas, carries out task sequences found in procedural memory, and adds new information gathered from the environment, forming new sequences that are then stored in procedural memory.

production rules (cognitivism)

An element (along with *problem spaces, search control, data chunking, objects with attributes and values,* and *automatic subgoaling*) in Alan Newell's *Soar*, a *cognitive architecture* and *artificial intelligence* programming language, production rules provide a single representation of permanent knowledge in *long-term memory*. Within the program, the mission of the operator is to complete a goal. A goal is a result that an operator seeks to achieve in order to complete a set of tasks (i.e., the operator moving from an initial state to a final state or result). Arguing for a *unified theory of cognition*, Newell developed a set of principles for *cognitive processing* and human *problem solving*

with Soar. Soar stands for State, Operator, And Result.

The other elements in Soar, besides production rules, are defined as follows. *Problem spaces* are a single framework within which all tasks and subtasks associated with achieving a goal are to be resolved. As such, problem solving in Soar is a search through the problem space in which the program applies an Operator (set of operations) to a State to get a Result. *Search control* is the process of selecting appropriate problem spaces, states, and operators by comparing alternative paths to take. *Data chunking* is the process by which learners recall information in *working memory* outside of the context that the information first appeared. *Objects with attributes and values* provide a single representation of temporary knowledge in *working memory*. Attributes are data chunks. *Automatic subgoaling* is a single mechanism for generating goals. As an attempt to construct a *unified theory of cognition*, Soar focuses on analyzing a task and all related subtasks and developing an effective and efficient means for completing the task and subtasks. Current Soar research is being conducted at Carnegie Mellon University, Ohio State University, University of Michigan, University of Southern California, University of Hertfordshire, and University of Nottingham.

productions (cognitivism)

In John Anderson's *ACT theory*, a *cognitive architecture*, productions are representations of knowledge regarding task performance stored in long-term, *procedural memory*, which is one of two types of *long-term memory*. *Declarative memory* stores facts and ideas in a particular format. *Procedural memory* sequences and organizes knowledge from declarative memory in the form of productions. Productions include conditions and actions needed for completing task sequences. Productions are a means for the human brain to represent procedural knowledge in memory.

productive thinking (humanism)

According to a book of the same name published in 1945, productive thinking is Max Werthweimer's contribution to the application of *Gestalt theory* to education, learning, and *problem solving*. In 1912 Max Wertheimer, along with his colleagues, Wolfgang Kohler and Kurt Koffka of Germany, began the movement that opposed *behaviorism* and favored a *holistic* approach to how humans learn. In contrast to behaviorism, which focused on objective, *molecular* behavior that could be broken apart and analyzed, Gestalt theory focused on subjective, *molar* behavior that could not be separated from the individual's shaping influence of human perception.

Because the focus of study for Gestaltists is often human perceptual phenomena, Gestalt psychology is also referred to as *phenomenology*. To Gestaltists, the phenomenological experience that each human has is greater than the multitude of individual parts that make up the experiences. *Consciousness* determines behavior. Human values, beliefs, and attitudes influence tremendously the human conscious experience. Learning is a lifelong experience. Within Wertheimer's productive thinking approach, learning occurs through insight. After pondering a problem for a while, after considering all of the ramifications of it, a human reaches a solution all at once.

According to Wertheimer, humans do not learn by memorization of facts, by learning rules, which are quickly and easily forgotten, or by using logic. Instead, learning occurs according to Gestalt principles through an understanding of the entire problem considered by the individual without having an answer imposed by someone else. The answer comes to the individual as a sudden insight, after pondering all of the ramifications, possibilities, and effects beforehand. The instructor can guide learners toward insights, but the insight must come from the students, as they consider the nature of the problem and come up with their own set of solutions that are influenced and shaped by their life experiences.

programmed learning (behaviorism)

Though first developed by Sidney L. Pressey in the 1920s, and modeled after the *reinforcement theory* implicit within the *learning paradigm* of *behaviorism*, programmed learning was rediscovered and popularized by B.F. Skinner. Skinner's programmed learning involves the following set of learner behaviors. (1) *Small Steps*. Learners obtain small amounts of information and proceed from one task to the next in an orderly, step-by-step fashion. (2) *Overt Responding*. Learners must provide an overt response to a problem or step so that correct responses are reinforced and incorrect responses corrected. (3) *Immediate Feedback*. Learners are provided with an immediate response to let them know whether they have answered or performed correctly or incorrectly. (4) *Self-Pacing*. Learners work through the programmed learning activity at their own pace. Programmed learning techniques have been employed and reused in many current *computer-based training, Web-based training, multimedia applications,* and *electronic performance support systems*. Programmed learning has been proven to be an effective technique for *skills management* and *organizational learning*.

progressive education (humanism)

As the basis of John Dewey's progressive, pragmatic, and humanistic philosophy of education of the 1920s, progressive education postulates that learning is developing and that developing is learning, that truth is an instrument that humans utilize to solve problems and promote changes in a global society. As such, Dewey's progressive education is also called *instrumentalism*. Rejecting authoritarian teaching methods, Dewey regarded education as a tool to be used to integrate the citizen into the democratic culture and to change that culture to make it more democratic, more progressive. Thus, the individual human becomes an instrument to the progress of a democratic society. Dewey's progressive education has had a profound and lasting impact on education to this day, and his philosophy was regarded globally as radical and influential.

project zero (constructivism)

Developed by a research group that has conducted an extended set of projects at Harvard University's Graduate School of Education, project zero investigates learning processes to help individuals, communities, schools, and organizations create self-reflective, creative, and independent thinkers. Begun in 1967 by Nelson Goodman, and co-directed since 1972 by David Perkins and Howard Gardner (theorist of *multiple intelligences*), project zero is dedicated to understanding human cognitive development and the process of learning in the arts and other disciplines. Current project zero investigations include teaching for understanding, creating thinking cultures in classrooms, instituting assessment as an ongoing school and curriculum enhancement activity, using new computer technologies to enhance the classroom, bringing artists into the schools as teachers and mentors, and devising games for learner *collaboration* and *creativity*. The name of project zero came in 1967 from the perception that schools were doing "zero" regarding considering arts learning as a serious activity worthy of inclusion in the *curriculum design*. Later, project zero looked at all disciplines (arts, humanities, sciences, and social sciences) and investigated how to enhance deep critical and creative thinking of students.

psychological tools (constructivism)

These are an important aspect of Len Vygotsky's *social development theory*, which is an attempt to define human *cognition* in relation to the social interaction of the individual within his or her culture. To Vygotsky, human *consciousness* is completely a result of socialization and *enculturation*. For Vygotsky, social interaction plays a fundamental role in the development of all of the individual's cognitive abilities, including thinking, learning, and communicating. Instead of reacting to the environment directly in a way that an animal would react, humans filter their experiences through cultural and social lenses. Human thoughts, actions, and experiences are all socially and culturally mediated. Humans have what Vygotsky calls *psychological tools*. These include various systems for counting, mnemonic techniques, algebraic symbol systems, works of art, language, writing, schemes, diagrams, maps, and technical drawings. Of all of the tools available to humans, the most valuable to the species is language. Through language, humans construct their reality. Language itself is both an individual and a social phenomenon. With words, humans define and characterize their life experiences. Words allow humans to move from subjective thoughts to objective ones to be shared in society.

purposive behaviorism (behaviorism)

Later called cognitive behaviorism, Edward Chace Tolman's purposive behaviorism postulates that there is a purpose for all behavior of organisms. Looking at stimuli and responses alone is not an effective way of studying animal and human behavior. Unlike many other behaviorists, such as Skinner who believed in *operant conditioning*, Tolman's purposive behaviorism began to theorize about internal mental aspects of behavior. For example, as rats go through mazes, they create a *cognitive map* that they rely upon to successfully perform the task of getting through the maze and obtaining the reward (i.e., food). Tolman also referred to this purposeful behavior as *molar behavior*.

puzzle box (behaviorism)

Edward Thorndike's *puzzle box*, an early precursor of B.F. Skinner's Skinner box, is a controlled learning environment, typically a small, very confining box with a pole sticking up in the middle or a chain hanging from the top of the box. In Thorndike's experiment, an animal (typically a cat) seeks to get out of the box by pushing against the pole or pulling on the chain. In Thorndike's experiments of the cat in the puzzle box, he sought to keep track of the time it took for the animal to get out of the box, as well as how many times the cat tried, using various means, to get out before being successful. Thorndike noted from his experiments that the time it took for the cat to get out of the box decreased as the number of attempts increased. He concluded from these experiments that learning occurs in small, incremental steps rather than in huge jumps. He referred to this as *incremental learning,* opposed to *insightful learning.*

R

Psychology as the behaviorist views it is a purely objective experimental branch of natural science. Its theoretical goal is the prediction and control of behavior. Introspection forms no essential part of its methods, nor is the scientific value of its data dependent upon the readiness with which they lend themselves to interpretation in terms of consciousness. The behaviorist, in his efforts to get a unitary scheme of animal response, recognizes no dividing line between man and brute.

—John B. Watson, twentieth-century American psychologist

radical behaviorism (behaviorism)

Taking his *operant conditioning* and *behavior modeling* approaches a step further into the realm of societal uses of *behaviorism*, B.F. Skinner called for a radical behaviorism that could potentially change society. By radical behaviorism, Skinner meant that principles of reinforcement could be applied to human institutions for the betterment of society. Skinner's radical behaviorism declared that environmental events in society could be ascertained and manipulated to control human behavior in order to make people happier and more productive members of that society. Skinner's behaviorism is radical because it rejects any attempt to study scientifically mental events, such as *consciousness* and motivation. Acording to Skinner, environmental events that can be observed and measured, the organism's response to the events,

and the consequences of the organism's behavior are all valid subjects worthy of scientific analysis.

Given this context, Skinner's radical behaviorism matches the theory of John B. Watson, who is considered the founder of behaviorism. As noted by Watson, since *consciousness* cannot be reliably studied, then we should not bother studying it at all. Behavior is observable, and therefore behavior only is what should be studied. Watson felt that the study of *epistemology*, the study of *consciousness,* should be left to the philosophers. To Watson, Skinner, and the behaviorists that followed them, the thousands of years of study about what is knowledge (i.e., epistemology) was a waste of time and scientific effort. Thus, behaviorism is a radical approach to the study of psychology and how animals and people learn.

rational analysis (cognitivism)

In John Anderson's *ACT theory*, rational analysis is the postulate that human *cognition* optimizes the behavior adaptation of the organism to accomplish tasks in the environment. More simply stated, Anderson finds that the best way to study how human thinking, reasoning, and learning works is to study the tasks that humans perform. Within John Anderson's postulate for *rational analysis*, there are three basic *signatures* for studying human *memory*, thinking, and behavior. These three signatures are the *power law of practice, categorization*, and the *fan effect*. The power law of practice states that the more often one performs a particular task, the less time it takes to accomplish it. The fan effect states that the larger and tighter the fan of conceptual links there are in the brain to the task to be achieved, the more likely the central concept to accomplish that task will be activated in memory. Categorization is the Web (fan) of information that is organized in the brain, based upon the feedback obtained from the act of completing the task. The forming of categories of information in the brain is tied to the predictive usefulness of categorization to the mission of accomplishing the task.

reaction potential (behaviorism)

An aspect of Clark Leonard Hull's *drive stimulus reduction theory*, reaction potential refers to the likelihood that a particular stimulus will elicit a correct response from an organism in an experiment. An increase in reaction potential occurs if the strength of the stimulus is increased (i.e., *stimulus intensity dynamic*), if the timing of the reinforcement occurs immediately after the organism's response, and if the response matches closely with the usual behavior of the organism. A factor that can be a "wild card," that negatively impacts reaction potential, is *inhibitory potential*. Inhibitory potential refers to the resistance of a subject to repeating a response to a stimulus. In this instance, the more often the stimulus is repeated, the more likely the individual will resist making the intended response.

reactive system (educational technology)

A reactive system is an *agent* that continuously and continually reacts to inputs from its environment. In terms of *cognition* of *artificial intelligence* systems, a reactive system is an agent that is able to learn and apply knowledge from one task learned to a new set of tasks necessary to be performed. This relatively new type of advanced software technology has important implications for how humans think, learn, and apply knowledge to *problem-solving* situations.

recency principle (behaviorism)

The recency principle of Edwin Ray Guthrie, an important aspect of his *one-trial learning* postulate, is closely related to his *contiguity theory* that accepted all of Aristotle's *laws of association* except the postulate regarding frequency. Aristotle's postulate regarding frequency states that the more often two objects are experienced by an organism simultaneously, the more likely they will be remembered and learned. Guthrie rejected this notion. With Guthrie, one trial, one successful pairing of a stimulus with a response is sufficient for learning to occur by the organism. Given both his contiguity theory and his postulate regarding one-trial learning, Guthrie had to come up with his *recency principle*, which states that whatever the organism did last in the presence of a fixed set of stimuli will be repeated again when those stimuli recur. To Thorndike and his theory of *connectionism*, learning occurs in small increments. To Guthrie, with his one-trial learning, learning occurs in an all-or-none proposition after one successful experience, one successful pairing of a stimulus and a response. According to the recency principle, whatever is learned last is what is remembered and acted upon by the organism when the same set of stimuli is presented. The debate as to whether learning occurs all at once or in increments is known as the *continuity-noncontinuity controversy*.

reception learning (cognitivism)

Reception learning is the opposite of the *active learning* (i.e., *discovery learning*) espoused by Jerome Bruner. It involves the receipt of information by students from an instructor. Reception learning is referred to in David Ausubel's *subsumption theory*, which he first delineated in the 1960s and elaborated upon in the 1970s. Subsumption theory states that new material learned in a school setting should be related to previously presented ideas and concepts that become processed and extant in the cognitive structure of the brain. Opposing Bruner's *discovery learning* process, in which the student discovers and shapes content on his or her own, Ausubel believes that instructors must provide to the students contextual information, as well as *advance organizers,* which act as a bridge between new material and previous material studied. Ausubel's learning paridgm is more *instructor-centric* than *learner-centric*. In fact, Ausubel refers to the instructional aspects of the subsumption process as *expository teaching.* Ausubel further defines, from the learner's perspective, the subsumption process (new ideas placed by the instructor within the context of old ideas in some sort of conceptual structure) as reception learning which opposes *discovery learning,* in which the students construct and organize the content. Besides reception learning, Ausubel also refers to subsumption theory as meaningful verbal learning, which is learning (of primarily textual information) determined by the organization of the learner's prior knowledge that allows for the incorporation and reception of new knowledge. As noted, much of Ausubel's focus is on the reception of verbal and textual information.

Followers and adherents of David Ausubel and his theory, in an attempt to provide graphical depictions of words and idea linkages, developed visual word and idea maps of concept families and linkages to provide a pictorial, contextual structure to the information being studied. These are exemplified in *concept mapping, mind mapping,* and *knowledge mapping* techniques. All are based upon subsumption theory, a learning process in which new concepts and ideas enter the learner's *consciousness* by means of the instructor providing information in a traditional classroom setting. These new concepts and ideas fit within a broader context and categorization, an organized set of information previously supplied as well by the instructor. Reception learning is *instructor-centric* and fits squarely within the *industrial age educational paradigm.*

reciprocal determinism (constructivism)

An important aspect of Albert Bandura's *self-efficacy theory* and *social cognitive theory,* reciprocal determinism postulates that an individual's thoughts and behaviors determine and shape the environment, and the environment reciprocally determines and shapes the thinking and behavior of the individual. Since individual action is influenced by and is an influencer of the sociocultural environment, Bandura postulates that humans are both products and producers of their own environments and social systems in which they live, learn, and work. Beliefs in self-efficacy, of being able to complete learning and work tasks successfully and achieve a goal, influence the choices people make and the actions that they pursue. Humans engage in particular pursuits wherein they feel competent and confident. They avoid those pursuits wherein they feel incompetent and uncertain. Individuals with high self-efficacy greatly influence, and are greatly influenced by, their environment. They feel that they are influencing the environment and being positively shaped by it. Individuals with low self-efficacy feel that the environment is determining their behavior negatively, while they have little effect on any changes occurring in the environment. According to Bandura and social cognitivists, *self-regulated learning* mediates between knowledge and action. Through self-reflection, individuals make judgments about their thought processes, experiences, and individual competence. Previous attainments, prior knowledge, and skills are not good predictors of future success. The beliefs that individuals hold about their abilities, their attainments, and their influences on their environment greatly influence the way they will behave in the future. The beliefs of individuals are significant determinants of future successes or failures in learning and in life.

reductive bias (constructivism)

An important aspect of *cognitive flexibility theory* (albeit a negative one), reductive bias is a state of learner oversimplification in which the learner is deficient in *knowledge acquisition* because he or she seeks to reduce a complex situation to a quick, simple, and reductive answer. In business situations, this is referred to colloquially as employees performing "no brainers," which often lead to faulty *decision making*. Complex situations demand an increased level of thinking that some learners do not wish to bother with. These learners instead seek to simplify things too quickly. They pose the problem and solution as simpler and easier than they actually are. Instructors who try to provide too much information, too much structure, and who seek to provide everything but the answer fall into the trap of catering to unmotivated students who want things simplified so that they don't have to think too long or hard about the problem.

First espoused by R.J. Spiro, R.L. Coulson, P.J. Feltovich, and D. Anderson in the late 1980s and early 1990s, cognitive flexibility theory focuses on the construction of knowledge by learners who build structure and context within the learning space that they are studying. Typically, within the *conceptual landscape*, learners navigate through an unstructured hypermedia environment (also known as the *crisscross landscape*) via the Web or via an application and then create their own representations and maps *(conceptual maps)* of the *knowledge base* that they are traveling through. The instructor's role is to provide case studies and multiple perspectives of the *knowledge base*, with the learners applying that information to their own learning contexts as they build the conceptual map of the unstructured information.

Oversimplification and memorization are de-emphasized within the cognitive flexibility learning domain. The instructor should not try to reduce the information to a formula, oversimplify it, or try to structure it too much for the learners. Doing so defeats the entire purpose of the learners constructing the content and learning through the process, and leads to a state of learner oversimplification known as reductive bias.

reflective mode of cognition (humanism)

One of two modes of *cognition* along with the *experiential mode of cognition*, the reflective mode refers to a higher order of thinking, similar to *metacognition*, in which the learner takes in ideas encountered from the world, thinks through them, reflect upon them, and reuses them to construct new ideas and knowledge. The experiential mode of learning is more of a subconscious mode of thinking that occurs as humans experience events and objects in their contemporary work and learning environment.

According to Donald A. Norman, in his book from the 1990s, *Things that Make Us Smart: Defending Human Attributes in the Age of the Machine,* contemporary education focuses on the use of computers, technology, and *multimedia* that help in regard to the experiential mode of cognition, yet often inhibit learners with regard to thinking creatively and constructively by means of the reflective mode of cognition. Norman goes on to describe *physical artifacts* that humans interact with, such as pencils, calculators, and computers that are important for the experiential mode of cognition, as well as *cognitive artifacts,* such as reading, math, and language that are important for the reflective mode of cognition. Thus, Norman's concern about using technology in education is that it overemphasizes the experiential mode of cognition and seeks to immerse and entertain students instead of getting them to be thoughtful and reflective, thus strengthening the reflective mode of cognition.

reinforcement theory (behaviorism)

Springing from the major *learning paradigm* of *behaviorism,* reinforcement theory is any theory holding as its key postulate that learning cannot occur without reinforcement, without some type of reward or feedback. For example, in B.F. Skinner's *operant conditioning,* a stimulus (e.g., food for the pigeon or rat) and a *reinforcer* (e.g., a light) are used by the experimenter to generate a specific response (e.g., pressing a lever). The goal of B.F. Skinner's *operant conditioning* is to achieve behavior shaping, or *behavior modeling*, so that the animal is rewarded or reinforced for following a particular path or set of actions that are desired by the behavioral scientist. The animal is provided immediately with a reward (i.e., food) following a particular action. By using operant conditioning, the experimenter alters the behavior of the animal to perform along a desired path or result. When the animal is provided with a reward for performing the behavior, it is likely to repeat the *elicited behavior* on subsequent occasions.

In Gagne's *conditions of learning*, a primarily cognitivist approach to learning, reinforcement is a *cognitive process* in the form of feedback letting the learner know whether or not he or she has made the correct response. Without this reinforcement, the learner is unaware whether he or she has learned.

reinforcer (behaviorism)

An important term in all of the reinforcement theories within the *learning paradigm* of *behaviorism*, a reinforcer is anything that causes *drive reduction* in an organism. Typically, a reinforcer is a stimulus, of which there are two types. A *primary reinforcer* is one that has as its basis the survival of the organism. A *secondary reinforcer* is a stimulus that is paired with a primary reinforcer. Clearly a behaviorist in orientation, David Premack in his *Premack principle* regards all of the organism's responses as potential reinforcers for behavior. According to the Premack principle, an oft-repeated activity of an organism can be utilized to reinforce an activity occurring less frequently.

With regard to reinforcers and their frequency of occurrence, the Premack principle, also known as the *probability-differential hypothesis* has been questioned by the *disequilibrium hypothesis*. According to William Timberlake, the disequilibrum hypothesis postulates that each and all activities of an organism can be a reinforcer if the experimenter provides a *contingency schedule* whose purpose is to constrain the organism from accessing a particular activity. The contingency schedule creates in the organism a disequilibrium in which the restriction to activity access is itself a reinforcer.

relaxed alertness (cognitivism)

One of the three types of instructional methods for *brain-based learning*, relaxed alertness involves minimizing learner fear and creating a low stress but high challenge learning experience. The goal is to move the learner from logical thinking only (which occurs in more traditional learning experiences) to thinking at a deeper, more creative, almost subconscious level. The other two types of brain-based learning methods are *active processing* (when the learner analyzes and becomes aware of the form, meaning, and motivation behind *knowledge acquisition*) and *orchestrated immersion* (immersing students in a rich learning environment). In Renate and Geoffrey Caine's book *Making Connections*, the authors examine the close relationship between the way the brain works and the way people like to learn, all within a brain-based learning approach. Brain-based learning is closely allied to *metacognition*, which is being conscious of and aware of what one has learned. The brain is an immensely powerful processor, and brain-based learning seeks to get the brain working the way it should work. As long as the brain is not constrained from doing its normal work, learning will take place. Traditional rote learning (from the *industrial age educational paradigm*), however, inhibits learning by punishing the brain's natural processing activity. For brain-based learning to take place, teachers must create a realistic context for learning (a rich learning environment that encourages orchestrated immersion). They must let students work in teams and work through mistakes themselves. They must let their students constantly assess how and why they learn.

repair theory (cognitivism)

Kurt VanLehn's *repair theory* looks at how humans learn procedures inductively and by fixing "bugs" (i.e., mistakes) along the way. The theory postulates that when an individual seeking to perform a procedure reaches an impasse, he or she applies various approaches to overcome the impasse. These approaches are referred to as repairs. Some repairs get the learner back on track; others are false restarts. An *artificial intelligence* computer model entitled Sierra has been developed to test out repair theory for an *agent* seeking to complete a procedure. By identifying the bugs that a human or agent encounters while completing a set of procedures, the system developer can reuse these bugs in future attempts to allow the human or agent to complete the procedure on the next trial more quickly and with fewer errors.

response learning (behaviorism)

Within the *learning paradigm* of *behaviorism*, learning is regarded as occurring as a result of reinforcement (i.e., *reinforcement theory*). According to Tolman, an adherent of *cognitive behaviorism*, learning is not necessarily a result of reinforcement. Organisms can employ either response learning or *place learning* to obtain a specific reinforcement. Response learning occurs when an organism learns a specific set of responses that solve a problem, at which time the experimenter provides a specific reinforcement. Place learning involves the organism creating a *cognitive map* of its environment. Once the organism has located an object, its creation of a cognitive map of the environment allows it to reach that object again more readily and through multiple paths. Tolman contends that place learners are quicker studies than response learners and are not dependent on the reinforcement to perform an action.

S

Never let formal education get in the way of your learning.
—Mark Twain, nineteenth-century American writer

scaffolded knowledge integration framework (constructivism)

Developed by KIE (Knowledge Integration Environment) researchers at the University of California at Berkeley, the scaffolded knowledge integration framework is a *curriculum design* method for K–12 science instruction. It primarily involves *Web-based knowledge transfer* and is made up of four components: (1) Identify new goals for science learning that utilize the Internet. (2) Make things visible through film clips, photographs, etc. on the Internet. (3) Have the students actively engaged in the science learning process using *discovery learning* approaches. (4) Have the students work in pairs, and share information and discuss it among themselves to foster *collaboration*. The framework includes *multimedia applications* that focus on learner sharing and communication tools (i.e., *computer-mediated communication*).

scaffolded learning (constructivism)

Growing out of Vygotsky's *social development theory* and an important aspect of Collins, Brown, and Newman's *cognitive apprenticeship model*, scaffolded learning is a method to help learners quickly gain independence from the instructor. The instructor initially supports the learners by focusing on ways for them to work independently. The learning method refers to a scaffold that painters use to support themselves while painting. Using this analogy, the instructor provides a scaffold upon which the learners support themselves so that they can do their own painting, do their own learning beyond the initial point of instruction. The approach favors *collaborative learning* techniques allowing students to learn and work in teams, as they will do when they leave the classroom.

scenario planning (organizational learning)

First developed by Peter Schwartz in the the mid–1970s and still in use today, scenario planning is a technique used by managers to reduce uncertainty with regard to corporate *decision making*, specifically in relation to predicting future business events and scenarios. Not simply a matter of doing the right thing, managers must choose the right thing to do for the benefit of the corporation and its employees. Thus, scenario planning involves testing out possible decisions, avenues, and directions that managers could take against a set of possible future business situations. The more that a particular decision could play out well, even in multiple future situations, the more likely that the action would be successful. Scenario planning is thus a way to deal with uncertainty, while at the same time promoting *organizational learning* and *systems thinking*.

schema (cognitivism)

An important aspect of Roger Schank's theories of learning, including *conceptual dependency theory, contextual dependency theory,* and *script theory*, schema refer to a *knowledge structure* that is created in the mind as we experience new things in the environment and from which we create scripts. Schema is important to an understanding of how language processing and higher thinking work within Schank's script theory. Script theory postulates that human *memory* (which Schank regards as *episodic memory*) is based upon personally remembered episodes and experiences, i.e., *scripts* (a sequence of events and actions) that we call upon and apply to a *schema*. Scripts allow human beings to make inferences. The schema, the knowledge structure that is created, is highly dynamic and continually enhanced over time. As new experiences occur, new scripts get written, and the *schema* become further enhanced as a result of an ever-growing set of personal life episodes and experiences. Roger Schank's schema is an elaboration and enhancement of Jean Piaget's *schemata* discussed within his theory of *genetic epistemology*.

schemata (constructivism)

Jean Piaget's conception of schemata is inextricably linked to an understanding of an organism's *cognitive structure*. To Piaget, all organisms have cognitive elements that manifest themselves into overt (e.g., grasping) and covert (e.g., thinking) behavior. These sets of behaviors determine how an organism interacts with the environment as it develops. The more schemata utilized by the organism, the more it can respond to the environment. In Jean Piaget's *genetic epistemology*, the cognitive structure of the organism is modified through the dual processes of *assimilation* and *accommodation*. As the organisms interact with the environment, as they develop, the schemata themselves are modified in order to allow the individuals to deal with the changes occurring as a result of interactions with the environment through the process of development.

script theory (cognitivism)

This is an important learning theory of Roger Schank that began as *conceptual dependency theory* and became enhanced over time into his script theory. In the mid–1970s, Roger Schank delineated his conceptual dependency theory, which states that all *conceptualizations* can be defined in terms of a set of acts performed on objects in the environment by actors (i.e., by humans). This theory was Schank's initial attempt to define how knowledge is structured and how humans think and remember. A correlative Schank theory first elaborated upon in the mid–1970s, *contextual dependency theory*, looked at how humans represent meaning in sentences within the context of language understanding. Both led to his fully elaborated script theory, a delineation of how language processing and higher thinking works.

Script theory postulates that human memory (which Schank regards as *episodic memory*) is based upon personally remembered episodes and experiences, i.e., scripts (a sequence of events and actions) that we call upon and apply to a *schema*. Scripts allow human beings to make inferences. *Schema* refers to a *knowledge structure* that gets created as we experience new things in the environment from which we create more scripts. This knowledge structure (schema) is dynamic and continually enhanced over time. As new experiences occur, new scripts get written, and the *schema* become enhanced as a result of a growing set of personal life episodes and experiences. With both conceptual dependency theory and script theory as their theoretical basis, a number of *natural language processing* computer programs are being tested and developed.

search controls (cognitivism)

An element (along with *problem spaces, data chunking, objects with attributes and values, production rules,* and *automatic subgoaling*) in Allen Newell's *Soar,* a *cognitive architecture* and *artificial intelligence* programming language, search control is the process of selecting appropriate problem spaces, states, and operators by comparing alternative paths to take. Within the program, the mission of the operator is to complete a goal. A goal is a result that an operator seeks to achieve from completing a set of tasks (i.e., the operator moving from an initial state to a final state or result). Arguing for a *unified theory of cognition,* Newell developed a set of principles for *cognitive processing* and human *problem solving* with Soar. Soar stands for State, Operator, And Result.

The other elements in Soar, besides production rules, are defined as follows. Problem spaces are a single framework within which all tasks and subtasks associated with achieving a goal are to be resolved. Problem solving in Soar is a search through the problem space in which the program applies an Operator (set of operations) to a State to get a Result. Data chunking is the process by which learners recall information in *working memory* outside of the context that the information first appeared. Objects with attributes and values provide a single representation of temporary knowledge in *working memory.* Attributes are data chunks. Production rules provide a single representation of permanent knowledge in *long-term memory.* Automatic subgoaling is a single mechanism for generating goals.

As an attempt to construct a *unified theory of cognition,* Soar focuses on analyzing a task and all related subtasks and developing an effective and efficient means for completing the task and subtasks. Current Soar research is being conducted at Carnegie Mellon University, Ohio State University, University of Michigan, University of Southern California, University of Hertfordshire, and University of Nottingham.

secondary reinforcer (behaviorism)

Most advocates of *reinforcement theory* have tried to provide a more specific response to the definition of a reinforcer. In early reinforcement theories, a reinforcer is anything that reinforces behavior. For Hull, a reinforcer is anything that causes *drive reduction* in an organism. Generally speaking, a reinforcer is a stimulus, of which there are two types. A primary reinforcer is one that has as its basis the survival of the organism. A *secondary reinforcer* is a stimulus that is paired with a primary reinforcer. Both are important to understanding animal and human behavior. The strength of the secondary reinforcer is dependent entirely upon its close association with the primary reinforcer. Pavlov firmly believed, based on his *classical conditioning* method, that conditioning of the organism is dependent completely upon primary reinforcers. Secondary reinforcers, neutral until associated with the primary reinforcer, gain importance as further conditioning occurs in the organism.

self-directed learning (constructivism)

In 1975, Malcolm Knowles published his book *Self-Directed Learning: A Guide for Learners and Teachers,* in which he defined self-directed learning as a process in which individual learners, without the help of others, construct their own learning activity. In particular, they identify their own *learning objectives,* find learning resources, implement learning strategies, and determine their own *learning outcomes.* Self-directed learning is an important aspect of Knowles *andragogy,* in which the adult learner is self-motivated to learn on his or her own in order to increase knowledge and skills related to work enhancement and job promotion.

In Patricia Cross's 1981 book, *Adults as Learners,* she noted that 70 percent of adult learning is self-directed learning. According to Cross and others, educators can foster self-directed learning for adult learners by doing the following: (1) Be a manager of the learning experience rather than an information provider. (2) Help the learners set their own learning goals and objectives. (3) Provide examples of others' previous work to act as models. (4) Help learners help themselves in gathering resources. (5) Teach self-evaluation techniques. (6) Create and maintain an atmosphere of trust and openness for the self-directed learners. As a *learner-centric* versus *instructor-centric* paradigm for adult learning, self-directed learning is closely associated with *lifelong learning*.

self-efficacy theory (constructivism)

In 1997, Albert Bandura, a Stanford University psychology professor, published his book, *Self-Efficacy: The Exercise of Control*. Bandura postulated that those with high self-efficacy expectancies generally perform better in learning and life situations than those with low self-efficacy expectancies. Bandura first talked about self-efficacy with the publication in 1977 of a seminal paper entitled "Self-Efficacy: Toward A Unifying Theory of Behavioral Change." To Bandura, high self-efficacy is characterized by being confident that one will accomplish a particular goal. Low self-efficacy, on the other hand, is characterized by being uncertain that the goal can be accomplished. By believing that one can accomplish a particular goal, the goal seeker increases the likelihood of successful *behavior modeling* and the likelihood that he or she will persist until the goal is achieved.

An outgrowth of Bandura's *social learning theory*, self-efficacy is achieved through positive past experiences, *reinforcement* from the environment, and encouragement from mentors. Another important factor for success is the act of observing and modeling oneself after others who have already successfully achieved the goal. Those who expect successful achievement of goals anticipate successful outcomes (i.e., one expects to receive the benefits of achieving the goal as a result of all the hard work necessary to achieve it). Three aspects of success in academic and other life endeavors are having the necessary knowledge and skills to achieve the goal, high self-efficacy beliefs, and high outcome expectations. High self-efficacy

alone does not always meet with success. Some people may have the requisite knowledge and ability to accomplish the goal and have high self-efficacy. As a result, they can envision the successful outcome and consequently achieve it. Others may have the requisite knowledge and ability to accomplish the goal, but have low self-efficacy and therefore are not able to achieve it. Still others may think they have the requisite knowledge and ability to accomplish the goal (when in fact this is not the case), still have high self-efficacy, but fail due to the disconnect between self-perception and reality.

Self-efficacy theory is reminiscent of Norman Vincent Peale's power of positive thinking. What makes it different from Peale is that Bandura has identified self-efficacy as a cognitive mechanism underlying all forms of psychotherapy. Therefore, self-efficacy theory could easily be placed within the *learning paradigm* of *humanism* in addition to *constructivism*.

self-pacing/self-paced instruction (behaviorism)

Self-pacing refers to the fourth of a set of learner behaviors that are to be followed within *programmed learning*, more popularly known as self-paced instruction. Self-pacing means quite simply that the learner goes through a learning program at his or her own pace. Thus, self-paced instruction has as its most critical feature the fact that the learner has control over the time it takes to complete the program.

Though first developed by Sidney L. Pressey in the 1920s, and modeled after the *reinforcement theory* implicit within the *learning paradigm* of *behaviorism*, programmed learning was rediscovered and popularized by B.F. Skinner. Skinner's programmed learning involves the following learner behaviors. (1) *Small Steps*. Learners obtain small amounts of information and proceed from one task to the next in an orderly, step-by-step fashion. (2) *Overt Responding*. Learners must provide an overt response to a problem or step so that correct responses are reinforced and incorrect responses corrected. (3) *Immediate Feedback.* Learners are provided with an immediate response to let them know whether they have answered or performed correctly or incorrectly. (4) *Self-Pacing.* Learners are to work through the programmed learning activity at their own pace.

Programmed learning techniques have been employed and reused in many current *computer-based training, Web-based training, multimedia applications,* and *electronic performance support systems.* Programmed learning has been proven to be an effective technique for *skills management* and *organizational learning.*

self-reflection (constructivism)

Humans capable of analyzing their own *cognitive processes,* their own thoughts, perceptions, actions, and behavior to gain a better understanding of themselves and of their role in the environment, are capable of a high degree of self-reflection. An important aspect of *self-regulated learning* as espoused by Dale Schunk and Barry Zimmerman, self reflection is one of three essential phases along with forethought and performance in the self-monitoring process. *Artificial intelligence* systems that are able to analyze their own internal processing mechanisms are also said to be capable of self-reflection. Internal diagnostics that trace problems and report solutions are regarded as a means of system self-reflection. Generally speaking, humans capable of self-reflection are better able to positively influence themselves, others around them, and their environment.

self-regulated learning (constructivism)

An outgrowth of *social learning theory* and of what Albert Bandura now calls *social cognitive theory,* self-regulated learning, as espoused by Dale Schunk and Barry Zimmerman, is an essential ingredient of *problem solving* that is closely related to *self-efficacy.* Self-regulated learners are self-motivated, self-aware, proactive learners who view the activity of learning as something they do for themselves versus something that is done to or for them. Three phases of self-regulated learning are forethought, performance, and self-reflection. The cognitive processes involved in these three phases are: (1) Forethought: goal-setting, high self-efficacy, and strategic planning; (2) Performance: attention focusing, self-instruction, and self-monitoring; and (3) Self-reflection: self-evaluation, attributions, and adaptivity.

Poor self-regulated learners have nonspecific goals, low self-efficacy, low interest in tasks leading up to goals, lack of focus, and inability to self-monitor progress. Strong self-regulated learners have specific goals, high self-efficacy, a high interest in task completion, focus, and the ability to self-monitor progress toward the goals.

self-regulation (cognitivism)

Within Alan Schoenfeld's model of *mathematical problem solving,* an important element to successful mathematics learning is the process of self-regulation. Self-regulation is the ability of the learner to self-monitor his or her own *cognitive processes.* A technique to achieve self-regulation is the *think aloud protocol,* in which participants engaged in a *problem-solving* activity by talking out loud to share what they are thinking. A finding of the think aloud protocol was that the entire process was an exercise in *mathematical metacognition,* in which the participants were able to become cognizant of, supervise, and change their own cognitive processes in order to be better problem solvers and more productive at reaching their task goals. Being able to assess personal status and progress, make adjustments to strategy, and adjust actions and procedures to meet task goals while the task is in process is essential to the self-regulation process.

semantic encoding (cognitivism)

One of Robert Gagne's *cognitive processes* associated with an instructional event within his *conditions of learning,* semantic encoding refers to what happens when new information is stored in *long-term memory* as a result of the instructor providing learning guidance. Gagne's conditions of learning theory describes a hierarchy of different types of learning, which require different instructional strategies and *instructional designs* based upon specific *learning outcomes*.

As delineated in the conditions of learning theory, there exists a hierarchical set of *cognitive processes* that occur in relation to nine *instructional events*. The nine instructional events and their respective cognitive processes (in parentheses) are: (1) Gain attention (reception) in order to focus upon the task at hand. (2) Inform learners of the objective (expectancy) in order to provide up front what are the projected *learning outcomes* for the course or module. (3) Stimulate recall of prior learning (retrieval) in order to stimulate prior knowledge previously remembered and gained. (4) Present the stimulus (selective perception) in order to initiate new information. (5) Provide learning guidance (*semantic encoding*) in order to structure the new information in a form that can be stored and remembered. (6) Elicit performance (responding) in order to stimulate learner recall through learners' active responses. (7) Provide feedback (reinforcement) in order to ensure that learning has occurred. (8) Assess performance (retrieval) in order to determine if the learners' performance is appropriate, correct, and in line with the projected learning outcomes. (9) Enhance retention and transfer (generalization) in order to place the new knowledge gained into *long-term memory*. For Gagne, these hierarchies provide a rationale for *sequencing of instruction*.

sensory memory (cognitivism)

Also referred to sometimes as the sensory store or the sensory register, sensory memory is the part of memory that holds the raw physical characteristics of a sight, sound, or touch stimulus for a short period. From sensory memory, the sensation moves to *short-term memory* and then *long-term memory*.

According to theory posed in 1967 by Ulric Neisser, currently professor of cognitive psychology at Cornell University, there are three *sensory memories* studied by cognitive psychologists: *echoic memory, haptic memory,* and *iconic memory*, all of which are aspects of human cognitive processing that deal with sensory stimuli from the outside world. Once the sensations are perceived and enter the sensory memory, echoic, haptic, and iconic memory information then move from *short-term memory* to long-term memory. *Memory* itself is an important aspect of learning theory, for it is generally regarded that learning takes place through memory as sensations in which various types of sensory information pass from the sensory store to short-term memory to long-term memory.

sequencing of instruction (cognitivism)

Sometimes referred to as an *instructional sequence* in its noun form, sequencing of instruction is an important principle at the center of many cognitivist learning theories, including but not limited to Gagne's *conditions of learning* and Merrill's *component display theory* and *instructional transaction theory*. In the conditions of learning theory, for example, Gagne describes a hierarchy of different types of learning which require different instructional strategies and *instructional designs* based upon specific learning outcomes. For Gagne, these hierarchies provide a rationale for the sequencing of instruction. For Merrill, the instructional sequences are then arranged on the basis of the specific type of instructional transactions (e.g., Merrill's *instructional transaction theory*) that are to occur and *knowledge objects* to be manipulated by the learner. Thus, instructional sequences are determined by the type of learning to occur, the goals and objectives of the learning activity, the state and *knowledge base* of the learner at the start of and during the course of the learning activity, and the *knowledge objects* to be manipulated by the learner.

serial processing (educational technology)

In the world of computers, serial processing is processing that occurs in a single given sequence and order. An example of serial processing is the single desktop PC that is not attached to a computer network and that performs one particular computer task at a time. Serial processing contrasts with *parallel processing*. In the world of networked computers, parallel processing refers to an array of computer networks in which many events are considered and acted upon by the systems at once. In other words, with parallel processing, more than one computer processor is devoted to executing the same program or same sets of programs simultaneously, or in parallel. By having many processors working in parallel, more sophisticated, media-rich applications such as *multimedia* and *hypermedia* can be consumed by users.

In relation to *artificial intelligence* systems, *agents* which simulate *cognition* utilize parallel processing techniques to perform an array of *problem-solving* activities. The *Internet* itself is an example of the effective usage of parallel processing systems. Some *artificial intelligence* systems utilize serial processing. In this case, the agents know which tasks are to be performed and in what order. The results of one action are known and recorded before the next action is considered and undertaken by the agent. In terms of understanding *cognition*, most cognitive scientists assume that human thinking employs both serial processing and parallel processing.

shaping (behaviorism)

The goal of B.F. Skinner's *operant conditioning* is to achieve behavior *shaping*, or *behavior modeling*, so that the animal is rewarded for following a particular path or set of actions that is desired by the behavioral scientist. In particular, shaping, as opposed to *trial-and-error learning*, involves an incremental modification of the organism's desired response to a particular set of stimuli from the experimenter. The desired behavior is divided into minute actions, each of which is reinforced to lead the organism to a final learning goal that otherwise would not have been achieved without a significant amount of trial and error.

shared cognition theory (constructivism)

Somewhat similar to Albert Bandura's *social learning theory* and *social cognitive theory*, the shared cognition theory of Brown, Collins, and Duguid focuses on how groups influence the learning of individuals and their *cognitive processes*. In the past, many cognitivist theories of learning focused strictly on the individual thinking process and ignored the group and the influence of the group on the learner. Shared cognition theory basically states that an individual's thinking is shaped by the shared thinking activity that occurs among groups of learners. The impact of social interaction is great on the individual learner and his or her own cognitive processes. According to shared cognition theory, social interaction shapes the individual mind.

shared cognitive maps (organizational learning)

In a study of cultural, learning, and communication aspects of organizations, Linda Smircich in 1983 defined organizational cognition as a system of shared knowledge and beliefs of individuals within the organization based upon common *knowledge structures* (i.e., *shared cognitive maps*) and communication *rules*. For proponents of *cognitive behaviorism*, a *cognitive map* is important for studying *learning and performance*. A cognitive map is the body of knowledge that an organism or *agent* has about the surrounding environment. It is a mental picture that allows the organism to navigate through various paths within that environment.

A cognitive map is also closely related to Roger Schank's concept of *schema*. An important aspect of Roger Schank's theories of learning, including *conceptual dependency theory*, *contextual dependency theory,* and *script theory*, schema refers to a *knowledge structure* that is created in the mind as humans experience new things in the environment and from which they create scripts. Schema is important to an understanding of how language processing and higher thinking works within Schank's script theory.

According to Kim Langfield-Smith in 1992, shared cognitive maps are based upon the shared knowledge and belief systems of the entire organization as well as those of specific subcultural groups used for daily interactions and group *decision making*. Her study was based upon the interactions and communications of individuals within a fire department organization. Also related to organizational cognition, Daniel Wegner's theory of transactive memory, elaborated upon in 1995, is a network model for describing shared cognitive maps, by which individuals in the organization access shared memory in their organizational environment in much the same fashion as a group of networked computers share memory. This theory falls squarely in line with *information processing theory* and *network models* such as the *PDP memory model* in which human cognition and memory are described in computer terms and relations.

Anand, Manz, and Glick in 1998 adapted Wegner's theory of transactive memory and applied it to an *organizational memory* approach to understanding organizational cognition and the concept of shared cognitive maps. These researchers define organizational memory as knowledge acquired by group members through their interactions and communications (i.e., *tacit knowledge*) as well as knowledge extant and available to individuals in the organization through *knowledge bases* (i.e., *explicit knowledge*).

Ultimately, according to Langfield-Smith, organizations share cognitive maps that are primarily domain specific and transitory (i.e., not of long duration). Some maps are thus related to a specific subculture, whereas others span the organization, are shared by all, and tend to be more explicit and of longer duration.

short-term memory (cognitivism)

Sometimes called *working memory*, short-term memory is working conscious thought. It is opposed to *long-term memory*. Short-term memory is an important aspect of human cognitive information processing. Short-term memory processes knowledge that is very active and dynamic. However, short-term memory also processes knowledge taken in from long-term memory typically of two types: declarative and procedural. In John Anderson's *ACT theory*, a *cognitive architecture*, *declarative memory* is a type of *long-term memory* that stores facts and ideas in a semantic network structure (i.e., a *network model*). *Procedural memory*, another type of long-term memory, takes sequences of declarative knowledge in the form of *productions* and makes further logical inferences about them. Each production contains a set of conditions and actions found within declarative memory. Short-term memory, or short-term conscious thought, retrieves declarative information of facts and ideas, carries out task sequences found in procedural memory, and adds new information gathered from the environment, forming new sequences that are then stored in procedural memory.

signatures (cognitivism)

Within John Anderson's postulate for *rational analysis* (human cognition optimizes the behavior adaptation of the organism to accomplish tasks in the environment), there are three basic *signatures* for studying human *memory*, thinking, and behavior. Part of his *ACT theory,* these three signatures are the *power law of practice*, the *fan effect*, and *categorization*. The power law of practice states that the more often one performs a particular task, the less time it takes to accomplish it. The fan effect states that the larger and tighter the fan of conceptual links there are in the brain to the task to be achieved, the more likely the central concept to accomplish that task will be activated in memory. Categorization, in this *schema*, is the Web (fan) of information that is organized in the brain, based upon the feedback obtained from the act of completing the task. The forming of categories of information in the brain is strictly tied to the predictive usefulness of categorization to the mission of accomplishing the task.

single loop learning (organizational learning)

Chris Argyris's single loop learning is the first of two types of learning that must take place in organizations in order for them to undergo successful transformation. Single loop learning is part of Argyris's *action research*. Action research, part of Argyris's *theory of action*, is a strategy to help managers move from *single loop* learning (learning that corrects errors by changing routine behavior) to *double loop* learning (learning that corrects errors by examining the underlying culture of the organization) in order to enhance corporate *decision making*.

Argyris's theories of action are underlying rules by which the organization operates. Often these rules are unstated and even unknown. As such, single loop learning does NOT attempt to bring to the surface, examine, and point out certain actions (and most importantly their underlying theories) that occur within the organization that are just and competent, and distinguish them from actions that are unjust and incompetent. Rather, single loop learning merely seeks to make adjustments to individual behavior that conforms to the *theories of action* of the organization. Single loop learning by itself (and without double loop learning) can be part of the problem of corporate ossification. For example, if the underlying rule that it is important to remain in control and to win is unquestioned, various types of inappropriate and harmful behavior can be reinforced by encouraging behavior that follows these unquestioned and unacknowledged corporate rules. In single loop learning, the object is to have the individual behavior conform to the goals of the organization without questioning whether the goals are just or competent, or without seeking out and examining those goals and rules that are unstated but nevertheless govern individual behavior within the organization.

situated cognition theory (constructivism)

Similar to Brown, Collins, and Newman's *cognitive apprenticeship* and related as well to the *shared cognition theory* of Brown, Collins, and Duguid, situated cognition theory (also by Brown, Collins, and Duguid) has as its main postulate the thesis that learning and *cognition* are situated. This means that "know what" and "know how" are inextricably intertwined. It means that individual working knowledge must be tied completely to conceptual knowledge. It declares that learning situations must produce knowledge through work activity. And most important, situated cognition theory states that through mental cues, the learner must return mentally to the situation and the environment in which the knowledge was first obtained in order to successfully retrieve and reuse it for another situation. By ignoring the situated nature of cognition, traditional education falls short of the important goal of providing useful information that learners can carry over into their personal and work lives.

Situated cognition is distinguished from, yet intertwined with, shared cognition theory. According to shared cognition theory, social interaction shapes the individual mind. For both situated cognition theory and shared cognition theory, knowledge is like language. Knowledge is a result of the group and individual learning activities and situations that occur. Knowledge is tied totally to a context in use, which exists in both an individual and a social context. Situated cognition theory, shared cognition theory, cognitive apprenticeship, and Jean Lave's *situated learning* all share the belief that learning occurs within a social context, and that this social nature of learning greatly enhances the ability and usefulness of the individual mind to remember, retrieve, and reuse knowledge.

situated learning (constructivism)

Greatly influenced by Vygotsky's *social development theory* as well as by John Dewey's *instrumentalism,* Jean Lave's situated learning theory has the following three postulates: (1) Classroom learning by its very nature is out of context and irrelevant. (2) Knowledge presented in the context of work settings and applications is most relevant and effective. (3) Learning is a highly social, interactive activity that involves a great deal of *collaboration* and mentoring. In her research work, Jean Lave performed anthropological studies of how individuals learned to perform particular skilled trades across cultures. Examples of these trades included Yucatec midwives, native tailors, navy quartermasters, and meat cutters. Through her observations, she witnessed both *apprenticeship learning* and *scaffolded learning,* in which the learners, with the guidance and assistance of mentors, were able learn the individual crafts of the particular observed trades almost unintentionally. From these cultural studies, Lave and Wenger came to the conclusion that knowledge transfer is closely tied to the social situation in which the knowledge is learned. Out of context, the knowledge itself is meaningless.

Unlike *discovery learning,* which assumes that knowledge is constructed by the individual, or the cognitivist approaches, which are often based on *information processing theory* and which focus on inputs, outputs, and *schemas,* situational learning focuses entirely on the learning experience as a shared, social, almost unintentional learning event. In situated learning, the learners participate in a *community of practice.* The social interaction process that occurs between newcomers and old-timers within the community of practice is referred to by Lave as *legitimate peripheral participation.* As the novice gains knowledge and moves closer to the community's center, he or she becomes more actively engaged in the culture and eventually takes on the role of mentor, helping new, uninitiated individuals into the community of practice.

Brown, Collins, and Newman further developed situated learning theory in their theory of *cognitive apprenticeship,* in which learners acquire skills and knowledge within a particular domain through a process of mentoring.

Six Thinking Hats (organizational learning)

Developed by Edward de Bono in the 1980s and still in widespread use within corporations worldwide, Six Thinking Hats is a method for incorporating his *lateral thinking* (i.e., the generation of novel solutions to problems) into organizations. The six hats represent six modes of thinking. They are not as much labels as they are directions that thinking can take, especially within corporate meetings when decisions need to be made. During a meeting, there are literally six colored hats. Each participant dons a hat and tries to take on the perspective of a "purple hat" thinker, for example.

The Six Thinking Hats are: white, red, purple, yellow, green, and blue. White hat thinking is looking at the facts and figures and the data. Red hat thinking emphasizes feelings and emotions and is characterized by intuitive thinking. It is pretty much the opposite of white hat thinking. Purple hat thinking focuses on the exercise of judgment, caution, and logic. It involves looking very carefully at a suggestion to determine if it matches up with the facts of the situation. It tends toward analysis, a critical perspective, and doubt. According to de Bono, there is too much purple hat thinking in organizations, which tends to stifle *creativity* and lateral thinking. Yellow hat thinking focuses on the positive, optimistic perspective of a proposal or suggestion. The focus here is on exploring the benefits and examining the advantages of the suggestion. The yellow hat thinker will also be the first to acknowledge the insight of the individual making the suggestion. Green hat thinking is the hat often missing from organizations. It represents the creative, innovative approach that involves changes that make the purple hat thinker most uncomfortable. Green hat thinking typically involves synthesis and the exercise of creativity for *problem solving*. Blue hat thinking is that which focuses on the process itself. This hat is the hat of *metacognition*, of thinking about the thinking process over and above the facts and feelings of the proposal on the table. Blue hat thinking is that of the observer, someone who is viewing the process from an objective, outsider's perspective. Blue hat thinking helps the group move toward a solution, while avoiding the pitfalls of the group being dominated by one particular hat, especially the purple hat.

The overall purpose of using Six Thinking Hats is to make for more productive meetings and more effective problem solving and *decision making*. It requires all participants to use all six hats instead of sticking to their more comfortable and dominant thinking hat perspective. The method is simple to learn and use. It has been incorporated into educational settings and classrooms in addition to business settings. It is a simplification and enhancement of de Bono's *CoRT thinking*, which provides 60 thinking lessons to help motivate and direct learners to develop creative solutions to problems, write more creatively, and become more active, self-confident, and effective thinkers.

skills management (organizational learning)

An important approach for *organizational learning* and *knowledge management*, skills management is a specific technique used for training employees in organizations. First, job skills are correlated to skills assessments (i.e., tests to see if the individual can do a particular job). The assessments determine skill gaps (i.e., shortcomings in ability to perform a particular job). The skill gaps are then correlated to specific training exercises (i.e., interventions found in many *electronic performance support systems, multimedia applications, computer-based training, and Web-based training*). By means of these interventions, the individual is able to fill in skill gaps and be a more productive employee for the organization.

Skinner box (behaviorism)

A direct descendant of Edward Thorndike's *puzzle box*, the Skinner box is an *operant chamber*, a controlled learning environment, typically a cage, where an animal (e.g., a pigeon or rat) can obtain food (the stimulus) by performing a particular response (e.g., pressing a lever). The Skinner box keeps track of the number of responses that the animal makes. The main focus of Skinner's experiments in the Skinner box is to study *operant conditioning* and the relationship between the stimulus and the response of the animal within the controlled environment.

small steps (behaviorism)

This term refers to the first of a set of learner behaviors that are to be followed within *programmed learning*, also more popularly known as *self-paced instruction*. Though first developed by Sidney L. Pressey in the 1920s, and modeled after the *reinforcement theory* implicit within the *learning paradigm* of *behaviorism*, programmed learning was rediscovered and popularized by B.F. Skinner. Skinner's programmed learning involves the following learner behaviors: (1) *Small Steps*. Learners obtain small amounts of information and proceed from one task to the next in an orderly, step-by-step fashion. (2) *Overt Responding*. Learners must provide an overt response to a problem or step so that correct responses are reinforced and incorrect responses corrected. (3) *Immediate Feedback*. Learners are provided with an immediate response to let them know whether they have answered or performed correctly or incorrectly. (4) *Self-Pacing*. Learners are to work through the programmed learning activity at their own pace.

Programmed learning techniques have been employed and reused in many current *computer-based training, Web-based training, multimedia applications,* and *electronic performance support systems*. Programmed learning has been proven to be an effective technique for *skills management* and *organizational learning*.

Soar (cognitivism)

A *cognitive architecture*, Soar is an ongoing *artificial intelligence* research project centered at Carnegie Mellon University. Soar was started in the mid–1980s under the guidance of Allen Newell, one of the principles involved as well in the *logic theorist*, GPS *General Problem Solver*, and *GOMS*. Arguing for a *unified theory of cognition*, Newell developed a set of principles for *cognitive processing* and human *problem solving* with Soar. Soar stands for State, Operator, And Result.

Soar has developed as well into an artificial intelligence programming language in which the following items are incorporated into the model: *problem spaces, search control, data chunking, production rules, objects with attributes and values,* and *automatic subgoaling.* Problem spaces are a single framework within which all tasks and subtasks associated with achieving a goal are to be resolved. As such, problem solving in Soar is a search through the *problem space* in which the program applies an Operator (sets of operations) to a State to get a Result. *Search control* is the process of selecting appropriate problem spaces, states and operators by comparing alternative paths to take. *Data chunking* is the process by which learners recall information in *working memory* outside of the context that the information first appeared. *Production rules* provide a single representation of permanent knowledge in *long-term memory. Objects with attributes and values* provide a single representation of temporary knowledge in *working memory. Automatic subgoaling* is a single mechanism for generating goals.

Soar deals with analyzing a task and all related subtasks and developing an effective and efficient means for completing the task and subtasks to reach a goal. Current Soar research is being conducted at Carnegie Mellon University, Ohio State University, University of Michigan, University of Southern California, University of Hertfordshire, and University of Nottingham.

social and cultural artifacts (constructivism)

Arising out of Lev Vygotsky's *social development theory*, activity theory is a learning framework in which individuals act on objects (through social and cultural artifacts that include language, norms, and modes of behavior) to achieve specific *learning outcomes.* Vygotsky and his Russian colleagues, Alexander Luria and Alexei Leont'ev, formulated in the 1920s and 1930s the concept of an activity as a unit of analysis within a social and cultural framework. The three elements of activity theory are the actor, the object, and the community. The actor's activities are different from each other as a result of the object focused upon. The actor transforms the object into an outcome. The actor's relationship with the object is mediated through the social and cultural artifacts. *Consciousness* exists in the individual as a result of the actor working with the object and moving toward an outcome within the culture. Personality formation and learning cultural meanings and modes become intrinsically intertwined. The term "object" is thus an object of a learning exercise and is related to the motivation of the actor in achieving a particular outcome. The core of activity theory is that thinking, reasoning, and learning is a culturally and socially mediated phenomenon.

social cognitive theory (constructivism)

Albert Bandura, known for his *observational learning* theory of the mid–1960s and his *social learning theory* of the mid–1970s, published a book in 1985 entitled *Social Foundations of Thought and Action: A Social Cognitive Theory.* In it, Bandura enhanced his social learning theory to include his updated perspective on what he meant by social cognitive theory. According to Bandura, social cognitive theory is an explanation of how humans think and why they are motivated to follow particular actions in society. He views human action as a result of the interplay of cognitive, behavioral, and environmental factors that influence the individual to act within a social and a cultural context. Social cognitive theory considers how people think and how their thinking influences their behavior and their performance in the environment.

social development theory (constructivism)

Len Vygotsky's social development theory is an attempt to define human *cognition* in relation to the social interaction of the individual within his or her culture. According to Vygotsky, human *consciousness* is completely a result of socialization and *enculturation*. Social interaction plays a fundamental role in the development of all cognitive abilities, including thinking, learning, and communicating. Instead of reacting to the environment directly in a way that an animal would react, humans filter their experiences through cultural and social lenses. Human thoughts, actions, and experiences are all socially and culturally mediated. Being able to differentiate individual consciousness from others and from the environment is key to the individual's ability to learn and develop. Being able to observe and interact with others and appraise self-performance in the context of the culture and society one lives in is also critical to self-control and self-maintenance as well as to the maintenance and survival of the entire culture.

Humans have what Vygotsky calls *psychological tools*. These include various systems for counting, mnemonic techniques, algebraic symbol systems, works of art, language, writing, schemes, diagrams, maps, and technical drawings. Of the tools available to humans, the most valuable to the species is language. Through language, humans construct their reality. Language itself is both an individual and a social phenomenon. With words, humans define and characterize their life experiences. With words, humans are able to move from subjective thoughts to objective ones to be shared in society.

Parents can increase their child's potential to develop as a cultured person by increasing the area of the *zone of proximal development*. This is an area at the lower end of the zone determined by the child's ability to think and solve problems on an individual basis in order to complete tasks. The higher end of the zone is determined by the parent's ability to provide a learning environment in which the child is able to collaborate with others, including adults and others more expert in the culture, in order to solve problems and complete tasks. This higher end of the zone is very similar to what Bandura discusses in *behavior modeling.* It is also closely related to *social learning, cognitive coaching, apprenticeship learning,* and *situated learning.* Thus, the zone of proximal development, an important aspect of Vygotsky's social development theory, is an area where learning occurs for the individual within a social context.

social learning theory (constructivism)

In 1977 Albert Bandura, a Stanford University psychology professor, published *Social Learning Theory,* in which he postulated that human learning is a continuous reciprocal interaction of cognitive, behavioral, and environmental factors. Sometimes called *observational learning,* social learning theory focuses on *behavior modeling,* in which the child observes and then imitates the behavior of adults or other children around him or her.

In his research on social learning theory, Bandura studied how violence portrayed in mass media can have a tremendously negative impact on the behavior of certain types of children watching violent television shows. What he noted was that some children will observe and then imitate the behavior of the characters on the television screen. From these observations, he determined that certain types of children learn to perform violent and aggressive actions by observing and then modeling their behavior after what they have seen. He referred to this as direct learning through instantaneous matching of the observed behavior to the modeled behavior.

Another aspect of Bandura's social learning theory is *critical theory*, in which the learner assesses and appraises the model being observed by internalizing it and then trying to imitate it.

Another important aspect of social learning theory is Bandura's *appraisal theories of emotion*, sometimes simply referred to as *emotion theory. Appraisal theories of emotion* attempt to predict what kinds of situations and emotional states elicit specific types of emotional responses that can either enhance or inhibit the quality and effectiveness of the learning experience. Learning theorists have long noted that emotions play an important factor in the receptivity of the learner to the learning experience. For example, a learner in an emotional state of anger and tension will have far more difficulty absorbing information and sharing ideas with fellow learners than a learner whose emotional state is one of relative calmness and serenity. In short, appraisal theories consider the impact of emotional states and responses on the social learning process.

Social learning theory states that learning can occur through the simple process of observing and then imitating others' activities. More recently, Bandura has turned his research focus to *self-efficacy* and renamed his social learning theory *social cognitive theory*.

socio-cognitive conflict (constructivism)

An important aspect of *socio-constructivist theory*, socio-cognitive conflict is an initial state that occurs among individuals in a *collaborative learning* environment. In this environment, different perspectives and idea conflicts within the group of learners lead to increases in individual cognitive development among the participants. Learner *problem solving* within the group is not so much a result of imitation as it it a result of individuals seeking to coordinate answers and resolve conflict. Through conflict, increases in individual cognitive development, as well as more sophisticated social interaction within the group, result.

socio-constructivist theory (constructivism)

Developed by a group of psychologists, known as the Geneva School, who study how social interaction affects cognitive development, the theory uses as its theoretical basis Jean Piaget's *genetic epistemology* and its postulates regarding *assimilation, accommodation*, and individual cognitive development. Its main thesis, as posed by W. Doise and G. Mugny, is that by interacting with others and by sharing with others one's vision of reality and the environment, an increase in cognitive development occurs in the individual. This in turn leads to more sophisticated interactions and communications within the *collaborative learning* group, which leads to further increases in individual cognitive development. Initial conflicting views among the group (i.e., *socio-cognitive conflict*) actually results in increased learning for the individuals in the group. The individuals, in essence, try to resolve idea conflicts, which results in individual cognitive progress in intelligence and communication.

sociocultural theory (constructivism)

Based upon Vygotsky's *zone of proximal development* (i.e., the qualitative difference between *problem solving* for individuals versus groups), sociocultural theory seeks to create a model that maps each individual cognitive change to each set of social interactions occurring within the group. Developed into a computer model by P. Dillenbourg and J. Self in the early 1990s, sociocultural theory treats *collaboration* as a key process for the development of higher-level individual thinking. Thus, sociocultural theory focuses on the causal relation between social interaction and individual cognitive development. Higher-level thinking that occurs in *collaborative learning* is internalized by each individual, which results in further gains in social interaction and the group construction of knowledge.

solo taxonomy theory (constructivism)

In the 1950s, the Dutch husband-and-wife team, of Pierre and Dieke van Hiele developed a theory of geometry and mathematics education that followed in the tradition of Piaget's *genetic epistemology*. Their solo taxonomy theory noted how children move through a series of stages, which are as follows: (1) Recognition. The child recognizes shapes holistically. (2) Analysis. The child analyzes the component parts of a figure including its angles and sides. (3) Relationships. Children begin to understand relationships between figures. (4) Deduction. The child begins to understand theories, postulates, and proofs for mathematical systems. (5) Axioms. The child can deal with highly abstract axioms and theories that are not necessarily tied to objects or pictorial models.

The theory is important within the *learning paradigm* of *constructivism*, for the van Hieles emphasized how children must learn for themselves in a *discovery learning* fashion in order to understand fully mathematics and higher-level thinking. They must struggle with the concepts and experience what the van Hieles call a "crisis of thinking" in order to achieve a more mature state of cognition and *consciousness*. Merely mimicking the teacher's expressed thoughts or memorizing theories and postulates of mathematics without grappling with the concepts and working them through will not lead learners to this higher level of mathematics thinking that is applicable to other types of higher thought as well.

spatial intelligence (constructivism)

One of Howard Gardner's eight *multiple intelligences,* spatial intelligence, sometimes referred to as visual-spatial intelligence, is the ability to visualize and create mental images and the ability to perceive the visual and spatial world accurately and represent it through symbols and pictures. Children who possess spatial intelligence can solve puzzles, find routes and paths, and build blocks with adeptness. Examples of spatial intelligence activities are painting, drawing, sculpting, and mapping. Individuals who possess spatial intelligence, and are provided with the right cultural and educational background in art, are apt to pursue careers as painters, sculptors, or cartographers. Gardner suggests that spatial intelligence needs to be developed in the individual, and that it must not be given less focus in favor of *verbal-linguistic intelligence* and *logical-mathematical intelligence,* which most schools tend to emphasize in their *curriculum design*.

spatial reasoning (constructivism)

An aspect of *cognitive robotics*, spatial reasoning deals with the robot's ability to determine the position of objects in a given space as the robot moves through or interacts with the environment. Understanding topological relationships between objects within a particular environment is crucial for a robot's ability to act within it. The key to spatial reasoning is the robot's ability to be intelligent enough to understand what is occurring in the environment and to take action based upon that understanding. The goal, of course, is for the robot to achieve a cognitive ability that approaches that of human *problem solving* in a given situation and environment.

speed up learning (cognitivism)

Within the field of *artificial intelligence* and *machine learning*, speed up learning is learning that occurs in the system that allows it to complete tasks more quickly and efficiently over time without external input. In John Anderson's *ACT theory*, his concept of the *power law of practice* (i.e., the more often one performs a particular task, the less time it takes the system or organism to accomplish it) is similar to the concept of speed up learning. Speed up learning is not as high an order of machine learning as *inductive learning*, or learning that occurs in a system that acquires new knowledge not explicitly or implicitly provided previously from an outside source. Speed up learning is a function of many *artificial intelligence* applications and *neural networks* that simulate how the mind works with regard to retrieving, sifting through, and processing information.

spiraled organization (constructivism)

Inspired by Piaget's *genetic epistemology* and its emphasis on the learner's individual development in stages, Jerome Bruner suggested the approach of the spiraled organization for the development of educational curriculum. The spiraled organization involves reteaching learners ideas in more complex forms as they grow older and mature. The assumption behind the spiraled organization is that learners gain new knowledge by relating it to existing knowledge and past experience. Essentially, the spiraled organization is a constructivist approach that emphasizes the tenet that learners learn best by building on what they already know from current and past education and experience.

spoken language systems (educational technology)

These are systems that permit *voice recognition systems* to interact with people or *agents*. These systems engage the users in dialogue and are considered an advanced form of *artificial intelligence*. The goal of spoken language systems is the attempt to understand the user's speech and discussion and to respond appropriately within the dialogue. Voice recognition systems are merely a combination of computer hardware and software that can recognize the human voice and essentially take dictation and record digitally what is being said. Voice recognition does not imply the understanding of what the human voice says (as is the case with spoken language systems). The attempt of a computer or agent to understand human language (i.e., understand what is being said) falls under the research discipline known as *natural language processing*. Spoken language systems are important to the goal of natural language processing. Voice recognition, on the other hand, is simply the conversion of spoken human words that are converted into computer text.

spreading activation (cognitivism)

Developed by Collins and Loftus in the mid–1970s, spreading activation is a *memory* model that utilizes the metaphor of a road map to describe how ideas in memory are organized. Cities on the road map are ideas. Distance between cities is represented as the links or highways between ideas. The closer two ideas are on the map, the greater is the strength of the association between the ideas. For *cognition*, spreading activation provides in essence a model of how concepts are diffused throughout the brain. The model is to a certain extent a basis for *concept mapping*, which is a learning process originally developed by Joseph D. Novak and later enhanced by William Trochim at Cornell University. Learners, often in a *cooperative learning* situation, work together to produce a graphical or pictorial view of the concepts being studied and how they are intertwined and interrelated.

Spreading activation is also a useful model for the creation of more efficient *neural networks*. Spreading activation has also been utilized and enhanced by Anderson as a model for computerized searches through a large body of information. In John Anderson's *ACT theory*, a *cognitive architecture*, *declarative memory* is a type of *long-term memory* that stores facts and ideas in a semantic network structure (i.e., a *network model*) similar to that described in the spreading activation model. Spreading activation is also a process whereby specific items can be quickly retrieved from long-term memory by specific cues that link the items to a network of related ideas.

staged self-directed learning model (constructivism)

In 1975 Malcolm Knowles published *Self-Directed Learning: A Guide for Learners and Teachers*, in which he defined self-directed learning as a process in which individual learners, without the help of others, construct their own learning activity. In particular, learners identify their own learning goals, find learning resources, implement learning strategies, and determine their own learning outcomes. Self-directed learning is an important aspect of Knowles andragogy, in which the adult learner is self-motivated to learn on his or her own in order to increase knowledge and skills related to work enhancement and job promotion. In her 1981 book, *Adults as Learners,* Patricia Cross notes that 70 percent of adult learning is self-directed learning.

More recently, Gerald Grow, as a follow-up to Knowles's self-directed learning, created the staged self-directed learning model (sometimes simply referred to as SSDL model), which seeks to help instructors match their teaching styles to the levels of self-direction of their students. Students who are categorized as dependent learners (i.e., the least self-directed) should be provided instruction from teachers who employ the authority-expert (i.e., the most restrictive of teaching styles) approach. Students who are categorized as interested learners (i.e., the next level up from dependent) should be provided instruction from teachers who employ the salesperson/motivator approach. Students who are categorized as involved learners (i.e., those pretty close to being self-directed), should be provided instruction from teachers who employ the facilitator approach. Students who are categorized as self-directed (i.e., the highest level of self-direction) should be provided instruction from teachers who employ the delegator approach (i.e., the least restrictive style). In short, the more dependent the learner, the more authoritative and *instructor-centric* the learning experience should be. The more independent the learner, the less authoritative and *learner-centric* the learning experience should be.

Stanford-Binet Intelligence Scale—4th Edition (cognitivism)

This scale is similar to the *Wechsler Adult Intelligence Scale* (i.e., WAIS), which is used as a measure of cognitive ability and intellectual aptitude for adults. The Stanford-Binet Intelligence Scale is used by schools to determine the earliest age at which an individual child can perform a particular task. Over a century ago, Sir Frances Galton of Great Britain sought to determine a measurement for human intelligence. Taking up Galton's drive to come up with an intelligence measure, Alfred Binet, in Paris, developed a series of questions to give to schoolchildren to measure aptitude and to predict future performance in school. Lewis Terman of Stanford University incorporated Binet's questions and enhanced the test to create the *Stanford-Binet Intelligence Scale*. In addition to measuring both verbal and nonverbal areas of a child's intellectual development, the Stanford-Binet Intelligence Scale (the 4th edition is the most recent), provides a quantitative score for *mathematical problem solving* and reasoning as well as a memory score to determine *short term memory* abilities. The test is used for school placement, giftedness, learning disabilities, brain disorders, as well as for tracking individual development over time. It is an important tool used by experts in *cognition* who seek to determine and measure *cognitive processes* of humans.

stimulus array (humanism)

Within James J. Gibson's *information pickup theory*, the stimulus array includes the physical environment (what Gibson calls environmental *affordances*) that we perceive. These environmental affordances include the physical landscape, the land, sky, and water. Also within the stimulus array are *invariants*, such as shadow, texture, color, and layout that help determine what we perceive. To Gibson, the act of perception is a dynamic between the organism and the physical environment. Developed by Gibson from the 1950s through the 1970s, information pickup theory is a *Gestalt theory* and approach to perception and learning.

Gestalt, the German word for shape, or configuration, is a way of describing how humans perceive the world as a meaningful whole, instead of as isolated stimuli. Humans see complete shapes such as buildings, houses, trees, and lakes, not merely lines, incomplete shapes, and patches of color. To adherents of Gestalt theory, dissection and analysis of individual parts are a distortion of reality. To Gestaltists, the whole is greater than the sum of the parts. Thus, given this philosophical background, Gestaltists study *molar behavior* (i.e., the whole) versus *molecular behavior* (i.e., the parts).

In terms of learning, Gibson postulates that the learner must have a rich, complex learning environment within which to interact. Learning should be based upon visual cues that the learner obtains from interacting in the environment. To increase learning, the instructor must provide realistic settings within which the learners can learn and perform a series of activities.

stimulus intensity dynamism (behaviorism)

An aspect of Hull's later *drive stimulus reduction theory*, stimulus intensity dynamism refers to Hull's postulate that the greater the intensity of a particular stimulus, the higher the probability that a correct response will be performed by the organism. Stimulus intensity dynamism is defined in terms of three thresholds: (1) Absolute, which is the smallest amount of stimulus energy needed for sensation to occur in the organism. (2) Terminal, which is the point at which any additional increases in stimulus intensity have no effect on the organism. (3) Difference, which is the smallest change in stimulus intensity that is noticed by the organism. Thus stimulus intensity dynamism is a way to measure changes in stimuli and the organism's perception of that stimuli.

stimulus-response association (behaviorism)

In general terms within the *learning paradigm* of *behaviorism*, the stimulus-response association is the relationship between a given stimulus and a given correct response to that stimulus. The stimulus-response association is an important element within Clark Leonard Hull's *drive reduction theory,* which states that organisms, especially humans, learn to perform behaviors that have the effect of reducing their biological drives. Hull's drive reduction theory is based upon Hull's mathematical formulation known as *Hull's Law*. The equation reads as follows:

E = H x D, where

D = Drive: the strength of a biologically-based homeostatic need.

H = Habit: the strength of a particular stimulus-response association.

E = Energy or Response Potential: the energy for performing the behavior, which is directly related to the probability of the behavior being completed.

From this formula, one can see that the stimulus-response association is tied directly to Hull's notion of habit and *habit strength*.

In Hull's *drive reduction theory*, habit strength is the measure of a bond formed between a particular stimulus and a given response. The more the stimulus leads to obtaining a basic need (such as water), the greater the habit strength becomes. Also, the more quickly that the need is fulfilled and met with a positive reward, the more likely that the habit strength will be regarded as high. Also, the higher the habit strength, the more likely that the response will be repeated successfully by the organism. Animal trainers seeking increased and repeated performance of particular tasks seek stimuli and responses that can be combined for a high habit strength to ensure successful learning of the desired act. Hull's formula helps to explain *behaviorism* in humans better than earlier theories of Skinner and Thorndike, which were able to look fairly accurately at the *stimulus-response association* of animals. By utilizing this equation, Hull was able to consider the drive and motivation of humans more explicitly as he considered such factors as environment, emotion, and prior training (habit strength) that would affect the stimulus-response association.

stimulus sampling theory (behaviorism)

William Kaye Estes's stimulus sampling theory is a statistical, probability-based learning theory that seeks to provide quantitative data to support Guthrie's *contiguity theory*. According to Estes, an organism has either a zero or one probability of completing a task desired by the experimenter. More likely, at the beginning of the experiment, the organism will perform an action, but not the one desired by the experimenter. Correct responses from the organism are labeled A_1; incorrect responses are labeled A_2. The total number of stimuli that accompany the experiment are labeled S. The stimuli elements of S are attached to either A_1 or A_2. Stimulus elements conditioned to A_1 elicit A_1 responses; stimuli elements conditioned to A_2 elicit A_2 responses. The constant proportion of S that is experienced by the organism at the beginning of the experiment is labeled as theta. The experiment ends at the time that the organism makes the correct A_1 response.

During the experiment, the state of the system is defined as the proportion of stimulus elements that are attached to A_1 and A_2 responses. If all of the stimulus elements at the beginning of the experiment are conditioned to A_1, then the correct response probability is 100 percent. If half of the stimulus elements at the beginning of the experiment are conditioned to A_1, then the correct response probability is 50 percent. If none of the stimulus elements at the beginning of the experiment are conditioned to A_1, then the correct response probability is 0 percent. Thus, the correct response probability is entirely dependent on the state of the system. As an increasing number of elements become conditioned to the correct response, learning occurs, up to a point. As more and more elements become conditioned to the correct response, the rate of learning goes down. When all of the stimulus elements are conditioned to the correct response, no more learning occurs. This Estes refers to as a negatively accelerated learning curve. If a set of stimulus elements is replicated between one experiment and the next, the probability of transfer is high. If none of the stimulus elements is replicated between one experiment and the next, the likelihood of transfer is zero. Thus, in a new learning situation, the probability of a correct response is entirely dependent on the proportion of stimuli in S that are conditioned to the A_1 response. Through probability and statistical sampling techniques, Estes's stimulus sampling theory predicted learning and learning rates for both animals and humans.

structuralism (humanism)

Not really a part of any modern *learning paradigm* although closest to that of *humanism*, structuralism, a late-nineteenth-century learning theory espoused by Edward Titchener, opposed its contemporary theory of *functionalism,* which states that *consciousness* could not be reduced to basic elements. Structuralism, like Wundt's *voluntarism*, was the belief that consciousness could indeed be reduced to basic elements, that it could be studied scientifically. However, in voluntarism the emphasis was on the human will, on an active mind. With structuralism, the focus was on *laws of association* and on a passive mind. In fact, the structuralists sought to prove via the scientific method Aristotle's notion that simple ideas are transformed into more complex ones through the laws of association. Structuralists also thought that an understanding of consciousness should be studied for its own sake and not for the good of human culture, as was thought by the functionalists. They opposed the possibility of unconscious processes. They also opposed the study of animals as a way to discover how humans behaved. As a result, structuralism was a short-lived phenomenon.

structural learning theory (cognitivism)

Developed by J. Scandura in the mid–1970s, structural learning theory is a rule-based approach to human *problem solving*. Most often applied to mathematics instruction, structural learning theory assumes that *working memory* follows a *cognitive process* that involves holding both rules and data. Structural learning theory is also an approach for rule identification based upon a hierarchy for specific learning and problem-solving tasks. With structural learning, instructors are to provide to the students the simplest solution to a mathematical problem since they are trying to master simple and basic rules. Then, once the simple rules and paths to problem solving are learned, the instructors should provide more complex paths and variations based upon higher-order rules and logic.

structure of intellect model (cognitivism)

Beginning in the mid–1960s, J.P. Guilford and his colleagues at the University of Southern California developed the structure of intellect (SI) model, which is regarded as a general theory of human *intelligence*. In the structure of intellect model, intelligence is made up of operations, contents, and products. Operations include cognition, memory, divergent production, convergent production, and evaluation components. Contents include visual, auditory, symbolic, semantic, and behavioral components. Products include units, classes, relations, systems, transformations, and implications.

Since Guilford regards each of the above dimensions as independent of one another, one could conceive of well over a hundred different components of intelligence. He and his colleagues developed a series of tests that seek to measure intelligence in relation to these components. Based upon the theory, Guilford postulated that there are thirty distinct *problem-solving* skills (i.e., convergent and divergent operations), thirty different memory operation skills, thirty different *decision-making* skills (i.e., evaluation operations), and thirty different language skills (i.e., cognitive operations). The structure of intellect model seeks to match various types of learning abilities to specific learning situations in general education, reading, mathematics, remedial and gifted education, training, and

career counseling. Structure of Intellect Systems, a company founded by Mary Meeker, a student of Guilford, provides testing, evaluation, and assessment of learners based upon the structure of intelligence model.

structuring (cognitivism)

This is one of three *modes of learning* (a general human learning model) delineated by D.E. Rumelhart and Donald A. Norman in the late 1970s and early 1980s. The main point of modes of learning is that *instructional design* and *curriculum design* should match with these three learning modes: *accretion*, *structuring*, and *tuning*. Accretion, the most common mode, is a process of *knowledge acquisition*, whereby new knowledge enters into human *memory*. Structuring (and restructuring), the most difficult mode, involves the creation of new *schema* or *knowledge structures*, which involve reflection that leads to a state of *metacognition*. Tuning, the most time-consuming mode, is the process of taking the new knowledge and using it to perform tasks to facilitate expert human performance.

subsumption theory (cognitivism)

David Ausubel's subsumption theory, first delineated in the 1960s and further elaborated upon in the 1970s, states that new material learned in a school setting should be related to previously presented ideas and concepts that become processed and extant in the *cognitive structure* of the brain. Opposing somewhat Bruner's *discovery learning* process, in which students discover and shape content on their own, Ausubel believes that teachers must provide to the students contextual information, as well as *advance organizers*, which act as a bridge between new material and previous material studied. Thus, Ausubel's learning paradigm is more *instructor-centric* than *learner-centric*. In fact, Ausubel refers to the instructional aspects of the subsumption process as *expository teaching*. Ausubel further defines, from the learner's perspective, the subsumption process (new ideas placed by the instructor within the context of old ideas in some sort of conceptual structure) as *reception learning*. It opposes *discovery learning,* in which the students construct and organize the content. Besides reception learning, Ausubel also refers to subsumption theory as meaningful verbal learning, which is learning (of primarily textual information) determined by the organization of the learner's prior knowledge that allows for the facile incorporation and reception of the new knowledge.

As noted, much of Ausubel's focus is on the reception of verbal and textual information. Followers and adherents of David Ausubel and his theory, in an attempt to provide graphical depictions of words and idea linkages, developed visual word and idea maps of concept families and linkages to provide a pictorial, contextual structure to the information being studied. These are exemplified in *concept mapping, mind mapping,* and *knowledge mapping* techniques. All are based upon subsumption theory, a process in which new concepts and ideas enter the learner's consciousness and fit within a broader context and categorization. Interestingly, all of these mapping techniques emphasize a cooperative, *constructivist* learning approach, whereby the students construct these maps and construct the content, with the instructor acting as a facilitator rather than as a distributor of information. In his *discovery learning* process, Bruner also has come to a more cognitivist approach, like that of Ausubel's subsumption theory, when he maintains that the learners need a *schema* that they can refer to and then build additional content as they make their inferences, interconnections, hypotheses, and learning decisions.

survival anxiety (organizational learning)

In a *transformational learning* situation, survival anxiety is an emotional state that a manager or worker may have as a result of not being able to learn, to change, to grow, and to meet the ever-mounting demands of the current business environment and organiza-

tion. Survival anxiety involves especially a fear to learn, usually because there is a fear to admit either that we do not know something or that in some way we feel lacking in knowledge, resources, or skills. Survival anxiety is obviously detrimental to *organizational learning* and the *learning organization.*

symbol systems theory (cognitivism)

Gavriel Salomon's symbol systems theory is similar to Lee Cronbach and Richard Snow's *aptitude-treatment interaction* and Howard Gardner's *multiple intelligences.* All three theories focus upon the individual differences and *learning styles* of students and how learning content and sequences, as well as types of media, should be tailored to take into consideration these differences. Symbol systems are patterns and sequences of symbolic expressions through which learners acquire new information. Examples of types of symbol systems, are printed text, pictures, numbers, graphs, and musical scores. Salomon's theory looks at the effects of media in relation to the learners' varying types of *cognitive processes* required for mastering specific sets of skills. Some media, such as educational television programs, require more processing than other types, such as reading books. Each media type follows specific rules and conventions.

According to Salomon, media should be provided, organized and sequenced within the instruction, based upon the learner's background, knowledge, and skills required. Salomon's theory also emphasizes the fact that media and the learner affect and influence each other. Salomon finds that the learner's *schema* has an important influence on *knowledge acquisition.* Media also create in the learner new schemata that are a result of the new cognitive processes and connections occurring as learning takes place.

symbolic concept acquisition (cognitivism)

A program within *Soar* developed by Craig Miller, symbolic concept acquisition seeks to model *cognitive processes* in humans, particularly *inductive learning.* Symbolic concept acquisition, in particular, models how humans learn and apply classification rules to the environment and use these to perform specific tasks. For example, a round, relatively heavy object may be a baseball; a somewhat round, but very light object may be a balloon. By having certain rules, certain classes of objects are predicted and are interacted with by humans. Letting go of one object may result in it hitting the foot. Letting go of the other object may result in it escaping up into the sky. The objective of the program and Soar is to discover the process of how humans learn, acquire new information, classify it, and utilize it to perform tasks. The assumption is that *knowledge acquisition* is tied to *knowledge representation* and interaction with *knowledge objects* within a given learning environment. The overall goal is to create a *cognitive architecture* that matches closely with human thinking and learning.

symbolic interaction (constructivism)

A term later used to describe the early developmental learning theories of Charles Cooley and George Herbert Mead, symbolic interaction is a process of learning and maturation that is characterized by the following postulate. Individuals develop personality and self-identity by interacting with others and by defining themselves through certain symbols and tags. First, the child only views things from his or her own selfish perspective. He or she is the center of the universe. Second, the child interacts with others and pretends to be others (soldiers, doctors, teachers, etc.) through role-playing activities. Third, the child uses symbols (e.g., language, signs, signals, and facial expressions) to communicate with others and to define the self in relation to the nonself.

Similar to Piaget's *genetic epistemology*, symbolic interaction involves a series of interactions that resemble what Piaget defined in the dual processes of *accommodation* and *assimilation*. As with Piaget's developmental theory, symbolic interaction focuses upon the child being actively engaged in the process of learning through his or her interactions

and experiences in life. Symbols greatly aid in the *knowledge acquisition* process, for they help learners name, classify, and remember objects encountered in the environment. They also increase the learner's ability to think and perform *problem-solving* activities and help learners be more active rather than passive as they interact with others and the environment. Symbol sharing is intimately tied to *knowledge sharing, knowledge representation*, and the development of individuality within the context of a social environment.

synchronous learning (educational technology)

A type of *distance learning*, synchronous learning is *computer-mediated communication* in which the learners and the instructor are communicating over the *Internet* at the same time as part of their course activities. With synchronous learning, interactions and communications occur simultaneously through the use of *videoconferencing*, voice or text *chat,* or *audio-conferencing*. Synchronous learning derives its meaning from the data processing world, in which the term "synchronous" refers to computer interactions or processes that occur at the same time rather than at various points of time. Synchronous learning is opposed to *asynchronous learning*. Asynchronous learning is *computer-mediated communication* in which the learners and the instructor are NOT communicating over the *Internet* at the same time as part of their course activities. Instead, interactions and communications are occurring non-simultaneously through the use of e-mail, mail lists, class Web sites (where lectures, lecture notes, *chat* text, syllabus, case studies, video and audio files, and research deliverables are posted) for consumption at any time. Most Internet-based distance learning courses employ both synchronous and asynchronous learning methods and techniques, where they are used for the creation of *virtual learning communities*, the *electronic campus*, and the *universal campus network*.

systems thinking (organizational learning)

In Peter Senge's paradigm for the *learning organization*, systems thinking is a mode of thinking, a process in which one not only analyzes the entire organization and breaks it down into its constituent parts, but also considers carefully the relationships between all of the parts. With systems thinking, which is the *fifth discipline*, one must focus on all or almost all of the interactions and interrelationships that occur within the organization being studied. Systems thinking is an important and necessary milestone to be achieved for the enterprise to become a learning organization. It allows one to look more carefully at the overall corporate situation and make informed decisions that are based upon an understanding of how the entire organization operates within a social context. With systems thinking, one looks at all of the aspects and interrelations occurring within the system (i.e., the enterprise) before making judgments about the direction that the organization should take to be effective as a whole and within the society at large.

T

There are things known, and there are things unknown. And in between are the doors.
—James Douglas Morrison, twentieth-century American poet and lead singer of "The Doors"

tabula rasa (behaviorism)

According to seventeenth-century English philosopher John Locke, the human mind at birth is a blank slate, a tabula rasa. To Locke, there is nothing in the mind that is not first derived from the senses. Locke's *empiricism,* which is succinctly summed up through his concept of the mind as a tabula rasa, is not really part of any one *learning paradigm*, but an influence on all. Empiricism is the philosophical belief that the basis for the understanding and attainment of human knowledge (i.e., *epistemology*) is through sensory experience. Through the senses, humans gather information and process it. The human mind is thus a direct result of life and learning experiences. From sensory experience, humans derive simple ideas. From a combination of simple ideas, complex ideas are formed.

In the eighteenth century David Hume, often regarded as a radical empiricist, argued that we can be sure of nothing, for all of our knowledge is based upon subjective and personal sensory experience. From a philosophical perspective, empiricism, especially in its most radical form (that of David Hume), was thus a tremendous influence on the learning paradigm of *behaviorism*, in which the study of mental events was regarded as irrelevant and off-limits. Human behavior, not human thought, should be the focus of learning research. To the behaviorists, behavior can be scientifically observed and analyzed. This is not the case with human thought.

Opposed to this radical form of empiricism is *cognitivism*, whose philosophical roots go back to Immanuel Kant. Immanuel Kant, opposing Hume, stated that there are *innate categories of thought* or faculties that are not derived from sensory experience. These faculties influence and provide meaning to human sensory experiences. For Kant, the mind itself is the source of knowledge. For empiricists, the source of knowledge is the sensory world.

tacit knowledge (organizational learning)

From a knowledge management perspective, tacit knowledge is knowledge that is stored in people's heads and shared among immediate colleagues. It is often harder to capture; yet it contains valuable information related to creative and innovative solutions to business problems, and it needs to be disseminated throughout the organization. *Explicit knowledge,* on the other hand, is knowledge that is extant in the form of corporate memos, reports, policies and procedures within the business enterprise. Thus, explicit knowledge resides in formal documents of the organization. Even though these documents may be *digitized* and provided to employees within a *digital library*, they are often less important than *tacit knowledge*.

tact (behaviorism)

This term refers to the second of four categories of human *verbal behavior* delineated by B.F. Skinner. According to Skinner, verbal behavior (i.e., language) of humans can be entirely defined and explained within the context of *reinforcement theory*. For Skinner, both human talking and listening are actions that are directly influenced, just like any other behavior, by reinforcement from the environment. Skinner classified verbal behaviors that are responses to reinforcement into four categorizations. (1) *Mands*. These are commands and utterances that require an immediate response. An example of a mand is, "Watch out for the baseball." (2) *Tact*. These are words that represent specific objects recognized by the human in the environment, expressed out loud, and reinforced not only by the sound of the word but also by an observer's recognition that the word corresponds to the object and to the sound of the word itself. (3) *Echoic Behavior*. When the human repeats exactly the same set of words stated verbatim by another, this action is known as echoic behavior. It is a first step toward learning more complex verbal behavior beyond repeating what another has said. (4) *Autoclitic Behavior*. This is behavior that is entirely dependent upon other verbal behavior to qualify responses, to express relationships, and to provide a grammatical frame to the verbal behavior. Overall, Skinner's view of human verbal behavior is that it is based entirely upon the environment and environmental responses. He rejects the cognitive processes that are delineated by cognitivists as they seek to define natural language processing of humans.

taskability (cognitivism)

Within a *cognitive architecture*, taskability refers to the ability of a system (e.g., Newell's

Soar) to have an *agent* perform various tasks and do *problem solving* without having to be reprogrammed each time by the system developers. Closely related to a *unified theory of cognition*, cognitive architecture refers to a model of mental processing for human problem solving, learning, and task completion. An example of a cognitive architecture is Newell's *Soar,* which is a framework for understanding how humans and *artificial intelligence* computer systems "think" and learn. Soar is a widely recognized cognitive architecture that uses concepts such as *chunking* and *problem space* to describe how the human brain works to solve problems and complete tasks.

taxonomy (organizational learning)

An important concept for *knowledge management* and *Web-based knowledge transfer*, the term taxonomy refers to a method for creating a hierarchical structure of information within a domain of knowledge for an organization or a business enterprise. The taxonomy orders information in logical and contextual ways so that seemingly random pieces of information extant in the organization as *tacit knowledge* take on additional meaning and context through a multilayered information structure. The taxonomy provides a common language within the *learning organization* to facilitate *knowledge sharing* for employees with diverse backgrounds and experience levels. By capturing the domain of knowledge by means of the taxonomy, the employees of an organization are able to access a wealth of information and materials that they may not have known existed or that were relevant to their need. The taxonomy is often tied to an *electronic performance support system* that involves a system for *natural language processing* as well as *a machine tractable dictionary*. As a result of having a taxonomy that is integrated with these *artificial intelligence* technologies, employees can become more productive and valuable to the organization by having a specific and targeted set of knowledge readily available and accessible via the computer.

taxonomy of educational objectives (cognitivism)

As postulated in the mid–1950s by a group of educational psychologists who compiled a book with the same title, the taxonomy of educational objectives, also known as Bloom's taxonomy, is Benjamin Bloom's (and colleagues') classification of the goals of education regarding the development of *intelligence* within three categories or domains: the cognitive domain (emphasizing mental processes), the affective domain (emphasizing feeling and emotion), and the psychomotor domain (concerned with motor skills). Within the cognitive domain, the domain most often noted by educators and experts in *cognitive psychology*, there exist six levels arranged in a hierarchy, in which the lowest level involves recall of facts and the highest level involves evaluation and assessment. The six levels and their corresponding actions, as synthesized by Carla Lane in *The Distance Learning Technology Resource Guide,* are as follows:

1. Knowledge: arrange, define, duplicate, label, list, memorize, name, order, recognize, relate, recall, repeat, and reproduce state;
2. Comprehension: classify, describe, discuss, explain, express, identify, indicate, locate, recognize, report, restate, review, select, and translate;
3. Application: apply, choose, demonstrate, dramatize, employ, illustrate, interpret, operate, practice, schedule, sketch, solve, use, and write;
4. Analysis: analyze, appraise, calculate, categorize, compare, contrast, criticize, differentiate, discriminate, distinguish, examine, experiment, question, and test;
5. Synthesis: arrange, assemble, collect, compose, construct, create, design, develop, formulate, manage, organize, plan, prepare, propose, set up, and write;
6. Evaluation: appraise, argue, assess, attach, choose, compare, defend, estimate, judge, predict, rate, core, select, support, value, evaluate.

Since the time of publication of *The Taxonomy of Educational Objectives,* Bloom's taxonomy has been repeatedly used to evaluate *curriculum design* within this hierarchy of learner actions. *Instructional design* specialists utilize the taxonomy to arrange educational content from relatively simple *learning and performance* activities to higher-level learning and performance activities.

teachback (constructivism)

In the mid–1970s, Gordon Pask espoused his *conversation theory,* which stated that for both living organisms and *artificial intelligence* machines, learning results from the continuing conversations on a focused subject matter that these entities engage in over time on several language levels. Similar to *social development* theory, *cognitive coaching,* and *apprenticeship learning,* conversation theory emphasizes *teachback,* which is the process by which one entity teaches another entity what they have learned. Pask's theory also emphasizes the entities' joint learning activities that focus on the relationships between concepts. Learners come to understand these concept relationships in one of two ways. They either obtain information sequentially, or they look at the complete set of information and seek a higher-order relationship that is not necessarily sequential. Conversation theory is an outgrowth of *cybernetics,* in which it is postulated that learning is completely determined by the subjective social interaction of the learners and is enhanced as the conversation continues.

team learning (organizational learning)

One of the disciplines for the *learning organization* in Peter Senge's *The Fifth Discipline,* team learning is a process of suspending assumptions previously held by individuals and entering into a team dialogue with the goal of having the individuals within the team think together. It does not involve a win-lose situation, where one person's views become the dominant one for the group. Team learning is closely related to another of Senge's disciplines, which is *building shared vision.* The goal is to have the team see the bigger picture, the one that is beyond the perspective of each individual on the team. According to Senge, teams rather than individuals are the fundamental atoms of the organization. For him, without team learning, there can be no *organizational learning*.

technical curriculum design (organizational learning)

Historically speaking, technical curriculum design is a term used in reference to the development of courses and programs within vocational and industrial arts learning. Currently, the term is used in reference to *organizational learning* and *skills management*. Technical curriculum is developed primarily to enhance the skills and performance of employees within an organization. Technical curriculum design follows primarily the *instructional design* process. Instructional design is a method that developers of technical curriculum use to create effective learning applications in the form of *multimedia applications, hypermedia applications, computer-based training, Web-based training,* etc.

Typically, there are four phases to the instructional design process, which are: (1) Analysis Phase. The instructional design team analyzes the audience and its needs and analyzes the tasks to be performed within the learning activity. (2) Design Phase. The instructional design team defines learning goals, objectives, and strategies. (3) Development Phase. The instructional design team develops the instructional content. (4) Implementation/Evaluation Phase. The content or course is delivered to the learners and feedback is obtained on the effectiveness of the product. Most products of technical curriculum design are very task-oriented, very structured, and follow most of the tenets that B.F. Skinner laid out in his approach to *programmed learning*.

technology integration (educational technology)

An umbrella term used often by educational administrators and *instructional technology* specialists within the world of education, technology integration refers to the process of integrating the computer, computer software, *computer-mediated communication*, and the *Internet* into the *curriculum design* of educational programs and courses. This is a noble goal of most educational institutions. However, most efforts in technology integration have difficulty achieving success due to problems inherent in schools that are still fully enmeshed in the *industrial age educational paradigm*. As schools move to the *digital age educational paradigm*, their attempts at achieving technology integration are likely to become more successful.

telecommuting (educational technology)

An important element for *knowledge management, knowledge sharing, Web-based knowledge transfer,* and *organizational learning*, telecommuting is the act of using the computer from home to perform work and learning activities online while being connected via the *Internet* to a corporate or educational Web site. Employers encourage employee telecommuting, for it reduces corporate overhead. Educational institutions encourage learners to engage in telecommuting instead of coming to classes, for it reduces educational overhead as well. In both environments, brick-and-mortar costs are reduced, *virtual learning communities* are created, and learning and work occur without the usual costs associated with people traveling to a physical location to share information.

theory of action (organizational learning)

Chris Argyris's theory of action is a set of rules that individuals, especially managers, use within organizations for what they regard as their corporate survival. These theories of action are composed of values, theories, beliefs, rules, policies, and procedures that people in organizations follow to plan and carry out all work. These rules in actual use, however, are typically simplified and translated by the managers as follows: (1) Remain in control. (2) Win; don't lose. (3) Repress negative feelings about yourself and the organization. (4) Always be rational and define your objectively clearly. However, by following these narrow rules, the possibility of learning in organizations is, according to Argyris, quite minimal. To solve the problem, Argyris poses his method, which he refers to as *action research*.

Action research is a strategy to help individuals in organizations move from *single loop* learning (learning that corrects errors by changing routine behavior) to *double loop* learning (learning that corrects errors by examining the underlying culture of the organization) in order to enhance *decision making* within a fluid work environment. The strategy goes back to the 1940s, when it was used during World War II to make command and control decisions in the military. The goal of action research is to integrate action and reflection for the management practitioner in the midst of great organizational change. Its method is useful in helping managers make more reflective, informed decisions and to develop a culture of inquiry in *decision-making* activities. Action research also emphasizes *collaboration*, cooperation, and sharing of information and experiences among management peers.

By developing these action research skills, managers can stop following the four narrowly defined rules that they previously used for what they thought was their survival. Instead, they can grow, develop, and learn as individuals and as good corporate citizens. By developing high levels of action research skills, managers within organizations can more easily innovate and deal with organizational change, promote *organizational learning*, and respond more effectively to problem situations requiring attention and action.

theory of teaching in context (cognitivism)

Developed by the Teacher Model Group at the University of California at Berkeley, the theory of teaching in context is an attempt to define why teachers do what they do when they are teaching. It is a model that seeks to define the interactions of the teacher's goals, beliefs, attitudes, and knowledge as they are focused on the teaching situation. It is also a method that seeks to predict what teachers will do in ordinary and extraordinary classroom situations. The goal is to help teachers learn how to monitor better their own teaching and the impact that it has on the learners.

Theory X / Y (organizational learning)

Somewhat opposed by William Ouchi, whose *Theory Z* is often referred to as a Japanese management style, Douglas McGregor's Theory X / Theory Y (first espoused in the early 1960s) is based to a great extent upon Maslow's *hierarchy of needs theory* from the mid–1950s. From an *organizational learning* perspective, Maslow's theory postulates that the leader of an organization must satisfy the human needs of his or her employees. Human needs range from lower-order needs (e.g., food, shelter, and safety) to higher-order needs (e.g., belongingness, esteem, and self-actualization). All of these needs are important factors for motivating humans to learn and perform well within the enterprise. Theory X workers who are not well motivated and who are regarded by management as lazy and unproductive are dominated by satisfying lower-order needs. Management's strategy is to control Theory X workers by strict discipline, threats of punishment within a rigid environment. Theory Y workers, on the other hand, are regarded by management as more creative and productive employees who enjoy learning and performing on the job. They wish to participate in management and in the *decision making* that occurs within the organization. They are dominated by satisfying higher-order needs, such as belongingness, esteem, and self-actualization. McGregor postulates that Theory Y is a better approach toward motivating employees in organizations than Theory X. McGregor's Theory X / Y tends to view how employees perform from the manager's perspective. Ouchi's Theory Z focuses on how employees view management. It is interesting to note that McGregor perceived schools as following Theory X from the 1930s through the 1950s, and Theory Y from the 1960s on.

Theory Z (organizational learning)

William Ouchi's Theory Z, often referred to as Japanese management style (though it is in fact a combination of Japanese and American styles), is a response to Douglas McGregor's *Theory X / Y*. Theory Z focuses on the employee and the perceptions and needs of employees. Theory Z employees have a great need to be supported and appreciated by management. They seek to build cooperative and close working relationships with their peers. Theory Z employees have a high degree of self-discipline, order, organization, and a sense of cohesiveness within the organization. They wish to learn from each other and participate greatly in management *decision making*. Important from an *organizational learning* perspective, Theory Z emphasizes the implementation of employee job rotation so that employees can learn new concepts, procedures, and skills. Continual education and training is emphasized as well so that employees can remain productive and be more valuable as participants in the organization over time. By doing a variety of jobs, by continually learning new things, Theory Z workers learn about the key issues that are important to the organization and can help steer it toward a productive, successful, and ethical future. Family, culture, and social context are important factors that Theory Z employees seek to incorporate into the business enterprise. It is interesting to note that Theory Z has a close parallel to that of *learner-centric learning paradigms* of *constructivism*, in which the control of the activities and the *learning environment* is placed in the hands of the employees, or the learners, rather than in the hands of the supervisors, or the teachers.

think aloud protocol (cognitivism)

Alan Schoenfeld's think aloud protocol is a technique within his *mathematical problem-solving model*, in which participants engaged in a *problem-solving* activity talk out loud to share what they are thinking about while performing a task. This is done in an attempt to reveal the inner *cognitive processes* that the participants are following as they seek to complete a goal set out for them by the researchers. The researchers, in turn, seek to understand better how both novice and expert problem solvers complete tasks. A finding of the think aloud protocol was that the entire process was an exercise in *metacognition*, in which the participants were able to become cognizant of, supervise, and change their own cognitive processes in order to be better problem solvers and more productive at reaching their task goals. This awareness and ability to self-monitor cognitive processes is known as *self-regulation*.

thinking mathematically (humanism)

Closely related to the *culture of mathematics*, which is a philosophical and social orientation to the study of mathematics, thinking mathematically involves learners being able to look at the world from a mathematical point of view. It involves achieving over time a level of competence with the mathematical theorems and postulates, and their applications, while using them to better understand the world and society. Within a *constructivist learning environment*, novice learners are introduced into thinking mathematically by a process of *social development, apprenticeship learning,* and *cognitive coaching*, and by participating in the process of acquiring mathematical knowledge within a cultural, interactive context. Through a series of *mathematical problem-solving* activities within the group, and guided by the instructor, the novice learners slowly become part of the culture of mathematics, in which they become adept at thinking mathematically. Similar to the process of *enculturation* and similar to the learning process described in Jean Lave's *situated learning*, the learners over time come to participate in a *community of practice*. As the novice gains experience at thinking mathematically and moves closer to the community's center, he or she becomes more actively engaged in the culture of mathematics and eventually takes on the role of mentor helping new, uninitiated individuals into the community of practice.

thought control (behaviorism)

Critics of *behaviorism* sometimes claim that coercive agents, seeking to control an individual's behavior, thoughts, and feelings, use *behavior modification* and *operant conditioning* methods to perform *behavior control,* which is a set of coercive techniques used to alter the behavior, attitude, and thoughts of the subject whether they are deemed functional or dysfunctional. Behavior control occurs against the will of the subject. With thought control, the subject is willingly subjected to the coercive agent's methods because of a desire to change and often to become part of the group or cult. The control often involves complete *behavior control* whereby the coercive agent seeks to control all aspects of life: where the person lives, what the person eats, wears, sleeps, duties performed, etc. With behavior control, the victim knows who the "enemy" is, or the agent attempting to exert control. In thought control, the victim does not really know if the controlling agent is a friend or a foe. In thought control, the victim willingly goes along with the process of control because he or she is seeking a change of behavior.

To avoid *cognitive dissonance*, people ultimately find a way to adjust their beliefs to fit the new experience no matter how poor the logic or rationalization may be to others. According to Leon Festinger, in attempting to avoid cognitive dissonance, some individuals are easily subjected to behavior control (i.e., the control of an individual's entire physical existence), thought control (i.e., the control of an individual's thought processes), and *emotion control* (i.e., the control of an individual's emotional life).

tractable (cognitivism)

Within artificial intelligence studies, tractable refers to how easily information can be understood by machines. Specifically, it refers to *knowledge objects* in which information can be extracted by *artificial intelligence* programs from dictionaries or *machine tractable dictionaries*, using human *natural language* instead of computer languages. An important *artificial intelligence* research focus, *natural language processing* is an attempt to make computer programs able to understand spoken or written natural languages. This would mean that computers would be able to understand meaning. Research is currently being conducted into compiling dictionaries of words and their meanings that are tractable (that a computer can "read" and "understand").

Thus, an objective of *computer lexicography* is the development of *machine tractable dictionaries* to facilitate computer-based natural language processing.

This area of AI research is also closely associated with *computational linguistics,* which involves the use of statistics and statistical programs to identify word patterns and recurrences. And, it is associated with *voice recognition,* which is sometimes referred to as natural language recognition. Natural language processing is the ultimate goal of AI research, giving the computer the ability to understand meanings of human words and to allow computers and humans to communicate. The path to that goal, according to more than a few AI researchers, is through the creation of the machine tractable dictionary and the creation of tractable *knowledge objects.*

transactive memory (organizational learning)

Daniel Wegner's theory of transactive memory elaborated upon in 1995 is a network model for describing *shared cognitive maps,* in which individuals in the organization access shared memory in much the same fashion as a group of networked computers share memory. This theory falls squarely in line with *information processing theory* and *network models* such as the *PDP memory model,* in which human cognition and memory are described in computer terms and relations. Anand, Manz, and Glick in 1998 adapted Wegner's theory of transactive memory and applied it to an *organizational memory* approach to understanding *organizational cognition.* These researchers define organizational memory as knowledge known by group members through their interactions and communications (i.e., *tacit knowledge*) and knowledge extant and available to individuals in the organization through *knowledge bases* (i.e., *explicit knowledge*).

transformational learning (organizational learning)

As a response to an organization's resistance to change, transformational learning is opposed to *adaptive coping.* Adaptive coping is a management learning strategy in which the individual does not challenge old, preset assumptions within a company or institution regarding its policies, procedures, and culture but instead works within the old framework and seeks to provide small, incremental enhancements to the organization. Unlike adaptive coping, in which the manager tries to slowly but surely change the organization's culture and business practices, transformational learning is a more radical process and solution in which operational assumptions are directly challenged and procedures are changed quickly. Typically, a new procedure is put in place in parallel to the old procedure. As the people in the organization learn to adapt to the significant change resulting from the new system, the parallel old system is eventually dropped. To facilitate the change process, shared learning and mentoring are encouraged by management in the transformed organization. In the current business and technological environment, with the rapid change that is occurring to meet twenty-first century business challenges, transformational learning is a far superior strategy to that of adaptive coping.

trial-and-error learning (behaviorism)

An important aspect of Edward Thorndike's *incremental learning* (i.e., learning that occurs in small steps over time rather than in large leaps), trial-and-error learning is the trying of different solutions in a problem-solving situation until an effective solution is finally discovered by the organism. In Edward Thorndike's *puzzle box* experiments, a cat is placed in a very confining box with a pole sticking up in the middle or a chain hanging from the top of the box. The cat seeks to get out of the box by pushing against the pole or by pulling on the chain. In the puzzle box experiments, Thorndike sought to keep track of the time it took for the cat to get out of the box, as well as how many times the cat tried, using various means, to get out before being successful. Thorndike observed that the time it took for the cat to get out of the box decreased as the number of attempts increased. He concluded from these experiments that learning occurs in small, incremental steps rather than in huge jumps. He referred to this as incremental learning as opposed to *insightful learning.* Thorndike also concluded that the most basic, yet most successful type of learning was *trial-and-error learning,* in which the animal tries different means and methods to get out of the puzzle box. He originally referred to trial-and-error learning as "selecting and connecting."

triarchic theory (cognitivism)

Robert Sternberg's triarchic theory, presented in *The Triarchic Mind: A New Theory of Intelligence* published in the late 1980s, states that *intelligence* is based upon three elements, which are: (1) functions of governments of the mind; (2) stylistic preferences; and (3) forms of mental self-government. Sternberg further subdivides the government functions into legislative (to create, plan, imagine, and formulate), executive (to do and implement), and judicial (to judge and evaluate). He subdivides the stylistic preferences into internal (individuals working by themselves) and external (individuals working with others). He subdivides the forms of mental self-government into monarchic (people with singular goals that they seek to accomplish), hierarchic (people with multiple goals who can easily prioritize), oligarchic (people who view goals as being equal in weight and therefore have difficulty prioritizing), anarchic (people, operating without rules or structure, who create their own *problem-solving* techniques and solutions on the fly). His theory is regarded as a general theory of human intelligence.

tuning (cognitivism)

This is one of three *modes of learning* (a general human learning model) delineated by D.E. Rumelhart and Donald A. Norman in the late 1970s and early 1980s. The main point of modes of learning is that *instructional design* and *curriculum design* should match with these three learning modes: *accretion, structuring,* and *tuning.* Accretion, the most common mode, is a process of *knowledge acquisition,* whereby new knowledge enters into human *memory.* Structuring (and restructuring), the most difficult mode, involves the creation of new *schema* or *knowledge structures,* which involve reflection that leads to a state of *metacognition.* Tuning, the most time-consuming mode, is the process of taking the new knowledge and using it to perform tasks to facilitate expert human performance.

U

unified theories of cognition (cognitivism)

In 1990, Allen Newell postulated in *Unified Theories of Cognition* that *cognitive psychology* has reached the point in its evolutionary development that it is now able to design a *cognitive architecture* and a working model of human learning and intelligence. Also, Allen Newell asserts that the cognitive processing that occurs in human brains can be replicated in computer models with *agents* acting as human learners seeking to complete goals. Newell is at the center of several cognitive architectures and *artificial intelligence* programming languages, including the *Logic Theorist, GPS, GOMS,* and *Soar*. This unified theory proposed by Newell embodies subcategories of cognitive behavior, such as the ability to process language, the ability to perform mathematical problems, and the ability to memorize information. An important goal for all of the artificial intelligence applications is the program's ability to measure agent and human learner performance toward the attainment of a goal.

universal campus network (organizational learning)

An important and large goal within the areas of *organizational learning* and *knowledge management*, the universal campus network is an *electronic learning environment* that spans across individual schools and organizations.

In the near future, the learning marketplace may well demand a tighter educational certification process for most professions, much as in law and medicine, thereby forcing colleges and universities to provide more standardized courses among themselves. In so doing, the universities will need to create a structure for *knowledge sharing* and degree sharing between schools. Multiple universities offering the same degree may establish partnerships with each other to give students the best possible curriculum and instruction in the areas that make up a discipline. Once local geographic boundaries are broken down via *Web-based education* and students are no longer restricted to particular geographic areas to obtain their education, we may experience a more capitalistic approach to education with the birth of a universal campus network. Implementation of the universal campus network may allow students to consume the best possible interactive courses and content via the *Internet*, no matter what their parent institution is. Professional or regional associations may take the lead regarding certification and promotion of partnerships between industry and education and between educational institutions working together to build the electronic content and the electronic sharing of information within the disciplines.

V

The purpose of computing is insight, not numbers.
—Richard Hamming, twentieth-century American mathematician and computer scientist

verbal behavior (behaviorism)

According to B.F. Skinner, verbal behavior (i.e., language) of humans can be defined and explained within the context of *reinforcement theory*. For Skinner, both human talking and listening are actions that are directly influenced, just like any other behavior, by reinforcement. Skinner classified verbal behaviors that are responses to reinforcement into four categorizations. (1) *Mands*. These are commands and utterances that require an immediate response. An example of a mand is, "Watch out for the baseball." (2) *Tact*. These are words that represent specific objects recognized by the human in the environment, expressed out loud and reinforced not only by the sound of the word but also by an observer's recognition that the word corresponds to the object and to the sound of the word itself. (3) *Echoic Behavior*. When the human repeats exactly same the set of words stated verbatim by another, this action is known as echoic behavior. It is a first step toward learning more complex verbal behavior beyond repeating what another has said. (4) *Autoclitic Behavior*. This is behavior that is entirely dependent upon other verbal behavior to qualify responses, to express relationships, and to provide a grammatical frame to the verbal behavior. Overall, Skinner's view of human verbal behavior is that it is based entirely upon the environment and environmental responses. He rejects the cognitive processes that are delineated by cognitivists as they seek to define natural language processing of humans.

verbal-linguistic intelligence (constructivism)

Howard Gardner's theory regarding human *intelligence-multiple intelligences*-posits that our culture and school systems focus far too much attention as a measure of success on verbal-linguistic intelligence and *logical-mathematical intelligence*. Gardner's theory suggests that there are at least eight other types of human intelligence that are just as significant and that need to be considered within our culture and schools. Gardner's eight intelligences are: verbal-linguistic intelligence; logical-mathematical intelligence; *musical intelligence*; *spatial intelligence*; *bodily kinesthetic intelligence*; *interpersonal intelligence*; *intrapersonal intelligence*; and *naturalist intelligence*.

Examples of verbal-linguistic intelligence activities are reading, listening, speech-making, writing, debate, poetry writing, storytelling, joke-telling, learning foreign languages, and learning grammar, syntax, and vocabulary. As an adherent of *constructivism*, especially Vygotsky's *social development theory*, Gardner believes strongly that intelligence cannot be defined or measured without consideration of the individual's cultural and social context. Each individual's development of particular types of intelligence is partially inherent but also shaped very much by environment, culture, and upbringing.

vestibule training (organizational learning)

An early precursor of *apprenticeship learning* and *on-the-job training,* vestibule training is close to the job training first utilized by owners of factories during the industrial revolution in the 1800s. Since factory owners needed trained workers to produce goods, they developed classrooms right next to the factory floor that were furnished with the kind of machines used on the factory floor. Trainees were taught in a group of about ten in the "vestibule" how to operate the machines before being assigned to a machine on the main factory floor. The key point of vestibule training is that the classroom was an exact model of what the workers would be dealing with on the factory floor. With vestibule training, the instructor provided immediate feedback to the trainees.

Similar to what is currently called *direct instruction*, vestibule training involves an expert who already knows how to perform a set of job tasks directly instructing novices on how to complete the job. This method of training is still in fairly wide use, especially in the computer industry where workers are trained on new or updated software applications, for the likelihood of successful skills transfer is quite high. Its downside is that vestibule training is human-resource-intensive and expensive, especially if many trainees need to learn the same set of job tasks at a time. Another downside of vestibule training is that both the trainer and the trainee are, during the training, off the production line or normal course of work. In the computer industry, vestibule training is being replaced by *computer-based training, Web-based training,* and *multimedia appli-*

cations that simulate through the *learning environment* the actual on-the-job activity.

videoconferencing (educational technology)

One of the earliest examples of *multimedia applications* used for *distance learning,* videoconferencing involves using in effect a video phone to allow instructors and learners in multiple locations to see and hear one another in real time (i.e., live) and interact. With the advent of the *Internet,* videoconferencing has moved to the PC desktop, wherein each learning participant has mounted on his or her own personal computer a video camera, microphone, and speakers. As each participant speaks, the others in the videoconference can see and hear one another as the video, voice, and sound data are carried over the network and delivered to each participant's computer screen and speakers.

virtual learning community (educational technology)

This is a term that falls under the umbrella of CMC, *computer-mediated communication,* a term popularized by John December. CMC is human communication via the computer. Primarily *Internet*-based, CMC focuses on the group dynamics, team-based learning activities, and associated *collaboration* and communication technologies, that closely dovetail with the constructivist learning theories embodied in *collaborative learning, cooperative learning,* and *situated learning,* among other theories within the educational *learning paradigm* of *constructivism.* CMC is a process and a technology whereby humans can create, exchange, enhance, and access information over the *Internet* to enhance communication and to create virtual learning communities. Virtual learning communities are groups of people who use the computer to engage in *Web-based knowledge transfer, Web-based education,* and *Web-based training* within a *virtual learning environment* over the Internet.

virtual learning environment (organizational learning)

Within current *knowledge management* circles, a virtual learning environment is a reference to the creation of *enterprise-wide learning* by building an *electronic learning environment* that promotes *business transformation, organizational learning*, and the achievement of a state of corporate *metacognition*. Through *agents, electronic performance support systems*, and other *just-in-time training* approaches, organizations can move from the *industrial age educational paradigm* to the *digital age educational paradigm*. As a result of the *Internet*, organizations are able to build and maintain a *knowledge construction* factory (versus the old industrial age factory that produced widgets). Organizations can also create an infrastructure for enterprise-wide learning via a virtual learning environment (including both *Web-based education* and *Web-based training components*) that is all encompassing and used by internal employees, customers, and even the public, while being entirely separate from the brick-and-mortar organization.

visual texture perception (humanism)

In *Gestalt theory*, humans instinctively structure and order visual information received from the world of phenomena. As humans attempt to structure the information perceived, they seek visual cues in order to group things into ordered sets. These visual cues are referred to as visual texture perception, which follows the Gestalt *principle of closure*. An important aspect of Gestalt theory, the principle of closure states that humans have a strong, universal tendency to complete incomplete perceptions and experiences. For example, if an individual perceives a set of lines that are broken, but nevertheless form a shape such as a rectangle or triangle, he or she will complete the figure and identify it as a rectangle or a triangle. Thus, the individual provides a *perceptual organization* to that which is perceived or experienced. This perceptual organization is applied to all life experiences as the individual grows and learns and as the *perceptual field* expands. The principle of closure also follows the *law of Pragnanz*, which states that humans respond to the world of phenomena to make it as meaningful as possible given the current conditions and situation. In German, pragnanz mean "essence." A constant human goal is to provide meaning, essence, structure, and form to all of life's experiences. Using visual texture perception (i.e., using visual cues), humans group visual phenomena experienced in the environment into ordered sets.

voice recognition (educational technology)

This is a combination of computer hardware and software that can recognize the human voice and essentially take dictation and record what is being said digitally. Voice recognition does not imply the understanding of what the human voice says (as opposed to spoken language systems). The attempt of a computer or an *agent* to understand human language through spoken language systems (i.e., understand what is being said) falls under the research discipline known as *natural language processing*. Voice recognition is simply the conversion of spoken human words into computer text. It is useful for certain *computer-based training* or *multimedia applications*, in which the learner is not able to use his or her hands to type at the computer keyboard.

voluntarism (humanism)

Not really a part of any modern *learning paradigm*, though closest to that of humanism, voluntarism is a late-nineteenth-century theory of learning espoused by Wilhelm Maximillian Wundt. Voluntarism was the belief that *consciousness* can be studied scientifically, that one could study the human mind and human will systematically. Wundt believed that one could ascertain the basic elements of which all consciousness consists, not through directly studying the mind, but through studying the mind's products (e.g., religion, myth, art, language, and culture). By observing cultural behaviors in the field, Wundt hoped to discover the elements of thought by means of the products of human will.

Waterlogic (organizational learning)

A coined term from Edward de Bono, developer of *lateral thinking, CoRT thinking,* and
Six Thinking Hats, Waterlogic, as opposed
to what is normally thought of as traditional
logic, is a thinking process that allows one's
thoughts to flow toward a solution to a problem. Waterlogic is not bound by traditional
logic and static, overly cautious, overly critical thinking, but rather focuses on creativity
and "outside the box" thinking for *problem
solving* and *decision making* in organizations.
Waterlogic allows the manager to be logical,
while still being creative and innovative.

Web-based education (educational technology)

Within *organizational learning* and *knowledge
management* circles, Web-based education is
electronic courseware offered to adult learners over the *Internet* within a business organization that is often, though not always,
directed toward management and management education. From a strictly academic
perspective, Web-based education is
courseware in any subject delivered within a
universal campus network in which programs
are offered and degrees awarded. No matter
what the environment, Web-based education
often employs both *hypermedia* and *multimedia* components.

Web-based knowledge transfer (organizational learning)

This is a process that involves sharing information within an organization via the Web to
promote and facilitate *knowledge management* and *organizational learning* for the enterprise. With the rise of the digital economy
and the *Internet*, enterprises are better able
to disseminate and share information within
and outside of the corporation on a global
scale through *Web-based knowledge transfer*.
In so doing, these organizations become more
cognizant of who they are and who their customers are. As knowledge managers, industry trainers and school educators are focusing
more and more of their attention on the evolution of *knowledge objects* from analog to
digital, from paper-based information to electronic information that is indexed and cataloged in order to facilitate Web-based
knowledge sharing. An important goal in both
industry and schools is to build the *digital
library*, the active storehouse of knowledge

that comprises the *electronic learning environment* in industry and the *electronic campus* curriculum and content in education.

Web-based training (educational technology)

Sometimes simply referred to as WBT, Web-based training is electronic courseware offered within a business to adult learners over the *Internet*. Typically, Web-based training is delivered within an *electronic learning environment* that is available strictly to an internal audience of corporate employees. It often employs both *hypermedia* and *multimedia*. It is an important element of an *electronic performance support system*, which is a *computer-based training* system that provides *on-the-job training* to workers as needed, while they are learning to perform new job tasks.

Wechsler Adult Intelligence Scale (cognitivism)

Sometimes referred to by the acronym WAIS, the Wechsler Adult Intelligence Scale is used as a measure of cognitive ability and intellectual aptitude for adults. Over a century ago, Sir Frances Galton of Great Britain sought to determine a measurement for human *intelligence*. Taking up Galton's drive to come up with an intelligence measure, Alfred Binet in Paris developed a series of questions to give to schoolchildren to measure aptitude and to predict future performance in school. Lewis Terman of Stanford University incorporated Binet's questions and enhanced the test to create the *Stanford-Binet Intelligence Scale*. The WAIS-R, the 1981 revision of the original Wechsler Adult Intelligence Scale, is an intelligence test developed for adults who are between the ages of 16 and 74. The test is subdivided into 11 modules, which include information, digit span, vocabulary, arithmetic, comprehension, similarities, picture completion, picture arrangement, block design, object assembly, and digit symbol. Using the test, a full scale IQ is scored, with 100 being an average or mean score. The standard deviation for the WAIS is an indicator of how far above or below an individual is from the average score. A modified version of the WAIS is provided to very young children between the ages of four and six-and-a-half years. Another modified version of the WAIS is used for children between six-and-a-half and fifteen years. The test is used for school placement, giftedness, learning disabilities, brain disorders, and for tracking individual development over time. It is an important tool used by experts in *cognition* who seek to determine and measure human *cognitive processes*.

working memory (cognitivism)

Sometimes called *short-term memory*, working memory is short-term conscious thought as opposed to *long-term memory*. Working memory is an important aspect of human cognitive information processing. Working memory processes knowledge that is very active and dynamic. However, working memory also processes knowledge taken in from long-term memory, typically of two types: declarative and procedural. In John Anderson's *ACT theory*, a *cognitive architecture*, *declarative memory* is a type of long-term memory that stores facts and ideas in a semantic network structure (i.e., a *network model*). *Procedural memory*, another type of *long-term memory*, takes sequences of declarative knowledge in the form of *productions* and makes further logical inferences about them. Each production contains a set of conditions and actions found within declarative memory. Working memory, or short-term conscious thought, retrieves declarative information of facts and ideas, carries out task sequences found in procedural memory, and adds new information gathered from the environment, forming new sequences that are then stored in procedural memory.

. . . the imagination reveals itself in the balance or reconciliation of opposite or discordant qualities.
—Samuel Taylor Coleridge, nineteenth-century English writer

Xanadu (educational technology)

This is a project launched in the 1960s by Ted Nelson, the individual who coined the term *hypertext.* Its purpose was to conduct new research and development of a text creation machine that employed many of the features originally envisioned by Vannevar Bush's *Memex.* The obvious allusion that gave the project its name is a reference to Samuel Taylor Coleridge's poem "Kubla Khan," in which seemingly discordant images are intermixed to create an otherworldly realm of "A sunny pleasure dome with caves of ice!" The goal of the Xanadu project was the intermixing and matching of portions of text from various sources to form hypertext works. Xanadu is important in the realm of educational technology, for it is an ancestor of *hypermedia,* the *Internet,* the *digital library,* and the *virtual learning environment.*

Z

zone of proximal development (constructivism)

This area of potential individual and cultural development of the child is an important aspect of Len Vygotsky's *social development theory*, which is an attempt to define human *cognition* in relation to the social interaction of the individual within his or her culture. To Vygotsky, human *consciousness* is completely a result of socialization and *enculturation*. For Vygotsky, social interaction plays a fundamental role in the development of all of the individual's cognitive abilities, including thinking, learning, and communicating. Through language, humans construct their reality. Language itself is both an individual and a social phenomenon. With words, humans define and characterize our life experiences. With words, humans are able to move from subjective thoughts to objective ones to be shared in society.

The zone of proximal development is an important aspect of social development theory, for it defines how children can reach their full potential as mature, intelligent, and socially responsible adults. Parents can increase their children's potential to develop as mature, cultured persons by increasing the area of the zone of proximal development. This is an area at the lower end of the zone determined by the child's ability to think and solve problems on an individual basis in order to complete tasks. The higher end of the zone is determined by the parent's ability to provide a positive communication and *learning environment* in which the child is able to collaborate with adults who are more expert in the culture in order to solve problems and complete tasks. This higher end of the zone is very similar to what Bandura discusses in *behavior modeling*. It is also closely related to *social learning*, cognitive coaching, *apprenticeship learning*, and *situated learning*. The zone of proximal development, an important aspect of Vygotsky's social development theory, is an area where learning occurs for the individual within a social and a collaborative context. The zone is a region of potential mastery of life and learning situations that can be increased by the quality and quantity of the child's communications and interactions with adult mentors, guides, and peers.

Appendix: Paths through the A-to-Z Content

Though it is recommended that a reader peruse through the content by following his or her own interests, predilections, and paths, we nevertheless provide here a set of four main paths through the content based upon the learning paradigm(s) of interest to you. These paths are *behaviorism, cognitivism, constructivism,* and *humanism.* Also listed are the terms related to *organizational learning* and *educational technology.* Remember that the most dominant paradigm for the term is the one selected here.

Behaviorism

altered states of consciousness
autoclitic behavior
behavior control
behavior modeling
behavior modification
behavioral repertoire
behaviorism
classical conditioning
cognitive array model
cognitive behaviorism
cognitive map
connectionism
contiguity theory
contingency schedule
continuity-noncontinuity controversy
disequilibrium hypothesis
drive reduction theory
drive stimulus reduction theory
Ebbinghaus experiments
echoic behavior
elicited behavior
emitted behavior
emotion control
empiricism
error factor theory
extinction
goal gradient
habit family hierarchy
habit strength
Hull's law
hypothetical deductive theory
identical elements theory of transfer
immediate feedback
imitative learning
incremental learning
inhibitory potential
instrumental conditioning
intervening variable
latent learning
law of effect
law of exercise
law of frequency
law of readiness
laws of association
learning and performance
logical deductive
mands
motivation
olfactory system
one-trial learning
operant chamber
operant conditioning
originality theory
overt responding
place learning
Premack principle
primary reinforcer
probability differential hypothesis

programmed learning
purposive behaviorism
puzzle box
radical behaviorism
reaction potential
recency principle
reinforcement theory
reinforcer
response learning
secondary reinforcer
self-pacing/self-paced instruction
shaping
Skinner box
small steps
stimulus intensity dynamism
stimulus-response association
stimulus sampling theory
tabula rasa
tact
thought control
trial-and-error learning
verbal behavior (behaviorism)

Cognitivism

accretion
ACT theory
active processing
advance organizers
algo-heuristic theory
analogical learning
anchored instruction
artificial intelligence
artificial life
Atkinson-Shiffrin memory model
automatic subgoaling
bounded rationality
brain-based learning
categorization
cell assembly
chunking
CMN-GOMS
cognition
cognitive architecture
cognitive complexity theory
cognitive load
cognitive load theory
cognitive processes
cognitive psychology
cognitive robotics
cognitively guided instruction
cognitivism
common sense reasoning
complete rationality
component display theory

computational linguistics
computer lexicography
concept acquisition
conceptual dependency theory
conceptualization
conditions of learning
consciousness
contextual dependency theory
control of variables strategy
CPM-GOMS
crisscross landscape
crystallized intelligence
curriculum as prescription
curriculum design
data chunking
data mining
declarative knowledge
declarative memory
deductive learning
directed behavior
discourse theory
dual coding theory
dynamic memory
echoic memory
elaboration theory
elaborative rehearsal
episodic memory
Experiential Learning of David Kolb
expert system
explanation-based generalization
explicit memory
expository teaching
fan effect
field dependent thinking
field independent thinking
fluid intelligence
functional context training
fuzzy logic
game theory
General Problem Solver
goal-based scenarios
goal reconstruction
GOMS
haptic memory
Hebb's rule
iconic memory
implicit memory
inductive learning
informatics
information processing theory
innate categories of thought
instructional design
instructional events
instructional sequence
instructional transaction theory

instructor-centric
intelligence
intelligence augmentation
keystroke level model
kinematics
knowledge objects
knowledge representation
knowledge structure
layers of necessity
learning by being told
learning objectives
learning objects
learning outcomes
learning styles
levels of processing
logic theorist
long-term memory
machine learning
machine tractable dictionary
magical number seven
maintenance rehearsal
mastery learning
mathematical metacognition
mathematical problem solving
maximum rationality hypothesis
means-ends analysis
memory
mind mapping
Model Human Processor
modes of learning
natural GOMS language
natural language
natural language processing
network model
neural networks
neuron
objects with attributes and values
orchestrated immersion
passive learning
PDP memory model
phase sequence
power law of practice
problem spaces
procedural knowledge
procedural memory
productions rules
productions
rational analysis
reception learning
relaxed alertness
repair theory
schema
script theory
search controls
self-regulation

semantic encoding
sensory memory
sequencing of instruction
short-term memory
signatures
Soar
speed up learning
spreading activation
Stanford-Binet Intelligence Scale - 4th Edition
structural learning theory
structure of intellect model
structuring
subsumption theory
symbol systems theory
symbolic concept acquisition
symbolic interaction
taskability
taxonomy of educational objectives
theory of teaching in context
think aloud protocol
tractable
triarchic theory
tuning
unified theories of cognition
Wechsler Adult Intelligence Scale
working memory

Constructivism

accommodation
active learning
activity theory
andragogy
appraisal theories of emotion
aptitude-treatment interaction
assimilation
barriers to learning
bodily kinesthetic intelligence
case-based reasoning
Chain of Response model
chaos theory
co-emergence
cognitive apprenticeship
cognitive coaching
cognitive flexibility
cognitive structure
cohort groups
collaboration
collaborative learning
community of practice
complex systems
concept mapping
conceptual landscape
conceptual map
constructionism

constructivism
constructivist learning environment
conversation theory
cooperative learning
critical theory
curriculum as experience
cybernetics
deschooling
developmental learning
dialectic method
differentiation
discovery learning
dynamic assessment
emotion theory
enactivism
engaged learning
equilibration
experience-based learning
facial action coding system
generative learning
genetic epistemology
Godel's theory of incompleteness
inquiry-based learning
insightful learning
instructionism
interiorization
interpersonal intelligence
intrapersonal intelligence
knowledge media design
learner-centric
learning web
legitimate peripheral participation
logical-mathematical intelligence
mental constructs
metamathetics
mindtools
minimalism
minimalist model
multiple intelligences
musical intelligence
naturalist intelligence
Nurnberg funnel
observational learning
pansophism
pedagogy
personal curriculum design
PIGS
problem-based learning
project zero
psychological tools
reciprocal determinism
reductive bias
scaffolded knowledge integration framework
scaffolded learning
schemata

self-directed learning
self-efficacy theory
self-reflection
self-regulated learning
shared cognition theory
situated cognition theory
situated learning
social and cultural artifacts
social cognitive conflict
social development theory
social learning theory
socio-cognitive conflict
socio-constructivist theory
sociocultural theory
solo taxonomy theory
spatial intelligence
spatial reasoning
spiraled organization
staged self-directed learning model
teachback
verbal-linguistic intelligence
zone of proximal development

Humanism

academic rationalism
adult education
affordance
apprenticeship learning
cognitive artifacts
cognitive consistency
cognitive dissonance
contextual awareness
cultural reproduction
culture of mathematics (humanism)
enculturation
epistemology
experiential learning of Carl Rogers
experiential mode of cognition
formal discipline theory of transfer
functionalism
Gestalt theory
holistic learning
humanism
information pickup theory (humanism)
instrumentalism
invariants
law of Pragnanz
lifelong learning
life space
molar behavior
molecular behavior
perceptual field
perceptual learning
perceptual organization

phenomenonology
physical artifacts
principle of closure
productive thinking
progressive education
reflective mode of cognition
stimulus array
structuralism
thinking mathematically
visual texture perception
voluntarism

Organizational Learning

action learning
action research
adaptive coping
building shared vision
business transformation
change adept organization
contribution
CoRT thinking
creativity
criterion-referenced instruction
critical consumerism
critical thinking (organizational learning)
decision making
decision support systems
digital age educational paradigm
direct attention thinking tools
direct instruction
disconfirmation
double loop learning
electronic performance support system
enactment effect
enterprise-wide learning
explicit knowledge
exploration/exploitation
Fifth Discipline
hierarchy of needs theory
industrial age educational paradigm
inert knowledge
infoglut
information architecture
information design
intellectual capital
just-in-time training
knowledge acquisition
knowledge assets
knowledge base
knowledge construction
knowledge management
knowledge mapping
knowledge sharing
knowledge sources

lateral thinking
learning organization
management thinking
mental models
metacognition
negotiation
on-the-job training
organizational learning
parallel thinking
personal mastery
practice field
problem solving
scenario planning
single loop learning
Six Thinking Hats
skills management
survival anxiety
systems thinking
tacit knowledge
taxonomy
team learning
technical curriculum design
theory of action
Theory X / Y
Theory Z
transformational learning
universal campus network
vestibule training
virtual learning environment
Waterlogic
Web-based knowledge transfer

Educational Technology

adaptive response
Adventures of Jasper Woodbury
agents
ASK systems
assistive technology
asynchronous learning
audio-conferencing
Cabri-geometry
chat
class Web site
cognitive overhead
computer-assisted instruction
computer-based training
computer-mediated communication
decentering
digital library
digital objects
digitize
disorientation
distance learning
distributed network system

educational technology
electronic campus
electronic learning environment
e-mail
embedded training
handle
human-computer interaction
hypermedia
hypermedia applications
hypertext
instructional technology
intelligent tutoring systems
Internet
knowledge space
learner control
learning environment
level of competence
mail list
Memex
metadata

multimedia
multimedia applications
navigation
nonlinearity
parallel processing
performance objectives
performance tracking
reactive system
serial processing
spoken language systems
synchronous learning
technology integration
telecommuting
videoconferencing
virtual learning community
voice recognition
Web-based education
Web-based training
Xanadu

Selected Books and Scholarly Articles Annotated

Anand, Vikas, Manz, Charles C., and Glick, William H. (organizational learning)

Anand, Vikas, Manz, Charles C., and Glick, William H. "An Organizational Memory Approach to Information Management." Academy of Management Review 23 (1998), pp. 796–807.

In this article, Anand, Manz, and Glick adapt Daniel Wegner's theory of transactive memory (i.e., a network model for describing shared cognitive maps) and apply it to an organizational memory approach to understanding organizational cognition. These researchers define organizational memory as knowledge known by group members through their interactions and communications and knowledge accessible and available to individuals in the organization through knowledge bases. Thus, individuals in the organization access shared memory in a similar fashion to the way memory is shared by networked computers.

Anderson, John Robert (cognitivism)

Anderson, John Robert. *Language, Memory, and Thought*. Mahwah, NJ: Lawrence Erlbaum Associates, 1976.

This work is John Anderson's first book-length elaboration of his ACT theory. As explicated in his book, ACT stands for Adaptive Control of Thought. ACT theory is a cognitive architecture, an attempt at a unified theory of cognition. ACT theory considers the principles of operation that govern human cognition, learning, and memory. In the book, Anderson proposes that cognition arises from the interactions of declarative memory and procedural memory. Dr. Anderson is the Walter VanDyke Bingham Professor of Cognitive Psychology and Computer Science at Carnegie Mellon University.

Anderson, John Robert. *Rules of the Mind*. Mahwah, NJ: Lawrence Erlbaum Associates, 1993.

Anderson's book defines the application of ACT theory to the creation of artificial intelligence learning systems for mathematics, cognitive psychology, and computer systems programming. This enhancement is called ACT-R (where R stands for Rules of cognition). The book includes a simulation on a disk of how ACT-R operates for procedural learning. According to Anderson in his book, much of his research on ACT-R simulation has gone beyond his original intent of understanding human cognition in Act theory and now is part of an attempt to improve the quality of American mathematics education through ACT-R and intelligent tutoring systems.

Anderson, John Robert. *The Architecture of Cognition*. Mahwah, NJ: Lawrence Erlbaum Associates, 1995.

An oft-cited Anderson work, *The Architecture of Cognition* (first published by Harvard University Press in 1983) is his explication of his enhancement to his original ACT theory. The enhancement, ACT* (pronounced ACT-star) theory, is a process model describing the information flow that occurs in human cognition, learning and memory. It is a synthesis of his ideas from cognitive psychology, artificial intelligence, and the process of how human cognition works.

Additional books by John Anderson include the following: *Cognitive Skills and Their Acquisition*. Mahwah, NJ: Lawrence Erlbaum Associates, 1980; *Cognitive Psychology and Its Implications*. San Francisco, CA: W. H. Freeman and Company,

1980; *The Adaptive Character of Thought*. Mahwah, NJ: Lawrence Erlbaum Associates, 1990.

Argyris, Christopher (organizational learning)

Argyris, Christopher, and Schon, Donald. *Theory in Practice: Increasing Professional Effectiveness*. San Francisco, CA: Jossey-Bass, 1974. Latest edition is Argyris, Christopher, and Schon, Donald (contributor) *Theory in Practice: Increasing Professional Effectiveness*. San Francisco, CA: Jossey-Bass, 1992.

Theory in Practice is a landmark book within the learning paradigm of organizational learning. It discusses Argyris's action research. Based upon Argyris's theory of action, action research, also referred to as action science, is a strategy to help managers move from single loop learning (learning that corrects errors by changing routine behavior) to double loop learning (learning that corrects errors by examining the underlying culture of the organization) in order to enhance decision making within a fluid and ever-changing work environment.

Other books on organizational learning and action research by Chris Argyris include: *Integrating the Individual and the Organization*. New York: John Wiley & Sons, Inc., 1964; *Organizational Learning: A Theory of Action Perspective*. Reading, MA: Addison-Wesley, 1978; Argyris, Christopher, Putnam, Robert, and Smith, Diana. *Action Science: Concepts, Methods and Skills for Research and Intervention*. San Francisco, CA: Jossey-Bass, 1985; *Overcoming Organizational Defenses: Facilitating Organizational Learning*. Boston, MA: Allyn and Bacon, 1990; *Knowledge for Action*. San Francisco, CA: Jossey-Bass, 1993; *Action Science*. San Francisco, CA: Jossey-Bass, 1996; Argyris, Chris and Schon, Donald. *Organizational Learning II*. New York: Addison-Wesley, 1996; *On Organizational Learning*. 2nd edition. London: Blackwell Publishers, 1999; *Flawed Advice and the Management Trap: How Managers Can Know When They're Getting Good Advice and When They're Not*. London: Oxford University Press, 1999. To say the least, Christopher Argyris is a prolific writer on the subject of organizational learning and action research.

Atkinson, R.C., and Shiffrin, R.M. (cognitivism)

Atkinson, R.C., and Shiffrin, R.M. "Human Memory: A Proposed System and Its Control Processes." In K.W. Spence and J.T. Spence, editors, *The Psychology of Learning and Motivation*, Vol. 2. New York: Academic Press, 1968.

This chapter delineates the first significant levels of processing memory model, in which it is postulated that humans process sensory data and information from the environment through three distinct levels: sensory memory, short-term memory, and long-term memory. Previous theories of how people remember and learn focused on a simple model in which information either goes directly into short-term memory or long-term memory. The Atkinson and Shiffron model, though the core idea of it remains current, has been superseded by Craik and Lockhart's level of processing theory that postulates that the human mind processes information and learns at a number of different levels simultaneously.

Ausubel, David Paul (cognitivism)

Ausubel, David Paul. *The Psychology of Meaningful Verbal Learning*. New York: Grune and Stratton, 1963.

This book is Ausubel's first explication of his subsumption theory, which states that new material learned in a school setting should be related to previously presented ideas and concepts that become processed and extant in the cognitive structure of the brain. Opposing somewhat Bruner's discovery learning process, in which the student discovers and shapes content on his or her own, Ausubel believes that teachers must provide to the students contextual information, as well as advance organizers that act as a bridge between new material and material previously studied. Author of a plethora of books and articles defending his subsumption theory and promoting cognitivism, David Ausubel is a Distinguished Professor Emeritus, Graduate School, The City University of New York.

Ausubel, David Paul. *The Acquisition and Retention of Knowledge: A Cognitive View*. Dordrecht, The Netherlands: Kluwer Academic Publishing, 2000.

This book explicates the cognitive conditions under which learning occurs. It defines how learning and memory are influenced by cognitive structure, frequency, motivation, and most importantly, cognitive processes. In short, it seeks to answer the question, "How do humans learn and remember content?"

Additional books by David Ausubel include: *Learning Theory and Classroom Practice*. Ontario, Canada: The Ontario Institute for Studies in Education, 1967; and *Educational Psychology, A Cognitive View.* New York: Holt, Rinehart and Winston, Inc., 1968.

Baecker, Ron (constructivism)

Baecker, Ron. "The Web of Knowledge Media Design." The Knowledge Media Design Institute at the University of Toronto. Available online at <http://www.kmdi.org/presentation.pdf>.

A coined term from Ron Baecker of the Knowledge Media Design Institute (http://www.kmdi.org/) at the University of Toronto, knowledge media design refers to the analysis, design, development, and evaluation of media (e.g., multimedia, hypermedia, and Internet content) utilized to support human thinking, learning, communicating, and knowledge sharing. The paper was delivered on January 23, 1997, at the OISE auditorium at the University of Toronto to launch the Knowledge Media Design Institute.

Bandura, Albert (constructivism)

Bandura, Albert. *Social Learning Theory.* New York: Prentice-Hall, 1976.

This book is Bandura's explication and elaboration of his social learning theory. In particular, Bandura postulates that human learning is a continuous reciprocal interaction of cognitive, behavioral, and environmental factors. Sometimes called observational learning, social learning theory focuses on behavior modeling, in which the child observes and then imitates the behavior of adults or other children around him or her.

Bandura, Albert. "Self-Efficacy: Toward a Unifying Theory of Behavior Change." *Psychological Review* 84 (1977), pp. 191–215.

This is an important early article that espouses Bandura's ideas on social learning theory. In particular, the paper elaborates upon Bandura's self-efficacy theory, the essence of which is that an individual's perceived ability to perform a task successfully affects performance of that task and similar tasks in the future

Bandura, Albert. *Social Foundations of Thought and Action: A Social Cognitive Theory.* New York: Prentice-Hall, 1985.

In this book, Bandura enhances his social learning theory to include his updated perspective on what he means by social cognitive theory. To Bandura, social cognitive theory is an explanation of how humans think and why they are motivated to follow particular actions in society. He views human action as a result of the interplay of cognitive, behavioral, and environmental factors that influence the individual to act within a social and a cultural context.

Bandura, Albert. *Self-Efficacy: The Exercise of Control.* New York: William H. Freeman & Co., 1997.

This is Bandura's recent work that further elaborates upon his self-efficacy theory as it describes methods for its implementation in real-life situations that include education, health, psychopathology, athletics, business, and international affairs. Having a strong belief in one's capabilities has a tremendous affect upon one's successfulness in life and life's achievements. In short, Bandura states that some of us can accomplish an individually desired goal in life; some of us can, but think we are unable to do so; and some of us do not have the capability to do so, but think we can.

Belsky, Janet (cognitivism)

Belsky, Janet. *The Psychology of Aging: Theory, Research, and Interventions.* 3rd edition. New York: Wadsworth Publishing Co., 1998.

This book explores both research and practice in the psychology of aging. With regard to both crystallized intelligence (as measured via intelligence tests) and fluid intelligence (as measured by the mind's adapting to new situations) and whether they decline with age, Belsky finds that intelligence indeed can decline with age, due to losses in health, job, and relationships that have an impact on the mental and physical state of the individual. However, Belsky does point out that a measure of this decline may be a result of negative self-fulfilling prophecies that are extant both in the individual aging person and those that he or she interacts with.

Bloom, Benjamin S. (cognitivism)

Bloom, Benjamin S. *Taxonomy of Educational Objectives: The Classification of Educational Goals.* London: Longman Group, 1969. This was first published as Bloom, Benjamin S., and Krathwohl, David R. *Taxonomy of Educational Objectives: The Classification of Educational Goals, by a Committee of College and University Examiners. Handbook I: Cognitive Domain.* New York: Longmans, Green, 1956.

The taxonomy of educational objectives, also known as Bloom's taxonomy, is Benjamin Bloom's (and colleagues') classification of the goals of education regarding the development of intelligence within three categories or domains: the cognitive domain (emphasizing mental processes), the affective domain (emphasizing feeling and emotion), and the psychomotor domain (concerned with motor skills).

More recent books by Bloom and colleagues that follow up on the original taxonomy are: Krathwohl, David R., and Bloom, Benjamin S. (editor). *Taxonomy of Educational Objectives, Handbook 1: Cognitive Domain*. Boston, MA: Addison-Wesley, 1984. Krathwohl, David R., Bloom, Benjamin S., and Masia, Bertram B. *Taxonomy of Educational Objectives, Handbook I1: Affective Domain*. Boston, MA: Addison-Wesley, 1999.

Blumenfeld, Phyllis C., Soloway, Elliot, Marx, Ronald W., Krajcik, Joseph S., Gudzial, Mark, and Palincsar, Annemarie (constructivism)

Blumenfeld, Phyllis C., Soloway, Elliot, Marx, Ronald W., Krajcik, Joseph S., Gudzial, Mark, and Palincsar, Annemarie. "Motivating Project-Based Learning: Sustaining the Doing, Supporting the Learning." *Educational Psychologist* 26 (1996), pp. 369–398.

This work is an important paper regarding inquiry-based learning by several researchers at the University of Michigan. Somewhat in the same vein as Jerome Bruner's discovery learning, inquiry-based learning is an instructional design method of the University of Michigan Digital Library (UMDL) Project. The focus of inquiry-based learning is to use online resources from the Internet to enhance the science learning activity of middle school students. The above individuals (along with a host of others) are actively involved in inquiry-based learning research at UMDL. More information on UMDL is available online at <http://www.si.umich.edu/UMDL/>.

Bransford, John D. (cognitivism)

Bransford, John D. et al., "Anchored Instruction: Why We Need It and How Technology can Help." In Nix, D., and Sprio, R. editors. *Cognition, Education and Multimedia*. Mahwah, NJ: Lawrence Erlbaum and Associates, 1990.

This chapter by Bransford and colleagues of the Cognition and Technology Group at Vanderbilt University delineates the technology-based learning theory of anchored instruction, which is a method of linking (or anchoring) new concepts

to the learner's knowledge and experience to help make these new concepts easier to learn and remember.

Other recent Bransford titles include: Bransford, John D. *The Ideal Problem Solver: A Guide for Improving Thinking, Learning, and Creativity*. 2nd Edition. San Francisco, CA: William H. Freeman and Company, 1993. Bransford, John D., Brown, Ann L., Cocking, Rodney R. *How People Learn: Brain, Mind, Experience, and School* (Expanded Edition). Washington, D.C.: National Academy Press, 2000.

Brown, John Seely, Collins, Allan, and Duguid, Paul (constructivism)

Brown, John Seely, Collins, Allan, and Duguid, Paul. "Situated Cognition and the Culture of Learning." *Educational Researcher*. 18 (1989), pp. 32–42.

This article introduces situated cognition, defines apprenticeship learning, and explicates shared cognition theory. Somewhat similar to Albert Bandura's social learning theory and social cognitive theory as well as Jean Lave's situated learning, the shared cognition theory of Brown, Collins, and Duguid focuses on how groups influence the learning of individuals and their cognitive processes. In the past, many cognitivist theories of learning focused strictly on the individual thinking process and ignored the group and the influence of the group on the learner. Shared cognition theory basically states that our individual thinking is shaped by the shared thinking activity that occurs among groups of learners.

Bruner, Jerome S. (constructivism)

Bruner, Jerome S. "The Act of Discovery." *Harvard Educational Review* 31 (1961), pp. 21–32.

This article is a classic for the learning paradigm of constructivism and the elaboration of Bruner's discovery learning theory. The key concept of discovery learning is that learners are more likely to remember concepts if they discover them on their own, apply them to their own knowledge base and context, and structure them to fit into their own background and life experiences. The assumption of discovery learning is that the learner is mature enough, self-motivated enough, and experienced enough to actively take part in the formation and structuring of the learning content. The instructor's role is as a facilitator, a coach, and a guide, who points the way and assists the learners through their active learning activities.

Other books by Jerome S. Bruner include: *Acts of Meaning*. Cambridge, MA: Harvard University Press, 1990; *Actual Minds, Possible Worlds*. Cambridge, MA: Harvard University Press, 1986; *Child's Talk: Learning to Use Language*. New York: Norton, 1983; *On Knowing: Essays for the Left Hand*. Cambridge, MA: Harvard University Press, 1979. First published in 1962 by Belknap Press of Harvard University; *Going Beyond the Information Given*. New York: Norton 1973; *Toward a Theory of Instruction*. Cambridge, MA: Harvard University Press, 1966; *The Process of Education*. Cambridge, MA: Harvard University Press, 1960; Bruner, J., Goodnow, J., and Austin, A. *A Study of Thinking*. New York: Wile, 1956.

Bush, Vannevar (educational technology)

Bush, Vannevar. "As We May Think." *Atlantic Monthly* (July, 1945), pp. 101–108. Available online at <http://www.ps.uni-sb.de/~duchier/pub/vbush/vbush-all.shtml>.

Bush's very famous article is the first to describe as a precursor of both hypermedia and the Internet, a system of traversing knowledge by means of a vast set of global associational links. In the mid–1940s, Bush sought to improve the antiquated state of libraries and library systems. He envisioned a day when the world's print-based knowledge would all be placed in a machine (using microfilm) that would be, on behalf of researchers everywhere, stored, indexed, and retrieved. It would include within this global library a vast set of interconnections between the data. Researchers would be able to browse through the content of this system that he called the memex. Though the memex machine was never built or implemented, its idea is now manifest in the huge global knowledge base that is now available online through the Internet. Nevertheless, important issues regarding indexing, organizing, and annotating in some sort of orderly fashion all of the knowledge available on the Internet is still an unfinished item.

Buzan, Tony (cognitivism)

Buzan, Tony. *Use Both Sides of Your Brain*. 3rd edition. London: Dutton, 1991.

In 1968, Tony Buzan of the U.K. was Editor of the *Mensa International Journal* when the BBC asked him to host a ten-part educational series called *Use Your Head*. This television series be-

gan a 25-year collaboration with the BBC that included the production of many television and radio programs, as well as the development of corporate videos and books. Contents from this series became part of his book, *Use Both Sides of Your Brain*. Chapters 6 through 9 introduces Buzan's mind maps, explain the laws for creating them, define advanced methods and uses, and explain study techniques related to mind maps. A prolific writer, Buzan is author of 15 books to date.

Buzan, Tony. *The Mind Map Book*. London: Penguin Group, Dutton, 1993.

This book defines the method Buzan calls mind mapping. A learning process similar to that of concept mapping, mind mapping is a visualization activity that learners use to organize information, often as a collaboration activity. Originally developed by Tony Buzan of the U.K., mind mapping is also a software product of The Bosley Group, entitled MindMapper. Information on the software is available online at <www.mindmapper.com>.

Additional books by Tony Buzan include (but are certainly not limited to): *Make the Most of Your Mind*. New York: Simon and Schuster, 1986; and *Head First*. London: Harper Collins Publishers, 2000.

Caine, Renate Nummela, and Caine, Geoffrey (constructivism)

Caine, Renate Nummela, and Caine, Geoffrey. *Making Connections: Teaching and the Human Brain*. Alexandria, VA: Association for Supervision and Curriculum Development, 1991.

This book, republished by Addison-Wesley in 1994, outlines the research and theory of Renate and Geoffrey Caine that define how the brain absorbs and processes information and how this applies to learning. According to the Caines, the brain is a complex and vast human computer hardware mechanism that has millions of built-in patterns and inputs. As the human learns and works in the environment, millions of software programs are created and enhanced over time. Brain-based learning de-emphasizes memorization, listening to lectures, and textbook reading and instead emphasizes hands-on learning tasks that actively engage the learner in the learning process through active problem solving.

Other books that elaborate upon the theory and methods for brain-based learning by the Caines include *Unleashing the Power of Percep-*

tual Change: The Potential of Brain-Based Teaching. Alexandria, VA: Association for Supervision and Curriculum Development, 1997; *Education on the Edge of Possibility*. Alexandria, VA: Association for Supervision and Curriculum Development, 1997; *Mindshifts: A Brain-Compatible Process for Professional Development and the Renewal of Education*. 2ⁿᵈ edition, Tucson, AZ: Zephyr Press, 1999. The latter book includes a third co-author, Sam Crowell.

Card, Stuart, Moran, Thomas, and Newell, Allen (cognitivism)

Card, Stuart, Moran, Thomas, and Newell, Allen. *The Psychology of Human-Computer Interaction*. Mahwah, NJ: Lawrence Erlbaum Associates, 1983.

This important work lays out the GOMS theory of cognitive skills that occur in human-computer interaction tasks. Based upon information processing theory, all cognitive processes occur within a problem space, which is also the fundamental premise of Newell and Simon's GPS and Newell's Soar theory. GOMS has developed into a family of techniques that includes keystroke level model (i.e., KLM), CMN-GOMS, natural GOMS language, and CPM-GOMS. The GOMS family is a prominent model for human-computer interaction and human learning still used today to measure the usefulness of computer user interface designs and human task performance.

Carpenter, T.P., and Moser, J.M. (cognitivism)

Carpenter, T.P., and Moser, J.M. "The Acquisition of Addition and Subtraction Concepts." In Lesh, R. and Landau, M., editors. *The Acquisition of Mathematics Concepts and Processes*. New York: Academic Press, 1983, pp. 7–44.

In this chapter, Carpenter and Moser explicate their theory of cognitively guided instruction (CGI). CGI is closely related to scaffolded learning, in which the student is initially provided a great deal of support and basic knowledge of the subject by the instructor. Then gradually, as information is learned and built up over time, the student is encouraged to combine the previous knowledge and solve more complex problems independently.

Carpenter, T.P., editor. *Children's Mathematics: Cognitively Guided Instruction*. London: Heinemann, 1999.

This book is a recent collection of papers that discuss the theory and process of cognitively guided instruction as a method for teaching mathematics to schoolchildren.

Carroll, John M. (constructivism)

Carroll, John M. *The Nurnberg Funnel: Designing Minimalist Instructions for Practical Computer Skills*. Cambridge, MA: MIT Press, 1990.

In perhaps his best-known book, John Carroll, currently professor at Virginia Tech, derived his minimalist model. For over ten years thereafter, Carroll has followed up on his original thesis through his research and writing. His basic assumption is that adult learners are not stupid. They have a low tolerance for being guided through a process in detail and for having to read through a great deal of content before performing a set of tasks. Thus, developing content within the minimalist model means creating a concise set of task-oriented information that allows the learners to get up and running quickly on the activity that they need to perform on the job with the computer.

Other books by Carroll as author or editor that elaborate upon and enhance his original work include: *Making Use: Scenario-based Design of Human-computer Interactions*. Cambridge, MA: MIT Press, 2000; Editor. *Minimalism: Beyond "The Nurnberg Funnel."* Cambridge, MA: MIT Press, 1998; van der Meij, H. & Carroll, J.M. "Principles and Heuristics for Designing Minimalist Instruction." *Technical Communication* 42 (1995) pp. 243–261; Editor. *Scenario-based Design: Envisioning Work and Technology in System Development*. New York: John Wiley and Sons, 1995; Moran, T.P., and Carroll, editors. *Design Rationale: Concepts, Methods and Techniques*. Hillsdale, NJ: Erlbaum, 1996.

Chen, Zhe, and Klahr, David (cognitivism)

Chen, Zhe, and Klahr, David. "All Other Things Being Equal: Children's Acquisition of the Control of Variables Strategy." *Child Development*. 70 (1999), pp. 1098–1120.

This article discusses a recent four-year pilot project led by Carnegie Mellon University psychology professor David Klahr and postdoctoral fellow Zhe Chen, with regard to control of variables strategy (CVS), which seeks to teach at the primary school level the scientific method of experimentation. With CVS, all possible variables in an experiment are identified and controlled with one variable being tested to determine various results. By keeping all variables but one constant in the experiment, the children are able to draw conclusions that would otherwise be unable to determine in a more open-ended experiment where all variables are left open to chance. CVS directly opposes Bruner's discovery learning process and insists that the cognitive process skills of the scientific method must be overtly taught. The goal of CVS is to develop scientific thinking in children at an early age.

Collins, Allan, Brown, John S., and Newman, S.E. (constructivism)

Collins, Allan, Brown, John S., and Newman, S.E. "Cognitive Apprenticeship: Teaching the Crafts of Reading, Writing, and Mathematics." In L. B. Resnick, editor. *Knowing, Learning and Instruction: Essays in Honor of Robert Glaere.* Mahwah, NJ: Lawrence Erlbaum Associates, 1989, pp. 453–494.

In this chapter, Collins, Brown, and Newman explicate the cognitive apprenticeship model based upon the following four elements: content, methods, sequence, and sociology. Content refers to problem-solving strategies, planning and revision management strategies, and learning strategies to reconfigure content. Method refers to a scaffolded learning approach, whereby the instructor initially supports the learners only to help them gain independence to carry out learning and problem-solving tasks later. Sequence refers to providing information that moves from the simple and familiar to more complex tasks with problem-solving scenarios that the learner resolves. Sociology refers to using collaborative learning techniques allowing students to learn and work in teams, as they will do when they leave the classroom.

Collins, Allan, and Loftus, Elizabeth (cognitivism)

Collins, Allan, and Loftus, Elizabeth. "A Spreading-Activation Theory of Semantic Processing." *Psychology Review* 82 (1975), pp. 407–428.

This paper elaborates upon spreading activation theory. Developed by Loftus and Collins in the mid–1970s, spreading activation is a memory model that utilizes the metaphor of a road map to describe how ideas in memory are organized. Cities on the roadmap are ideas. Distance between cities is represented as the links or highways between ideas. The closer two ideas are on the map, the greater is the strength of the association between the ideas. For cognition, spreading activation provides in essence a model of how concepts are diffused throughout the brain.

Cooley, Charles H. (constructivism)

Cooley, Charles H. *Human Nature and the Social Order.* New York: Schocken Books, 1964.

An important work in relation to Charles Cooley and George Herbert Mead's theory of symbolic interaction, Cooley's primary contribution to SI theory is that there is no sharp distinction between the individual and society. The self is a product of social interaction. A term later used to describe the early developmental learning theories of Charles Cooley and George Herbert Mead, symbolic interaction is a process of learning and maturation that is characterized by the following postulate: Individuals develop personality and self-identity by interacting with others and by defining themselves through certain symbols and tags.

Cowan, Nelson (cognitivism)

Cowan, Nelson. *Attention and Memory: An Integrated Framework.* Oxford Psychology Series, No. 26. New York: Oxford University Press, 1995.

University of Missouri professor of cognitive psychology, Dr. Cowan in this book elaborates upon his thesis that attention and memory cannot be considered independently of each other. He goes on to define how information processing theory correlates with our understanding of visual and auditory perceptions. In a recent article, which is a follow-up of George Miller's magical number seven thesis, Cowan also seeks to explain how sensory storage is extremely limited, even more limited than was previously thought.

For more information, see Cowan, Nelson. "The Magical Number 4 in Short-term Memory: A Reconsideration of Mental Storage Capacity." *Behavioral and Brain Sciences* 24 (2001). (Note that this article is to come out in print in 2001.)

Craik, F. and Lockhart, R. (cognitivism)

Craik, F., and Lockhart, R. "Levels of Processing: A Framework for Memory Research." *Journal of Verbal Learning and Verbal Behavior* 11 (1972), pp. 671–684.

This book explicates Craik and Lockhart's level of processing theory, which postulates that the human mind processes information and learns at a number of different levels simultaneously. The more levels experienced, the deeper the processing that occurs. Rote memorization is ultimately unsuccessful for long-term memory because deep processing does not occur and the information remains temporarily in short-term memory. When information is given in context, it can be processed and placed in long-term memory. Though still following the Atkinson-Shiffron memory model, in which there are three processing levels (sensory memory, short-term memory, and long-term memory), Craik and Lockhart improved on the model by defining how some information can be processed more deeply.

Cronbach, Lee J., and Snow, Richard E. (constructivism)

Cronbach, Lee J., and Snow, Richard E. *Aptitudes and Instructional Methods: A Handbook on Interactions.* New York: Irvington, 1975.

This book by Lee Cronbach and Richard Snow defines their theory of Aptitude Treatment Interaction. ATI postulates that learning content and interaction should be adapted to the varying aptitudes and emotional states of the students. Optimal learning occurs when the instructional content matches the learner's aptitude.

Cross, K. Patricia (constructivism)

Cross, K. Patricia. *Adults as Learners: Increasing Participation and Facilitating Learning.* San Francisco, CA: Jossey-Bass, 1981.

This book delineates K. Patricia Cross's views of adult learning, in particular her chain of response model. In Patricia Cross's Chain of Response model, otherwise known as COR, participation in the adult learning experience is a direct result of a set of variables. These include self-esteem, attitude, goals, life changes, barriers, awareness of learning opportunities, and previous learning participation, all of which are determining factors for the success of the adult learning activity. All of these variables form links in the process that can predict how successfully adult learners will perform in their upcoming adult education experience.

de Bono, Edward (organizational learning)

de Bono, Edward. *Lateral Thinking.* Reissue edition, London: HarperCollins, 1990.

This is the latest reissue of de Bono's lateral thinking exposition. In the late 1960s and early 1970s, Edward de Bono developed his theory of lateral thinking, the generation of creative and innovative solutions to business problems. In lateral thinking, there are four steps to innovation. (1) Focus on dominant ideas that come to mind that polarize perception of a problem. (2) Look at multiple perspectives of the problem. (3) Relax the logical thinking process typically taught in schools as part of the scientific method. (4) Allow "outside of the box" ideas to come to mind and be considered even though they do not fit into the logical, scientific thinking pattern. Lateral thinking was later incorporated in Edward de Bono's CoRT thinking and six thinking hats, both of which emphasize the importance of creativity to problem solving and decision making.

de Bono, Edward. *Six Thinking Hats.* London: Little, Brown, and Co., 1999.

This is the latest edition of de Bono's six thinking hats exposition. Developed by Edward de Bono in the 1980s and still in widespread use within corporations worldwide, Six Thinking Hats is a method for incorporating his lateral thinking (i.e., the generation of novel solutions to problems) into organizations. The six hats represent six modes of thinking. They are not as much labels as they are directions that thinking can take, especially within corporate meetings where decisions need to be made.

A prolific writer, other books by Edward de Bono include: *Textbook of Wisdom.* Penguin/Viking, 1996; *Parallel Thinking—From Socratic Thinking to de Bono Thinking.* Penguin, 1994; *Water logic.* Viking Penguin, 1993; *Serious Creativity.* Harper Business, 1992; *Teach Your Child How to Think.* Penguin, 1992; *Six Action Shoes.* Harper Collins, 1991; *I am Right, You are Wrong.* Penguin, 1990; *Letters to Thinkers.* Harrap, 1987; *The CoRT Thinking Program.* Easterville: SRA, Ohio 1986; *Six Thinking Hats.* Little, Brown and Company, 1985; *Atlas of Management Thinking.* Maurice Temple Smith Limited, 1981; *Future Positive.* Penguin, 1979; *The Happiness Purpose.* Penguin, 1977; *The Greatest Thinkers–30 Minds That Shaped Our Civilisation.* London: Weidenfeld and Nicolson, 1976; *Po: Beyond Yes and No.* Penguin, 1972; *Lateral Thinking: Creativity Step by Step.* Perennial Library, 1970; *The Mechanism of*

Mind. Penguin, 1969; *The Five Day Course in Thinking.* Penguin, 1968.

December, John (educational technology)

December, John. "Computer-Mediated Communication Information Sources." Madison, WI: December Communications, Inc., 2000. < http://www.december.com/cmc/info/ >

This Web site, developed and maintained by John December, is an online digital library of information on a variety of topics related to CMC or computer-mediated communication. Primarily Internet-based, CMC focuses on the group dynamics, team-based learning activities, and associated collaboration and communication technologies that closely dovetail with the constructivist learning theories embodied in collaborative learning, cooperative learning, and situated learning, among other theories within the educational learning paradigm of constructivism.

For further discussions of computer-mediated communication technologies and culture, see Jones, Steven G. *Cybersociety 2.0: Revisiting Computer-Mediated Communication and Community (New Media Cultures, V. 2).* London: Sage Publications, 1998; and Ess, Charles and Sudweeks, Fay, editors. *Culture, Technology, Communication: Towards an Intercultural Global Village (SUNY Series in Computer-Mediated Communication).* Albany, New York: SUNY Press, 2001.

Dewey, John (humanism)

Dewey, John. *Democracy and Education.* Reprint edition of original 1916 work. New York: Simon and Schuster, 1997.

This classic book provides the basis of Dewey's progressive, pragmatic, and humanistic philosophy of education, otherwise known as instrumentalism (and sometimes referred to as progressive education), which postulates that learning is developing and that developing is learning. Instrumentalism regards truth as an instrument that humans utilize to solve problems and promote changes in a global society. Rejecting authoritarian teaching methods, Dewey regarded education as a tool to be used to integrate the citizen into the democratic culture and to change that culture to make it more democratic, more progressive.

Dewey, John. *How We Think.* Reprint edition of 1910 work. Mineola, New York: Dover Publications, 1997.

In this book, John Dewey defines critical thinking as reflective thought, where one withholds judgment, remains skeptical, and questions assumptions, yet keeps an open mind to solutions that will surface through a close intellectual and emotional examination of the problem and its social context.

Other books by Dewey that espouse his pragmatic and progressive philosophy include: *Human Nature and Conduct.* Reprint edition of 1922 work. Carbondale, IL: Southern Illinois University Press, 1988; and *Freedom and Culture.* Reprint edition of 1938 work. Amherst, NY: Prometheus Books, 1989.

Eisner, E.W., and Vallance, E. (humanism)

Eisner, E.W., and Vallance, E. *Conflicting Conceptions of Curriculum.* Berkeley, CA: McCutchan Publishing, 1974.

One of a multitude of curriculum design books that focus on categorizing curriculum, Eisner and Vallance's book identifies five orientations toward curriculum: academic rationalism, the development of cognitive processes, curriculum as technology, self-actualization, and social reconstruction-relevance. Eisner and Vallance's most important contribution was in relation to academic rationalism. Academic rationalism focuses upon the responsibility of educators and the educational curriculum to have our youth share the intellectual fruits of the great minds of the past to help promote cultural reproduction and enculturation.

Ellis, Willis D. (humanism)

Ellis, Willis D. (with an Introduction by K. Koffka). *A Source Book of Gestalt Psychology (International Library of Psychology).* London: Routledge Press, 1999.

Routledge is currently reissuing a psychology series of 204 volumes originally published between 1910 and 1965. The titles include works by key psychology figures such as C.G. Jung, Sigmund Freud, Jean Piaget, and the Gestaltists, including Wertheimer, Kohler, and Koffka. Each volume is organized according to a themed mini-set, such as this one on the Gestaltists. In 1912, Max Wertheimer, along with his colleagues Wolfgang Kohler and Kurt Koffka of Germany, began the movement that opposed behaviorism and favored a holistic approach to how humans learn. In contrast to behaviorism, which focused on objective, molecular behavior that could be broken apart and analyzed, Gestalt theory focused on subjective, molar behavior that could not be separated from the individual's shaping influence of human perception. As the behaviorists looked back to a radical form of empiricism as their philosophical foundation, the Gestaltists looked back to Kant's theory of innate categories of thought and of the shaping influence of the individual's perceptions of his or her experiences in the environment.

Ericsson, K., and Simon, H. (cognitivism)

Ericsson, K., and Simon, H. *Protocol Analysis*. Cambridge, MA: MIT Press, 1984.

In this book, Ericsson and Simon provide a method for testing Ernst and Newell's and Newell and Simon's GPS, General Problem Solver, which was a computer simulation that involved tracking human behavior while performing a given set of computer tasks. The technique was to use protocol analysis, in which the verbal reports of a person solving a task while he or she is in the act of completing that task are used as indicators of cognitive processes that are occurring.

Ernst, G., and Newell, A. (cognitivism)

Ernst, G., and Newell, A. GPS: *A Case Study in Generality and Problem Solving*. New York: Academic Press, 1969.

This case study by Ernst and Newell is the first evocation of what Newell and Simon later defined as the General Problem Solver (GPS), which is a theory of human problem solving explicated in the form of a computer simulation program. The General Problem Solver is also an enhancement to Allen Newell and Herb Simon's logic theorist, which some consider to be the first artificial intelligence program.

Estes, William Kaye (behaviorism)

Estes, William Kaye. "Toward A Statistical Theory of Learning." *Psychological Review* 57, 1950, pp. 94–107.

This seminal article established Estes's statistical theory of learning processes, in particular, his stimulus sampling theory. William Kaye Estes's stimulus sampling theory is a statistical, probability-based learning theory that seeks to provide quantitative data to support Guthrie's contiguity theory. According to Estes, an organism has either a zero or one probability of completing a task desired by the experimenter. More likely, the organism at the beginning of the experiment will

perform an action, but not the one desired by the experimenter. Later on, through repeated conditioned learning activities, the organism will respond correctly and perform the desired action.

Estes, William Kaye. *Learning Theory and Mental Development*. New York: Academic Press, 1970.

Learning Theory and Mental Development shows Estes moving toward a more cognitive versus strictly behavioral view of learning. Though a proponent of behaviorism, to Estes, learning and mental development need to be studied together. This line of thought led Estes to his later cognitive array model. Sometimes simply called the array model, Estes's cognitive array model is his approach to cognition, learning and performance, and memory.

Estes, William Kaye. *Statistical Models in Behavioral Research*. Mahwah, NJ: Lawrence Erlbaum Associates, 1991.

In this book, Estes explains the use of statistics for explicating scientific models. He further notes that the book is a product of his applying statistics to learning theory models for over forty years.

Estes, William Kaye. *Classification and Cognition*. New York: Oxford University Press, 1994.

Estes's book explains how categorizations and classifications of stimuli features that are encountered by humans in the environment are stored in sets or arrays. Estes's array model focuses not on past stimuli events, but on present events that will be encountered again and reused in the future. To Estes, the essence of human thinking and memory is classification and categorization. Nevertheless, Estes never strayed too far from his statistical modeling approach to learning.

Fancher, Raymond E. (cognitivism)

Fancher, Raymond E. *The Intelligence Men: Makers of the I.Q. Controversy*. New York: W.W. Norton and Co., 1987.

In this book, Fancher provides a thorough discussion of the history, background, and people involved in the making of intelligence tests to determine IQ or an individual's IQ.

Fancher, Raymond E. *Pioneers of Psychology*, 3rd edition. New York: W.W. Norton and Co., 1987.

This book traces the evolution of psychology from Descartes, Locke, and Kant, to Galton, Binet, and William James, to Skinner, Piaget, and the contemporary cognitivists currently doing research in artificial intelligence.

Festinger, Leon (humanism)

Festinger, Leon. *A Theory of Cognitive Dissonance*. Stanford, CA: Stanford University Press, 1957.

This book outlines and explicates Festinger's cognitive dissonance theory. Festinger notes that cognitive dissonance results from individuals' grappling with contradictory beliefs, attitudes, and behaviors. Cognitive dissonance is alleviated or eliminated as the conflicting beliefs (and their importance) are reduced in the mind of the individual. Other methods to reduce cognitive dissonance include modifying the dissonant beliefs to make them less conflicting or creating additional or new beliefs that cancel out the earlier beliefs that were in conflict. The theory is particularly relevant to human problem solving and decision making.

Gagne, Robert (cognitivism)

Gagne, Robert. *The Conditions of Learning*, 4th edition. New York: Holt, Rinehart and Winston, 1985.

This book defines Robert Gagne's conditions of learning theory, which describes a hierarchy of different types of learning that require different instructional strategies and instructional designs based upon specific learning outcomes. As delineated in the conditions of learning theory, there exists a hierarchical set of cognitive processes that occur in relation to instructional events. The theory was originally set forth on behalf of military training applications in Gagne's article, "Military Training and Principles of Learning." *American Psychologist*, 17 (1962), pp. 263–276.

Other books by Gagne include *Instructional Technology Foundations*. Hillsdale, NJ: Lawrence Erlbaum Associates, 1987; Gagne, Robert, and Driscoll, Marcy P. *Essentials of Learning for Instruction*, 2nd edition. Englewood Cliffs, NJ: Prentice-Hall, 1988; Gagne, Robert, Briggs, Leslie J., and Wager, Walter W. *Principles of Instructional Design*. 4th edition. Fort Worth, Texas: Harcourt Brace College Publishers, 1992; and Gagne, Robert, and Medsker, Karen L. *The Conditions of Learning Training Applications*. Harcourt Brace College Publishers, 1995.

Gardner, Howard (constructivism)

Gardner, Howard. *Frames of Mind: The Theory of Multiple Intelligences*. New York: Basic Books, Inc., 1983. The latest (10th anniversary) edition was published in 1993 by Basic Books.

This work by Howard Gardner established his theory of multiple intelligences. According to Gardner, there is no one type of intelligence that humans possess. Instead, there are multiple intelligences, which the school systems must foster through interactive, constructivist learning environments. In particular, our school systems focus far too much attention as a measure of success on verbal-linguistic intelligence and logical-mathematical intelligence. Gardner's theory suggests that there are at least eight other types of human intelligence that are just as significant and that need to be fostered within our culture and schools.

Gardner, Howard. *The Unschooled Mind: How Children Think and How Schools Should Teach*. New York: Basic Books, Inc., 1993.

Gardner argues that the current educational approach that focuses upon book learning in our schools is outmoded for childhood learning and even harmful for later adult learning. Gardner invokes schools and instructors to create "Christopherian confrontations" for students to grapple with, whereby they encounter gaps and conflicts between belief and reality like that faced by Christopher Columbus, who sought to prove that the world is round, not flat. The goal of the confrontation is to challenge beliefs and belief systems and to look at things from multiple perspectives.

Gardner, Howard. *The Disciplined Mind: Beyond Facts and Standardized Tests, the K–12 Education That Every Child Deserves*. New York: Penguin U.S.A., 2000.

In this book, Howard Gardner argues that K–12 education should encourage a deep understanding of three classic educational principles: truth, beauty, and goodness. Understanding these principles requires mastery of the major disciplines that human beings have created and developed over the millennia.

Gardner, Howard. *Intelligence Reframed: Multiple Intelligences for the 21st Century*. New York: Basic Books, Inc., 2000.

This recent book revisits and enhances Gardner's theory of multiple intelligences. In the book, Gardner delineates the modern history of intelligence as well as reintroduces his educational plan, which focuses upon deeper understandings of a variety of subjects that use multiple instructional approaches and perspectives.

Other books by Howard Gardner include, but are not limited to: *Creating Minds: An Anatomy of Creativity Seen Through the Lives of Freud, Einstein, Picasso, Stravinsky, Eliot, Graham, and*

Gandhi. New York: Basic Books, Inc., 1994; *Leading Minds: An Anatomy of Leadership*. New York: Basic Books, Inc., 1996; *Extraordinary Minds*. New York: Basic Books, Inc., 1998.

Gery, Gloria (educational technology)

Gery, Gloria. *Electronic Performance Support Systems: How and Why to Remake the Workplace through the Strategic Application of Technology*. Tolland, MA: Gery Performance Press, 1991.

This book is the benchmark for the discussion of electronic performance support systems. Coined by Gloria Gery, also referred to by the acronym EPSS, an electronic performance support system is a computer-based training system designed to provide employees with on-the-job access to training information as needed while job tasks are being performed online. The primary goal of most EPSSs are to provide knowledge workers with learning information just when they need it.

Also by Gloria Gery are the following articles: "Preface to the Special Issue on Electronic Performance Support Systems." *Performance Improvement Quarterly*, 8 (1995), pp. 3–6; "Attributes and Behavior of Performance-centered Systems." *Performance Improvement Quarterly*, 8 (1995), pp. 47–93. A previous book on computer-based training by Gery is: *Making CBT Happen: Prescriptions for Successful Implementation of Computer-Based Training in Your Organization*. Tolland, MA: Gery Associates, 1987.

Gibson, James J. (humanism)

Gibson, James J. *The Perception of the Visual World*. Boston, MA: Houghton-Mifflin, 1950.

This book elaborates upon Gibson's Gestaltist approach to perceptual learning. According to James J. Gibson, perceptual learning is an active process of information pickup. In his information pickup theory, Gibson proposes that there exists in the environment a set of affordances, which includes the physical landscape (i.e., land, sky, and water) that make up the stimulus array. Also within the stimulus array are invariants, such as shadow, texture, color, and layout that help determine what we perceive. To Gibson, the act of perception is a dynamic between the organism and the physical environment.

Other books on perceptual learning by Gibson include: *The Senses Considered as Perceptual Systems*. Boston: Houghton-Mifflin, 1966; and *The Ecological Approach to Visual Perception*. Boston: Houghton-Mifflin, 1979.

Godel, Kurt (constructivism)

Godel, Kurt. *Collected Works. Volume 1. Publications 1929-1936*. Solomon Feferman, editor. Oxford University Press, 1986.

This volume includes discussion of Godel's theory of incompleteness. Within metamathematics (i.e., the study of what is mathematics and what is the nature of mathematical reasoning), Godel's theory of incompleteness is an example of a current metamathematical proposition. Godel's theory sought to dispute over 3,000 years of proofs by mathematicians that a mathematical system, such as the number system, can be complete and consistent. Godel's theory said that the number system is not complete and is not consistent. Since mathematics cannot prove what is not provable, new emphasis has been placed on the cultural, social, and collaborative aspects of mathematics learning and its effective usage in solving real-world problems.

Guthrie, Edwin R. (behaviorism)

Guthrie, E.R., and Horton, G.P. *Cats in a Puzzle Box*. New York: Rinehart Press, 1946.

The title of the book says it all. The book seeks to prove Guthrie's contiguity theory (i.e., learning is a result of an organism's association between a specific stimulus and response) by means of a series of experiments with cats. By photographing the cat's movements in the puzzle box, Guthrie observed that cats learned to repeat their movement sequences based upon their last escape from the box. The cats improved their escape ability by unlearning movements that were not successful to their mission. Thus, the key thing about contiguity theory is that learning occurs immediately at the time of the response to the stimulus.

Guthrie, Edwin R. *The Psychology of Human Conflict*. New York: Harper and Row, 1938.

This book by Guthrie discusses the psychology of how humans react and learn from changes in the environment, especially as they react in human conflict situations.

Guthrie, Edwin R. *The Psychology of Learning*. Revised Edition. New York: Harper and Row, 1952.

In this revision of this classic book, first published in 1935, Guthrie discusses his contiguity theory and what he means by associative learning, in which he regards learning as being a direct result of the organism's association between a specific stimulus and a specific response. The revised 1952 book revisits his observations that sought to prove his contiguity theory through his experiments with cats seeking to escape puzzle boxes.

Harrison, Colin, and Caglayan, Alper (educational technology)

Harrison, Colin, and Caglayan, Alper. *Agent Sourcebook: A Complete Guide to Desktop, Internet, and Intranet Agents.* New York: John Wiley and Sons, 1997.

A relatively new type of software technology, agents guide software users and provide electronic performance support as they seek to complete software tasks online. According to the *Agent Sourcebook* by Colin Harrison and Alper Caglayan, there are three basic types of agents: (1) desktop, (2) Internet, and (3) intranet. The book goes on to define these three types of agents. In general, agents are a practical application of electronic performance support, where learners gain access to information at the moment of need.

Hergenhahn, B.R., and Olson, Matthew H. (behaviorism)

Hergenhahn, B.R., and Olson, Matthew H. *An Introduction to Theories of Learning*, 6th edition. Upper Saddle River, NJ: Prentice-Hall, 2001.

This book covers early notions of learning going back to the Greeks and includes detailed chapters on and discussions of the theories of Thorndike, Watson, Skinner, Hull, Pavlov, Guthrie, Estes, Piaget, Tolman, Bandura, Hebb, Bolles, as well as a host of others.

Horn, Jack (cognitivism)

Horn, Jack. "Organization of Data on Life-span Development of Human Abilities." In R. Goulet and P.B. Baltes, editors. *Life-span Developmental Psychology*: *Research and Theory*. New York: Academic Press, 1970.

In this chapter, Jack Horn argues that aging does not have a negative impact on either crystallized or fluid intelligence. Horn argues that because crystallized intelligence (as measured by intelligence tests) is based on learning and experience, it can remain relatively stable over time, despite the effects of aging. Horn also argues that the central nervous system structures (necessary for the adaptability aspects of fluid intelligence) continue to develop and do not decline with age.

Illich, Ivan (constructivism)

Illich, Ivan. *Deschooling Society.* London, UK: Pelican Books, 1976.

In this book, Illich argued that education's top-down management style, which was typical of modern technological organizations, was robbing students of their creativity and personal decision-making abilities. Learners, in effect, needed to be deschooled, that is, deprogrammed from the industrial age educational paradigm whose principles and policies get in the way of the natural curiosity and self-motivation of the learner. A prolific author and social commentator, his articles have appeared in the *New York Review*, the *Saturday Review, Esprit, Kursbuch, Epreuves, Temps Modernes, Le Monde,* and *The Guardian.*

Johnson, David W., and Johnson, Roger T. (constructivism)

Johnson, David W., and Johnson, Roger T. *Cooperation and Competition: Theory and Research.* Edina, MN: Interaction, 1989.

Johnson and Johnson's book advances the theory of social interdependence and postulates that individual outcomes are affected by others' actions and interactions through the cooperative learning experience.

Johnson, D.W., Johnson, R.T., and Smith, K. A. *Active Learning: Cooperation in the College Classroom.* Edina, MN: Interaction, 1991.

Johnson, Johnson, and Smith advocate active learning and class participation and provide ten chapters on cooperative learning theory and how to implement it.

Johnson, D.W., Johnson, R.T., and Smith, K. *Academic Controversy: Enriching College Instruction through Intellectual Conflict.* Washington, DC: George Washington University Press, 1996.

Johnson, Johnson, and Smith argue for the value of introducing conflict into the collaborative learning environment. They provide evidence of its utility, citing research studies and providing a method for its application in the college classroom.

Jonassen, David H. (constructivism)

Jonassen, David H. *Computers as Mindtools for Schools: Engaging Critical Thinking.* 2nd edition. New York: Prentice-Hall, 1990.

In this book, David H. Jonassen of Pennsylvania State University develops his thesis that computers, multimedia, hypermedia, the Internet, and other educational technologies (i.e., mindtools) should be used to actively engage learners in constructivist, higher-order thinking and reasoning. Instructional design too often focuses first on technology and is too often concerned with a highly structured curriculum design that is developed at the expense of a learner-centric, active learning approach to education. To Jonassen, mindtools are catalysts to facilitate, support, guide, and extend human cognitive processes, knowledge acquisition, and knowledge sharing.

Jonassen, David H., Peck, Kyle L., Wilson, Brent G., Pfeiffer, William S. *Learning with Technology: A Constructivist Perspective.* New York: Prentice-Hall, 1998.

Technology as a constructivist thinking tool for enhanced learning is discussed in this book.

Kanter, Rosabeth Moss (organizational learning)

Kanter, Rosabeth Moss. *Rosabeth Moss Kanter on the Frontiers of Management.* Boston, MA: Harvard Business School Press, 1997.

A prolific author of 15 books and a plethora of scholarly articles on organizational change and a professor of management at Harvard University, R.M. Kanter within her book, *Frontiers of Management*, outlines her perspective on what she means by the change adept organization. The change adept organization is defined as one that anticipates, responds to, and adapts to ongoing changes that continuously occur within the business enterprise. According to Kanter, the ways to foster a change adept organization are by using the three Cs, which are concepts, competence, and connections. Concepts encourage imagination that lead to new innovations. Competence encourages skill development through knowledge sharing and exchange. Connections encourage collaboration as well as joint ventures that are both internal and external to the organization.

Kanter, Rosabeth Moss. *Evolve!: Succeeding in the Digital Culture of Tomorrow.* Boston, MA: Harvard Business School Press, 2001.

Her most recent book discusses how large corporations can manage the transition to the E-culture, the digital culture of the twenty-first century.

Kieras, David E. (cognitivism)

Kieras, David E. "Towards a Practical GOMS Model Methodology for User Interface Design." In M. Helander, editor. *Handbook of Human-Computer Interaction.* Amsterdam: Elsevier/North Holland, 1985.

In this chapter, Kieras explicates the use of GOMS for user task modeling and user interface design. First developed by David Kieras in the mid-to-late 1980s, Natural GOMS Language is a high-level syntax and technique for GOMS that helps better define and evaluate GOMS applications for usability. Using this technique, the goals of the users are broken down into a hierarchy that becomes increasingly more detailed and delineated down to the operator level to represent better all of the sets of tasks occurring in a GOMS application that the users are to perform.

Kieras, David E. "The GOMS Model Methodology for User Interface Design and Analysis." *Proceedings of ACM INTERCHI 1993 Conference on Human Factors in Computing Systems—Adjunct Proceedings.* Amsterdam, the Netherlands: 1993. p. 228.

This tutorial introduces the use of GOMS for user task modeling and user interface design. In the tutorial, Kieras provides an overview of GOMS and the Natural GOMS Language. He also shows how to obtain task time, learning time, and knowledge transfer rates using the technique. The usefulness of this technique is to better understand how humans perform computer-related tasks.

Knowles, Malcolm S. (constructivism)

Knowles, Malcolm S. "Andragogy, not Pedagogy!" *Adult Leadership* 16, (1968), pp. 350–352, 386.

This article is Knowles's first evocation of his theory of andragogy, which states that the approach toward adult learning is far different from pedagogy, the teaching of children.

Knowles, Malcolm. *Self-Directed Learning: A Guide for Learners and Teachers.* Cambridge, MA: Cambridge Book Co., 1988. (Paperback edition of the original 1975 hardbound work.)

In 1975, Malcolm Knowles published this book in which he defined self-directed learning as a process whereby individual learners, without the help of others, construct their own learning activity. In particular, they identify their own learning goals, find learning resources, implement learning strategies, and determine their own learning outcomes. Self-directed learning is an important aspect of Knowles's andragogy, in which the adult learner is self-motivated to learn on his or her own in order to increase knowledge and skills related to work enhancement and job promotion.

Subsequent books that further elaborate upon Knowles's andragogic philosophy of education include: *Andragogy in Action*. San Francisco, CA: Jossey-Bass, 1984; *The Adult Learner: A Neglected Species*. 3rd edition. Houston, TX: Gulf Publishing, 1984; *The Modern Practice of Adult Education: From Pedagogy to Andragogy*. New York: Cambridge Book Company, 1988; *Self-Directed Learning: A Guide for Learners and Teachers*. New York: Cambridge Book Company, 1988; *Designs for Adult Learning*. Alexandria, VA: American Society for Training and Development, 1995; Knowles, Malcolm S., Holton, and Elwood F., Swanson, Richard A., *The Adult Learner: The Definitive Classic in Adult Education and Human Resource Development*. 5th edition. Houston, TX: Gulf Publishing Company, 1998.

Kolb, David A. (cognitivism, organizational learning)

Kolb, David A. *Experiential Learning: Experience as the Source of Learning and Development*. New York: Prentice-Hall, 1983.

Providing first a historical perspective on experiential learning, David A. Kolb in this book outlines how experiential learning has its roots in Kurt Lewin's Gestalt theory and his concept of life space, John Dewey's instrumentalism, and Jean Piaget's genetic epistemology. In the book, Kolb goes on to create a model for experiential learning by matching types of cognitive processes with specific types of instructional design strategies that are based upon his four learning styles. These four learning styles are tied to four types of learners: reflectors, theorists, pragmatists, and activists. David A. Kolb is a professor in the Department of Organizational Behavior, Weatheread School of Management, Case Western Reserve University.

Smith, Donna M., and Kolb, David A. *The User's Guide for the Learning-Style Inventory: A Manual for Teachers and Trainers*. Boston, MA: McBer and Company, 1986.

This is a follow-up book on learning styles by Smith and Kolb that provides methods and techniques for implementing experiential learning.

Osland, Joyce S., Kolb, David A., and Rubin, Irwin M. *Organizational Behavior: An Experiential Approach*. 7th edition. New York: Prentice-Hall, 2000,

This book by Kolb and colleagues focuses on experiential learning from an organizational learning and behavior perspective. It provides group learning exercises and problem-solving situations and simulations to promote experiential learning for the various types of learning styles of employee audiences addressed. Its twin goals are to have

employees learn specific, new work-related content and through that experience to learn more about oneself, one's learning style, as well as one's learning strengths and weaknesses.

Landa, Lev Nakhmanovich (cognitivism)

Landa, Lev Nakhmanovich. *Algorithmization in Learning and Instruction*. Englewood Cliffs, NJ: Educational Technology Publications, 1974.

This classic work by Landa, a former, leading Soviet Union learning theorist now in the United States, explains how the concept of algorithmization can be applied to teaching and learning problems. This book defines Lev Landa's algo-heuristic theory, which focuses on identifying cognitive processes that learners undergo while performing learning tasks and problem-solving activities to obtain knowledge to perform operations. A key aspect of the theory is that algo-heuristic principles can be taught through prescriptions (i.e., sets of specific instructions for problem solving) and demonstrations of operations that follow the prescriptions.

Landa, Lev Nakhmanovich. *Instructional Regulation and Control: Cybernetics, Algorithmization, and Heuristics in Education*. Englewood Cliffs, NJ: Educational Technology Publications, 1976.

Algo-heuristic theory is further explicated in this second classic work. Landa defines in the book when to use algorithmic approaches for instructional design and when to use heuristic techniques.

Lane, Carla (educational technology)

Lane, Carla. "Distance Learning Resource Guide." From the Distance Learning Resource Network, 2001. Available online at <http://www.dlrn.org/library/dl/guide.html>.

As quoted from the Web site, <http://www.dlrn.org/about.html>, "The Distance Learning Resource Network is a dissemination project for the Star Schools Program, a federally funded distance education program which offers instructional modules, enrichment activities and courses in science, mathematics, foreign languages, workplace skills, high school completion and adult literacy programs." Dr. Carla Lane's Distance Learning Resource Guide is a compendium of educational technology information that includes chapters on the following

Chapter 1: What is Teleconferencing?

Langfield-Smith, Kim (organizational learning)

Langfield-Smith, Kim. "Exploring the Need for a Shared Cognitive Map." *Journal of Management Studies.* 29 (1992), pp. 349–368.

This article follows upon the research done by Linda Smircich on organizational cognition. According to Kim Langfield-Smith in this paper, shared cognitive maps are based upon the shared knowledge and belief systems of the entire organization as well as those of specific subcultural groups used for daily interactions and group decision making. Ultimately, according to Langfield-Smith, organizations share cognitive maps that are primarily domain specific and transitory (i.e., not of long duration). Some maps are thus related to a specific subculture, whereas others span the organization, are shared by all, and tend to be more explicit and of longer duration.

Langton, Christopher G. (cognitivism)

Langton, Christopher G., editor. *Artificial Life: An Overview (Complex Adaptive Systems)* Cambridge, MA: MIT Press, 1995.

This edited book includes introductory articles that appeared in the first three issues of the key journal in this discipline, *Artificial Life*, with an introduction by Christopher Langton, Editor-in-Chief of *Artificial Life*, founder of the discipline, and Director of the Artificial Life Program at the Santa Fe Institute. Artificial life, sometimes called Alife, is the study of man-made systems that perform behaviors characteristic of living beings. Artificial life is the attempt to explain the behavior of existing carbon-based life forms by creating human-made, computerized "life" forms, within a computer simulated model, that are able to adapt to that environment and perform actions independent of an external human agent. Each article begins with an abstract and a list of Alife key words.

Lave, Jean (and Wenger, Etienne) (constructivism)

Lave, Jean. "A Comparative Approach to Educational Forms and Learning Processes." *Anthropology and Education Quarterly* 8 (1982), pp. 181–187.

In this article, Lave used her cross-cultural anthropological studies to provide a basis for how people learn. The article studies the cognitive processes various craft persons follow as they utilize knowledge gained in a situated, social context. The purpose of the article is to question ultimately traditional classroom-based learning that does not emphasize the socially organized nature of learning.

Lave, Jean. *Cognition in Practice: Mind, Mathematics, and Culture in Everyday Life*. Cambridge, UK: Cambridge University Press, 1988.

The book by Jean Lave argues that mathematics is a practical discipline that ought to be taught in real-life settings. It should not be taught as a theoretical approach in a classroom-only situation.

Lave, Jean, and Wenger, Etienne. *Situated Learning: Legitimate Peripheral Participation*. Cambridge, UK: Cambridge University Press, 1991.

The authors propose in this book that situated learning is a process of participation in a community of practice. Participation in the learning activity is at first legitimately peripheral but after a time it increases gradually toward greater social engagement and complexity. In Jean Lave's situated learning theory, the social interaction process that occurs between newcomers and old-timers within the community of practice is called legitimate peripheral participation. All learners, new and seasoned, participate in a community of practice, which is a social, interactive group that has at its center seasoned practitioners who provide cognitive coaching and apprentice learning to novices who are in the process of learning a particular skilled craft or trade.

Lindeman, Eduard Christian (humanism)

Lindeman, Eduard Christian. *The Meaning of Adult Education*. Norman, OK: The Oklahoma Research Center for Continuing Professional and Higher Education, 1926.

This remarkable book, published in 1926, is a forward-thinking elaboration of adult education, lifelong learning, and the nature of adult students and how they learn. In the book, Lindeman defines how adults differ markedly from traditional youthful students in terms of maturity, self-direction, and the application of life experience to their studies. The book also delineates how much adult education is a social learning activity that involves adults thinking and learning together. Lindeman's views are very much a foreshadowing of Malcolm Knowles assumptions and postulates of andragogy and its distinction from pedagogy. In the 1960s and 1970s, adult education became widespread in colleges across the United States. The emphasis on adult education that Lindeman prophesied about in 1926 is a result of current demographic, cultural, and technological changes occurring in society.

Mager, Robert F. (organizational learning)

Mager, Robert F. *The New Mager Six-Pack*. The set includes *Preparing Instructional Objectives, Measuring Instructional Results, Analyzing Performance Problems, Goal Analysis, How to Turn Learners On . . .Without Turning Them Off*, and *Making Instruction Work*. Atlanta, GA: Center for Effective Performance, 1997.

Published by the Center for Effective Performance, <http://www.cepworldwide.com>, an organization dedicated to Robert Mager's CRI philosophy and its implementation in business organizations, this "six-pack" set provides several Mager titles, the most famous of which is *Preparing Instructional Objectives*, originally published through Belmont, CA: Fearon Publishers, Inc., 1975. This classic work popularized Mager's use of criterion-referenced instruction, which includes the establishment of performance objectives for planning the development of effective technical instruction along with the establishment of measurable learning outcomes to assess the quality of its implementation.

Maltzman, Irving (behaviorism)

Maltzman, Irving. "On the Training of Originality." *Psychological Review* 67 (1960), pp. 229–242.

Emeritus professor of psychology at UCLA, Irving Maltzman defines in this article his originality theory. Originality theory is a behaviorist study of what makes up human creativity. Through a specific set of behavior modeling activities, Maltzman believes that creativity in humans could be increased. His focus is more on language creativity rather than other aspects of creativity, such as drawing, sculpting, or musical composition. He concludes in this article that creativity could be increased by means of the practice of evoking uncommon responses in word associations.

Mead, George Herbert (constructivism)

Mead, George Herbert. *Mind, Self, and Society*. Chicago: University of Chicago Press, 1962.

This is a critical book, along with that of Charles Cooley's *Human Nature and the Social Order*, related to symbolic interaction theory. In Mead's book, mind refers to symbols that define objects in the real world, the meaning of which is constructed by each individual. Mind inhibits inappropriate actions by using imaginative rehearsals. The self comes forth as the individual acts symbolically toward himself or herself and others. Society is essentially organized interaction patterns among individuals. A term later used to describe the early developmental learning theories of Charles Cooley and George Herbert Mead, symbolic interaction is a process of learning and maturation that is characterized by the following postulate. Individuals develop personality and self-identity by interacting with others and by defining themselves through certain symbols and tags.

Merrill, M. David (cognitivism)

Merrill, M. David, "Component Display Theory." In Reigeluth, Charles, editor. *Instructional Design Theories and Models*. Mahwah, NJ: Lawrence Erlbaum Associates, 1983.

This article by David Merrill explicates his component display theory, also known by the acronym CDT, which emphasizes that the learner should have control over the sequencing of instruction, based upon the instructional components (e.g., presentation forms) provided by the lesson. Merrill's original component display theory seeks to identify the components from which instructional sequences could be constructed. His later instructional transaction theory seeks to integrate the components into what he calls instructional transactions. An instructional transaction is composed of each and every interaction required for the learner to obtain knowledge on a particular set of job tasks.

Merrill, M. David, Li, Zhongmin, and Jones, Mark K. "Instructional Transaction Theory: An Introduction." *Educational Technology* 31 (1991), pp. 7–12.

This elaboration and enhancement of Merrill's original theory is delineated in this co-written article, "Instructional Transaction Theory: An Introduction." In the paper, the authors explain how instructional transactions are instructional algorithms and patterns of learner interactions, designed to aid learners acquiring particular types of knowledge or skills.

Merrill, M. David, Li, Zhongmin, and Jones, Mark K. "Instructional Transaction Theory: Classes of Transactions." *Educational Technology* 33 (1992), pp. 12–26.

This co-written article, "Instructional Transaction Theory: Classes of Transactions," defines a class hierarchy for various types of instructional transactions based upon knowledge structures.

Merrill, M. David. "Instructional Transaction Theory: Instructional Design Based on Knowledge Objects." *Educational Technology* 36 (1996), pp. 30–37.

This is a more recent article outlining Merrill's instructional transaction theory, especially as it relates to knowledge objects. A prolific writer of a dozen books, 16 chapters in edited books, and 65 journal articles to date, Merrill is currently professor of instructional technology at Utah State University.

Miller, George A. (cognitivism)

Miller, George A. "The Magical Number Seven, Plus or Minus Two: Some Limits on Our Capacity for Processing Information." *The Psychological Review* 63 (1956), pp. 81–97.

In this now famous article, George A. Miller of Harvard University espouses the theory that the human brain's capacity to retain information in working memory is very, very limited. In fact, he postulated that the human brain processes only from five to nine information items at a time. Also, the time limit for retaining this small set of information is no more than twenty seconds. Working within the tradition of information processing theory, in which the mind processes information similarly to the way a computer processes data, Miller theorized that humans are far more limited with regard to initially retaining new information than was previously thought.

Neisser, Ulric (cognitivism)

Neisser, Ulric. *Cognition and Reality.* San Francisco, CA: William H. Freeman, 1976.

Dr. Neisser, Cornell University professor of cognitive psychology, defines in this book what he means by echoic memory and the recall of auditory information, iconic memory and the recall of visual information, and haptic memory and the recall of touch information.

Neisser, U., and Libby, L.K. "Remembering Life Experiences." In E. Tulving and F.I.M. Craik, editors. *The Oxford Handbook of Memory*. New York: Oxford University Press, 2000, pp. 315–332.

This paper is a further elaboration of Neisser's findings on memory, which is included in this edited book, *The Oxford Handbook of Memory*.

Nelson, Theodore Holm (educational technology)

Nelson, Theodore Holm. "The Hypertext Proceedings of the World Documentation Federation, 1965."

The first usage of the term "hypertext" appears in this paper by Ted Nelson, who was the inventor of the term and chief strategist for the Xanadu project. Its purpose was to conduct new research and development of a text creation machine and approach that employed many of the features originally envisioned by Vannevar Bush's Memex. The goal of the Xanadu project was the intermixing and matching of portions of text from various sources to form hypertext works. Xanadu is an incomplete concept for a worldwide library of text that was a precursor and partial fulfillment of what we know today as the Internet.

Nelson, Theodore Holm. *Literary Machines.* Swarthmore, PA: Self-published, 1981. Currently reprinted and available through Eastgate Systems, Inc. Watertown, MA: 2001.

In this book, Ted Nelson introduces and defines Xanadu, an incomplete but novel electronic publishing system, which has great similarities to what we now know as the World Wide Web. It does offer "improvements" that the Internet is still seeking to include. An example of an improvement is a royalty system, whereby electronic authors would be paid for their Web-published works.

Newell, Allen, and Simon, Herbert (cognitivism)

Newell, Allen, and Simon, Herbert. *Human Problem Solving*. Englewood Cliffs, NJ: Prentice-Hall, 1972.

This work defines what Newell and Simon mean by the General Problem Solver (GPS), which is a theory of human problem solving explicated in the form of a simulation program. The General Problem Solver is an enhancement to Allen Newell and Herb Simon's logic theorist, which some consider to be the first artificial intelligence program. Both programs are from the middle 1950s. The goal of GPS was twofold: (1) to solve problems that require intelligence, and (2) to understand better how humans perform problem-solving activities.

Newell, Allen (cognitivism)

Newell, Allen. *Unified Theories of Cognition (The William James Lectures)*. Cambridge, MA: Harvard University Press, 1994.

Allen Newell postulated in this book that cognitive psychology has reached a point in its evolutionary development that it is now able to design a cognitive architecture and a working model of human learning and intelligence. This working model is based to a large extent on information processing theory. Cognitive psychologists use computer programs to replicate how they believe the human brain operates. Allen Newell asserts in his book that the cognitive processing that occurs in human brains can be replicated in computer models with agents acting as human learners seeking to complete goals.

Norman, Donald (humanism)

Norman, Donald. *Things That Make Us Smart: Defending Human Attributes in the Age of the Machine*. Boston, MA: Addison-Wesley, 1994.

This book explores Norman's concern about technology and its use in education. He feels that currently there is a great deal of overemphasis on enhancing what he calls the experiential mode of cognition that seeks to immerse and entertain students instead of getting them to be thoughtful and reflective by strengthening what he calls the reflective mode of cognition through simpler activities such as reading. According to Norman, contemporary education focuses far too much time and energy on the use of computers, technology, and multimedia for learning, while often inhibiting learners' activities with regard to thinking creatively and constructively. Norman goes on to describe physical artifacts that we interact with, such as pencils, calculators, and computers that are important for the experiential mode of cognition as well as cognitive artifacts, such as reading, math, and language that are important for the reflective mode of cognition.

Novak, Joseph D. (constructivism)

Novak, Joseph D. *Introduction to Concept Mapping: A Handbook for Educators*. Ithaca, NY: Cornell University, Department of Education, 1986.

This book is an introduction and outline of Joseph Novak's approach to concept mapping. Concept mapping is a learning process originally developed by Novak and enhanced as a software program by Concept Systems and by William Trochim at Cornell University.

Novak, Joseph D. *Learning, Creating, and Using Knowledge: Concept Maps as Facilitative Tools in Schools and Corporations*. Mahwah, NJ: Lawrence Erlbaum Associates, 1999.

This book is a further explication of Novak's concept mapping method. With concept mapping, learners, often in a cooperative learning situation, work together to produce a graphical or pictorial view of the concepts being studied and their interrelationships.

Ouchi, William (organizational learning)

Ouchi, William. *Theory Z: How American Business Can Meet the Japanese Challenge*. Reading, MA: Addison-Wesley, 1981.

A professor of the Anderson School of Management at UCLA, William Ouchi in his book, *Theory Z*, sought to combine the best aspects of both Japanese and American management. *Theory Z* has been published in 14 foreign editions and ranks in the top ten of most widely held books in 4,000 U.S. libraries. William Ouchi's Theory Z is a response to Douglas McGregor's Theory X / Y. As noted in the book, Theory Z focuses on the employee and the perceptions and needs of employees. Theory Z employees have a high degree of self-discipline, order, organization, and a sense of cohesiveness within the organization. Continual education and training is emphasized as well so that employees can remain productive and be more valuable as participants in the organization.

Paivio, Allan (cognitivism)

Paivio, Allan. *Mental Representations: A Dual Coding Approach*. New York: Oxford University Press, 1986.

This book explicates and elaborates upon Paivio's dual coding theory. Dual coding theory is a theory of human cognition that states that human recognition and recall is enhanced by the parallel processing of verbal (i.e., spoken and textual) information along with nonverbal (i.e., image) information. Information recognition and recall is by contrast weakened if only one channel is used. If both verbal and image stimulation is provided to the learner, recognition and recall is enhanced.

Paivio, Allan. "Dual Coding Theory: Retrospect and Current Status." *Canadian Journal of Psychology* 45 (1991), pp. 255–287; and in Clark, J.M. and Paivio, A. "Dual Coding Theory and Education." *Educational Psychology Review* 3 (1991), pp. 149–170.

Allan Paivio discusses the past, present, and future status of his dual coding theory in this article from the *Canadian Journal of Psychology*. Paivio has a Ph.D. in Psychology and has spent over forty years researching imagery, memory, language, and cognition. Currently retired from the University of Western Ontario, Paivio has during his career published around two hundred essays, including articles, chapters of books, and five books.

Papert, Seymour (constructivism)

Papert, Seymour, and Harel, I., Editors. *Constructionism Research Reports and Essays*. Norwood, NJ: Ablex Publishing Corporation, 1991.

This series of essays explores the theoretical background for constructionism that was formulated and researched at the MIT Media Lab in the middle 1980s. Coined by Seymour Papert, developer of the Logo programming language for computer-aided instruction (CAI) applications that are created by children, and currently a professor at MIT, constructionism is a minimalist approach to teaching with the goal of producing in the learners the most learning for the least teaching. It is in the same vein as Bruner's discovery learning approach with its emphasis on a learner-centric orientation, in which the learner is actively engaged in constructing knowledge.

Papert, Seymour. *The Children's Machine: Rethinking School in the Age of the Computer*. New York: Basic Books, 1994.

This is another book by Papert that supports his constructionist viewpoint. The book discusses how schools can utilize constructionist approaches to learning with computers and change their entire approach to how children are taught.

Papert, Seymour A., and Negroponte, Nicholas. *The Connected Family: Bridging the Digital Generation Gap*. Marietta, GA: Longstreet Press, 1996.

This book discusses how children will learn more by randomly exploring the Internet for information versus by going through specific learning applications.

Papert, Seymour A. *Mindstorms: Children, Computers, and Powerful Ideas*. New York: Basic Books, 1999.

This book discusses Papert's development and use of Logo to help children use the computer to learn mathematics and physics principles and applications by themselves.

Pask, Gordon (constructivism)

Pask, Gordon. *Conversation, Cognition, and Learning: A Cybernetic Theory and Method*. New York: Elsevier Press, 1975.

This book delineates Pask's conversation theory, which is that for both living organisms and artificial intelligence machines, learning results from the continuing conversations on a focused subject matter that these entities engage in over time on several language levels. Similar to social development theory, cognitive coaching, and apprenticeship learning, conversation theory emphasizes teachback, which is the process in which one entity teaches another entity what they have learned. Pask's theory also emphasizes the entities' joint learning activities that focus on the relationships between concepts. Conversation theory is an outgrowth of cybernetics, in which it is postulated that learning is completely determined by the subjective social interaction of the learners and is enhanced as the conversation continues.

Pask, Gordon. "Learning Strategies, Teaching Strategies, and Conceptual or Learning Styles." In R.R. Schmeck, editor, *Learning Strategies and Learning Styles*. New York: Plenum Press, 1988, pp. 83–100.

Pask's most recent iteration of his conversation theory is presented in a chapter of this edition on learning strategies. In that chapter, Pask outlines what he means by global learners (i.e., learners that achieve understanding in large, holistic leaps) and sequential learners (i.e., learners that acquire understanding in small, connected chunks). Born in the UK in 1928, Pask died in 1996 of a protracted illness. He was a professor at Brunel University and the University of Amsterdam.

Petrina, S., and Volk, K. (organizational learning)

Petrina, S., and Volk, K. "Industrial Arts Movement's History, Vision, and Ideal: Relevant, Contemporary, Used but Unrecognized—Part I." *Journal of Technological Studies* 21 (1995), pp. 24–32.

This article outlines the history of the industrial arts movement, including a discussion of critical consumerism. In the 1920s, W.E. Warner developed a curriculum for schools within the industrial arts and technologies area that emphasized teaching children how to be more effective consumers and users of products they will buy as adults. This curriculum was known as critical consumerism.

Piaget, Jean (constructivism; cognitivism)

Piaget, Jean. *Jean Piaget's Selected Writings*. Nine-Volume Set that includes: Vol. I. The Child's Conception of Space, 1956; Vol. II. The Child's Construction of Quantities, 1974; Vol. III. The Origin of Intelligence in the Child, 1953; Vol. IV. The Child's Conception of Number, 1952; Vol. V. Insights and Illusions of Philosophy, 1972; Vol. VI. Language and Thought of the Child, 1959; Vol. VII. Principles of Genetic Epistemology, 1972; Vol. VIII. Mental Imagery in the Child, 1971. Vol. IX. The Child's Conception of the World, 1929. New York: Routledge Press, 1998.

This library of volumes, produced by Routledge Press provides researchers and students with the original works of Piaget that delineate his genetic epistemology approach to learning, knowledge, and intelligence, as well as his developmental concepts of assimilation, accommodation, interiorization, etc.

Reigeluth, Charles M. (cognitivism)

Reigeluth, Charles M., and Stein, F.S. "The Elaboration Theory of Instruction." in Charles M. Reigeluth, editor. *Instructional Design Theories and Models*. Mahwah, NJ: Lawrence Erlbaum Associates, 1983.

This chapter in Reigeluth's *Instructional Design Theories and Models* provides an outline and discussion of his elaboration theory, which is an instructional design method utilized for organizing and sequencing instruction. Reigeluth's key point is that instructional information should be provided to the learners in increasing order of complexity, which Reigeluth refers to as an elaborative sequence.

Reigeluth, Charles M., editor. *Instructional Design Theories and Models: A New Paradigm of Instructional Theory*. Vol. 2. Mahwah, NJ: Lawrence Erlbaum Associates, 1999.

Elaboration theory is most recently discussed in this compilation of essays. Also discussed in the book are a variety of methods of instruction (multiples approaches to increasing and promoting human learning and performance) and when to use these methods.

The theory is also discussed in Reigeluth, Charles M. "Lesson Blueprints Based Upon the Elaboration Theory of Instruction." In Charles M. Reigeluth, editor, *Instructional Design Theories in Action*. Hillsdale, NJ: Erlbaum Associates, 1987; as well as in Reigeluth, Charles M. "Elaborating the Elaboration Theory." *Educational Technology Research & Development* 40 (1992), pp. 80–86.

Revans, Reg (organizational learning)

Revans, Reg. *The Origins and Growth of Action Learning*. Kent, England: Chartwell Bratt, 1982.

First discussed almost forty years earlier in an industry white paper in the mid–1940s ("Plans for the Recruitment, Education and Training in the Coal Mining Industry"), *The Origins and Growth of Action Learning*, which includes a reprint of the original paper, provides a history and elaboration of Revans's theory of action learning. Revans, originally a physicist, was concerned that organizations and industries that did not learn and change as quickly as their business environment changed were doomed to extinction. According to Revans, action learning is an executive training and development strategy in which a management team, guided by a facilitator, works collaboratively on the following actions: (1) Analyze a management problem (2) Develop a plan to address the problem. (3) Apply the solution. (4) Study the effects of the decision to determine what aspects were effective and ineffective. (5) Determine how to handle similar problems in the future. Revans theory, as espoused in his book, advocates the creation of action learning teams that focus on questions that would generate learning instead of attempting to use preexisting knowledge to gain new knowledge.

Revans, Reg. International Management Centres Multinational. "The Collected Sayings of Reg Revans: Action Learning in Brief." Available online at <http://www.mcb.co.uk/imc/al-inter/columns/revans.htm>.

This short piece from the Web is a synopsis of action learning with some good quotations from Reg Revans in his industry workshops that reveal his train of thought. To quote Revans himself, "When I was asked, towards the end of the Second World War, by the coal-owners to write an education plan for their industry, then the world's largest employer, I went through all of these previous steps and saw that I needed to trade my ignorance with the miners themselves. From that plan, published in October 1945, came action learning." Also noted by Revans, "At 80 I no longer judge others by what they already know, but by the questions they put to me." Both quotes are from Revans's Action Learning Workshop that was given on December 18, 1987.

Rosenbloom, Paul S., Laird, John E., and Newell, Allen (cognitivism)

Rosenbloom, Paul S., Laird, John E., and Newell, Allen. editors. *The Soar Papers: Research on Integrated Intelligence (Artificial Intelligence)*. Cambridge, MA: MIT Press, 1993.

This major work provides a history of Soar and the Soar artificial intelligence research work done during about a twenty-year period and begun by John E. Laird, Allen Newell, and Paul S. Rosenbloom at Carnegie Mellon in the early 1980s. The Soar Project is an investigation into artificial intelligence. Arguing for a unified theory of cognition, Newell and colleagues developed a set of principles for cognitive processing and human problem solving with Soar. The Soar Papers in this compilation include 63 articles related to this ongoing project. Topics include the Soar beginnings, the Soar architecture, its implementations, intelligent capabilities, domains of application, etc. Current Soar research is being conducted at Carnegie Mellon University, Ohio State University, University of Michigan, University of Southern California, University of Hertfordshire, and University of Nottingham.

Rumelhart, D. and Norman, D. (cognitivism)

Rumelhart, D. & Norman D. (1978). "Accretion, tuning and restructuring: Three modes of learning." In J.W. Cotton and R. Klazky (eds.), *Semantic Factors in Cognition*. Hillsdale, NJ: Erlbaum.

Schall, Maryan S. (organizational learning)

Schall, Maryan S. "Communication-Rules Approach to Organizational Culture." *Administrative Science Quarterly* 28 (1983), pp. 557–581.

Closely related to Smircich's paper noted below, Schall's article further defines organizational cognition, particularly in relation to common knowledge structures (similar to the concept of shared cognitive maps) and communication rules. In her article, Schall defines communication rules as tacit understandings among work groups in organizations. She also distinguishes between operative rules (similar to the concept of explicit knowledge) and formal rules (similar to the concept of tacit knowledge).

Schoenfeld, Alan (cognitivism)

Schoenfeld, Alan. *Mathematical Problem Solving*. Orlando, FL: Academic Press. 1985.

This book by Alan Schoenfeld was instrumental in changing the focus of education in mathematics. To Schoenfeld, mathematics is a problem-solving activity in which four sets of skills are needed. (1) Resources, which involve knowledge of mathematical propositions and procedures; (2) Heuristics, which are techniques for mathematical problem solving, such as the think aloud protocol; (3) Control, which involves decision making as to when and how to use resources and problem-solving techniques; and (4) Beliefs, which involve thinking mathematically (i.e., being able to look at the world from a mathematical point of view).

Schoenfeld, Alan H. "Learning to Think Mathematically: Problem Solving, Metacognition, and Sense-Making in Mathematics." *Handbook for Research on Mathematics Teaching and Learning*. D. Grouws, editor. New York: MacMillan, 1992, Pp. 334–370.

In this chapter, Schoenfeld delineates the dynamic nature of what thinking mathematically means. He first explores what is meant by problem-solving in a traditional curriculum design for mathematics. He then reviews how mathematics teaching should move from a content-oriented to a process-oriented exercise that involves mathematical metacognition, which is the ability to think about the process of thinking and problem solving, to be consciously aware of one's actions within the problem solving activity, and to be able to monitor and to control one's cognitive processes to be better mathematics problem solvers. To Schoenfeld, the most important aspect of mathematical metacognition is the concept of enculturation, wherein the learner comes to understand how the thinking and sharing processes involve a collaborative, social activity.

Schubert, William H. (humanism)

Schubert, William H. *Curriculum: Perspectives, Paradigm, and Possibility.* New York: Macmillan, 1986.

This large and comprehensive work, over 800 pages in length, outlines the historical context for curriculum and organizes curriculum into different schools of thought. It discusses the concept of cultural reproduction as an important goal of education. In the mid–1980s, William H. Schubert regarded cultural reproduction as one of the important orientations for curriculum design that is similar to academic rationalism. The goal of cultural reproduction is enculturation, which is the process of learning a culture through our interactions and communications at home, at school, and in the society at large. In education, cultural reproduction is the means by which important elements of the culture must be passed down from one generation to the next.

Schubert, William H. "Reconceptualizing and the Matter of Paradigms." *Journal of Teacher Education* 40 (1989), pp. 27–32.

This article is another important work that further elaborates upon Schubert's approach to curriculum design in relation to cultural reproduction and enculturation.

Shannon, Claude (cognitivism)

Shannon, Claude E. "A Mathematical Theory of Communication." *The Bell System Technical Journal* 27 (1948), pp. 379–423, 623–656.

This important article established Claude Shannon's postulates for information theory, which was an attempt in the late 1940s to solve the problem of communicating information efficiently over noisy data and communication lines by using probability and statistics, as well as employing various types of feedback and control

mechanisms. Information theory is important from a learning theory perspective in that it was a precursor to cybernetics, which postulates that no matter how complex and disordered our world appears to be, there lies an inherent self-organizing order that is self-adapting, self-regulating, and based upon mathematical principles and statistical calculations. As such, information theory is also an important precursor of chaos theory and artificial life.

Simon, Herbert A. (cognitivism)

Simon, Herbert A. *Models of Man: Social and Rational; Mathematical Essays on Rational Human Behavior in Society Setting.* New York: John Wiley, 1957.

One among many topics covered in this book is Simon's view of complete and bounded rationality. To Simon, the better the architecture of an artificial intelligence system, the more closely it approximates human cognitive processes to achieve what is considered complete rationality. This assumes, of course, that humans themselves are completely rational (though Herbert Simon, in this book states that they are not) as they go about solving complex task-based problems in the environment.

Simon, Herbert A. *Models of My Life.* Cambridge, MA: MIT Press, 1996.

This book is Herbert A. Simon's personal and intellectual biography. One of the developers of the logic theorist along with Allen Newell at Carnegie Mellon University, Simon was a key figure in artificial intelligence research and cognitive psychology for nearly half a century. At the time of his death in February 2001, Simon was the Richard King Mellon Professor of Computer Science and Psychology at Carnegie Mellon University, a post he had held since 1966. A polymath, Simon was the 1978 Nobel Prize winner for economics and was an instrumental voice regarding the study of decision making in organizational behavior circles.

Other recent books by Herbert A. Simon include his classic book on organizational behavior applied to decision making, *Administrative Behavior: A Study of Decision-Making Processes in Administrative Organizations.* 4th Edition. New York: Free Press, 1997; and *The Sciences of the Artificial.* 3rd Edition. Cambridge, MA: MIT Press, 1996, which explores the wide range of the following disciplines: economics, management, computer science, psychology and philosophy in order to better understand humans and their artifacts.

Smircich, Linda (organizational learning)

Smircich, Linda. "Concepts of Culture and Organizational Analysis." *Administrative Science Quarterly* 28 (1983), pp. 339–358.

This article defines five themes for understanding organizational culture, which include cross-cultural management, corporate culture, organizational cognition, organizational symbolism, and unconscious processes in the organization. For the purposes of this book, research by Smircich and others related to organizational cognition is our primary focus as their studies relate to organizational learning. To Smircich, organizational cognition is a system of shared knowledge and beliefs of individuals within the organization based upon common knowledge structures and communication rules.

Sternberg, Robert (cognitivism)

Sternberg, Robert. *The Triarchic Mind: A New Theory of Intelligence.* New York: Viking Press, 1988.

Robert Sternberg's triarchic theory, as espoused in his book, *The Triarchic Mind*, states that intelligence is based upon three elements, which are: (1) functions of governments of the mind; (2) stylistic preferences; and (3) forms of mental self-government. He further subdivides the government functions into legislative (to create, plan, imagine, and formulate), executive (to do and implement), and judicial (to judge and evaluate). He subdivides the stylistic preferences into internal (individuals working by themselves) and external (individuals working with others). He subdivides the forms of mental self-government into monarchic (people with singular goals that they seek to accomplish), hierarchic (people with multiple goals who can easily prioritize), oligarchic (people who view goals as being equal in weight and therefore have difficulty prioritizing), and anarchic (people, operating without rules or structure, who create their own problem-solving techniques and solutions on the fly). His theory is regarded as a general theory of human intelligence.

Other intelligence theory books by Sternberg that espoused earlier versions of his triarchic theory include: *Intelligence, Information Processing, and Analogical Reasoning.* Hillsdale, NJ: Erlbaum, 1977; and *Beyond IQ: A Triarchic Theory of Human Intelligence.* New York: Cambridge University Press, 1985.

Sticht, Thomas G. (cognitivism)

Sticht, Thomas G. "Applications of the Audread Model to Reading Evaluation and Instruction." In L. Resnick and P. Weaver, editors. *Theory and Practice of Early Reading.* Vol. 1. Mahwah, NJ: Lawrence Erlbaum Associates, 1975.

This chapter is Thomas Sticht's first espousal of his functional context training, which is an approach developed originally for the U.S. military and later developed for the U.S. Department of Labor and Department of Education for adult technical reading, and literacy training. The method focuses first on providing a familiar context for a set of new information. The learner then builds from simple and well-known concepts and procedures to more complex concepts and tasks.

Other follow-up works to Sticht's functional context approach are: "Comprehending Reading at Work." In Just, M., and Carpenter, P., editors, *Cognitive Processes in Comprehension.* Hillsdale, NJ: Lawrence Erlbaum Associates, 1977; "Adult Literacy Education." In *Review of Research in Education*, Vol. 15. Washington, DC: American Education Research Association, 1988; Sticht, Thomas G., Armstrong, William B., Hickey, Daniel T., and Caylor, John S. *Cast-off Youth: Policy and Training Methods from the Military Experience.* New York: Praeger Publishers, 1988.

Sweller, John (cognitivism)

Sweller, John. "Cognitive Load During Problem Solving: Effects on Learning." *Cognitive Science* 12 (1988), pp. 257–285.

This article defines Sweller's cognitive load theory. Cognitive load theory's emphasis is on the limitations of human working memory. Its principles are the following: (1) Working memory is limited, and once exceeded, no learning can take place. (2) Long-term memory is unlimited. (3) Learning involves actively engaging the working memory so that information is transferred, processed, and stored in long-term memory. In relation to instructional design, information should be presented to the student through working examples that have all of the data, diagrams, and steps included to provide the learner with a clear, simple view of the essential information needed in order to keep cognitive load at a minimum.

Sweller, John. *Instructional Design in Technical Areas*. Sterling, VA: Stylus Publishing, 1999.

Further exploration of cognitive load and instructional design is explored by Sweller in this book. John Sweller is a Fellow of the Academy of Social Sciences of Australia as well as a Professor of Education at the University of New South Wales, Australia. The book draws on his extensive research of more than 20 years to create clear and useful instructional design principles for mathematics and physical science lessons.

Tomlinson, Carol Ann (constructivism)

Tomlinson, Carol Ann. *How to Differentiate Instruction in Mixed Ability Classrooms*. Alexandria, VA: Association for Supervision and Curriculum Development, 1995.

This book introduces what is differentiated instruction, what is the rationale for differentiated instruction, and how to plan and implement differentiated instruction in the classroom. It also discusses how to differentiate content, process, and products, as well as instructional and management strategies for the differentiated classroom.

Tomlinson, Carol Ann. *The Differentiated Classroom: Responding to the Needs of All Learners*. Alexandria, VA: Association for Supervision and Curriculum Development, 1999.

The focus of this book is on differentiating curriculum to foster both gifted students and normal students. In differentiating the curriculum for gifted students, Tomlinson states that teachers must no longer be dispensers of knowledge, but must instead be organizers of learning opportunities. Also, in differentiated classrooms, teachers must ensure that each student competes against himself or herself as learning and development progresses, rather than competing against other students who have varying abilities, learning styles, and aptitudes.

Trochim, William (constructivism)

Trochim, William. "An Introduction to Concept Mapping for Program Planning and Evaluation." *Evaluation and Program Planning* 12 (1989), pp. 1–16.

Concept mapping is a learning process originally developed by Joseph D. Novak and enhanced as a software program by William Trochim at Cornell University. With concept mapping, learn-

ers, often in a cooperative learning situation, work together to produce a graphical or pictorial view of the concepts being studied and their interrelationships. If one sought to evaluate a program to determine whether it increases students' self-esteem, one could utilize the concept map to explicate all of the terms associated with self-esteem. The map thus created would not necessarily generate a theory with regard to the effectiveness of the program on self-esteem. However, the map would distinguish particular aspects of self-esteem normally not considered that could be useful to a new theory to be generated.

Trochim, William. "Concept Mapping: Soft Science or Hard Art?" Available online at <http://trochim.human.cornell.edu/research/epp2/epp2.htm>

Trochim, in this paper, provides a discussion of concept mapping and seeks to determine whether the activity is a "scientific" process or an "artistic" one. Ultimately, he determines that it is a little of both. Nevertheless, at the conclusion of the paper, Trochim feels that more research is needed on using concept mapping for building scientific theories. According to Trochim, concept maps provide frameworks within which theories might be stated. However, concept maps are not theories in and of themselves. They are instead tools to help create theories.

VanLehn, Kurt (cognitivism)

Brown, J.S., and VanLehn, K. "Repair Theory: A Generative Theory of Bugs in Procedural Skills." *Cognitive Science* 4 (1980), pp. 379–426.

VanLehn's repair theory was first postulated with a colleague (J.S. Brown) in this article. Repair theory looks at how humans learn procedures inductively and by fixing "bugs" (i.e., mistakes) along the way. This article reported on an extensive study and observation of children, who used repair theory methods to solve mathematics problems.

VanLehn, Kurt. *Mind Bugs*. Cambridge, MA: MIT Press, 1989.

This book is an elaboration of Kurt VanLehn's repair theory. The theory postulates that when an individual, seeking to perform a procedure, reaches an impasse, he or she applies various approaches to overcome the impasse. These approaches are referred to as repairs. Some repairs get the learner back on track; others are false restarts.

Vincent, Jill (educational technology)

Vincent, Jill. *Exploring 2-Dimensional Space with Cabri-Geometry II.* Victoria, Australia: Mathematical Association of Victoria, 2001.

This text is a workbook that provides numerous exercises and tasks using the Cabri-Geometry method. Cabri-geometry is one of the most popular, educational technology products used by learners worldwide. Its value to the learning theory school of constructivism is that the learner has direct control over the behavior of the geometric objects he or she has constructed in a highly visual, fast-feedback-oriented way. For more information on Cabri-Geometry, visit the Web site located at: <http://www-cabri.imag.fr/index-e.html>.

Vygotsky, Lev S. (constructivism)

Vygotsky, Lev S. *Thought and Language.* Cambridge, MA: MIT Press, 1962.

Originally published in Russia in the mid–1920s, this classic work explicates Vygotsky's social development theory. In particular, it discusses the relationship between words and consciousness and elaborates upon the thesis that speech and learning are based upon social interactions.

Vygotsky, Lev S. *Mind in Society.* Cambridge, MA: Harvard University Press, 1978.

Vygotsky's other classic work is *Mind in Society.* Its thesis is that human intelligence and learning are mediated through environmental objects and social activity.

Vygotsky, Lev S. *Educational Psychology.* Boca Raton, FL: CRC Press—St. Lucie Press, 1997.

Vygotsky's first published, but last translated, book is *Educational Psychology.* This work notes that the child's individual development and learning activity must be the focus of education, as well as the nurturing of creativity and reasoning.

Wadsworth, Barry J. (constructivism)

Wadsworth, Barry J. *Piaget's Theory of Cognitive and Affective Development: Foundations of Constructivism.* 5th edition. Boston, MA: Addison-Wesley Publishing, 1996.

As noted by Wadsworth, though concerned with cognition and how the brain develops, Jean Piaget's genetic epistemology's primary postulate is that all healthy brains at any stage of human development are concerned with one thing: the natural desire to be active, to be creative, and to learn new things that come from the stimulations,

observations, and interactions with the environment. Though there are strong environmental influences upon everyone, the learning process of the individual is self-directed.

Walsh, James P., and Fahey, Liam (organizational learning)

Walsh, James P., and Fahey, Liam. "The Role of Negotiated Belief Structures in Strategy Making." *Journal of Management Studies* 12 (1986), pp. 325–338.

This article follows upon the research done by Linda Smircich on organizational cognition. According to Walsh and Fahey in this paper, negotiated belief structures are the configurations of power and beliefs within an organization that are at the root of work group decision making. Organizations share knowledge and share cognitive maps that are primarily domain specific and transitory (i.e., not of long duration). Some shared cognitive maps are thus related to a specific subculture, whereas others span the organization, are shared by all, and tend to be more explicit and of longer duration.

Wegner, Daniel M. (organizational learning)

Wegner, Daniel M. "A Computer Network Model of Human Transactive Memory." *Social Cognition* 13 (1995), pp. 319–339.

This paper, which is also related to organizational cognition, is an elaboration of Daniel Wegner's theory of transactive memory. Transactive memory is a network model for describing shared cognitive maps, in which individuals in the organization access shared memory in much the same fashion as a group of networked computers share memory. This theory falls squarely in line with information processing theory and network models such as the PDP memory model in which human cognition and memory are described in computer terms and relations.

Wiener, Norbert (humanism)

Wiener, Norbert. *Cybernetics, or Control and Communication in the Animal and the Machine.* Cambridge, MA: MIT Press, 1948.

Wiener was a brilliant mathematician and professor at MIT who wrote many books and articles on stochastic processes, harmonic analysis, and Brownian motion. His own favorite work, which gained him great notoriety among a much wider audience than mathematicians, was *Cybernetics*. Cybernetics, a term coined by Wiener in this book, is closely related to chaos theory, which postulates that no matter how complex and disordered our world appears to be, there is an inherent self-organizing order that is self-adapting, self-regulating, and based upon mathematical principles and statistical calculations. As it relates to chaos theory, cybernetics has influenced studies and research in artificial intelligence and artificial life. Though its roots are in mathematics and engineering, cybernetics and its adherents seek to include a variety of disciplines, including but not limited to biology, neurophysiology, anthropology, psychology, and education.

Wiener, Norbert. *The Human Use of Human Beings*. New York: Doubleday, 1955.

Wiener's book elaborates upon the social impact of the application of cybernetics and technology on humans, both positive and negative.

Wiener, Norbert. *Invention: The Care and Feeding of Ideas*. Cambridge, MA: MIT Press, 1993.

This book discusses the framework upon which invention occurs, historically, politically, and socially. The book was published posthumously.

Wundt, Wilhelm Maximillian (humanism)

Wundt, Wilhelm Maximillian. *Volkerpsychologie* (Social Psychology), 10 vols., 1911–1920.

Wilhelm Maximillian Wundt is a famous nineteenth-century German psychologist who, in his lifetime, published 54,000 pages of books and scholarly articles. Wundt is the chief advocate of voluntarism, which is the belief that human consciousness can be studied scientifically, that one could study the human mind and human will systematically. He believed that one could ascertain the basic elements of which all consciousness consists, not through directly studying the mind, but through studying the mind's products (e.g., religion, myth, art, language, and culture).

Besides his ten-volume treatise on social psychology, Wundt's other major works include: *Vorlesungen uber die Menschen und Tier-Seele*, 1863, English translation, Lectures on Human and Animal Psychology, 1896; and *Grundzuge der physiologeschen Psychologie,* 1874, English translation, Principles of Physiological Psychology, 1904.

Index

About the Author

DAVID C. LEONARD was Assistant Dean at Mercer University, School of Engineering, Atlanta, where he developed and taught in the Internet-based distance learning master's degree program in technical communication management. He had also developed graduate and undergraduate technical communication programs and courses at the George Institute of Technology, the University of Maryland, and the University of Tennessee at Chattanooga. Leonard has co-authored two other Oryx Press publications, *Multimedia and the Web from A to Z* and *Multimedia from A to Z,* as well as other books and numerous articles.